AN INTERDISCIPLINARY APPROACH TO
MARKETING

Perspectives for the Christian Liberal Arts College

AN INTERDISCIPLINARY APPROACH TO

MARKETING

Perspectives for the Christian Liberal Arts College

Harwood Hoover Jr.

Professor of Marketing, Aquinas College

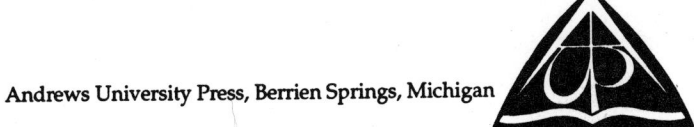

Andrews University Press, Berrien Springs, Michigan

The permissions granted for the use of copyright material are gratefully acknowledged. In addition to the specific acknowledgements found in the footnotes, figures, and pages of the text, the following uses are acknowledged:

The Miles and Snow Strategic Typology from R. Miles and C. Snow, *Organizational Strategy Structure and Process* (New York: McGraw Hill, 1978). Reproduced with permission.

Figure 20.4 from *Consumer Behavior*, Third Edition, by James F. Engle, Roger D. Blackwell, and David T. Kollat, copyright © 1978 by the Dryden Press, a Division of Holt, Rinehart and Winston Inc., reprinted by permission of the publisher.

Figure 2.10 from *Consumer Behavior*, Fourth Edition, by James F. Engle, Roger D. Blackwell, copyright © 1982 by the Dryden Press, a Division of Holt, Rinehart and Winston Inc., reprinted by permission of the publisher.

Figure 2.7 from *Consumer Behavior*, Fifth Edition, by James F. Engle, Roger D. Blackwell, Paul W. Miniard, copyright © 1986 by the Dryden Press, a Division of Holt, Rinehart and Winston Inc., reprinted by permission of the publisher.

All rights reserved
copyright © 1990 by Harwood Hoover, Jr.

No part of this book may be reproduced or transmitted in any form or by any means, electronic or mechanical, including photocopying, without permission in writing from the publisher.

Andrews University Press
Berrien Springs, MI 49104

ISBN 0-943872-64-2

Printed in the United States of America

PREFACE

There are many fine marketing texts. This book should complement rather than compete with those currently available. It is a shorter book than most introductions. This allows it to be used as an ancillary text by those who wish to add its theoretical, financial and ethical perspectives to the extensive taxonomies developed in the established texts. It is also sufficiently complete to stand on its own as an introduction. It might logically be used with innovative class formats requiring less than a semester to complete, or as a review text for graduate students preparing for case studies. Use as a primary text in full semester formats would also be possible where class sizes are small enough to allow profitable use of the extensive set of discussion questions which is provided.

This text develops perspectives useful in generating a realistic understanding of marketing. These perspectives include:

- An interdisiplinary perspective
- A complete and unified theoretical development
- Realistic inclusion of the financial dimensions
- Integrated treatment of the price-offering exchange
- A realistic information-based approach to the management discussion
- Recognition of the entrepreneur
- Complete integration of the international dimension
- A scripturally based ethical discussion

The author has felt the need for a text with these perspectives while teaching marketing over the last several years. Colleagues who have also felt the need for a presentation of one or more of these perspectives should comprise a logical target market for this book.

TABLE OF CONTENTS

Part I

Market Exchange and Market Niche

1 Marketing And Its Functions 3

    Marketing Defined 3
    The Functions of Marketing 4
    Functions for Parties to the Exchange 4
    Functions for Society 4
    Functions Comprising Marketing 7
    Questions for Study, Discussion, and Examination 10

2 Human Exchange: Satisfaction, Utility and Demand Behavior 13

    Exploring Utility: Psychology 14
    Exploring Utility: Consumer Behavior 24
    Satisfaction and Utility: Psychology and Microeconomics Related 30

Proceeding from Utility: The Microeconomics of Consumer Choice	32
Proceeding from Utility: Effects of Price Changes	37
Proceeding from Utility: Effects of Income Changes	37
Proceeding from Utility to Demand	41
Effects of Other Managerial Variables	48
Group Effects	52
Crossing National Boundaries	54
Chapter Summary	54
Questions for Study, Discussion, and Examination	59

3 Human Exchange: Supply Behavior and the Market Niche ... 67

The Supplying Firm: An Economist's Concept	68
The Firm and Profit-Maximization	69
Market Structure	71
Competitive Decisions to Supply	74
Supply and Demand in Markets	77
Pure Competition: A Polar Extreme Case of Market Structure	81
Monpoly: A Polar Extreme Case of Market Structure	85
Market Structures between Monopoly and Competition	86
Market Structure and Pricing Power	92
Regulation and Market Niche	92
Examples in Competitive Markets	94
Examples in Monopoly Markets	94
Examples in Oligopoly Markets	96
Examples in Monopolistically Competitive Markets	98
Heterogeneity, Psychology and Ecological Niche	98
Dynamics	100

	Crossing National Boundaries	101
	Chapter Summary	103
	Questions for Study, Discussion, and Examination	106

4 Quantifying the Market Niche: Financial Measurement 111

Breakeven	112
Contribution Margin	112
Three Dimensions of Marketing Controllable Profit	121
Exploring C.O.E. Within an Individual Offering	122
Contribution Margin in Time: The Future Pattern of C.O.E., Without Investment and with Investment	124
C.O.E. Across the Product Line: Solving the Problem in Year One	126
Longer Term Constraint: Society and Capital	129
The Capital Market	129
Capital Allocation	130
Aids to Conceptualization: Models of Capital Allocation . .	130
Adjustments: Non Profit Organizations	133
Crossing National Boundaries	133
Chapter Summary	137
Appendix A: Perspectives and Calculations for Evaluating C.O.E. in Time	139
Net Present Value	140
Ranking Investments: Internal Rate of Return	142
Payback	142
Return on Investment and Associated Calculations . .	146
Understanding Currency Fluctuations	146
Questions for Study, Discussion, and Examination	151

Part II

The Managerial Variables and the Market Niche

5 Adjusting the Exchange: the Interaction of Appropriate Price and Product Design 157

    Pricing the Homogeneous Product 158

    Pricing the Differentiated Product 161

    Pricing and Designing the Differentiated Product: Understanding the Differentiation 162

    Pricing and Designing the Differentiated Product: Other Factors Affecting Price 165

    Market Structure 166

    Options for Management Initiative 167

    The Response of the Market Niche 167

    General Strategic Direction 170

    Pricing the Monopoly Product 172

    Typical Pricing Objectives 172

    The Specialized Terminology of Pricing 173

    Perspectives in Product Design 173

    Product Classes 173

    Branding 173

    Competition Among Brands 177

    Packaging 177

    Crossing National Boundaries 178

    Chapter Summary 180

    Appendix B: Commonly Used Terms to Describe Pricing, Behavior, and Express Price 183

    Questions for Study, Discussion, and Examination 187

6 Adjusting the Exchange: Altering the Price—Product Interaction with Promotion ... 191

    The General Problem ... 192
    The Option ... 192
    Sales Promotion ... 192
    Public Relations ... 192
    Advertising ... 193
    Personal Selling ... 203
    Communication Feedback ... 210
    Useful Diagnostic Models ... 210
    Crossing National Boundaries ... 211
    Appendix C: Useful Diagnostic Models for Marketing Communication ... 214
        Adoption Process Model ... 221
        The Adoption Curve Model ... 221
        The AIDA Model ... 222
        The Multistage Flow Model ... 222

    Questions for Study, Discussion, and Examination ... 225

7 Adjusting the Exchange: Altering the Price-Product Interaction with Place ... 231

    Channels ... 231
    Forms of Channel Organization ... 232
    Entities and Their Typical Functions ... 234
    Wholesalers and Their Typical Functions ... 236
        1. Buying and Selling ... 236
        2. Transportation and Storage ... 236
        3. Standardizing and Grading ... 237
        4. Financing ... 237
        5. Risk Taking ... 238
        6. Market Information ... 238

Specific Wholesaler Types	238
Retailers and Their Typical Functions	239
The Market Niche of the Retailer and Retail Types	243
Technological Change in Retailing	247
Channel Dynamics	247
Physical Exchange: Transportation and Storage	249
Transportation Options: Their Costs and Customer Service Capabilities	251
Water	252
Pipeline	254
Rail	255
Motor Carriers or Trucks	256
Air	257
Transportation Ownership: Cost Versus Price	258
Pricing in Transportation Services	258
Innovation and Facilitating Transportation Services	259
Storage Options: Their Costs and Customer Service Characteristics	260
Integrated Physical Distribution: Transportation Plus Storage	262
Enhancing the Market Niche with Integrated Distribution Policy	263
Crossing National Boundaries	265
Chapter Summary	266
Questions for Study, Discussion, and Examination	268

Part III

Managing the Market Exchange Process

8 Gaining and Analyzing Information 277

    Environmental Scans 277

    Internal Scans or Audits 284

    Directed Information Gathering: Market Research 285

    A Market Research Project 285

    Market Research: The Management Problem 286

    Market Research: The Research Problem 286

    Market Research: Research Design 286

    Market Research: Field Work 293

    Market Research: Data Analysis Interpretation and Communication 293

    Information About the Future 295

    Trend Extension 296

    Trend Extension and Modeling 299

    Modeling 299

    Crossing National Boundaries 301

    The Normative Versus Empirical Perspective 302

    Chapter Summary 304

    Questions for Study, Discussion, and Examination 306

9 Information Synthesis and Organizational Strategy ... 313

Marketing Organization ... 314
Flexibility in Marketing Organization ... 318
Procedures to Facilitate a Whole Understanding and Strategic Choice ... 320
Strategic Choice ... 321
Varieties of Strategy: Conceptual Aids to Strategic Choice ... 323
Portfolio Models ... 323
PIMS Results ... 326
Contingency Models: A Product Life Cycle Example ... 329
The Experience Curve ... 329
Military Analogy ... 331
Game Theory ... 332
Positioning ... 337
Segmentation ... 344
Mergers, Acquisitions and Spinoffs ... 348
The Marketing Concept and Capital Shifting ... 350
Risk and Product Market Expansion ... 351
Strategic Response Patterns in a Changing Environment ... 353
Results of Strategy Selection ... 353
Crossing National Boundaries ... 354
The Normative Versus Empirical Perspectives ... 357
Chapter Summary ... 359
Questions for Study, Discussion, and Examination ... 364

10 Legal and Ethical Guidelines 371

Marketing Law in the United States 372
Antitrust Laws 372
Consumer Protection Laws 374
Intellectual Property Protection 376
Contract Law 376
Direct Economic Regulation 376
Law and Ethics 378
Marketing Ethics 379
Secular Ethics 380
Religious Ethics 382
Scriptural Ethics 382
    Positive Injunction 383
    Negative Injunction 384
    Governing Perspectives 385
Implications to Marketing Strategy 385
Crossing National Boundaries 386
Law 386
Ethics 388
Ethical Marketing 391
Chapter Summary 392
Questions for Study, Discussion, and Examination 397

List of Figures

Figure 1	Economies of Scale	6
Figure 2	Perception	15
Figure 3	Improvement in Satisfaction or Utility	21
Figure 4	Loss of Satisfaction or Utility	22
Figure 5	Need Structures and the Idea of Tensions	23
Figure 6	Consumer Behavior Models—The Howard Sheth Model	26
Figure 7	A Low Involvement Buyer Behavior Model—Engle-Blackwell	27
Figure 8	The Sheth Family Decision Making Model	28
Figure 9	The Webster and Wind Model of Organizational Buying Behavior	29
Figure 10	Buyer's Choice—The Consumer Behavior and Micro-Economic Perspective Related	31
Figure 11	Utility Curves	34
Figure 12	Diminishing Marginal Utility	34
Figure 13	The Budget Line	36
Figure 14	The Economist's Picture of Consumer Choice	36
Figure 15	Effects of Price Changes	38

Figure 16	Effects of Income Changes	40
Figure 17	Creating a Demand Curve	43
Figure 18	Backward Bending or Prestige Demand Curve	44
Figure 19	Perfectly Inelastic Demand	45
Figure 20	Relatively Inelastic Demand	47
Figure 21	Relatively Elastic Demand	47
Figure 22	Effect of Successful Product or Service Differentiation	50
Figure 23	Effect of Promotion or Communication	50
Figure 24	Effect of Place	51
Figure 25	The Economist's Portrayal of the Firm	70
Figure 26	Costs and Revenue	72
Figure 27	Definitions Explored	73
Figure 28	Supply Decisions of the Individual Firm: An Economist's Portrayal	75
Figure 29	The Supply Curve, Horizontal Summation of Individual Choice to Supply	78
Figure 30	Supply and Demand in a Market	80
Figure 31	Consumer Surplus	82
Figure 32	Pure Competition	84
Figure 33	Monopoly	87
Figure 34	Monopoly of the World Market for Lead Lifeboats	88
Figure 35	Price Effects of Shifting the Demand Curve	88
Figure 36	The Oligopoly Kinked Demand Curve	91
Figure 37	Market Structure and Pricing Power	93
Figure 38	Regulation of Competitive Markets	95
Figure 39	Price Control In Monopoly	97
Figure 40	The Product Life Cycle OR Innovation Life Cycle	102
Figure 41	Breakeven Analysis	113

Figure 42	Overhead, Incremental Costs and Incremental Revenues	115
Figure 43a	Product Profitability Analysis	116
Figure 43b	Contribution to Overhead and Earnings [C.O.E.]	118
Figure 44a	C.O.E. Analysis	119
Figure 44b	Three Dimensions of Contribution Margin	120
Figure 45	C.O.E. in the Individual Offering	123
Figure 46a	C.O.E. in Time: No Investment	125
Figure 46b	C.O.E. in Time: Investment	125
Figure 47	C.O.E. Across the Product Line	127
Figure 48	Example of a Linear Programming Approach to Short-Term Profit Maximization Across the Product Line	128
Figure 49	Marketing Decisions as Capital Allocations	131
Figure 50	Marketing Decisions as Capital Allocations: The BCG Model	132
Figure 51	Marketing a Japanese-Manufactured Product in the United States: Results in Dollars and Yen	135
Figure 52	Translated to C.O.E. in US Dollars	136
Figure 53	Currency Fluctuations and Results in the Reference Currency	138
Figure A-1	Cash Flow Benefits	141
Figure A-2	Compounding of $1.00 at 10%	143
Figure A-3	A Logical Development of the Net Present Value Calculation	144
Figure A-4	Converting NPV to IRR	145
Figure A-5	A Balance of Trade Deficit and Its Effect upon the Value of Currency	147
Figure 54	Buyer's Choice—The Consumer Behavior and Micro-Economic Perspectives Related	160
Figure 55	Linear Models and the Engle Blackwell Model	164

Figure 56	Options for Management Initiative and the Place of Price	168
Figure 57	Contribution Margin of the Individual Offering	169
Figure 58	Effects to Consider when Pricing	171
Figure 59	Consumer Goods Classes	174
Figure 60	Industrial Goods Classes	175
Figure 61	Consumer Behavior Perspectives Are Useful in Advertising	194
Figure 62	A Message Appeal May Appeal to any Level of Maslow's Hierarchy of Needs	200
Figure 63	Common Terms and Concepts to Describe Sales Presentations	207
	The Engle Blackwell Model of Consumer Behavior—High Involvement	215
	The Engle Blackwell Model of Consumer Behavior—Low Involvement	216
	Information Loop Concept	217
	A General Model of Communications	217
	Microeconomic Models	218
	Communications which Reduce Competition	219
Figure 64	The Terms Vertical and Horizontal as Used in Distribution	233
Figure 65	Sources of Power	235
Figure 66	Common Terms Describing Wholesalers	240
Figure 67	Axes to Characterize Retail Strategy	242
Figure 68	Common Terms for Retailer Types	244
Figure 69	Aspects of Retail Strategies for Representative Types	245
Figure 70	Integeration in Channels	250
Figure 71	Costs Versus Contribution to Customer Service by Mode	253
Figure 72	Customer Service and Revenue	264

Figure 73	Common Demographic Terms Used in Marketing	279
Figure 74	A National Economy	281
Figure 75	Leading Indicators in the U.S. Economy	282
Figure 76	An Experimental Design Using a Control Group	287
Figure 77	Statistical Inference	289
Figure 78	Sampling Procedures and Examples	290
Figure 79	Level of Confidence, Precision, and Sample Size	292
Figure 80	Established Measurement Devices	294
Figure 81a	Simple Trend Extension by Geometric Projection	297
Figure 81b	Simple Trend Extension by Geometric Projection	297
Figure 82	A Possible Use of Multiple Regression	298
Figure 83	Hierarchical Structures Organized by Function	315
Figure 84	The Product Manager in a Matrix Context	315
Figure 85	The Market Manager in a Matrix Context	317
Figure 86	The New Product Manager	317
Figure 87	The BCG Matrix	325
Figure 88	The General Electric Planning Grid	327
Figure 89	The Directional Policy Matrix	328
Figure 90	The Innovation Life Cycle or the Product Life Cycle	330
Figure 91	Attack Strategies, Governing Principles and Marketing Examples	333
Figure 92	Defense Strategies Governing Principles and Marketing Examples	334
Figure 93	Payoff Matrices	336
Figure 94	Probable Outcomes	338
Figure 95	Product Positioning	340
Figure 96	The Repositioning of Product B	340

Figure 97	Identification of a New Potential Market Niche	342
Figure 98	Repositioning Product B to The Ideal Position	343
Figure 99	Financial Viability of Alternative Segments	346
Figure 100	The Boston Consulting Group Matrix Classifying Firms or Subsidiaries Held	349
Figure 101	Product-market Expansion Grid	352
Figure 102	International Organizational Forms	356
Figure 103	International Product Market Portfolios	358
Figure 104	Sources of Power	360
Figure 105	The Nature of Rail Monopoly	377

PART I

MARKET EXCHANGE AND MARKET NICHE

The first part of this book introduces the market exchange process; this includes the social rationale for specialization and exchange, as well as the various perspectives from psychology, economics and finance which allow an integrated understanding of the process. Outcomes of this examination will include an understanding of consumer choice, markets, and the market niche of the firm. Financial characterization and measurement of the market niche are carefully developed as they will be useful in guiding the managerial perspectives which comprise the second and third parts of the book.

Chapter One

Marketing And Its Functions

Marketing Defined

The study of marketing is the study of *human exchange behavior*. It may therefore be seen as an intrinsically psychological study. However, the focus of most marketing study is upon *voluntary* exchange behavior *as guided and constrained* by ethical and legal ground rules. As these ethical and legal ground rules are socially derived and interpreted, the guidelines for marketing practice may be understood in terms of ethics, religion, psychology, sociology, political science or law. In this social view of exchange behavior, group expectations may be codified as law.

The study of marketing must include a careful examination of *two human decisions* essential to the exchange: The decision to provide or *supply* a good or service and the decision to accept or *demand* a good or service. Both supply decisions and demand decisions may be either individual or group decisions. Extensive examination of supply and demand behavior has been undertaken within the academic discipline of microeconomics, and ideas developed in this area will provide extremely powerful insights into marketing behavior.

Since exchanges are the result of individual or group decisions which create demand or supply, they may be studied form a point of view provided by any of several academic disciplines. *Psychology* and *economics* are particularly useful in describing an exchange as are *finance* and *accounting*. Within economics, *price theory* will provide a powerful perspective, as price is a critical component of the exchange. It is the component which, through continuous adjustment, can alter the desirability of any proposed exchange to either party. Prices, as developed and understood in microeconomic price theory, may be seen as being derived from psychological realities. At the same time, prices provide the inputs used by society's conventional modes of measuring the economic results of exchange. Prices of things sold add up to revenue, as prices of things purchased for transformation into goods and services add up to costs. In this way, the disciplines of finance and accounting become integral to the understanding of marketing.

The Functions of Marketing

The *functions of marketing* may be viewed from several perspectives. These perspectives include the function performed for the individual parties to the exchange, the function performed for society as a whole, and the functions comprising the marketing process itself.

Functions for Parties to the Exchange

For the individual parties to the exchange, the function of the exchange behavior is to *improve their satisfaction* with their situation. This may be seen as being strictly a material improvement, as a measurable improvement in a person's standard of living or in a firm's profit. But the term *satisfaction* is fundamentally psychological, and is defined in terms of gratification, pleasure, or contentment.[1] What satisfies an individual is dependent upon the psychology of the individual, and may or may not be material in nature. A person may improve *satisfaction* with life by giving belongings to the poor, according to religion. Alternatively, if one's value system is materialistic one will seek to improve satisfaction in a materialistic way.

Functions for Society

From a social point of view marketing activities perform the function of *matching* heterogeneous supplies with heterogeneous demands.[2] Even without considering the substantial *heterogeneity* of human psychology, a would-be economic planner is confronted with awesome physical *heterogeneity*. People come in different sizes and live in different places, and the raw materials needed to provide a standard of living for the race are equally diverse and scattered. Of course, the race might opt out of this complex matching chore. In that case each individual would produce and consume the same assortment of goods and services. Human experience has shown that this "Robinson Crusoe" approach fails to provide the low costs which come from specialization or large scale production and results in a lower standard of living.

The importance of the standard of living enjoyed by the human race should not be seen simply in terms of the level of luxury one enjoys as it might be seen in the United States. The world's population is undergoing unprecedented and explosive growth. Failure to realize the standards of living which are achievable through specialization and exchange could result in mass starvation.

Specialization and exchange results in a higher standard of living because people become more knowledgeable and efficient at an activity when they specialize in that activity. This, combined with the productive efficiency which comes with larger production runs and the use of modern equipment, yields a cornerstone of adequate human living standards, low unit costs. Given this, it becomes wise for people to produce a great deal of something and to exchange it for what they need or want to consume. This in turn requires some means of matching supplies and demands or facilitating exchange.

Consider for *example*, a primitive fishing economy. If there were no specialization and exchange, each individual would have to undertake the learning necessary to know how to build a canoe. Each individual would also have to obtain the tools necessary to build a canoe. The entire cost of the learning experience together with the tools' cost would have to be added to the cost of the single canoe produced by a single individual. This situation is depicted in figure 1 as point A. Note also in figure 1, that as more canoes are built by the individual who is now beginning to specialize, the *average total cost* per canoe begins to come down. The average total cost is simply the total cost of production divided by the number of units produced. This is illustrated by points B and C in figure 1. This effect is observable because, once the learning and tools have been obtained, the additional costs required to build any extra canoe are relatively low. In this example, the additional costs of an extra canoe are the $200.00 costs of direct materials and labor. These additional costs are called *incremental costs* or *marginal costs*.

This low incremental or marginal cost of producing extra canoes has served to bring the average total cost of the canoes down. This phenomenon, decreasing average total cost with increasing numbers of units produced, is referred to as *Economies of Scale* in production.

When this kind of cost pattern results from specialization, it becomes advantageous for individuals to specialize in their productive efforts and engage in exchange (marketing) behaviors with others in the community. This pattern of specialization and exchange should be to their advantage until such time as exchange or marketing costs completely consume the cost advantages achieved in specialized production. Alternatively, specialization and exchange may not be worthwhile when individuals find the extent of their

Figure 1
Economies of Scale

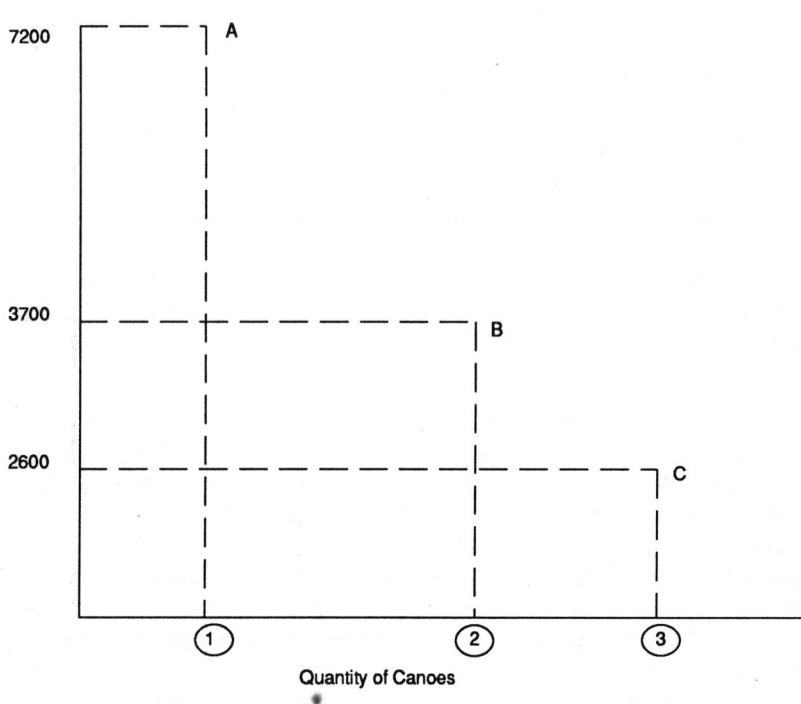

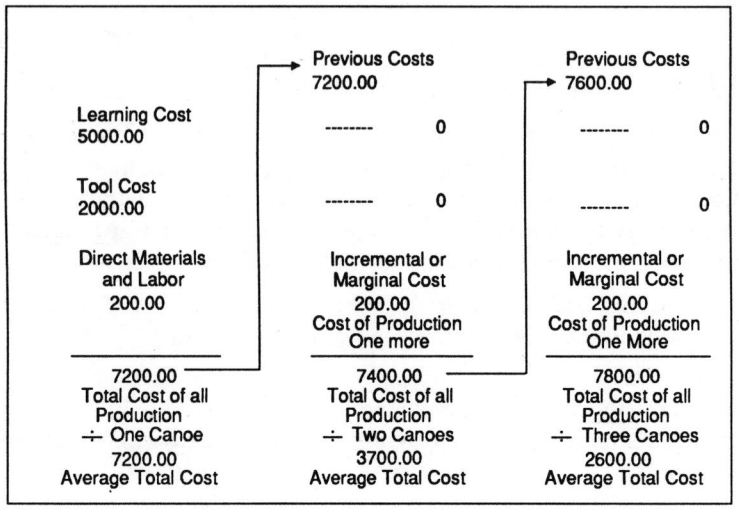

personal specialization in the work place to be intolerably demeaning. When sufficient individual freedom remains in a society, individuals may opt out of the specialization and exchange process when they are dissatisfied. An individual opting to engage in subsistence farming might feel the that marketing costs are too high ("I can achieve a higher standard of living by myself") or might feel that an improvement in daily lifestyle has been achieved.

When this kind of specialization of human skills and human production is added to the natural diversity and dispersion of raw materials, *supply* in the society *becomes heterogeneous* in the extreme. When psychological individuality is added to the natural physical and geographic heterogeneity of the human race, *demand* in the society *becomes heterogeneous* in the extreme. Society requires a mechanism to match these demands with these supplies, to decide who will produce what for whom. When authoritarian approaches are avoided, and individuals are left free to engage in voluntary exchange behavior, *marketing is the mechanism which matches* supplies with demands.

Alternative approaches have been attempted in some societies. These have utilized varying degrees of state authority (force) in place of voluntary exchange behaviors. Viewed from market societies, these state approaches are often seen as unsatisfactory because of the loss of freedom involved when state authority is used. State authoritarian approaches have to some extent fallen from favor in their originating societies. This has largely been a result of a pragmatic concern for quality and productivity rather than a result of a concern for human liberty. These societies have begun to experiment with market allocations, much as the United States has experimented with state ownership or control when there has been dissatisfaction with the market mechanism.[3]

Functions Comprising Marketing

Matching, the greater social function of marketing, which is driven by individual and group attempts to improve their satisfaction with a situation, is comprised of several lesser functions. These functions are generally referred to as the *functions of marketing*. Several lists of marketing functions exist. The following list is commonly used and recognized:[4]

1. Buying and selling
   [Facilitates the match by changing ownership]

2. Transportation and Storage
   [Facilitates the match by altering when and where things are available.]

3. Standardizing and Grading
   [Facilitates the match by clarifying the nature of the product being offered.]
4. Financing
   [Facilitates the match by providing the funds needed by producers, sellers or buyers.]
5. Risk Taking
   [Facilitates the match by risking assets in order to be ready for anticipated patterns of exchange.]
6. Market Information
   [Facilitates the match by letting buyers know more about sellers and what they offer. Facilitates the match by letting sellers know about buyers and what they want.]

The ways in which these functions contribute to the social matching process is straightforward. *Buying and selling* provides for legal exchange of title or stewardship, often the consummation of a match. *Transportation and storage* facilitates the exchange by moving items to places where they may be required and holding them for times when they may be required. *Standardizing and grading* facilitates the exchange by identifying classes or categories of goods or services and certifying their quality. Branding performs a part of this function in modern market societies. In this way, the buyer does not have to individually inspect each item purchased.

The production and distribution of any item also requires *financing* or the advance of funds. Without financing, an automobile manufacturer might require that the buyer provide cash for the automobile a year in advance of delivery. This would allow the firm to buy direct materials and labor in order to produce and deliver the car. In fact, not only are few auto buyers willing and able to do this, but most require that funds be advanced to them.

Sometimes funds or other assets are committed on a risk basis. *Risk taking* amounts to placing assets so as to facilitate an exchange which may or may not occur. By placing the assets in a way that facilitates the exchange, the owner of the assets hopes to encourage an exchange which will more than repay his costs of taking the risk. A dealer does this when inventory is purchased. None of it may be sold, but the dealer is willing to take the risk that buyers will be responsive to the great selection that the inventory investment has provided.

The match is further facilitated by *market information*. The perfect match between product and customer may have been created, but if the seller does not know who or where the buyer is, and the buyer has not heard of the product, this excellent potential match will never come to fruition. Promotional activities such as advertising and sales, and company information gathering such as market research activities provide this function in modern societies.

---

[1] Webster's definition of "satisfaction" includes the terms gratification, pleasure and contentment. Webster's definition of "satisfy" includes the concepts of fulfillment of needs, expectations, wishes, desires, or requirements. These terms and concepts convey the meaning of satisfaction as used in this book.

[2] This view of marketing's social role has been inspired by Wroe Alderson. See for example Wroe Alderson, *Marketing Behavior and Executive Action* (Homewood, Illinois: Richard D. Irwin, 1957), pp. 195-202. See also Wroe Alderson, *Dynamic Marketing Behavior* (Homewood, Illinois: Richard D. Irwin, 1965), p. 26. See also Shelby D. Hunt, James A. Muncy, and Nina M. Ray, "Alderson's General Theory of Marketing: A Formalization," in *Review of Marketing 1981*, eds. Ben M. Enis and Kenneth J. Roering (Chicago, Illinois: American Marketing Association, 1981), p. 271.

[3] During the 1980's the People's Republic of China and the Soviet Union engaged in extensive experimentations with the market mechanism in order to improve productivity. For its part, the United States has experimented with such extra market institutions as TVA and Amtrak.

[4] There have been many lists of marketing functions created. Most are roughly similar. This list appears in E. Jerome McCarthy and William D. Perreault Jr., *Basic Marketing*, 9th Edition (Homewood, Illinois: Irwin, 1987), p. 18, and is used with permission.

Questions for Study, Discussion and Examination

1. Could you define or explain to a friend who has not studied marketing, each of the following terms?
    a. Marketing
    b. Voluntary exchange
    c. Function
    d. Satisfaction
    e. Matching
    f. Specialization
    g. Exchange
    h. Standard of living
    i. Unit cost or average total cost
    j. Incremental cost or marginal cost
    k. Economies of scale
    l. Heterogeneity of supply
    m. Heterogeneity of demand
    n. Buying and selling
    o. Transportation and storage
    p. Standardizing and grading
    q. Financing
    r. Risk taking
    s. Market information

2. What kind of study is the study of marketing? To what extent is it psychology or economics or finance? How do these disciplines interact to describe marketing behaviors?

3. What was your last major purchase? Why do you think you bought it? To what extent you were unique in the way you came to your decision?

4. Of what use is marketing to individual members of society in their roles as consumers and in their roles as producers?

5. Are decisions to demand something individual or group decisions? Give examples.

6. Are decisions to supply something individual or group decisions? Give examples?

7. Of what use is marketing to society as a whole?

8. Why does specialization and exchange make sense in terms of unit costs and standards of living?
9. How fast is the world population expected to grow during the current period of time? (late 20th century). How fast should the production of goods and services grow to ensure that (on average) the human material standard of living does not fall? (You may wish to consult a library in order to derive exact numbers.)
10. How does marketing contribute to a standard of living?
11. From the point of view of the society, when are marketing costs too high?
12. How does an incremental or marginal cost differ from an average total cost?
13. What are the disadvantages of specialization?
14. Why is supply heterogeneous?
15. Why is demand heterogeneous?
16. What drives or motivates the market matching process in a free society? What alternative to the market matching process exist?
17. Discuss the pros and cons of voluntary exchange versus state authority to encourage the matching process. What drives each?
18. What contribution does each of the functions which comprise marketing make to the larger function which marketing itself provides to the society?
19. Could a voluntary exchange occur which results in one party gaining and another party losing? What logical problems or inconsistancies appear to exist in this situation? What resolutions do you see?
20. Does pursuit of satisfaction imply materialism? Why or why not?

CHAPTER TWO

Human Exchange: Satisfaction, Utility and Demand Behavior

This chapter explores the reasons people decide to *demand* goods or services, while the next chapter will explore the conditions under which people elect to *supply* goods or services. The two chapters, taken together, should provide a useful picture of voluntary human exchange, the first focusing on the buyer, and the second focusing on the seller.

People engage in voluntary exchange behaviors in order to improve their satisfaction with their situation. In the case of the buyer, this often means adjusting the assortment of goods or services which is owned or cared for. The study of this *demand aspect* of the exchange will proceed in two directions. First, the question of *what creates human satisfaction* or utility will be explored. Secondly, behavior patterns which can be explained in terms of the individual's *attempts to improve satisfaction* or utility will be presented. The first question has traditionally belonged to the psychologist or the more marketing specialized consumer behaviorist. The second has traditionally been the microeconomist's area of study. The terms *satisfaction*, used by psychologists and consumer behaviorists, or *utility*, used by economists, may be *used interchangeably* by the beginning student or the practical market analyst. Both economics texts and Webster's Dictionary define utility in terms of satisfaction.[1]

Exploring Utility: Psychology

Psychologists as well as philosophers and other groups have explored the question of what creates human satisfaction. Unfortunately, the question will not be quickly answered through reference to psychology. This is because psychologists are still engaged in a process of theory building and often do not shape a consensus. Psychological thought and research has proceeded down many separate tracks. This section will introduce useful perspectives provided by several of the areas of inquiry which characterize the field of psychology.

Psychologists studying *perception* have studied the way people attend to and organize incoming stimuli. This is important to marketing people because it addresses the effectiveness of attempts to communicate and the way people will organize stimuli into a meaningful image. Psychologists in the field of perception have given us the useful concepts of *perceptual vigilance*, an increased sensitivity to those stimuli which support one's current understandings and *perceptual defense*, a decreased sensitivity to those stimuli which conflict with one's current understandings.

This group has also contributed an understanding of *perceptual organization*, the mind's unconscious and automatic process of assigning meaning to incoming stimuli. Figure 2 illustrates the mind's tendency to do this. The stimulus is ambiguous. There is no necessary reason why the lines should be organized into either a three-dimensional box with the lower face or upper face closest to the observer. But the mind will not tolerate the ambiguity. It must organize incoming stimuli into meaningful perception. Principles of perceptual organization are owed in part to the "Gestalt" (pattern) school of psychology.[2] Therefore the term *Gestalt* has been used to refer to the resulting pattern or image. Perceptual psychologists have also contributed ideas concerning the effects of *perceptual sets*. A perceptual set, or the group of perceptions which the individual retains in memory, are believed to affect incoming perception. Some studies have found that the *way things are valued* by individuals affects such basic perceptions as the estimation of the size of the object.

Findings from the psychology of perception suggest that people will be extremely individualistic in what they will perceive and how they will organize their perceptions into unified images or Gestalts.[3] Whether something brings an individual satisfaction would logically depend upon how that something is perceived or viewed, how it is formed into an image or total Gestalt. Humankind becomes even more heterogeneous when its perceptual processes are understood.

Chapter 2   15

**Figure 2
Perception**

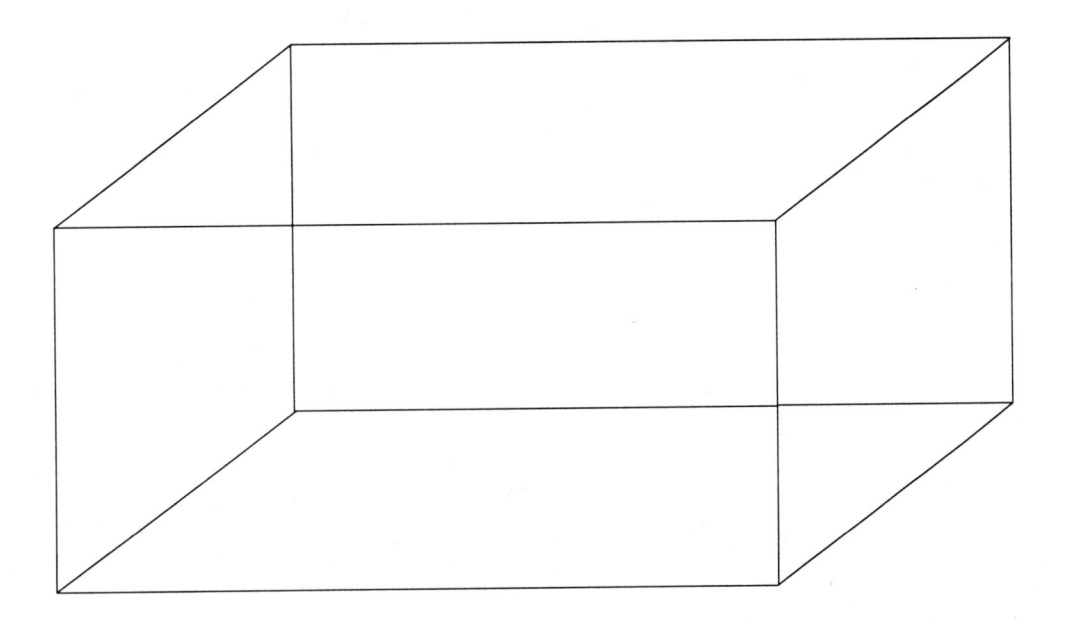

Is this a three-dimensional box with the upper face closest to you or the lower face closest to you? Or is it just a set of lines on a flat surface?

The mind is intolerant of ambiguity and organizes incoming stimuli into whole images or gestalts.

Social psychologists and sociologists have studied the interactions of group and individual behavior. The groups that an individual associates with or is even aware of can be expected to have substantial effects on a person's attitudes or predispositions to respond and thus on eventual responses. Groups can *act to change attitudes* by removing social support for the atttiude, generating disussion, and involving the individual in group decision making.[4] Important groups can also *support existing attitudes* by controlling exposure to information, determining the credibility of information sources and providing social support for the attitudes.[5] Groups also support or withdraw support for specific responses or behaviors. Groups found to be important to buying decisions include the individual's family, social class, work groups, and friendship groups.[6] Groups called *reference groups* are particularly important as they are defined as groups which people take as a frame of reference for self evaluation and attitude formation.[7] A reference group can be a *membership group* wherein the individual is an acknowledged member, an *aspirational group* that the individual would like to belong to, or a *dissociative group* whose behaviors and values the individual wishes to avoid.[8] Reference groups may have differing degrees of effect on different purchase decisions, sometimes affecting which brand name is preferred.[9]

Social psychologists have contributed other ideas concerning the change of attitudes and behaviors. Particularly useful for marketing people are such ideas as affective cognitive consistency and cognitive dissonance.[10] *Affective cognitive consistency* refers to one's feelings (affect) and thoughts (cognitions). These are seen as components of an attitude. When one's feelings and thoughts are consistent, the attitude toward the subject of the feelings and thoughts is stable and unlikely to change.[11] For example, I "feel" good about my car and I "think" that my car is safe, reliable and good looking. This stable attitude feels good, and information which is destabilizing is likely to be met with perceptual defense. On the other hand, if the destabilizing information is irrefutable (the car breaks down) then the attitude becomes unstable and likely to change. *Cognitive dissonance* refers to the relationship between cognitive elements and overt behavior. This allows it to be very useful in the context of purchase behavior. Cognitive dissonance is defined as:[12]

$$\text{Dissonance} = \frac{\text{Cognitive Elements Incongruent with Behavior}}{\text{Cognitive Elements Congruent with Behavior}}$$

Dissonance is psychologically uncomfortable. If one smokes cigarettes (behavior) one is unlikely to be able to totally avoid the information linking cigarette smoking with cancer (incongruent cognitive element). In this state of psychic discomfort the individual will seek to reduce dissonance by:[13]

1. Changing behavior (stop smoking)
2. Changing some element of environment (smoke filter tips)
3. Adding new cognitive elements (it won't happen to me because . . .)

Dissonance may be seen as resulting from psychic elements in conflict, creating a state of *tension* which is uncomfortable to the individual.[14] This state of tension between conflicting cognitive elements is a state nearly opposite in character to utility or satisfaction which has been defined in terms of gratification, pleasure or contentment. It is thus not only useful in explaining attitude stability or change, but is useful as an outcome of purchase behavior which stands in stark contrast to satisfaction or utility.

Social psychologists have thus provided us with insights concerning group effects on what an individual sees as giving satisfaction. They have provided insights into attitude stability and change and into cognitive dissonance, a concept which will be useful by virtue of its contrast with satisfaction or utility.

The contrast between satisfaction and dissonance provides marketing practitioners with a way to view the buyer's behavior as a *learning* process. When buyers experiment with some products and experience satisfaction, then experiment with other products and experience dissonance, there is a reward and punishment mechanism in place which conforms to the learning theorist's idea of *operant conditioning* or instrumental learning.[15] In operant conditioning the individual learns to associate his overt behavior with rewards or punishment. Thus, some purchase behavior is rewarded while some is punished.

Often overt behavior such as purchase of a product is not involved in the learning process. Sometimes an individual *learns to associate* certain feelings or emotions with products, ideas or images. For example an individual may have learned over a life time to associate warm feelings of home, family and community with certain images. The images might include white clapboard homes, well kept lawns, oak and elm trees, picket fences, kids and dogs. This association has become established because over the period of a lifetime, times of warm, comfortable and secure feelings have also been times when these other images were perceived. There may or may not be any causal relationship between the feelings and the images. That they have been perceived simultaneously a sufficient number of times to be associated with one another is enough. This kind of learning is called *classical conditioning*.[16] Advertisers use classical conditioning when they run advertisements which encourage the association of appropriate feelings with their product or service. For example, a presidential candidate might run ads using pictures of white clapboard homes, well kept lawns, oak and elm trees, picket fences, kids and dogs. These ads, if well executed, might then *evoke* (or call forth) warm feelings of home, family and community in certain audiences. What remains to be done is to encourage association of these feelings with the candidate. It may only be necessary to mention and show the name, repeating the advertisement to encourage the association.

Both operant conditioning and classical conditioning are examples of *associative learning*.[17] Important terms involved in this kind of learning include *drive*, which is the underlying motivation or need which the individual is trying to deal with.[18] In the example of the presidential campaign, the individual's drive, might be the need for security or fellowship such as might be found in the home. The *cue* is the stimulus which calls forth a *response*.[19] The warm feelings are called forth when the individual views the images of small town America. These images are the cues which call forth the emotional response. If the advertising is successful, a new association will be formed, and the candidate's name will be a new cue which calls forth the same emotional response. Rewards in these systems of learning are referred to as *reinforcement*.[20] In terms of an individual's reaction to purchases or the election of candidates, satisfaction is positive reinforcement. Removal of dissatisfaction is negative reinforcement and dissonance or dissatisfaction is punishment.[21]

Associative learning occurs in all kinds of animals. Man's greater cognitive capacity allows a different kind of learning to occur. In *cognitive learning* the human ability to reason and develop new insights is the mechanism of learning.[22] A solid understanding of this will await knowledge concerning just how people think, but in the meantime practitioners may view it as a rational process. In this process the buyer can be expected to apply reason to the chore of improving satisfaction with the situation. Industrial and professional selling approaches which use rational appeals based upon economic and engineering logic are hoping to stimulate cognitive learning.

Another group of psychologists have concerned themselves with the measurement of psychological phenomena. These people are involved in the field of *psychometrics*. The focus of this group is to devise and perfect measurement techniques for such difficult psychological constructs as personality, associations, perception and lifestyle. As challenging as this seems, useful measurements have been developed and standardized. The Edwards Personal Preference Schedule and Activities Interest and Opinion (AIO) Measures have been used to measure personality and lifestyle.[23] Projective techniques such as the Thematic Apperception Test (TAT) can give insights into associations that people make[24] and elaborate multivariate statistical techniques have been used to assemble approximations of how one product is perceived vis-a-vis another.[25] Market research people have participated in these developments and have applied them, providing useful information for marketing decisions.

Clinical psychologists deal with questions of human satisfaction and dissatisfaction on a one to one professional basis. They specialize in the areas of motivation, personality and psychopathology or abnormal psychology. In trying to solve the complex riddle of why an individual is satisfied or dissatisfied with life, they have developed many useful insights, constructs and theories.

In *Freudian* theory much of an individual's motivation is thought to be unconscious. The personality is structured in three parts: the id, ego, and superego. The id is the reflection of basic animal needs such as the need for sex. The superego is the reflection of social expectations, and the ego must somehow forge a workable personality. According to Freud, *the personality develops in response to tension*, which may come from physiological growth, frustrations, conflicts and threats.[26] People may deal with tension by identification, the adoption of the features of another's personality, or displacement of energy into socially acceptable channels. This last behavior is termed sublimation.[27]

Many other theories of personality use tension concepts. Sullivan "conceives of *personality* as an *energy system* whose *chief work* consists of activities that will *reduce tension.*"[28] He conceives of the organism as a *tension system* which varies between the limits of absolute relaxation (euphoria) to the absolute tension, exemplified by extreme terror.[29] To Sullivan the chief sources of tension are the needs of the organism and anxiety.[30]

Sullivan provides a *useful reconciliation* of the *tension* concept, which is central to many theories of personality with the *satisfaction* concept which is central to the understanding of markets.

> Tensions can be regarded as *needs* for particular energy transformations which will dissipate the tension, often with an accompanying change of "mental" state, a change of awareness, to which we can apply the general term *satisfaction.*[31]
>
> —*Harry Stack Sullivan*

Thus the marketing practitioner finds respectable support for a practical generalization to the effect that a decrease in tension is equivalent to an increase in satisfaction. This would also be equivalent to an increase in utility because satisfaction and utility are synonymous for practical marketing purposes.

However, one must then confront situations when it appears that it is an increase in tension which brings satisfaction. The thrills of increasing sexual excitement, of downhill skiing, of flying an open canopy airplane certainly brings some form of satisfaction. Recognition of these situations would support the idea that it is an ideal level of tension or balance of tensions which is sought, not necessarily the absolute minimum level of tension. This perspective is reflected in the work of Garner Murphy whose position is that *motives are tension gradients* in a tissue and that *"in general" tension reduction* is equivalent to satisfaction while tension increase is equivalent to discomfort.[32] Murphy acknowledges that pleasure is sometimes associated with increased tension.[33] An appropriate marketing generalization might therefore be that *adjustment of tension toward an ideal level*, balance or equilibrium constitutes *a gain in satisfaction* or utility. In like fashion, *adjustment of tension away from an ideal level*, balance or equilibrium constitutes *a loss of satisfaction* or utility. This generalization is illustrated in figures 3 and 4.

Another personality psychologist, Murray relates satisfaction not to the achieved level or balance of tension but to the process of adjustment.[34]

> It is important to note that it is not a tensionless state, as Freud supposed which is generally most *satisfying* to a healthy organism, but the *process of reducing tension*, and other factors being equal, the degree of *satisfaction* is roughly proportional to the amount of tension that is reduced per unit of time . . .
>
> —*Murray and Kuckohn*

The idea that satisfaction or utility is related to the achievement of an ideal level or balance of tension within the human organism can be very useful to marketing practitioners. *First* it serves to provide a *concise way of thinking about the many elaborate sets of needs or motives that are often used to explain human behavior*. Take for example Maslow's hierarchy of needs which is displayed in figure 5.[35] Maslow's more basic needs may be thought of as tensions which are a result of basic biological requirements. Then, as one ascends the hierarchy of needs, the tensions which must be addressed are increasingly a function of perceptions and cognitions. *Secondly*, relating the adjustment of tensions to satisfaction or utility is helpful because it provides a *useful interim concept* while psychologists seek a cleaner more measurable set of concepts to express the idea. In their close observation of individuals who are searching for satisfaction, clinical psychologists have come up with many concepts which are useful, but difficult or impossible to measure. One might for example, have measurement difficulty with Freud's concepts of id, ego, and superego. *Better precision and predictability in marketing will come with further theoretical development in psychology.*

Chapter 2 21

Figure 3
Improvement in Satisfaction or Utility

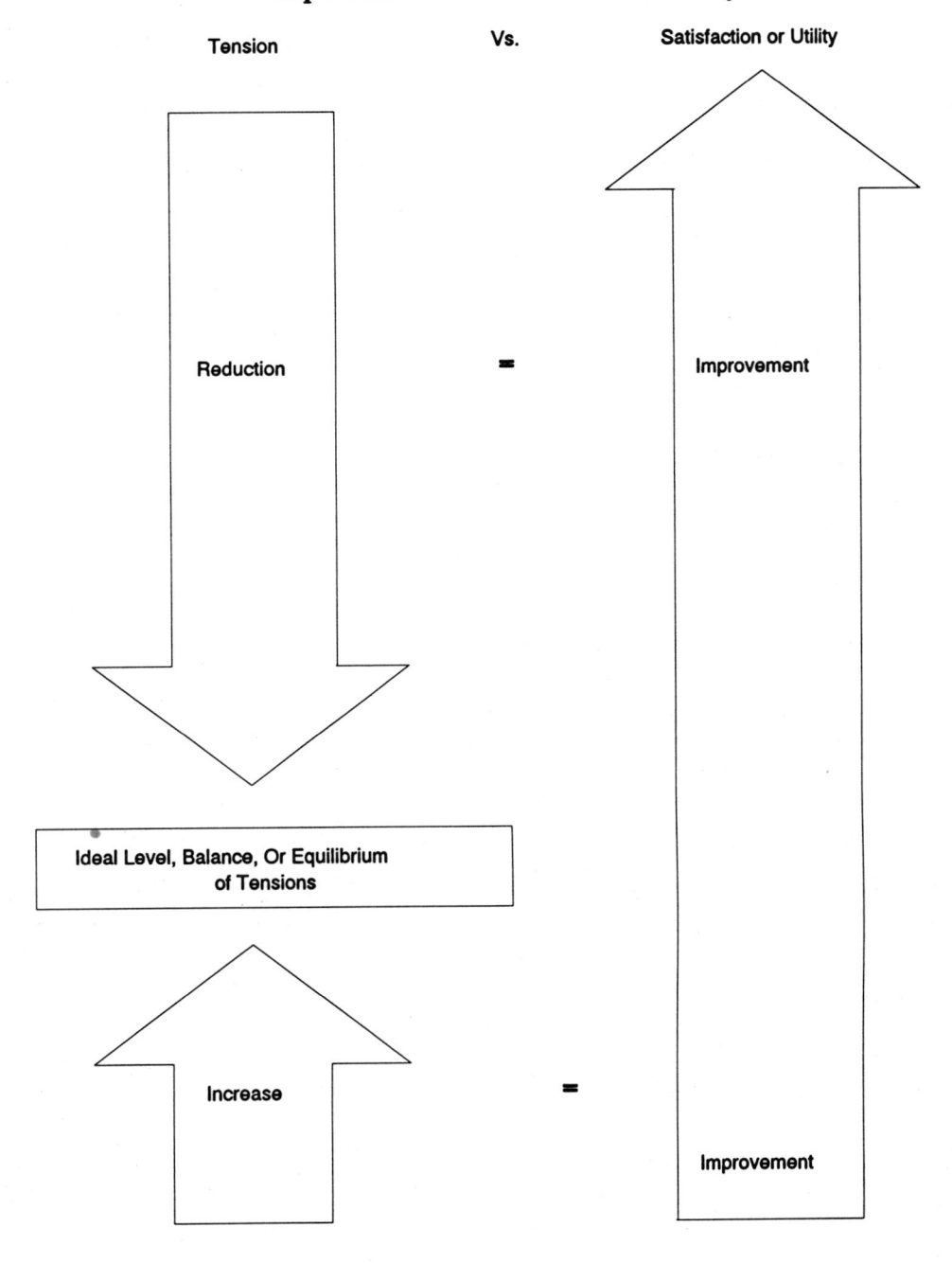

Tension   Vs.   Satisfaction or Utility

Reduction = Improvement

Ideal Level, Balance, Or Equilibrium of Tensions

Increase = Improvement

22 Part I

Figure 4
Loss of Satisfaction or Utility

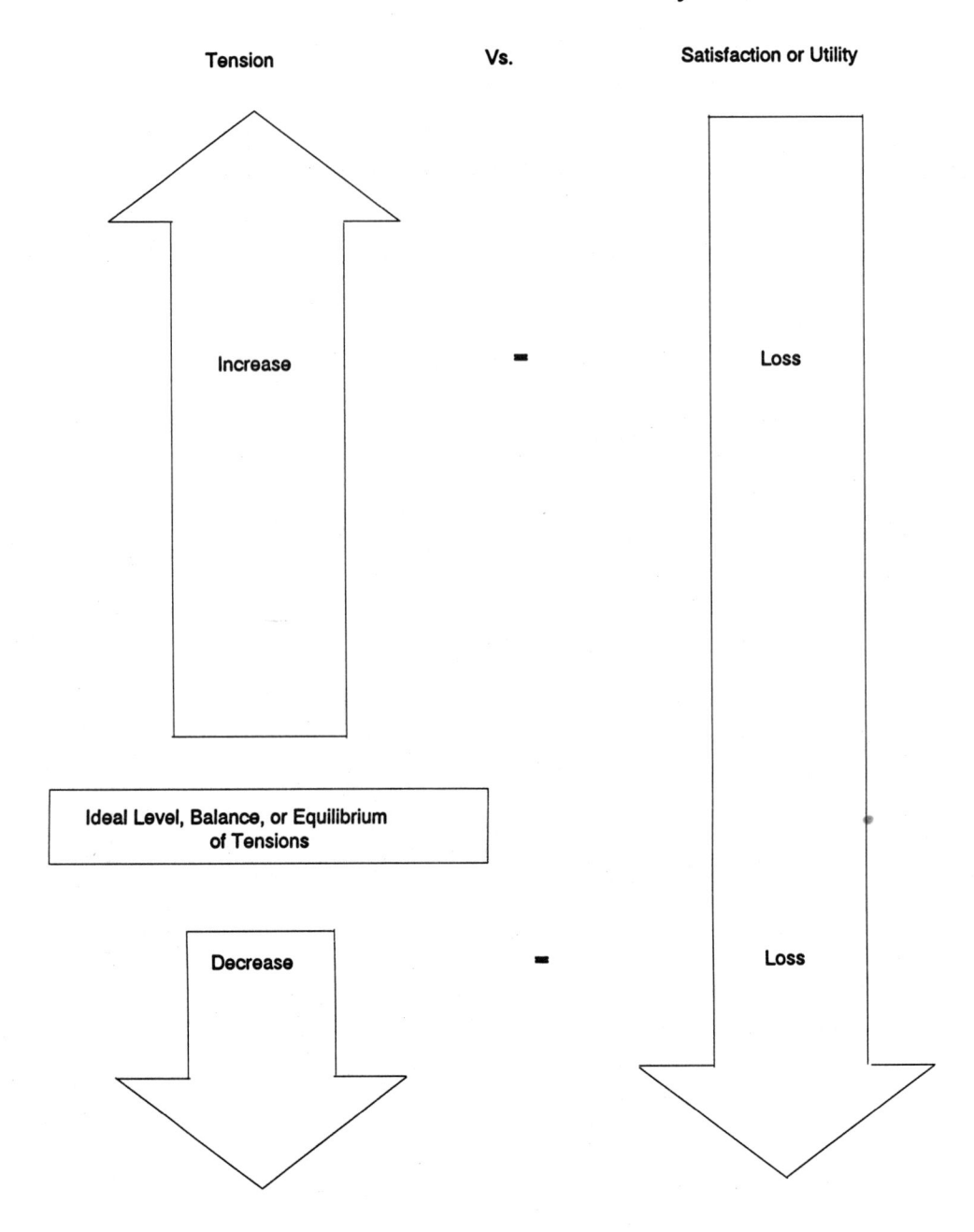

Tension   Vs.   Satisfaction or Utility

Increase   —   Loss

Ideal Level, Balance, or Equilibrium of Tensions

Decrease   —   Loss

Figure 5
Need Structures and the Idea of Tensions

Maslow's Heirarchy from Motivation and Personality, 2nd ed., by Abraham H. Maslow. Copyright 1954 by Harper and Row Publishers, Inc. Copyright 1970 by Abraham H. Maslow. Reprinted by permission of the publisher.

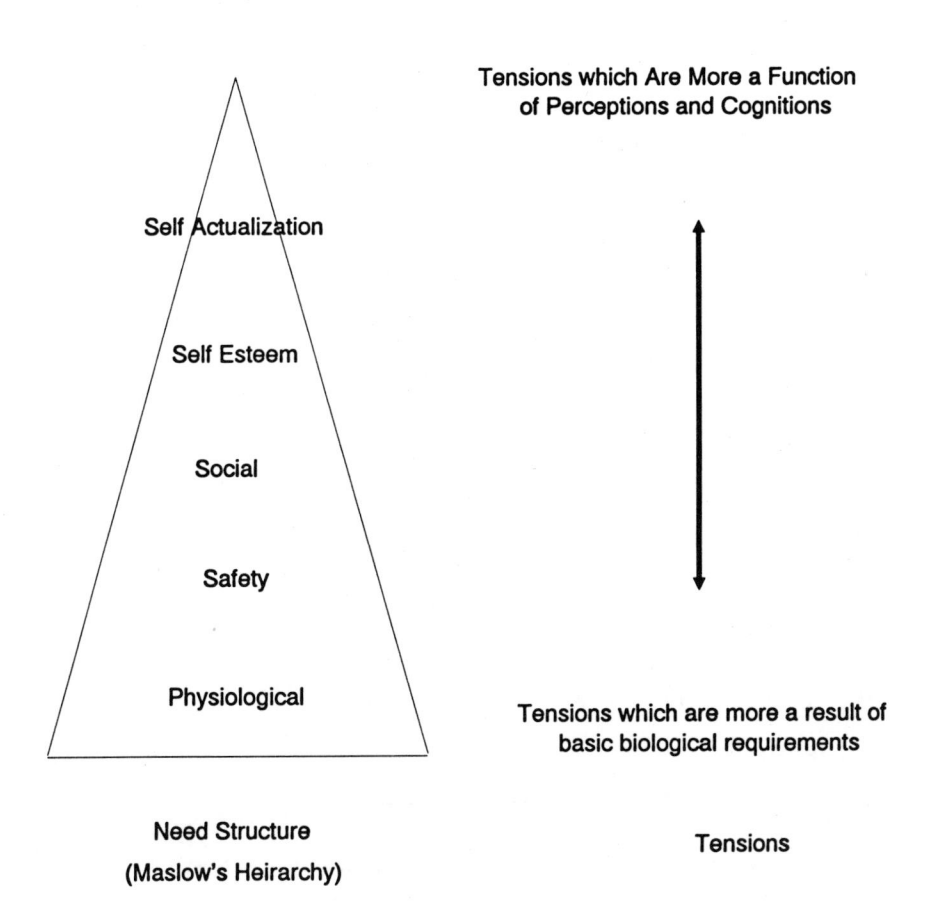

Pyramid labels top to bottom: Self Actualization, Self Esteem, Social, Safety, Physiological

Tensions which Are More a Function of Perceptions and Cognitions

Tensions which are more a result of basic biological requirements

Need Structure
(Maslow's Heirarchy)

Tensions

Theoretical development will require an improvement in the understanding of reality through observation of reality and improvement in the components of theory, forcing theory to conform with, explain and predict reality. The components of theory are *theoretical units*, the basic building blocks, and the *relationships* which are believed to exist among the theoretical units.[36] For example in physics, a science which is now well developed, Aristotle suggested in an early theory that the basic building blocks of matter were earth, air, fire and water.[37] These were early theoretical units in physics. This theory did not always predict and explain reality well, so better theoretical units were thought of. These were atoms. While atoms provided better prediction and explanation there were still problems. The theory then advanced with the understanding of subatomic particles. The relationships among these particles are often well enough understood so that they can be expressed mathematically.

So, too, it is hoped that science will advance in psychology, and the understanding of human satisfaction or utility will improve. In this context *tension may be an interim theoretical unit* to be further explained by and replaced with more useful, precise and measurable theoretical units.

One group of psychologists prefers to work with *theoretical units which are physiological.* These physical, electrochemical realities are more easily measured than the theoretical units used by the clinical psychologists. The nature of the *physiological psychologists'* experimental work has largely limited them to animal studies, but they have developed some very interesting hypotheses. For example one theory holds that memory is synaptic facilitation.[38] That is, the synapses become accustomed to firing in certain ways, facilitating retrieval through resulting "associations." The eventual place and importance of the physiological psychologists' has been suggested by a noted clinical psychologist. Murray recognized the *physiological processes which underlie the psychological.*[39] Recent research has found support for Murray's position. Physiological psychologists may eventually explain more precisely and completely, the physiological correlates of what is now called satisfaction or utility.

Exploring Utility: Consumer Behavior

Marketing practitioners will not idly wait for the best answers. Marketing is practiced *now* and marketing practitioners want to *apply* what psychological knowledge is available now. Therefore much as the discipline of engineering developed to apply what was known in physics, so the discipline of consumer behavior seeks to develop and apply psychological knowledge in marketing. Much of consumer behavior comes straightforwardly from psychology and has simply been placed in the context of the attempt to understand how a buyer or potential buyer behaves.

An important tool that consumer behaviorists have developed is the consumer behavior or *Buyer Behavior Model*. Each of these models describes a logical linkage of psychological concepts which explain a purchase decision. Figure 6 contrasts two popular models, the Howard Sheth Model and the Engle Blackwell High Involvement Model.[40] These models are not only useful in guiding theory development in their own right, but they are also extremely useful diagnostic tools for practitioners.

Both models illustrate *the use of the central concept of satisfaction*. In each model, purchase or choice may lead to *satisfaction*. The models also make use of social influence concepts, perceptual concepts, and learning concepts. Both models use the term "motive" which has been defined in terms of tension by some clinical psychologists.[41] In the Engle Blackwell model, motives influence problem recognition.[42] Sufficient *problem recognition*, a perceived difference between the *ideal state* of affairs and the *actual situation*, then activates a decision process which may result in satisfaction or dissonance (dissatisfaction).[43] This may be seen as a learning process which is activated by tensions and then either punishes with tensions or rewards with satisfaction.

Another useful concept incorporated in the Engle Blackwell Model is the concept of *alternative evaluation*. It is important to understand that an individual often evaluates alternative choices by judging how each alternative stacks up according to various *evaluative criteria* or standards.[44] Many models have been proposed to describe exactly how this is done.[45] For introductory purposes it is sufficient to understand that the *satisfaction an individual anticipates* from an alternative is *a function of how that alternative scores according to the individual's standards of judgment or evaluative criteria*. This anticipated satisfaction is also a function of perceptual effects such as total image, pattern or Gestalt effects.

Consumer behaviorists have created useful models to describe special purchase situations. One model describes a low involvement purchase where an individual simply buys something and evaluates it later.[46] This is illustrated in figure 7. Other models describe important group purchase decisions such as the family choice process (figure 8) and the organizational purchase decision (figure 9).[47] *Organizational buying* can be expected to be somewhat more systematic in nature than consumer buying. Evaluative criteria are more explicit and profit oriented in nature, and image or Gestalt effects have somewhat less influence.

26   Part I

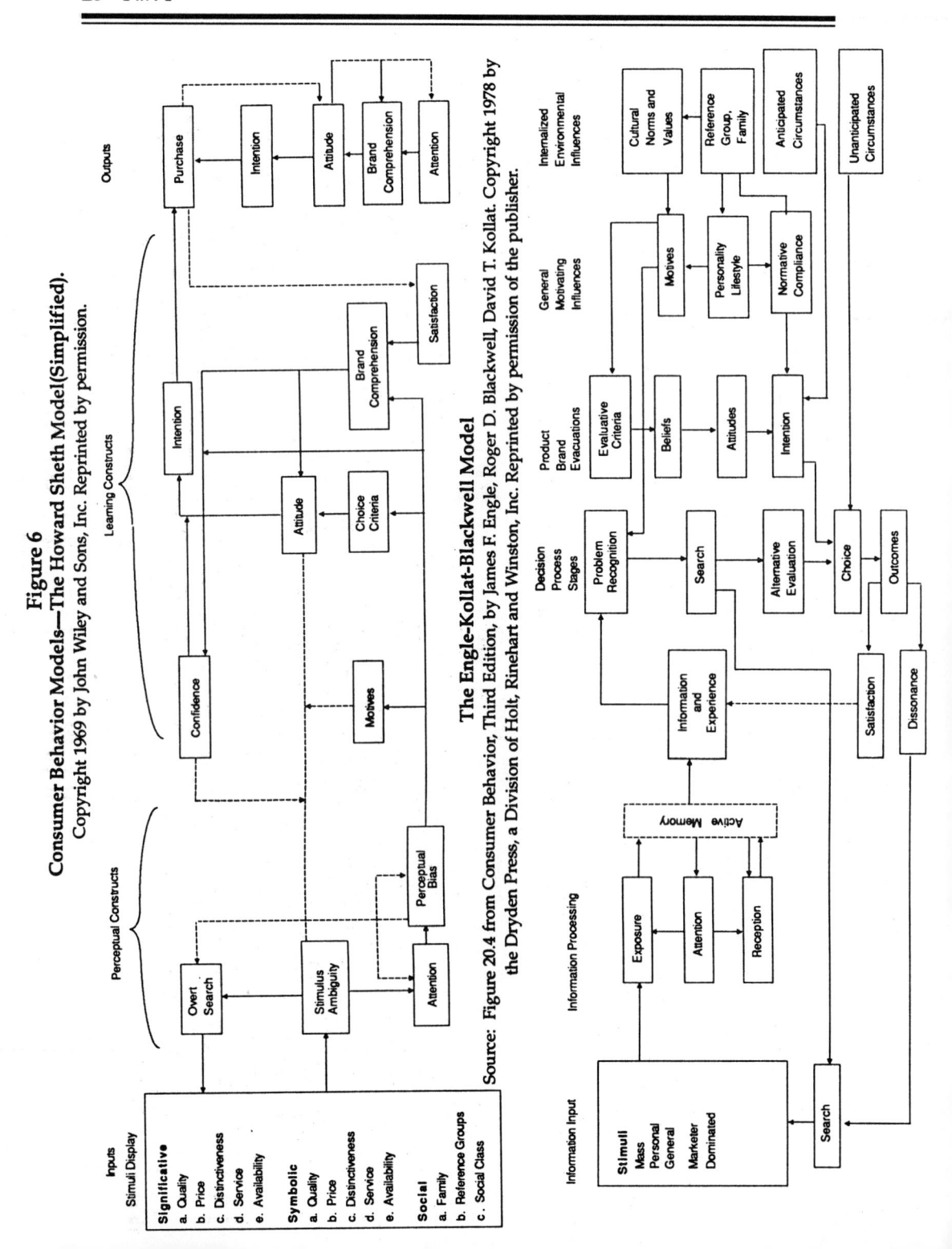

Figure 6
Consumer Behavior Models—The Howard Sheth Model (Simplified).
Copyright 1969 by John Wiley and Sons, Inc. Reprinted by permission.

The Engle-Kollat-Blackwell Model

Source: Figure 20.4 from Consumer Behavior, Third Edition, by James F. Engle, Roger D. Blackwell, David T. Kollat. Copyright 1978 by the Dryden Press, a Division of Holt, Rinehart and Winston, Inc. Reprinted by permission of the publisher.

Chapter 2 27

Figure 7
Above: A Low Involvement Buyer Behavior Model—Engle-Blackwell (Figure 2.10 from *Consumer Behavior*, Fourth Edition by James F. Engle and Roger D. Blackwell, copyright 1982). Below: The Engle-Blackwell High Involvement Model (Figure 2.7 from *Consumer Behavior*, Fifth Edition, by James F. Engle, Roger D. Blackwell, and Paul W. Miniard, copyright 1986). Both figures reprinted by permission of the Dryden Press, a Division of Holt, Rinehart and Winston, Inc.

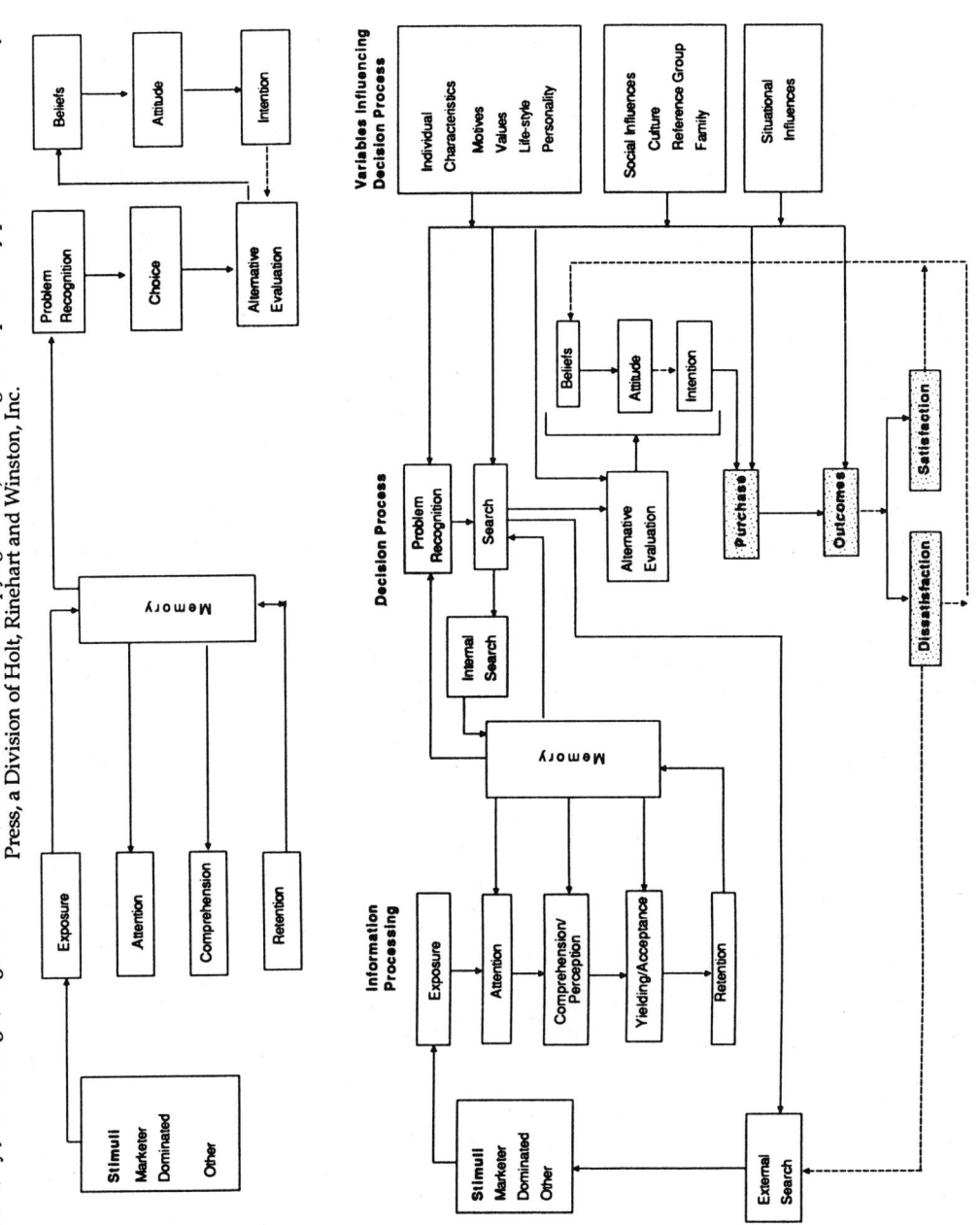

28 Part I

Figure 8
The Sheth Family Decision-Making Model

Source: Model from *Models of Buyer Behavior*, by Jagdish M. Sheth. Copyright 1974 by Jagdish M. Sheth. Reprinted by permission of Harper and Row, Publishers, Inc.

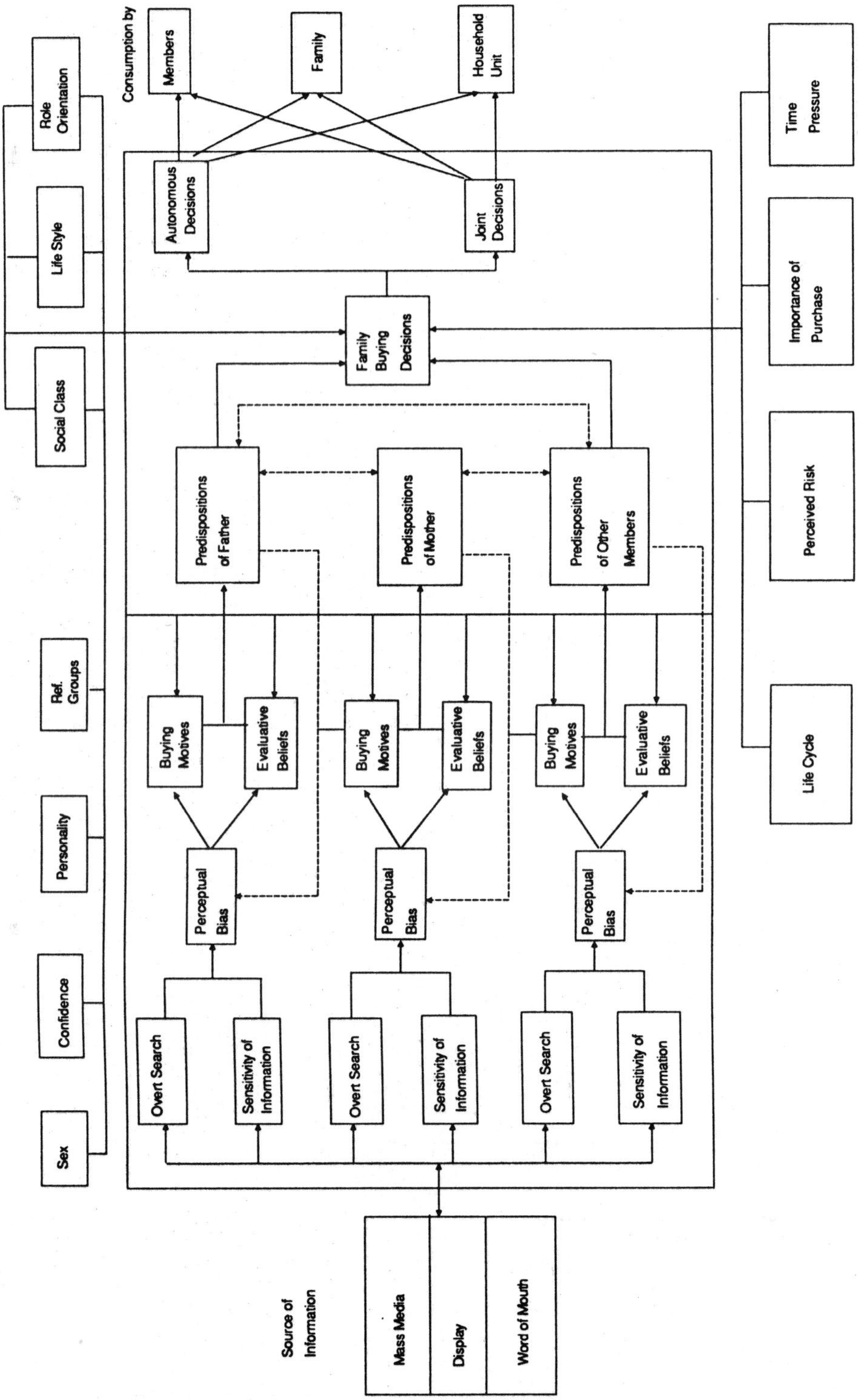

Figure 9
The Webster and Wind Model of Organizational Buying Behavior

Source: Reprinted with permission (*Journal of Marketing*, April 1972, 36, pp. 12-99; Frederick E. Webster Jr. and Yorham Wind). Published by the American Marketing Association, Chicago, IL.

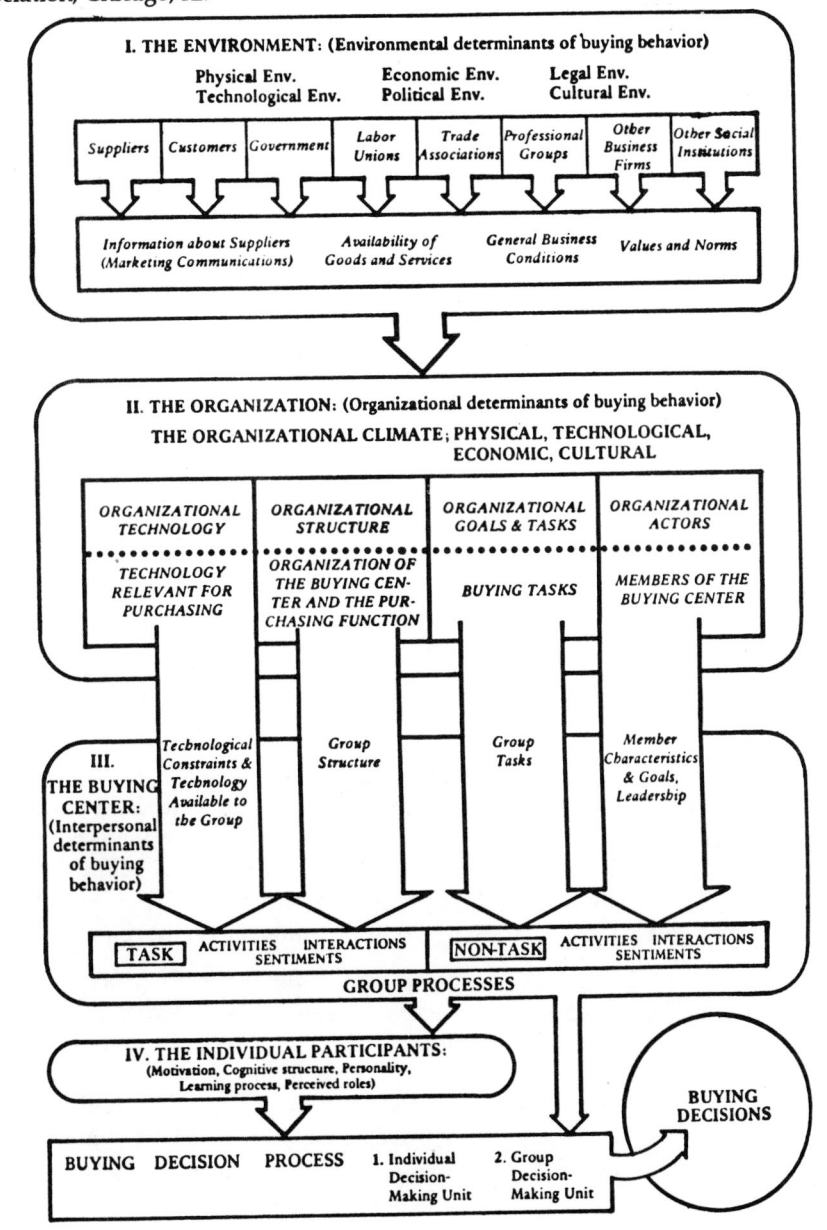

Satisfaction and Utility:
Psychology and Microeconomics Related

The student or marketing practitioner may think of the *psychological approaches* just described as related the exploration of the concept of *satisfaction*. The questions considered by psychologists and consumer behaviorists have included: what is satisfaction in essence, what characterizes the need to achieve it, and how is this reflected in the way buyers behave? The *microeconomist* does not generally focus on these questions but simply assumes that one product or service, by whatever means or mechanism, will be viewed by the consumer as providing more *utility* (or satisfaction) than an alternative product or service. This perspective has led the microeconomist to focus on a quite different set of questions which are equally useful to the marketing practitioner. The microeconomist's area of interest includes *what general kinds of behavior patterns are observable in markets, once it is given that an individual behaves so as to improve satisfaction.*

The relationship between psychology and economics can be better understood by examining the economist's concept of *marginal utility*. Marginal utility is the *added satisfaction* (or increment of utility) which is gained with an extra unit of consumption.[48] For example, with an extremely hungry individual, a slice of warm pizza might bring about a great improvement in satisfaction: a high added satisfaction or increment of utility. A clinical psychologist might call this "a reduction of the tension level created by hunger." The high level of added satisfaction would not always be the case, however. As the person ate more and more of the pizza, the next slice would not bring the same improvement in satisfaction. As the persons eats the pizza and becomes more full, each *extra* (added or incremental) slice contributes less and less to the individual's total satisfaction until such time as the last slice might even be left on the plate. While the first slice contributed great added satisfaction, the last slice was seen as contributing so little added satisfaction that it was left to cool. This general phenomenon of declining additional satisfaction with additional consumption is termed *declining marginal utility* by economists. Marginal utility and declining marginal utility are the economist's concepts which relate most directly to the understandings of psychologists.

Figure 10 illustrates a *useful relationship between psychology and economics* which will be of help in the analysis of markets. A person judges alternatives using that person's *evaluative criteria*. This may or may not be a conscious process for the individual and will be a *function of perceptual and cognitive processes*. The *resulting marginal utility* (MU) is then weighed against the *price* (p) as valued and perceived. Buyers can then be expected to make selections in accordance with the following general rules:

Figure 10
Buyer's Choice—The Consumer Behavior and Micro-Economic Perspective Related

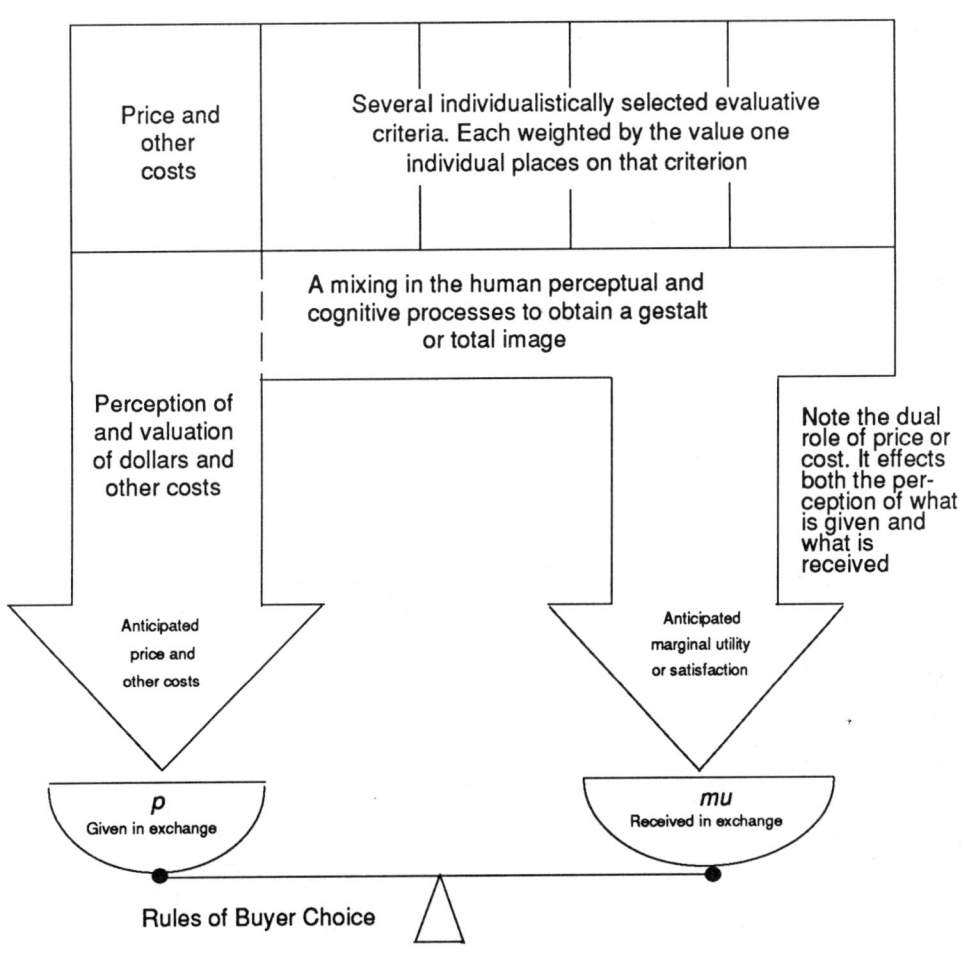

Price and other costs	Several individualistically selected evaluative criteria. Each weighted by the value one individual places on that criterion	
Perception of and valuation of dollars and other costs	A mixing in the human perceptual and cognitive processes to obtain a gestalt or total image	Note the dual role of price or cost. It effects both the perception of what is given and what is received

Anticipated price and other costs

Anticipated marginal utility or satisfaction

p Given in exchange

mu Received in exchange

Rules of Buyer Choice

1. The purchase of an alternative will not be considered unless mu > p
2. The choice of alternative 1 will be preferred to alternative 2 when $\frac{mu_1}{p_1} > \frac{mu_2}{p_2}$
3. The buyer is indifferent between alternative 1 or alternative 2 (could choose either) when $\frac{mu_1}{p_1} = \frac{mu_2}{p_2}$

1. The purchase of any given alternative will not be considered by the individual unless marginal utility is perceived to exceed price (or MU > P). Otherwise it is "not worth the price."
2. The choice of offering one will be preferred to offering two if it is seen as delivering greater satisfaction in relation to its price (price is also as valued and perceived) or when:

$$\frac{MU_1}{p_1} > \frac{MU_2}{p_2}$$

3. The buyer would not care which alternative were purchased (would be *indifferent* between alternatives) where:

$$\frac{MU_1}{p_1} = \frac{MU_2}{p_2}$$

These rules are stated in microeconomic terms, but should also be understood in terms of their underlying psychology. *Psychology* allows us to understand what creates certain perceptions of marginal utility and price. *Microeconomics* describes behavior given those perceptions of marginal utility and price.

Proceeding from Utility: The Microeconomics of Consumer Choice

The microeconomic concept of *declining marginal utility*, provides in addition to economies of scale, *one of the primary bases of human exchange.*

Consider for *example* the individual eating pizza who was described in the preceding section. Suppose this individual, while consuming the pizza, could also obtain a glass of cola. As pizza can make a person thirsty, the added satisfaction provided by the first glass of cola might be quite high. It is easy to imagine however, that in a situation where eight or ten glasses of cola were available to the pizza eater, the added satisfaction (marginal utility) provided by the last glass might not be as high as that provided by the first. There would thus be *declining marginal utility for both* pizza and cola.

A *basis for exchange* now exists. If the original pizza eater, who has an entire ten slice pizza and no cola, is joined at the table by an individual with a pitcher containing ten glasses of cola, *both* can be better off through exchange. In the first exchange, the pizza eater exchanges a last slice of pizza for a first cola. Something of low marginal utility has been exchanged for something of high marginal utility. The first party to the exchange now enjoys greater total satisfaction. But at whose expense? Clearly not at the expense of the other party to the exchange. That person has exchanged a last cola, an item with low marginal utility for a first slice of pizza, an item with high marginal utility. The second party to the exchange is better off as well. Both parties to the exchange must perceive themselves to be better off as a result of the exchange, or the exchange simply will not occur. In this way, diminishing marginal utility is an important basis of voluntary exchange.

The *understanding of the concepts of utility, marginal utility, and declining marginal utility now allows the exploration of observable patterns of human exchange* when prices change and when income changes. *In order to explore* these areas, *a graphic depiction* of the phenomenon of declining marginal utility will be useful. The economist's iso-utility curve is such a depiction.

The *iso-utility curve* is a means of describing consumer choice. Figure 11 illustrates such a curve. Each axis represents a mode of expenditure.[49] In this case the consumer can buy apples or oranges. The place where the axes intersect represents the zero point on each axis (no apples and no oranges). Moving away from this zero point on either axis represents the consumption of a larger quantity of the item represented by the axis.

The iso-utility curve is drawn within these axes. This curve represents a series of consumption packages with which the individual concerned would be *equally satisfied*. The term "iso-utility" is equivalent to "equal satisfaction." In the case of the individual's psychological preferences which are mapped in figure 11, the consumer is equally satisfied with the consumption packages marked A, B, C, D, E, and F. An infinite number of iso-utility lines may be drawn for any individual. Those lines lying above and to the right of another line indicate a greater level of satisfaction.

The *shape of* these iso-utility *lines conform* to the *assumption of diminishing marginal utility*. Because of their shape, the increases in utility that one obtains with the consumption of an extra item decreases as one has more of that item. This is illustrated by a comparison of points one and two in figure 12.

The iso-utility curve *should be seen in* the same *individual psychological sense* as the root term utility. While materialistic examples are often useful, charity to others, or another's level of consumption may be put on an axis.

The micro economist *uses the iso-utility curve to illustrate general patterns of behavior which can be expected when: 1) price changes or 2) income changes*. To illustrate these patterns a *budget line must be added* to the iso-utility lines.

The microeconomist assumes that the consumer maximizes utility as constrained (or limited) by the amount of resources that he or she has to spend. This is a the reasonable assumption if utility is interpreted in an individual psychological sense. *The budget line describes the financial limits to the consumer's*

Figure 11
Utility Curves

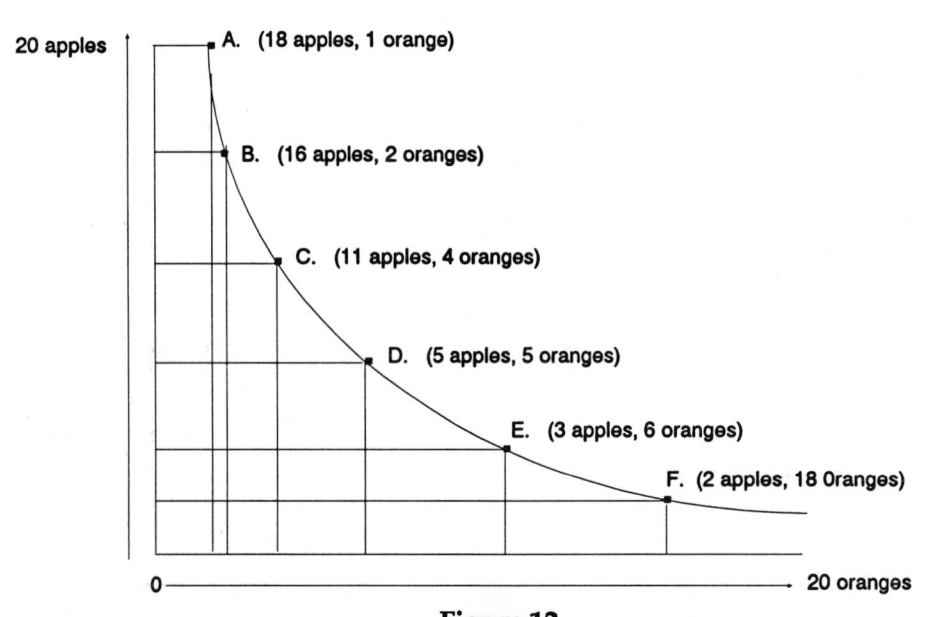

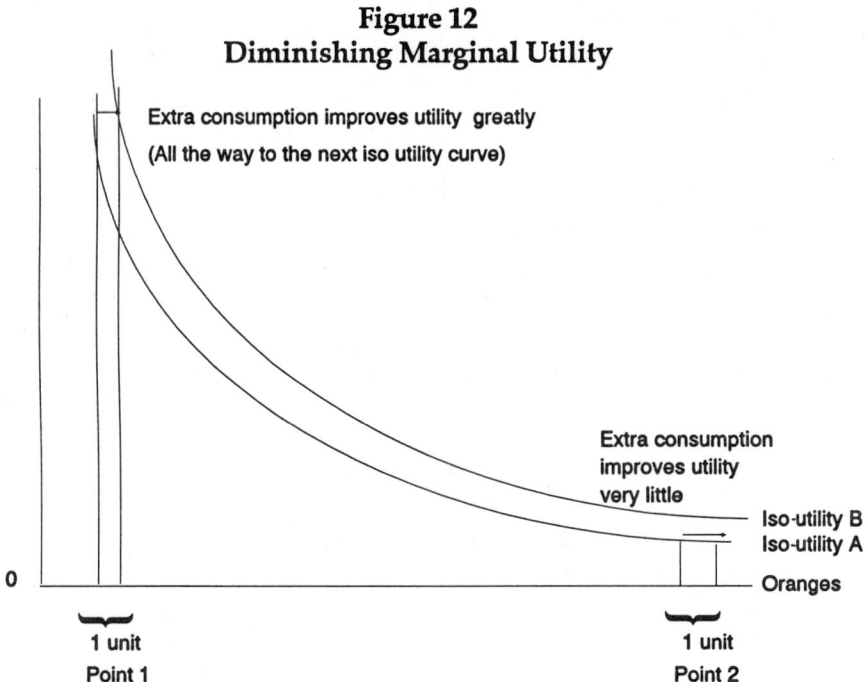

- 20 apples
- A. (18 apples, 1 orange)
- B. (16 apples, 2 oranges)
- C. (11 apples, 4 oranges)
- D. (5 apples, 5 oranges)
- E. (3 apples, 6 oranges)
- F. (2 apples, 18 Oranges)
- 20 oranges

Figure 12
Diminishing Marginal Utility

Extra consumption improves utility greatly
(All the way to the next iso utility curve)

Extra consumption improves utility very little

Iso-utility B
Iso-utility A

Oranges

1 unit
Point 1

1 unit
Point 2

behavior. The budget line is placed into the iso-utility diagram by first taking the person's entire budget and applying it to the first commodity (apples). Depending on the dollar amount of the budget and the price of the apples, this places a top limit on the number of apples the individual can consume. In similar fashion, the entire budget is then allocated to the second commodity, thus placing a top limit on the number of oranges which can be consumed. Connecting the resulting two points with a straight line forms the budget line. The straight shape of the line assumes that the consumer can exchange apples for oranges in a ratio which is dictated by their prices. Thus the expenditure of the entire budget allows the consumer to consume anywhere along the budget line. The budget line is illustrated in figure 13.

Putting the budget line together with the iso-utility curves completes *the micro-economists picture of consumer choice*. The consumer will now select that package or combination of goods which attains the highest iso-utility curve possible within the budget. This is illustrated in figure 14. The consumer maximizes utility subject to the budget constraint at the point where the budget line is briefly *tangent* to the highest attainable iso-utility curve. This occurs on iso-utility curve "B" in figure 14. This point is called the *consumer optimum*.

It is useful to note *what this geometric tangency implies*. *First* the slope of the budget line is the *price* of one item in terms of the other. For example, a 45 degree budget line implies that the price of apples in terms of oranges is one. *Second* the slope of the iso-utility curve is the *marginal utility* of one item in terms of the other. For example, a 45 degree iso-utility line implies that the marginal utility of apples in terms of oranges is one. *When these slopes are equal at the point of tangency the following relationship holds*:

$$\frac{\text{Marginal utility of oranges}}{\text{Price of apples}} = \frac{\text{Marginal utility of apples}}{\text{Price of oranges}}$$

or

$$\frac{MU_o}{p_o} = \frac{MU_a}{p_a}$$

This is the *same relationship* that was developed earlier in a more psychological context. (See rule three in figure 10.)

36 *Part I*

**Figure 13
The Budget Line**

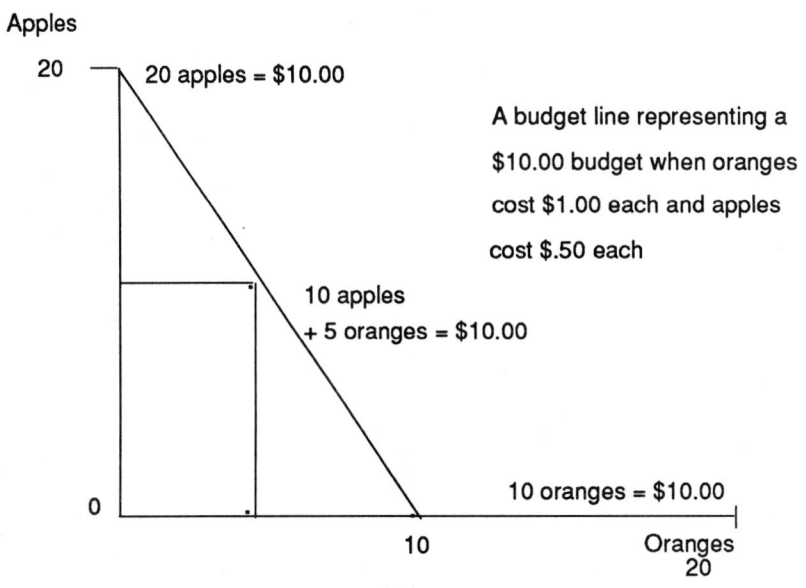

Apples

20 apples = $10.00

A budget line representing a $10.00 budget when oranges cost $1.00 each and apples cost $.50 each

10 apples + 5 oranges = $10.00

10 oranges = $10.00

Oranges

**Figure 14
The Economist's Picture of Consumer Choice**

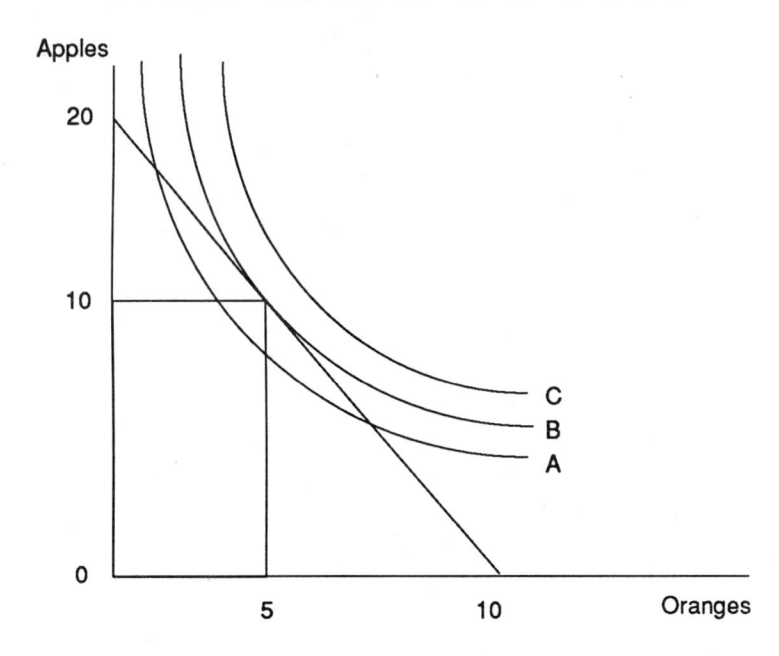

Apples

C
B
A

Oranges

The fact that the consumer optimum occurs where $\frac{MU_o}{P_o} = \frac{MU_a}{P_a}$ should have intuitive appeal. If $\frac{MU_o}{P_o} > \frac{MU_a}{P_a}$, the individual should prefer the consumption of more oranges (o) until this diminishing marginal utility for oranges resulted in $\frac{MU_o}{P_o} = \frac{MU_a}{P_a}$. If $\frac{MU_o}{P_o} < \frac{MU_a}{P_a}$ the individual would prefer the consumption of more apples (a) until the diminishing marginal utility for apples resulted in $\frac{MU_o}{P_o} = \frac{MU_a}{P_a}$.

Proceeding from Utility: Effects of Price Changes

To illustrate the effects of a change in price the economist simply adjusts the budget line to reflect the new reality. Figure 15 illustrates a doubling of the price of apples. This has resulted in a new budget line allowing a maximum of 10 apples instead of 20. The *consumer has responded* by *substituting* away from apples; from a consumption of 10 to a consumption of 4. The consumer is not able to entirely avoid apples, so the new higher price is also reflected in a loss in the consumer's standard of living. This is demonstrated by the move to a lower iso-utility curve. This is called an *income effect*. This situation demonstrates the general principle that *price changes* are met with *substitution effects* and *income effects*. In the case of a price increase, the consumer tries to substitute away from the now more expensive product. If it cannot be completely eliminated from the consumption package, a negative income effect is also experienced. In the case of price declines, consumers will substitute in the direction of more consumption of the item and will enjoy a positive income effect. Both of these phenomena are observable as gasoline and oil prices fluctuate. During past oil shortages, people in the U.S. substituted away from oil by purchasing smaller cars and home energy savings devices. They were unable to substitute away entirely and negative income effects were felt.

Proceeding from Utility: Effects of Income Changes

The iso-utility curves and the budget line can also illustrate some general principles of *consumer behavior* which are observable *when income rises or falls*.

Figure 15
Effects of Price Changes

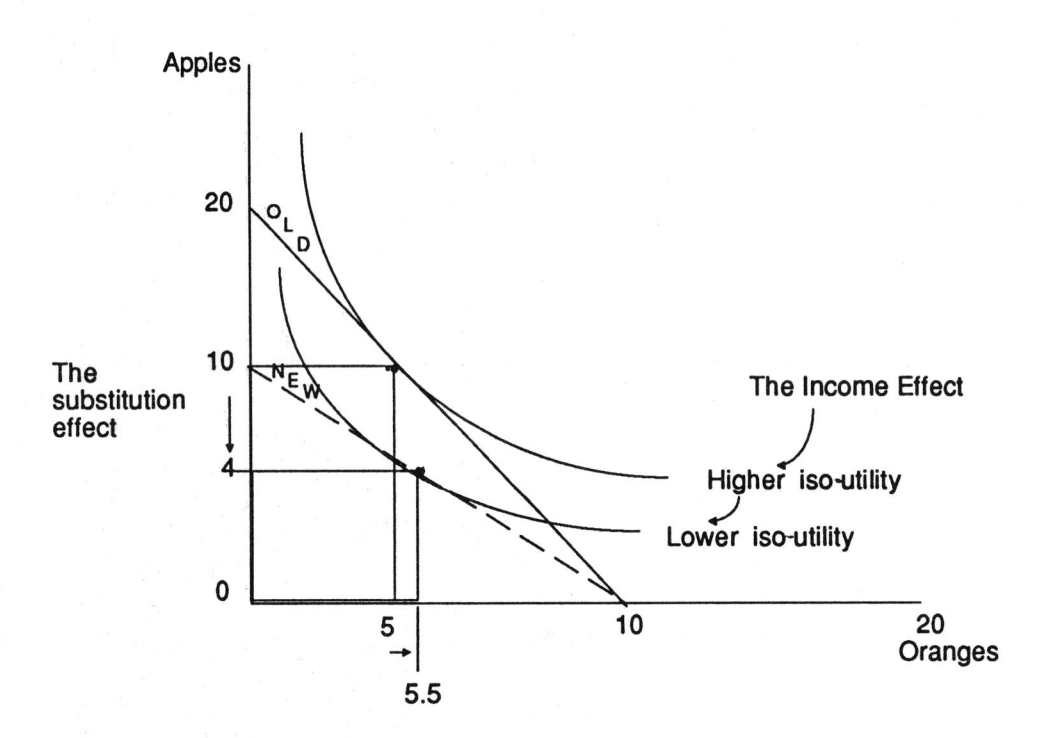

A rise in income is shown by simply moving the budget line out to represent the greater quantities of goods which can be purchased with the enhanced budget. If prices have not changed, the new budget line should be parallel to the old one. This expansion of the consumer budget is illustrated in figure 16 A, B, and C.

Comparison of these figures reveals a change in the consumption pattern with the change in income. The consumer depicted has preferred apples to oranges as income has expanded. Connecting the consumer optimum points or points of tangency results in a line called the *income expansion path* which demonstrates this preference.

A set of general rules called *Engle's Laws* summarize phenomena of this nature. Engle's laws are as follows:[50]

1. Goods which comprise an increasing proportion of the consumption package as income increases are *superior goods*.

    > Apples are the superior good in the example. In the U.S. automobiles and savings are superior goods.

2. Goods which comprise a constant proportion of the consumption package as income increases are *normal goods*.

    > There is no normal good in the example as the apple is a superior good and the orange is an inferior good. In the U.S. housing is a normal good.

3. Goods which comprise a declining proportion of the consumption package as income increases are *inferior goods*.

    > Oranges are the inferior good in the example. In the U.S. bus travel is considered an inferior good.

The practical market analyst is able to use this kind of information to predict changes in consumption patterns as income changes. Income information is available for many markets as a part of the broader numerical descriptions of markets known as *demographics*. For example, the availability of demographics including income figures allows estimation of how many of

40 *Part I*

Figure 16
Effects of Income Changes

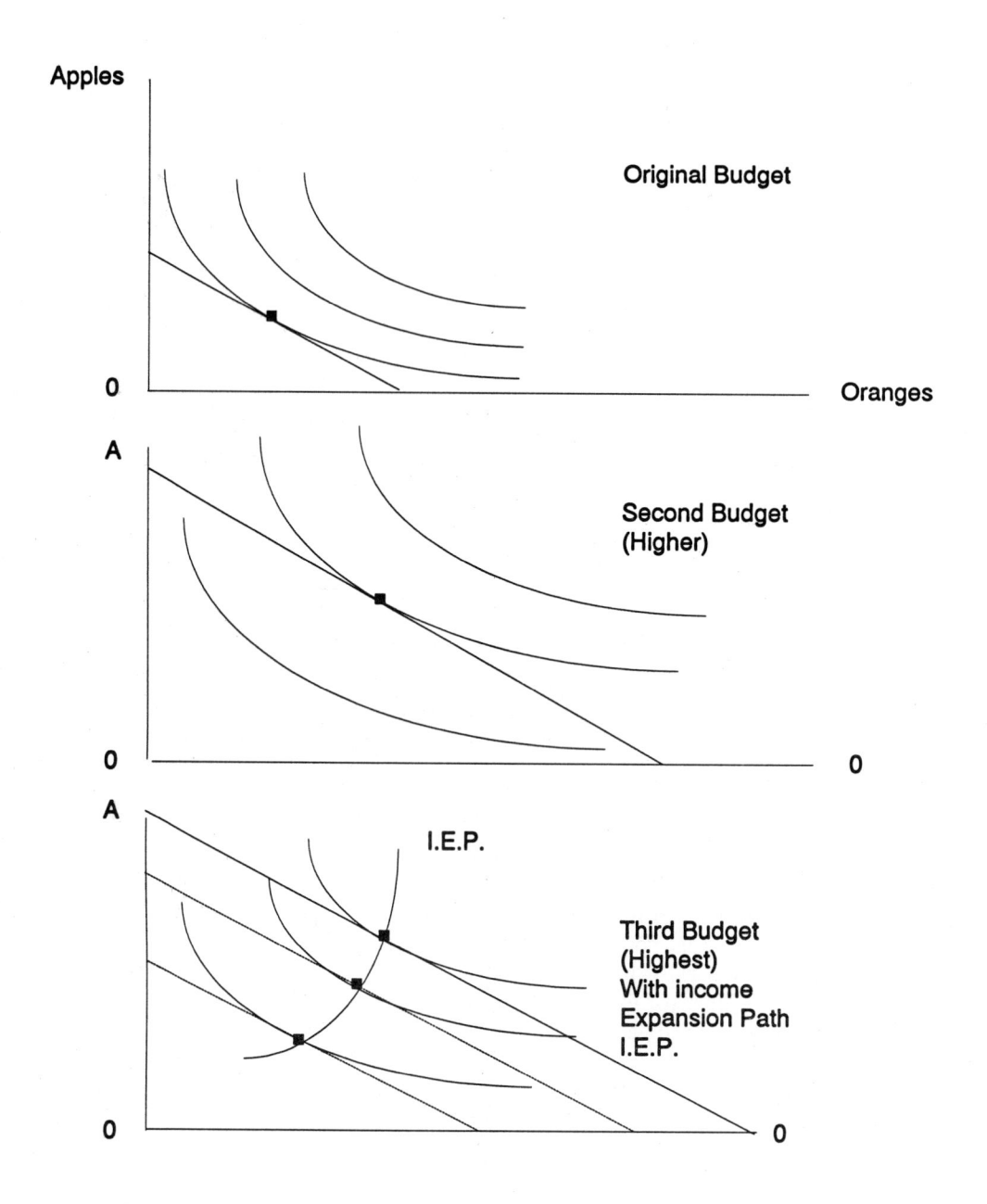

which sorts of automobiles might logically be purchased in communities having different income levels.

Proceeding from Utility to Demand

The *demand curve* is an important but somewhat limited tool which plays a critical role in the understanding of marketing. It is very powerful, though limited in focus. The demand curve describes how a number of people react to differing price levels for a product or service offering. The reaction focused upon is the number of units purchased. This is a powerful perspective, but the marketer will eventually want to understand how to adjust several interacting variables simultaneously and to understand the demand implications of these actions in specific target markets.

The demand curve may be understood as a *horizontal summation of individual choices to consume when the only variable being altered is price*. In order to understand the demand curve in this way, it is useful to think of a group of people simultaneously making a consumption choice as individuals. *Each individual makes* his or her *choice based upon* an individualistic assessment of *marginal utility* versus *price*. The resulting *units purchased are totaled up to create the demand curve*. This perspective is illustrated in figure 17.

In this example, the area to the left identifies the individuals to whom an offering of potatoes is made at varying prices. At the highest price considered ($100.00/pound) each individual compares the marginal utility of a potato purchase to the price and makes a decision. An understanding of this decision has been developed in earlier sections and summarized in figure 10 on page 31. This decision is duplicated for each price considered. The area to the right shows the resulting demand curve, where the purchase decisions of the individuals comprising the group are totaled up, showing the group's response to each level of price.

As price declines, the ratio of marginal utility to price $\frac{mu}{p}$ as perceived by each individual tends to improve, making the purchase more attractive in and of itself and more competitive vis a vis the other alternatives the individual has. It is important to note that this is only a general tendency and is not inevitable. Note for example the unusual decision behavior of Ethan. Ethan buys fewer pounds as the price drops. This may be because Ethan is using price as a communication of quality or exclusivity. Study of figure 10 shows that price can affect the total image of the product, impacting the perception of the offering itself. Thus price in some instances may contribute to the numerator as well as the denominator of the ratio $\frac{mu}{p}$. But Ethan's behavior is atypical. In most cases the ratio $\frac{mu}{p}$ improves as price declines and so more is purchased. Summing these individual purchase decisions horizontally results in the demand curve as illustrated in figure 17. The shape of the curve is downward sloping to the right, reflecting the increasing quantity typically demanded as price declines. This typically expected relationship is referred to as the *law of downward sloping demand*.

Note, however, the *substantial heterogeneity of individual response* which is in evidence. Fawn has avoided the product altogether, and Alfred's behavior is somewhat similar to Ethan's. Alfred does not seem to buy at the very highest price levels, perhaps being constrained by his budget, but he does show a tendency to buy less as the product becomes less expensive. Appropriate research might determine that Ethan and Alfred share an increased preference for the product when higher pricing communicates quality and exclusivity. In this case it might be wise for management to treat Ethan and Alfred as a separate *market segment*. A market segment is an aggregation of individuals whose response to product offerings is sufficiently similar to allow management to make useful generalizations about their behavior.

If Ethan and Alfred were treated as a separate segment of this market, their demand curve would demonstrate a substantially different shape than that displayed by the demand curve for the market as a whole. Ethan and Alfred, individuals participating in a market, can be used to demonstrate two important concepts in marketing. They have been used as an example of a market segment within a greater market. They also demonstrate a *backward bending or prestige demand curve*. This curve comprises figure 18.

Other important properties of demand curves may also be demonstrated by reference to the psychology of the individuals involved in the market. Consider for example a new group of six individuals composing the market. Unfortunately, all six individuals are diabetics for whom there is no substitute for insulin. If each individual requires one unit of insulin during the period of time considered by the demand curve, the demand curve would take on the perfectly vertical shape illustrated in figure 19. In this situation, the individuals will continue to demonstrate this demand pattern until the resources of the individuals, their third party payment support and charity have been exhausted. During this period when such budgetary limits have not yet been reached, the number of units demanded will *not* vary as the price varies. The term for this type of demand is *perfectly inelastic demand*. The term is easily remembered if one recognizes that *"elasticity" refers to* the change in the number of *units* demanded. When there is absolutely *no change*, the demand is *perfectly inelastic*.

Chapter 2   43

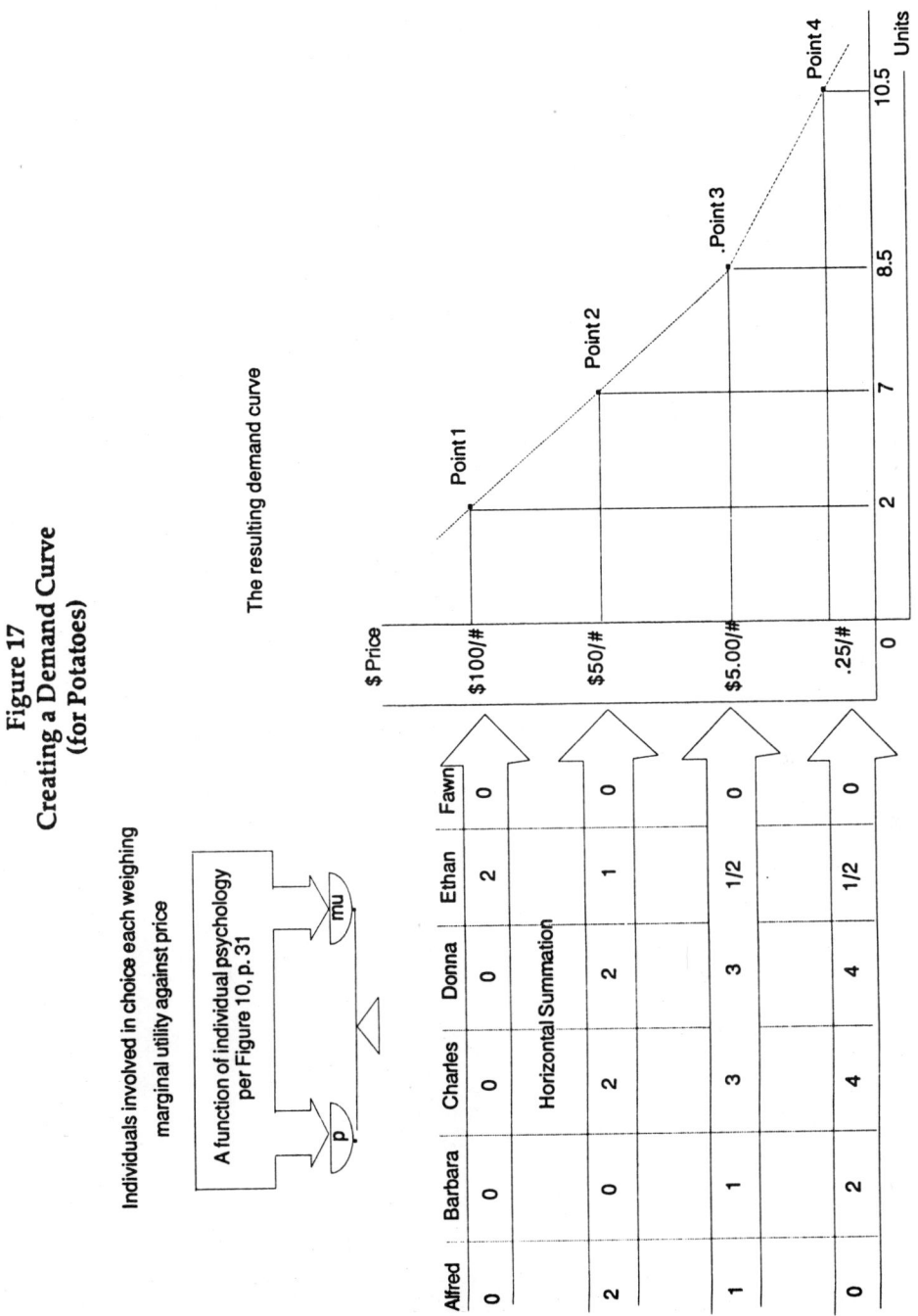

Figure 17
Creating a Demand Curve
(for Potatoes)

Individuals involved in choice each weighing marginal utility against price

A function of individual psychology per Figure 10, p. 31

The resulting demand curve

	Alfred	Barbara	Charles	Donna	Ethan	Fawn
$100/#	0	0	0	0	2	0
$50/#	2	0	2	2	1	0
$5.00/#	1	1	3	3	1/2	0
.25/#	0	2	4	4	1/2	0

Horizontal Summation

$ Price

Point 1 — 2
Point 2 — 7
Point 3 — 8.5
Point 4 — 10.5

Units

Figure 18
Backward Bending or Prestige Demand Curve

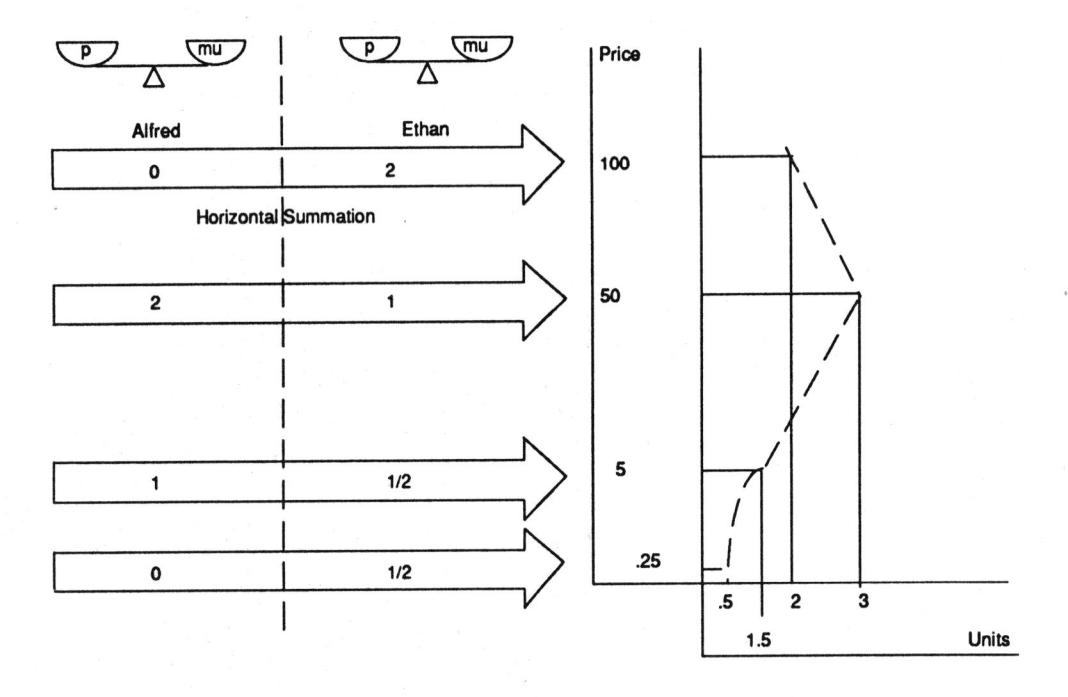

Chapter 2   45

Figure 19
Perfectly Inelastic Demand

Price per unit	Ambrose	Berry	George	Daffine	Ephriam	Francine	
$100	1	1	1	1	1	1	
$75	1	1	1	1	1	1	
$50	1	1	1	1	1	1	6 units
$25	1	1	1	1	1	1	

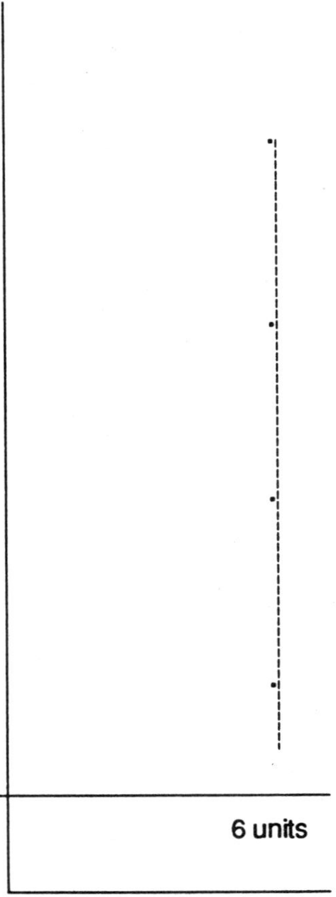

Relaxing the conditions of absolute need that characterized the diabetic's insulin example allows other forms of elasticity to be illustrated. For example, suppose the demand curve characterizes a commodity for which there is great need, but for which there are some substitutes. In other words some substitution effect can be expected when price increases. An example of this kind of commodity would be crude oil. During the OPEC embargo of the early 1970s crude oil prices went up by approximately 200% but consumption only declined by approximately 5%. This kind of relationship, only small changes in the number of units demanded to accompany large changes in price, is termed *relatively inelastic demand*. Figure 20 demonstrates relatively inelastic demand.

Continuing to relax the conditions of need in the marketplace would result in situations where a price change would be met with a great deal of substitution effect. Large changes in the numbers of units demanded would accompany relatively small changes in price. Movie tickets might be a useful example. If movie tickets became too expensive, many moviegoers could readily substitute various forms of home video. Figure 21 demonstrates this kind of demand, termed *relatively elastic demand*.

The general concept of *price elasticity of demand* which has just been demonstrated, has a specific, quantitative definition. Price elasticity of demand is defined as:

$$\frac{\text{Percentage Change in Units}}{\text{Percentage Change in Price}} = \frac{\frac{\Delta x}{x}}{\frac{\Delta p}{p}}$$

Relatively inelastic demand then is:

$$\frac{\text{The Smaller Percentage Change in Units}}{\text{The Larger Percentage Change in Price}} = \frac{\frac{\Delta x}{x}}{\frac{\Delta p}{p}} < 1$$

Relatively elastic demand becomes:

$$\frac{\text{The Larger Percentage Change in Units}}{\text{The Smaller Percentage Change in Price}} = \frac{\frac{\Delta x}{x}}{\frac{\Delta p}{p}} > 1$$

Chapter 2 47

Figure 20
Relatively Inelastic Demand

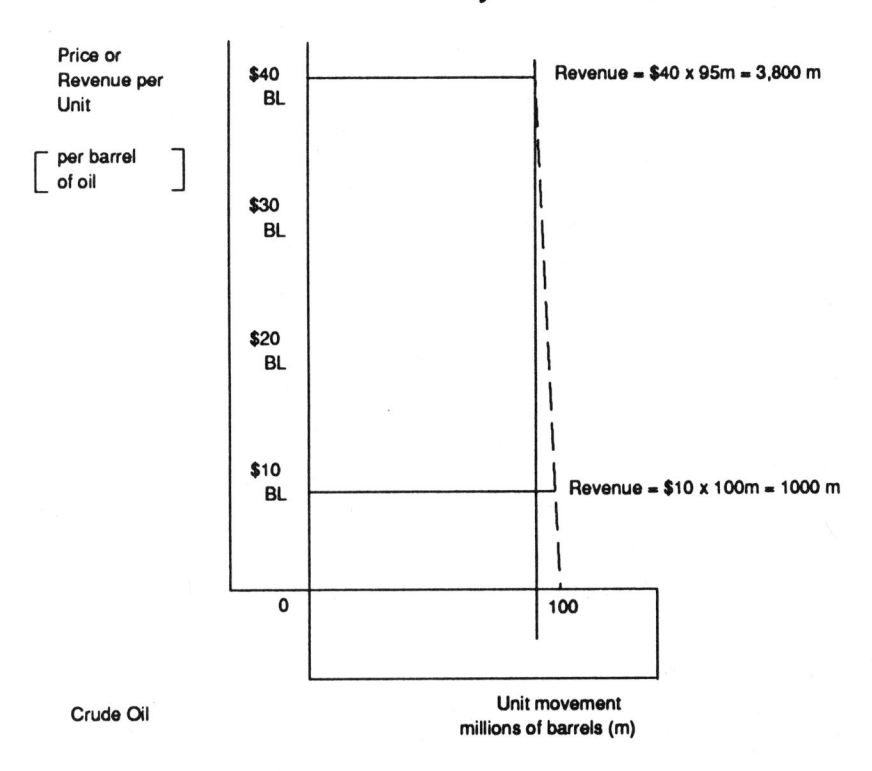

Price or Revenue per Unit

[per barrel of oil]

$40 BL — Revenue = $40 x 95m = 3,800 m

$30 BL

$20 BL

$10 BL — Revenue = $10 x 100m = 1000 m

0 — 100

Crude Oil

Unit movement millions of barrels (m)

Digure 21
Relatively Elastic Demand

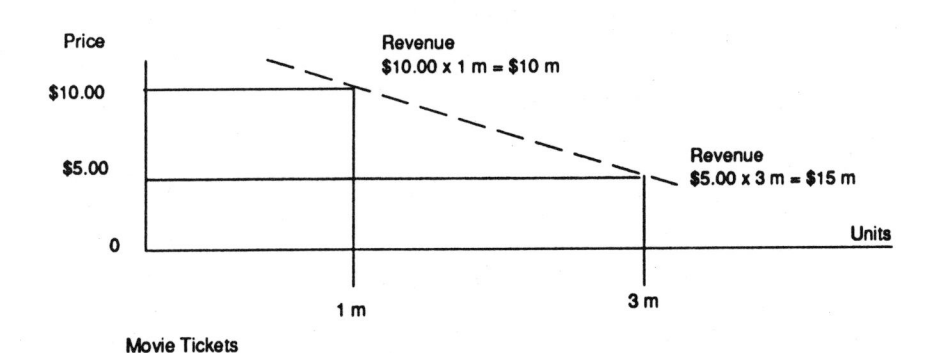

Price

$10.00 — Revenue $10.00 x 1 m = $10 m

$5.00 — Revenue $5.00 x 3 m = $15 m

0

1 m   3 m   Units

Movie Tickets

Perfectly inelastic demand becomes:

$$\frac{\text{No Change in Units}}{\text{Any Percentage Change in Price}} = \frac{\frac{\Delta x}{x}}{\frac{\Delta p}{p}} = 0$$

Perfectly elastic demand, which will be of interest later in the discussion is defined as:

$$\frac{\text{An Unlimited Change in Units}}{\text{Any Percentage Change in Price}} = \frac{\frac{\Delta x}{x}}{\frac{\Delta p}{p}} = \infty$$

The *managerial implication* of this is that *when demand is inelastic* the revenue derived from the market as a whole will rise when the price rises and fall when price falls. In similar fashion, *when demand is elastic*, the revenue derived from the market as a whole will fall when price is raised and rise when price is lowered. Figures 20 and 21 illustrate this.

While *these statements* are true they *can also be very misleading*. It does not necessarily follow that price moves by the individual firm will be greeted with the same elasticity that characterizes the market as a whole. Depending on the *nature of the competition,* the individual firm raising price in a market where demand is relatively inelastic may be met with perfectly elastic demand for its offerings, losing all unit movement and all revenue. Conditions under which this might be the case will be considered in the next chapter. The general statements about elasticity and revenues might also be misleading if management were to consider higher revenue preferable to lower revenue without *evaluating* the *costs* associated with each revenue level.

Effects of Other Managerial Variables

Demand curves are powerful, but marketers generally want to work with several variables simultaneously rather than focus on just the manipulation of price. Marketers are interested in unit movement, but are more interested in the translation of unit movement into the relationship between revenues and costs which each level of unit movement implies. Marketers therefore rarely work with demand curves, but work with something analogous. Marketers often use a series of spot estimates of the unit movements, revenues and costs which would be derived from a series of feasible combinations of the four managerial variables: *product* (or service), *promotion, place,* and *price.*

The *four managerial variables* mentioned, often referred to as the *four "ps" of the offering,* interact in the perception and cognition of individual consumers, resulting in anticipations of satisfaction or utility. The second section of this book will discuss some of the many ways in which these variables interact. This chapter will introduce each of the new variables in the context of the demand curve, the tool already used to discuss price.

The *product or service offering* itself might be *altered or enhanced.* The market reaction to this *investment,* taken by itself, might be illustrated by figure 22. Here *product differentiation* has been successful and the adjusted product is viewed as improved; a different and better product than the original. This results in higher anticipated satisfaction or utility, a new evaluation of the ratio $\frac{mu}{p}$ and thus, a new demand curve, lying to the right of the first.

The buyers view of a product or service and its value may also be altered by saying something about the product. This involves the managerial variable of *promotion* or communication. Suppose the potatoes discussed earlier have been found to have some heretofore unknown therapeutic value. They may for example enhanced one's "animal magnetism" or attractiveness to the opposite sex. If this virtue were promoted, the effect might be to enhance demand for the product. In the context of what the buyer thinks about the product, and thus the buyers anticipated satisfaction or utility, saying something about the product may be as or more effective than actually changing the product. Thus in the perception of the buyer, *promotion alters and enhances product.* The market reaction to successful *investment* in promotion, taken by itself, is illustrated in figure 23.

Anticipated satisfaction or utility can also be altered and enhanced by altering the time and place of the product's availability. *Investment in distribution* activities such as transportation, storage, and arrangements with other firms who distribute the product may *alter and enhance the product* in the perception of the buyer. The consumer often anticipates higher satisfaction with improved customer service. The isolated effect of successful *investments* in the managerial variable of *place* or distribution activity is illustrated in figure 24.

The effect of each of the four managerial variables of marketing: price, product, promotion, and place has been introduced. But each has been introduced in isolation. Marketing managers are more likely to view their work as a *creative mixing* of price, product, promotion and place.[51] Some combinations of these four variables are feasible or possible for the organization concerned

50 Part I

Figure 22
Effect of Successful *Product* or Service Differentiation

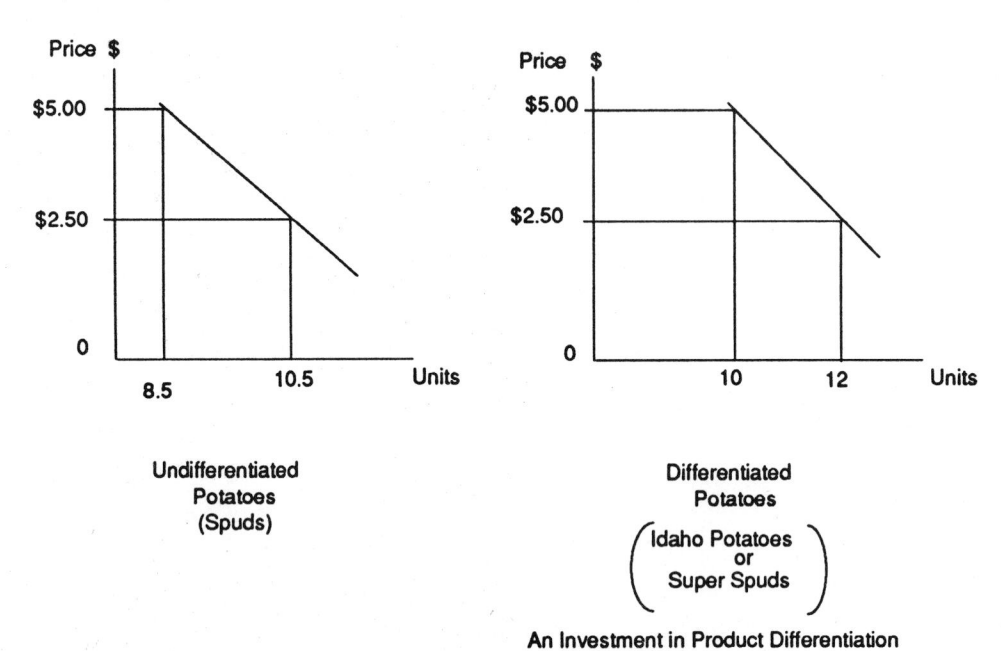

Price $ — Undifferentiated Potatoes (Spuds): demand curve from $5.00 at 8.5 units to $2.50 at 10.5 units.

Price $ — Differentiated Potatoes (Idaho Potatoes or Super Spuds): demand curve from $5.00 at 10 units to $2.50 at 12 units.

An Investment in Product Differentiation

Figure 23
Effect of *Promotion* or Communication

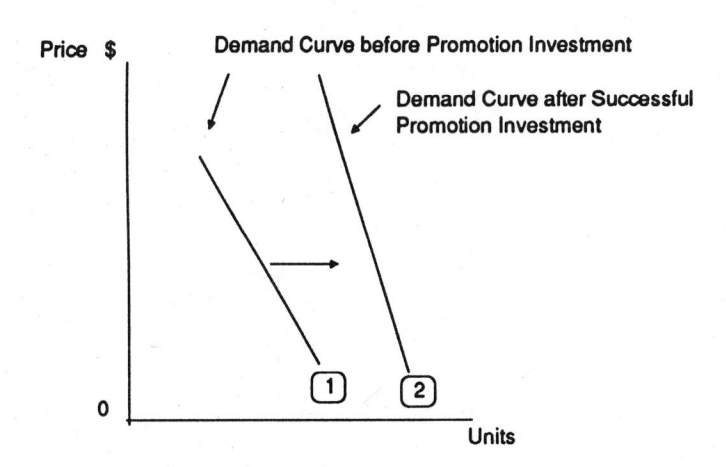

Demand Curve before Promotion Investment — ①
Demand Curve after Successful Promotion Investment — ②

Chapter 2 51

Figure 24
Effect of *Place*
(Time and Place of Availability)

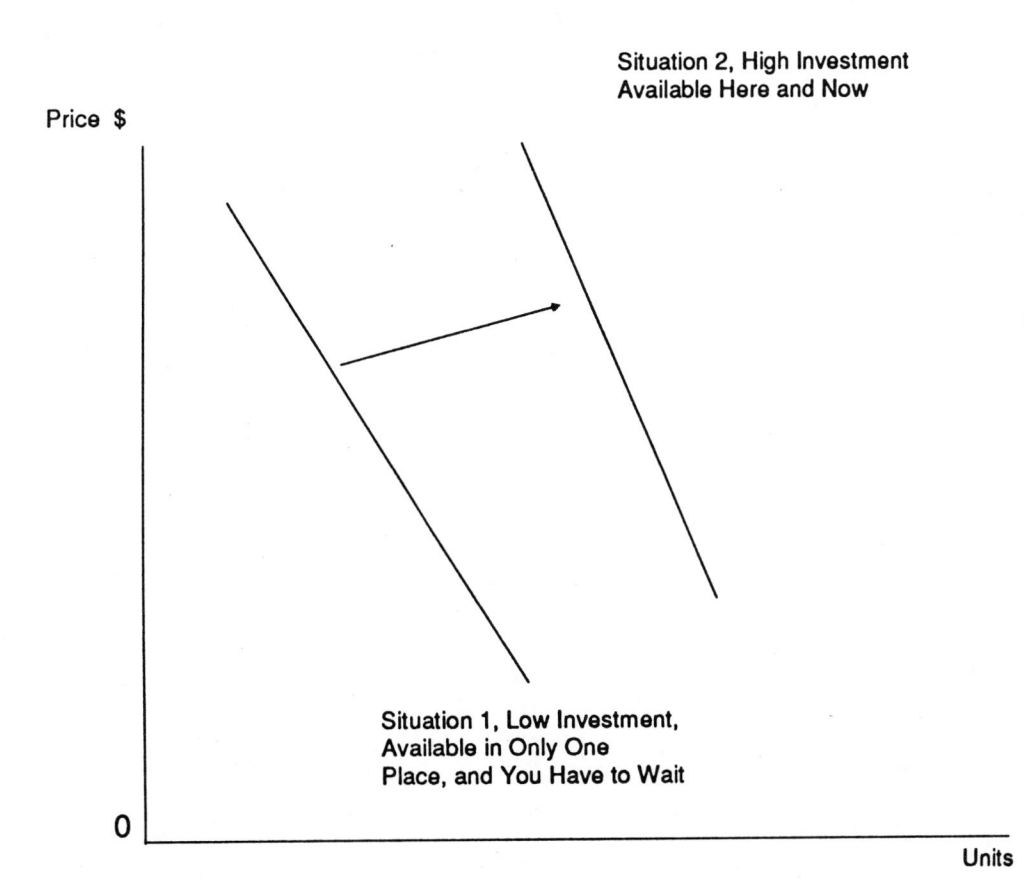

Price $

Situation 2, High Investment
Available Here and Now

Situation 1, Low Investment,
Available in Only One
Place, and You Have to Wait

0

Units

and some are not. *For each feasible* combination or "mix" of the four "ps" there will be a *reaction from the market* to which the offering is made. *Each mix* targeted at *each market* would result in *a number of units sold*. This has several important implications:

1. A *revenue* implication

   - Because *price* was specified in the mix and because the market reaction is in terms of units sold.

2. *Cost* implications

   - *Costs of product production.* Because product design was specified in the mix and because the market reaction is in terms of units sold. Remember the average total cost discussion in chapter one.
   - *Cost of promotion.* Because promotion was specified in the mix.
   - *Cost of place.* Because transportation, storage and arrangements with other firms to distribute the product were specified in the mix. Also, units sold, which will effect the costs of distribution, are part of the market reaction to the mix.
   - *Other costs* which might logically be seen as a part of the total cost of offering this particular mix. That is, costs which are incremental to the mix, appearing when the mix is offered and disappearing when the mix is not offered.

This perspective is analogous to that of the demand curve. In a demand curve, price is changed and the market reacts with units sold. In this more complex and realistic situation, the mix is changed and the market reacts with units sold.

It is the *job of marketing management* to *anticipate* these reactions and their associated costs and revenues. It then becomes the job of marketing management to *select* the *best combination* of a *marketing mix* and a *target market*. This combination, a marketing mix consisting of a specification of the four ps, and a target market consisting of a carefully identified group of individuals, forms a *marketing strategy*. The job of marketing management is a fascinating challenge for those interested in psychology, sociology, economics, finance, production, distribution, information systems, management, law, and competitive strategy.

Group Effects

Substantial group influence upon individual choice has been introduced in the discussion of such areas as social psychology and in the social influence component of the consumer behavior models. Interactions of individuals have been introduced with the Sheth Family Decision Model and the Webster and Wind Model of Organizational Decision Making. In these cases, reconciliation with the microeconomic decision model is fairly straightforward. The group becomes the unit of analysis. As a result of the interactions of the individuals in the group, the group is thought of as having a utility for something or a preference for something.

But a more complex picture is sometimes useful in the diagnosis of markets. Market behaviors should sometimes be seen as *complex exchange*, wherein there may be *several parties to the exchange*, and *things being exchanged besides the marketing mix* with its obvious price.[52] For *example*, selling pharmaceuticals may involve understandings of complex influences among pharmacists, their professional associations, medical doctors, their associations and hospitals and their associations. Pharmacists may prefer the offerings of pharmaceutical firms which have provided useful research information to their professional association. These kinds of understandings are needed in addition to understandings of the internal group dynamics of the organizations which are involved, such as the hospitals. The "currency" of these complex exchanges may include professional and community recognition and status. Complex exchanges can be diagnosed and a marketing mix devised to complement the pattern of exchange. This mix will eventually conform to all of the general rules which have been set forth in this chapter. But each individual mix must be seen in the full context of the other exchanges in the complex pattern. An incomplete understanding of the complex exchange pattern will result in a misunderstanding of the effective competition. An offering might then be rejected, largely because the offering firm simply did not fathom all of the sources of satisfaction and all of the prices and costs involved in the complex exchange.

Another form of group exchange behavior is peculiar to the organization which is essentially buying *inputs* or items to be converted into its product or service. When vending inputs it is important to recognize that any *demand* for the input is *derived* from the demand for the *intermediate customer's* end product. Little if any utility is generated in the purchase of an input beyond the utility of gaining a satisfactory or better input in the context of satisfactory or better service. This is not to say that successful strategies will not depend upon creative marketing mixes which differentiate the vendor from competition. It is to say that the individual purchasing is concerned primarily with putting a mix together to satisfy a third party. Such a buyer, sometimes a *purchasing agent* for the organization, is likely to display a fairly cold and rational set of purchase behaviors.

Crossing National Boundaries

Few if any *of the generalizations* made in this chapter *will change* when operating across national boundaries. Perceptions of product or service offerings will still be individualistic, satisfaction or dissatisfaction will essentially remain the same, and consumers will still pursue satisfaction subject to budget constraints. Demand curves will describe reactions to price, and marketing mixes will be greeted in the market place with unit movement, implying revenues and costs.

Most if not all *of the specifics will change*. Expectations and perceptions will be different, family relations will be different, and so what generates satisfaction in specific will be different. For the microeconomist, this simply means that the shapes of utility curves will differ, and demand curves will take on a different shape. For the marketing manager it means that extreme sensitivity to the individuals and their culture will be required if satisfaction in the specific culture is to be understood. It means that a change in the marketing mix will have to be considered. It also means that both what is feasible and what things cost will change. This will further strengthen the argument for an adjusted marketing mix.

Chapter Summary

This chapter has *explored the concept of satisfaction* and *what it implies for human exchange behavior*. The exploration of the concept of satisfaction has been the province of psychologists and more recently, consumer behaviorists. This exploration has provided many useful insights for management, including ideas about the roles of perception, group influence, learning, and measurement. Clinical and physiological views of satisfaction were explored, as well as the consumer's attempt to achieve satisfaction through specific buying behavior.

The question of what satisfaction means for human exchange behavior also led to the introduction of the consumer behaviorists' and microeconomists' models.[53] The microeconomic concepts of the consumer optimum, the effects of price and income changes, and demand were introduced.

Demand then led to the perspective of marketing management. The demand curve's description of the market's reaction to price with units sold was expanded to become the market reaction to the more complex marketing mix with units sold. This led to estimates of revenues and costs and choices of strategy. Instances of complex exchange and exchange for the purpose of further transformation and exchange were also introduced as making the analysis of the exchange process more interesting and challenging.

---

[1]Respected Economics texts define utility to mean satisfaction. See for example C. E. Furguson and J. P. Gould, *Microeconomic Theory*, 4th ed. (Homewood, Illinois: Richard D. Irwin, 1975), p. 12. See also Kalman J. Cohen and Richard M. Cyert, *Theory of the Firm: Resource Allocation in a Market Economy*, 2nd ed. (Englewood Cliffs, N.J.: Prentice Hall, 1975), p. 66. *Webster's New World Dictionary* defines utility (in Economics) as the power to satisfy the needs and wants of humanity. Advanced scholars may be wary of this synonymity and wish to draw distinctions. This should not prevent the beginning student or practical market analyst from developing the useful whole understanding of markets which rests upon the parallel nature of these concepts.

[2]Leon G. Schiffman and Leslie Lazar Kanuk, *Consumer Behavior*, 2nd ed. (Englewood Cliffs, N.J.: Prentice Hall, 1983), p. 148.

[3]See for example, J. S. Bruner and C. C. Goodman, "Value and Need as Organizing Factors in Perception," *Journal of Abnormal and Social Psychology* 42 (1947), pp. 33-44. See also, J. W. Atkinson and E. L. Walker, "The Affiliation Motive and Perceptual Sensitivity to Faces," *Journal of Abnormal and Social Psychology* 53 (1956), pp. 38-41.

[4]Paul F. Secord and Carl W. Blackman, *Social Psychology* (New York: McGraw Hill, 1964), p. 205.

[5]Ibid., p. 201.

[6]Schiffman, pp. 288-292.

[7]R. K. Merton, *Social Theory and Social Structure* (New York: The Free Press of Glencoe, 1957), pp. 131-194, as cited in Secord, p. 209.

[8]Foundation for Research on Human Behavior, "Group Influence in Marketing," *Group Influence in Marketing and Public Relations* (Ann Arbor: Foundation for Research on Human Behavior, 1956), pp. 1-12.

[9]Ibid., pp. 215-216.

[10]See David G. Meyers, *Social Psychology*, 2nd ed. (New York: McGraw Hill, 1987), pp. 61-72 for a contemporary introduction to Dissonance Theory. See M. J. Rosenburg, "An Analysis of Affective-Cognitive Consistency," in *Attitude Organization and Change*, eds., C. I. Hovland and M. J. Rosenburg (New Haven: Yale University Press, 1960), pp. 15-64. See also L. Festinger, *A Theory of Cognitive Dissonance* (New York: Harper and Row, 1957). Both theories are summarized in Secord, pp. 111-119.

[11]Rosenburg, p. 22.

[12]This is a simplification of Festinger for pedagogical purposes. Festinger's equation is:

$$\text{Dissonance} = \frac{\text{importance} \times \text{no. of dissonant elements}}{\text{Importance} \times \text{no. of consonant elements}}.$$

In Secord, p. 116.

[13] Secord, p. 117.

[14] Dissonance may be defined as "tension." See Meyers, p. 61.

[15] See Winfred F. Hill, *Psychology: Principles and Problems* (Philadelphia: Lippincott, 1970), p. 62. See also James F. Engle and Rodger D. Blackwell, *Consumer Behavior*, 4th ed. (Chicago: The Dryden Press, 1982), pp. 240-242.

[16] Hill, p. 62.

[17] Engle, p. 237.

[18] See Neal E. Miller and John Dollard, *Social Learning and Imitation* (London: Keegan, Trench and Co., 1945). See also Engle, p. 242; also Abraham H. Maslow, *Motivation and Personality*, 2nd ed. (New York: Harper and Row, 1970).

[19] Engle, p. 243.

[20] Ibid., p. 245.

[21] Schiffman, p. 182.

[22] See Engle, p. 237 and Schiffman, p. 185.

[23] See Engle, pp. 191-192, and Schiffman, p. 61, 93-94.

[24] See Mason Haire, "Projective Techniques in Marketing Research," *Journal of Marketing* 14 (April 1950), pp. 649-656.

[25] See Richard M. Johnson, "Market Segmentation: A Strategic Management Tool," *Journal of Marketing* 39 (February 1975), pp. 13-18.

[26] See Calvin S. Hall and Gardner Lindzey, *Theories of Personality*, 3rd ed. (New York: John Wiley and Sons, Inc., 1978), p. 49. See also Calvin S. Hall and Gardner Lindzey, *Theories of Personality* (New York: John Wiley and Sons, Inc., 1957), p. 46.

[27] Hall (1978), p. 51, Hall (1957), p. 40.

[28] Hall (1978), p. 187, Hall (1957), p. 141.

[29] Ibid.

[30] Ibid.

[31] Harry S. Sullivan, "Tensions Interpersonal and International; a Psychiatrist's View," in *Tensions that Cause War*, ed. H. Cantril (Urbana, Ill; University of Illinois Press, 1950), p. 85 as cited in Hall (1978), p. 188 and as cited in Hall (1957), p. 142.

[32] Gardner Murphy, *Personality: A Biosocial Approach to Origins and Structure* (New York: Harper, 1947). As characterized in Hall (1957), p. 510.

[33] Ibid.

[34] H. A. Murray and C. Kluckhohn, "Outline of a Conception of Personality," in *Personality in Nature, Society, and Culture*, 2nd ed.; eds. C. Kluckhohn, H. A. Murray and D. Schneider (New York: Knopf, 1953), pp. 36-37. As cited in Hall (1957), p. 180.

[35] Maslow's Hierarchy is set forth in Maslow, pp. 35-51.

[36] A complete discussion of theoretical units and their relationships is provided by Robert Dubin, *Theory Building* (New York: Free Press, 1969).

[37] Shmuel Sambursky, *Physical Thought from the Presocratics to the Quantum Physicists* (New York: Pica Press, 1975), pp. 77-79.

[38] See Clifford T. Morgan, *Physiological Psychology*, 3rd ed. (New York: McGraw-Hill, 1965), pp. 548, 549.

[39] Murray and Kluckhohn, p. 4. As cited in Hall (1957), p. 166.

[40] See John A. Howard and Jagdish N. Sheth, *The Theory of Buyer Behavior* (New York: John Wiley, 1969), p. 30. See also Engle, p. 500.

[41] Hall (1957), p. 510.

[42] Engle, p. 500.

[43] Ibid.

[44] This text will rely upon Webster's definition of a criterion as "A standard, rule or test by which a judgment of something can be formed." This is essentially compatible with Engle, pp. 414-436.

[45] Engle, pp. 421-427, 444-459.

[46] Ibid., pp. 34-39.

[47] The Sheth family decision-making model is owed to Jagdish N. Sheth, *Models of Buyer Behavior* (New York: Harper and Row, 1974), pp. 22-23. The model of organizational buying behavior is owed to Frederick E. Webster, Jr. and Yoram Wind, "A General Model for Understanding Organizational Buying Behavior," *Journal of Marketing* 36 (April 1972), pp. 12-19.

[48] This is not necessarily materialistic. The consumption described may be understood as another's consumption in the case of the donor, or as an option on future consumption in the case of the saver.

[49] This two-dimensional drawing is limited to the choice between two items. The real choice is "N" dimensional.

[50] A discussion of Engle's laws may be found in Cohen, pp. 85-86, Furguson, pp. 40-44.

[51] See Neil H. Borden, "The Concept of the Marketing Mix," *Journal of Advertising Research* (June 1964), pp. 2-7.

[52] See Richard P. Bagozzi, "Marketing as Exchange," *Journal of Marketing* 39 (October 1975), pp. 32-39.

[53] All microeconomic understandings used in this chapter are straightforward and in common use. See for example Cohen and Furguson.

Questions for Study, Discussion and Examination

1. Could you define or explain to a friend who has not studied marketing, each of the following terms? Can you give examples of each?
    a. Satisfaction
    b. Utility
    c. Perception
    d. Perceptual vigilance
    e. Perceptual defense
    f. Perceptual organization
    g. Gestalt
    h. Perceptual set
    i. Reference group
    j. Membership group
    k. Aspirational group
    l. Dissociative group
    m. Affective Cognitive Consistency
    n. Cognitive dissonance
    o. Operant conditioning
    p. Classical conditioning
    q. Evoke
    r. Associative learning
    s. Drive
    t. Cue
    u. Response
    v. Reinforcement
    w. Cognitive learning
    x. Psychometrics
    y. Tension
    z. Motives
    aa. Needs
    ab. Interim concept

ac. Theoretical unit
ad. Alternative evaluation
ae. Evaluative criteria
af. Marginal utility
ag. Declining marginal utility
ah. $\dfrac{mu}{p}$
ai. Iso utility curve
aj. Budget line
ak. Consumer optimum
al. Substitution effect
am. Income effect
an. Income expansion path
ao. Engles Laws
ap. Superior good
aq. Normal good
ar. Inferior goods
as. Demographics
at. Demand curve
au. Law of downward sloping demand
av. Market segment
aw. Backward bending demand curve
ax. Perfectly inelastic demand
ay. Relatively inelasic demand
az. Price elasticity of demand
ba. Relatively elastic demand
bb. Perfectly elastic demand
bc. Four "Ps" of the offering (the marketing "mix")
bd. Investment in product differentiation
be. Investment in promotion
bf. Investment in distribution
bg. Creative mixing
bh. Job of marketing management
bi. Complex exchange
bj. Derived demand
bk. Intermediate customer
bl. Purchasing agent

2. Why do you think an individual demands a product or a service? Is demanding a product or service the same as wanting it or as needing it? Distinguish between a demand and a want or a need. Does it make sense to distinguish between a want and a need? If so, how would you distinguish between them? (hint: Review the economist's budget line and clinical psychologist's definitions of satisfaction.)

3. What is the relationship between the terms satisfaction and utility?

4. How do the concepts of perceptual vigilance, perceptual defense and perceptual organization suggest that individuals deal with incoming information? Of what relevance is this to marketing practitioners? What does this suggest about the idea of a perfectly openminded person?

5. Of what value do the concepts of consistency, order and balance seem to be to people? Relate this to the concepts of perceptual vigilance, perceptual defense, perceptual organization, reference groups which are selected, affective cognitive consistency, cognitive dissonance and tension.

6. How does a person learn to behave in the marketplace? Give examples of operant conditioning and classical conditioning. Both are examples of what kind of learning?

7. Give an example of a marketplace learning experience of your own. Pick an example in which you will be able to demonstrate the concepts of drive, cue, response and reinforcement.

8. Discuss the terms drive, motive, need and tension. How would you relate them, how would you differentiate them?

9. Compare and contrast the concepts of want and need. How are they similar? How are they different? If you were to give a person only what that person needs what would you give?

10. Give an example of cognitive learning.

11. Can psychological concepts be measured? If so how can this be done?

12. What concepts from Freudian theory do you think might be useful to marketing people. Explain specifically how they might be relevant.

13. Explain the role of the concept of tension in the personality theories of Freud, Sullivan, Murphy, and Murray. Based on the brief summary in this book what do they seem to agree upon? Where do they seem to disagree? What is useful to marketing people?

14. How would you evaluate the status of theoretical development in the area of drives, motives, needs and satisfaction? Where do you think it is going? What is useful now?
15. Evaluate the role or potential role of the physiological psychologist in providing understandings which are useful to marketing.
16. What is the relationship of the discipline of consumer behavior to the discipline of psychology?
17. What is a buyer behavior model or consumer behavior model? How might one be used to develop theory or to improve the quality of marketing practice?
18. How is the concept of satisfaction used in the Howard Sheth and Engle Blackwell models of consumer behavior?
19. Given what you have read, what do you feel that you know about the nature of human satisfaction? What do you feel that you do not know? Describe instances in your life when you have felt satisfaction. What did it feel like? Describe instances in your life when you have experienced dissatisfaction. What did you feel like? What did you do about it?
20. How are buyers rewarded or punished in the Engle Blackwell model of consumer behavior? How is the decision process initiated and consummated in this model? How does this relate to satisfaction, dissatisfaction, and tension?
21. What are evaluative criteria? How, according to the Engle Blackwell model, are they used in alternative evaluation? Describe how you might have experienced this process. To what extent was the process you experienced clear, conscious, and explicit? To what extent was alternative evaluation somewhat more subjective (less explicit) and unconscious? Have you experienced both kinds of alternative evaluation?
22. What is a low involvement consumer behavior model? What is a low involvement product? Describe your experience with the purchase of these kinds of products.
23. Describe a family purchase decision you have experienced. Does the Sheth Family Decision Making Model help you to remember and describe this decision? Why or why not?
24. Have you ever sold anything to a business or other organization? Have you ever purchased anything for such an organization? Does the

Webster and Wind model help you remember, understand and describe that experience? Why or why not? If you have not had this experience, what do you imagine it would be like?

25. A purchase will not be made unless MU > P. This statement uses microeconomic terms. Explain it in psychological terms. How does perception enter in? How does it affect MU? How does it affect P? How do evaluative criteria enter in? What is the correct statement of MU > P in microeconomic terms?

26. Explain the choice of one product or service over another when $\frac{mu}{p_1} > \frac{mu}{p_2}$ explain it in terms of both psychology and microeconomics.

27. What is the correct statement of the following relationship in microeconomic terms? $\frac{mu_1}{p_1} = \frac{mu_2}{p_2}$ How does a person feel in this situation? Have you ever experienced this situation? If so describe it.

28. Describe a situation wherein you have experienced declining marginal utility. What did it feel like?

29. What is marginal utility in economic terms? In psychological terms?

30. Would the marginal utility of a package of 10 $1,000 bills be the same for you as it would be for an individual who has just inherited 100 million dollars? Why or why not? What does this suggest about pricing, about market segmentation, or about pricing in different market segments?

31. How is it possible for two people to be involved in a voluntary exchange and both be better off as a result? Isn't it necessary that one profits at the expense of another? Would an exchange be voluntary if one party to the exchange profited at the expense of the other? How much does this depend on equivalent intelligence or knowledge on the part of both parties to the exchange? What do you see the ethics of voluntary exchange to be?

32. What does the term iso-utility mean? What is an iso-utility curve?

33. What is a budget line? What do the utility curves and the budget line illustrate about what might be preferred versus what is demanded?

34. Of what interest is a preference without money behind it? Under what circumstances does a person have money to back up his/her preferences? What does this say about the market's valuation of that person's skills or products? Can you cite examples where this seems to be equitable to you? Where it does not? Is it always equitable or always inequitable?

35. What is occurring at the point of consumer optimum? In terms of iso-utility curves and the budget line? In terms of the marginal utility and prices of the products or services being considered?

36. What general results can be expected when the price of a product or service changes? Can you give an example of this?

37. What general results can be expected when an individual's income changes? How can the study of demographics make this knowledge more useful in marketing practice?

38. What is a demand curve? How is it related to individual choice? Why is it usually expected to slope downward to the right?

39. Explain the following characteristics of demand curves in terms of the nature of human choice and the concept of $\frac{mu}{p}$.

   a. A demand curve for a market segment which differs substantially in slope from the demand curve for the greater market from which the segment was taken.
   b. A backward bending or prestige demand curve.
   c. Perfectly inelastic demand, relatively inelastic demand, relatively elastic demand and perfectly elastic demand.

40. What value does the expression below have in each of the situations named in 39c above? What can this imply about revenue? Under what circumstances?

$$\frac{\frac{\Delta x}{x}}{\frac{\Delta p}{p}}$$

41. What are the four managerial variables of marketing? How does each, taken by itself, relate to the demand curve? Can you relate this to the idea of investment?

42. How does investment in the managerial variables of marketing affect the way the consumer views $\frac{mu}{p}$ for any given product? In this context, what is meant by creative mixing and the marketing mix? What does this have to do with perception and evaluative criteria?

43. What is the job of marketing management? How does it involve the anticipation of reactions? How is this related to the ideas expressed in

the demand curve? What is the importance of unit movement or unit sales?

44. What must a marketing strategy consist of?
45. What is complex exchange, can you give an example? How should the marketer approach such situations?
46. Explain how marketing might differ when selling into a market characterized by derived demand.
47. How should the marketing decision maker change his or her thinking when engaging in marketing activities which cross national boundaries? What ideas should remain unchanged?

CHAPTER 3

HUMAN EXCHANGE: SUPPLY BEHAVIOR AND THE MARKET NICHE

A *market match* occurs when resources are transferred or allocated through voluntary human exchange. A *voluntary exchange* occurs when something which is *voluntarily demanded* according to the principles developed in the last chapter is also *voluntarily supplied*. Thus the *study of supply behavior* is *important to the understanding of human exchange*.

Just as a consumer might behave so as to improve satisfaction, an individual or group involved in supply behavior endeavors to establish and expand a *market niche*.[1] A market niche is a position in the ecology of human exchange where the organization or firm may survive and grow. It is established by providing products and services, or performing functions, which the society values more highly than the products and services which are consumed in the process. This valuation process is performed using the complex, imperfect and often legally constrained mechanism of markets.

Within such market behavior there is an implicit *social reward structure for the suppliers*. Under some conditions a supplier is rewarded, as the valuation of what the supplier creates exceeds the valuation of what the supplier uses. In other conditions the supplier is punished and must either change the match by altering what is offered to the market and what is consumed in order to create it, or give up and leave the market. In general *the social reward structure for suppliers which is implicit in market behavior:*

1. *Rewards* sensitivity to what people really want or need and punishes insensitivity.

   [Note this is not responding to what people say they want or need or what they ought to want or need, but what they really want or need. This requires some psychological insight as introduced in chapter two.]

2. *Rewards* successful innovation (a better product in the eyes of the consumer or a better means of production or distribution) and punishes failure to improve.

3. *Rewards* the position of sole supplier, whether that is due to innovation or to the other suppliers' complete inability to follow the market mix. In similar fashion the reduction of effective competition is rewarded, whether by innovation or other means.

4. Does *not reward* producers of "me too" (homogeneous) products *unless* they can produce the product more efficiently than their competitors.

A complete understanding of why these generalizations make sense, together with an understanding of why consumers demand as they do, will form the basis of a solid understanding of marketing strategy. An understanding of these generalizations about the social reward structure for suppliers is encouraged in this chapter through the development of perspectives in microeconomics and psychology.

The Supplying Firm: An Economist's Concept

Much supply behavior can be understood using the economist's portrayal of the firm. The economist characterizes the supplying firm using the concepts of *average total cost* and *marginal cost* which were introduced in chapter one. The average total cost is the total cost of producing the items divided by the number of items built. According to arguments developed in chapter one, the average total cost is expected to fall as the quantity of items produced increases. Marginal cost is the incremental or added cost of producing one more unit.

To complete the economist's picture of average total cost it should be noted that after some point, for any given productive facility such as a plant or a farm, the amount being produced will exceed the amount the plant or farm was designed to produce. (The level of production will exceed the designed capacity.) This will result in certain economic inefficiencies such as the extra stacking and moving of materials, and overtime pay. It is for these reasons that the average total cost curve for any given productive facility is expected to be "U shaped." That is, it is expected to first move down as economies of scale reduce the average total cost of production and then move back up as design capacity is exceeded and inefficiencies are experienced.[2]

The marginal costs are reflected in the U-shaped average total cost curve. When marginal costs are low, their effect upon average total cost is to lower it. When marginal costs are high, their effect is to bring average total costs up. This effect can be illustrated using the example of a student's grade point average (G.P.A.). If a student's incremental grades (the grades for one semester) are *below* the average total grade point the effect is to bring the average total grade point down. If the incremental grades are *above* the average total gradepoint the effect is to bring the gradepoint up. Thus, marginal cost is expected to lie *below* average total cost when average total cost is falling and *above* average total cost when average total cost is rising. Putting average total cost and marginal cost together in this way results in the *economist's conventional way of portraying the firm*. This is illustrated in figure 25.

When using the economist's portrayal of the firm to describe a firm's supply behavior, the student or analyst should note one important assumption which is contained in the average total cost curve. The economist's idea of cost and the accountant's idea of cost differ in a significant way. The economist includes some amount of accounting profit in the average total cost curve. This amount of accounting profit is termed a *risk adjusted return to capital*. It is the amount of accounting profit that is required to keep capital in a firm or industry, given the amount of risk in that industry. In the economist's eyes, this amount of profit is seen as a cost of keeping investors' capital in that firm. Greater accounting profit would attract more capital, less accounting profit would cause capital to leave. This amount of accounting profit is adjusted for risk. In a risky business the risk adjusted return to capital might be 25% of revenue. In a stable business the risk adjusted return to capital might be 3% of revenue. Capital itself is economically defined as the durable goods produced by an economy in order to produce other goods.[3] Alternatively, capital "as created" may be socially defined as the excess of production over consumption when both are valued by the imperfect mechanism of markets. Thus, capital is created when individuals save or when firms make a profit. It is then attracted to investments in firms or repelled from such investments depending upon the return to capital which that firm offers.

The Firm and Profit-Maximization

Attempts on the part of the firm to improve its profits will be greeted with greatly different responses in the marketplace. These different responses may be explored using economists' graphs of the firm in markets. These graphs in turn will use lines depicting marginal cost and marginal revenue. This section

70   Part I

Figure 25
The Economist's Portrayal of the Firm

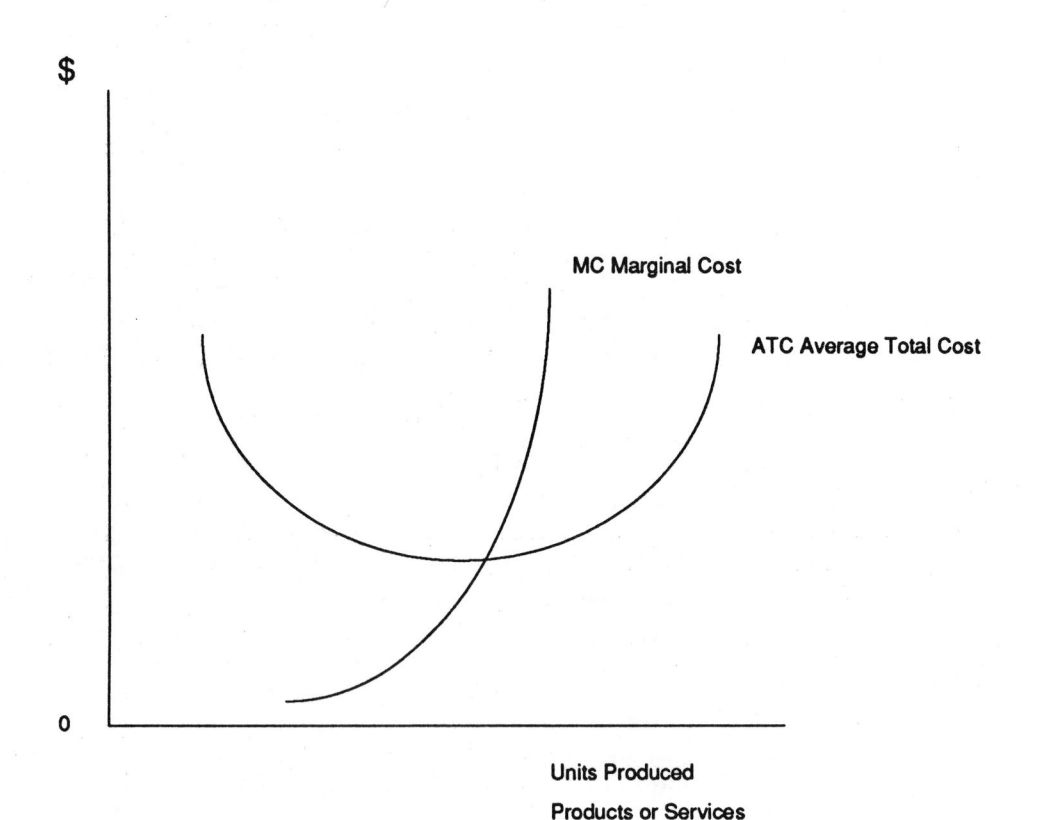

$

MC Marginal Cost

ATC Average Total Cost

0

Units Produced
Products or Services

develops the rationale behind the use of those lines. It also develops the rationale as to why maximum profit or minimum loss might be expected at the sales and production point where marginal cost equals marginal revenue (MC = MR).

Marginal costs have been defined as the additional or incremental cost associated with another unit of production. Marginal revenue has a parallel definition. *Marginal revenue is the additional or incremental revenue associated with another unit of production.* In cases where price does not change, the marginal revenue simply equates to the price of the last unit sold.

A straightforward graph of total costs and total revenues can be used to develop the understanding of marginal cost, marginal revenue and profit maximization. In the graph of total costs and total revenues (figure 26) it is straightforward to assume that maximum profit occurs where total revenues exceed total costs by the greatest distance. But how does this relate to marginal cost and marginal revenue?

The definition of marginal cost $\frac{\Delta TC}{\Delta \text{Units}}$ may be seen on the graph of total cost. It is simply the slope of the total cost line. Similarly, marginal revenue $\frac{\Delta TR}{\Delta \text{Units}}$ may be seen as the slope of the total revenue line. This compatibility of definitions is explored in figure 27.

The maximum profit point identified in figure 26, is also the point where the slope of the total revenue line equals the slope of the total cost line and therefore where MC = MR. It is due to this rationale that the intersection (or equality) of MC and MR is taken to indicate a maximum profit point in the graphs of the firm in markets.

Market Structure

Graphs of firms in markets are used by economists to describe and explore differences in market structure. *Market structure* is a term used to characterize markets according to the number and size of suppliers, the difficulty of entering the market (barriers to entry) and the degree to which the products involved are homogeneous or heterogeneous. Market structure is important in characterizing the niche of the firm because market structure predicts long run relationships between prices and costs.

Economists have developed elaborate theory concerning the behavior of the firm and its resulting profitability in each condition of market structure.[4] Not all of it will be needed for practical market analysis. It will be necessary

**Figure 26
Costs and Revenue**

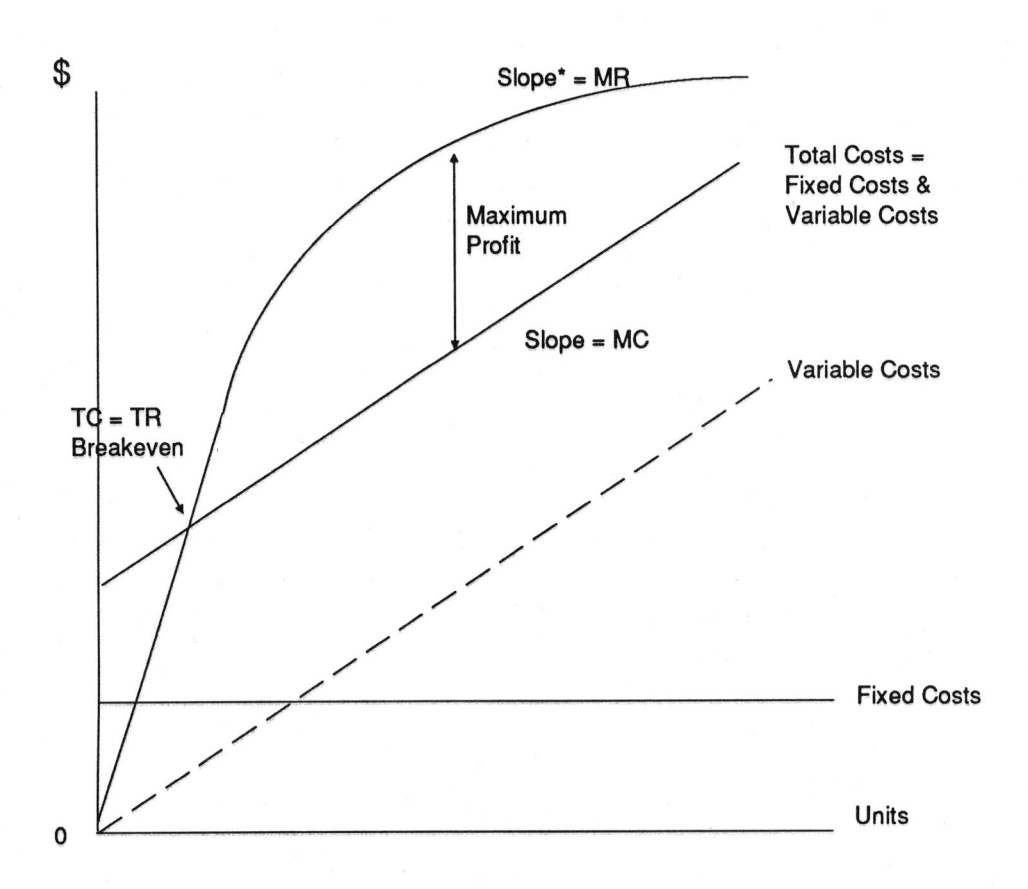

* Slope of a curved line is the 'instantaneous slope' or the first derivative.

Chapter 3   73

Figure 27
Definitions Explored

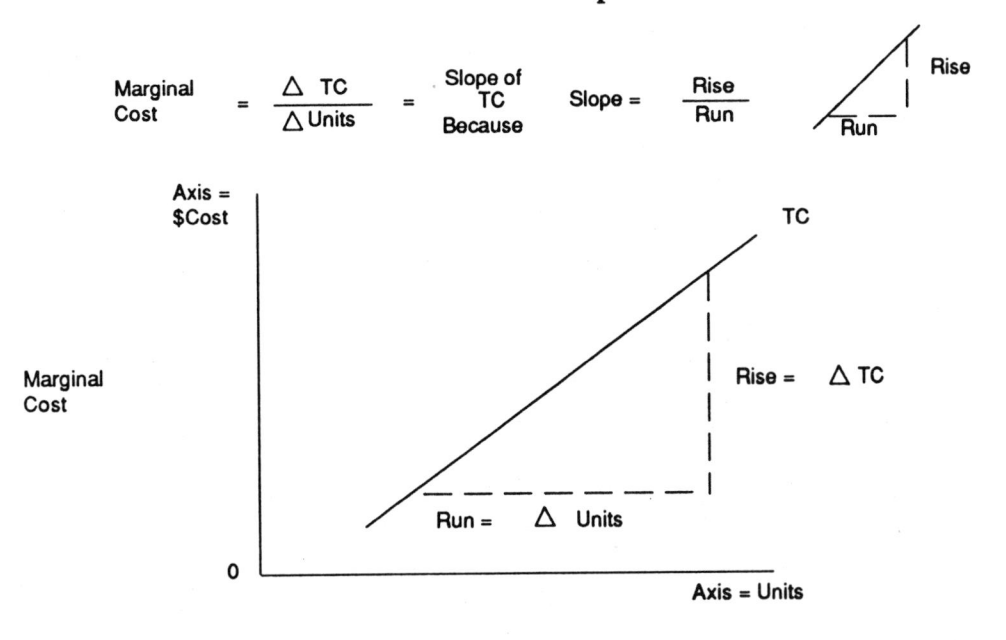

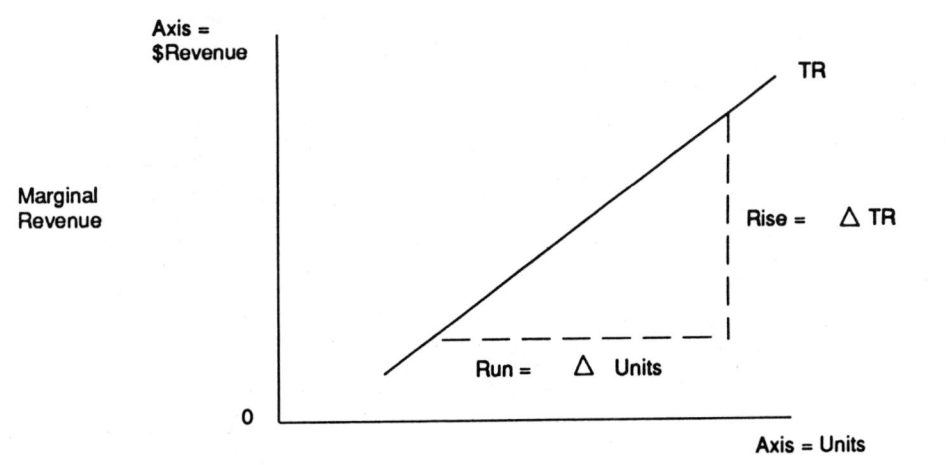

Marginal Cost $= \dfrac{\Delta \text{ TC}}{\Delta \text{ Units}} =$ Slope of TC Because   Slope $= \dfrac{\text{Rise}}{\text{Run}}$

Marginal Cost

Axis = $Cost

TC

Rise = Δ TC

Run = Δ Units

0

Axis = Units

Marginal Revenue $= \dfrac{\Delta \text{ TR}}{\Delta \text{ Units}} =$ Slope of TR Because   Slope $= \dfrac{\text{Rise}}{\text{Run}}$

Marginal Revenue

Axis = $Revenue

TR

Rise = Δ TR

Run = Δ Units

0

Axis = Units

to understand the polar extreme cases of market structure (monopoly and competition) quite well. It will also be useful to understand both the economic and the psychological reasons why any actual market under consideration may approximate or deviate from the classical behavior of the polar extreme cases.

Competitive Decisions to Supply

The polar extreme case of pure competition is characterized by a homogeneous or undifferentiated product, by many suppliers, by perfect information about the marketplace, and by low barriers to the entry of new firms in the marketplace.[5] Competitive market structure is also characterized by a *supply curve*, an abstraction similar to a demand curve which describes the number of units supplied to a marketplace at different levels of price. Like the demand curve, it is a horizontal summation of individual choices. In this case the choice focused upon is the individual firm's decision of whether to supply and how much to supply.

The individual decision to supply is as complex as the individual decision to demand. The second and third sections of this book will explore supply behavior in depth using a managerial focus. At this point, the economist's portrayal of the firm will be useful in approaching the question of supply behavior.

Figure 28 illustrates several possible relationships which might exist between the cost curves of the firm and the price of the good or service that the firm is selling in the market. The cost curves are shown as they have been developed and explained before. Figures 28c and 28d have a representation of average variable cost (AVC) added to the familiar ATC and MC. Average variable cost includes only those costs which vary with the number of units produced, while average total cost includes the fixed costs of the firm. For this reason AVC lies below ATC. The introduction of AVC is important for market analysis, and the next chapter will develop a more thorough and sophisticated understanding of these kinds of costs.

The level of price for the product or service being offered is given by a horizontal line, marked P = MR = AR in each picture. The horizontal line implies a constant price, such that the firm can sell all that it wants to sell at the constant market price and need not drop the price to sell more units. For this reason, price equals marginal revenue which in turn equals average revenue (P = MR = AR). In other words the extra revenue gained by selling another unit (MR) is the market price (P) and, if one were to total up all revenue and divide by the total number of units sold to get revenue per unit (AR) that result would also equal the market price (P).

Chapter 3 75

Figure 28
Supply Decisions of the Individual Firm: An Economist's Portrayal

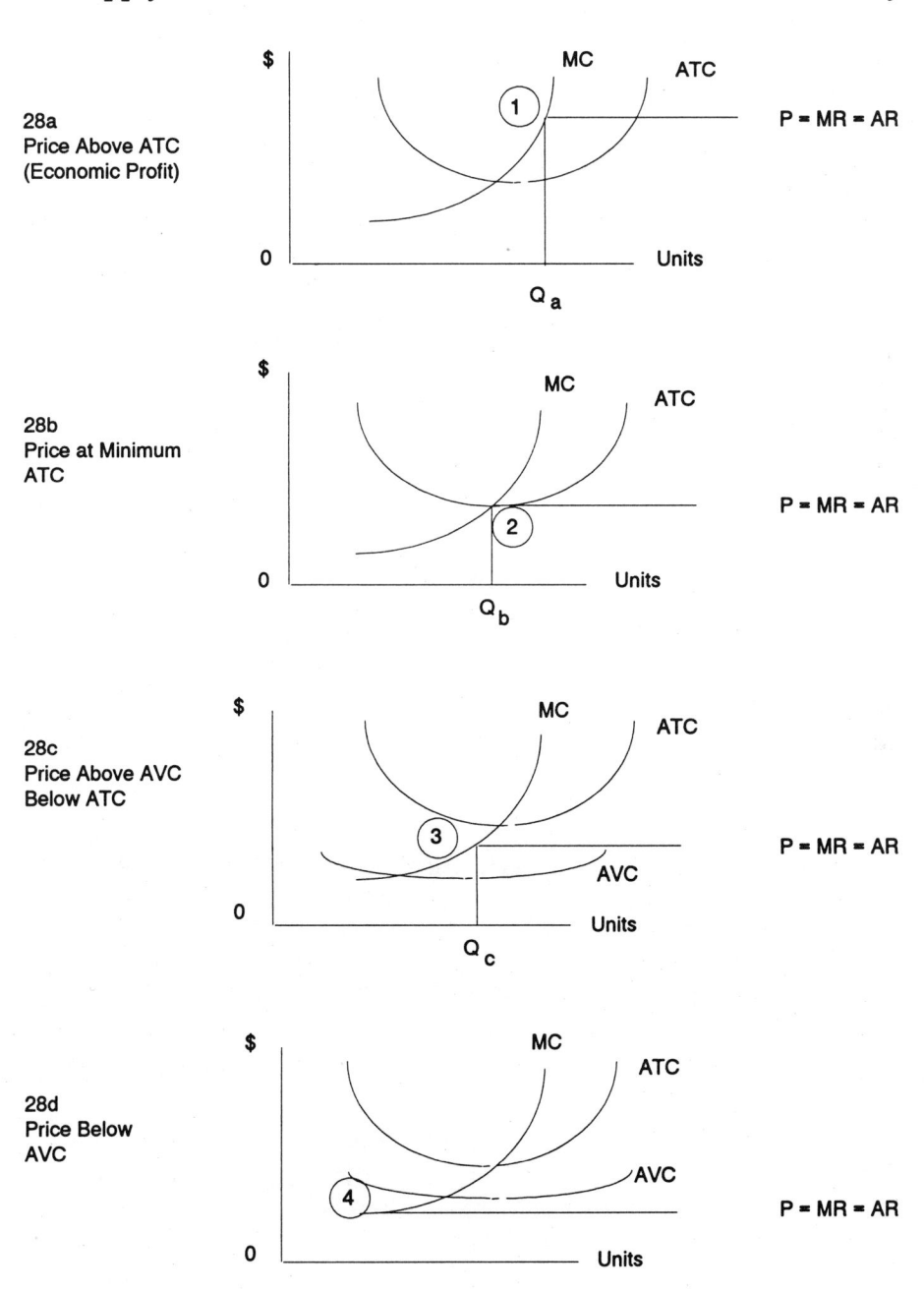

28a
Price Above ATC
(Economic Profit)

28b
Price at Minimum
ATC

28c
Price Above AVC
Below ATC

28d
Price Below
AVC

The firm displays substantially different reactions depending on the level of price. In figure 28a the price is quite high. The firm maximizes profit where MC equals (intersects) MR at point 1, thus electing to produce the relatively high quantity, Qa. In this situation price exceeds average total cost by a substantial amount. The firm is thus making profits over and above the risk adjusted return to capital which is included in ATC. Profits over and above the risk adjusted return to capital are termed *economic profits*. In figure 28a economic profit per unit is given by the distance from point 1 to the ATC curve. Total economic profit is given by multiplying that dollar amount by the number of units or quantity Qa. Figure 28a displays *two reasons why this relatively high price will bring forth a relatively large quantity supplied*. First the profit maximizing production for the *individual firm* is a *larger quantity*. Compare quantities Qa (Figure 28a), Qb (28b) and Qc (28c). This is because the high price allows the firm to continue to make a profit as quantity exceeds the design capacity of the productive facility, as represented by the cost curves. In terms of the economist's graph, profit can be made to the right of the lowest point or minimum cost point on ATC. The *second reason* this relatively high price brings forth a large quantity is that the *economic profit* will attract *more firms* into this industry. People investing capital will be looking for profits over and above risk adjusted returns. In the context of the ease of entry into competitive markets, this will mean more firms producing. This *second effect is not embodied in the supply curve itself*, but in shifts of the supply curve, as will be discussed later.

As *price declines, the amount produced by the individual firm will decline and economic profits will no longer attract new firms*. In Figure 28b, MC = MR at point 2, resulting in the firm cutting production back to the point of maximum efficiency at minimum average total cost. Because price equals minimum average total cost, there is no economic profit and no attraction for new firms.

In Figure 28c, the firm is sustaining an economic loss as price lies below average total cost. Firms will begin to leave the market at this point, but those in the market are still better off producing something. This is because price still exceeds (or covers) variable costs. Thus *each sale contributes something to fixed costs* even if not enough to cover average total cost. But, because marginal costs are increasing with quantity the firm selects a low production quantity.

Finally, in Figure 28d price is so low that it will *not cover variable costs*. There is now no incentive for the firm to produce at all and it ceases production.

While the complex world of *business decision making is not as neat* as these economist's models of supply choice, the *generalization* that *higher prices can provide incentive for more production* is quite often a good one.

A *supply curve can now be illustrated* using the same horizontal summation process that was used to illustrate the demand curve. Consider for example, the response of four farmers capable of supplying undifferentiated potatoes to a marketplace. The horizontal summation of individual choice is depicted in Figure 29.

Consider the farmer's reaction to an extremely low price of $.05/#. At this very low price some farmers may *make the decision to supply*. Farm B in Figure 29 has elected to supply twenty units, at $.05/#. This kind of *decision is a function of the psychology and or strategy of the decision maker(s) as well as the economics of the situation*. $.05/# may not cover variable costs and yet the decision makers may still elect to produce. This decision could be the result of sophisticated strategic thinking whereby farm B has elected to produce this crop at a loss as a part of an overall strategy. Alternatively it may be the result of simple habit, the farm family involved always having planted potatoes. It may be the result of poor accounting and a resulting unawareness of variable costs. For whatever reasons, farm B elects to supply at the low price.

Price increases have important effects on the decision process of the farmers. For farmers who have the opportunity and inclination to plant other crops, potatoes must compete for their investment and attention. As the price increases, the profitability of potatoes relative to the other crops improves and production may be shifted to potatoes. This could be the case for farmers A and C at the second price level of $5.00. Their production is added to supply at that price. Farm D may be in a poor potato climate and thus be a relatively inefficient producer of potatoes. Extremely high prices will encourage production even in such marginal cases and farm D begins production at $50.00. As the price continues to go up, each supplier is encouraged to produce more units. Horizontal summation of all of these individual supplier decisions results in the supply curve which ordinarily slopes upward to the right. In Figure 29 the curve takes on differing slopes. As it does with the demand curve, the slope demonstrates the property of *elasticity*. In parallel fashion to demand, supply may demonstrate perfect elasticity, relative elasticity, relative inelasticity or perfect inelasticity. *Perfectly inelastic supply*, indicated by a vertical supply curve, indicates that for whatever reason, no larger quantities are available, despite increases in the price.

Supply and Demand in Markets

The ideas necessary for the understanding of a *market* have now been introduced. A market consists of individuals or groups involved in exchange. One type of market, a competitive market, may be described using the economist's tools just demonstrated. The supply and demand curves describe

78   Part I

Figure 29
The Supply Curve, Horizontal Summation Of Individual Choice to Supply

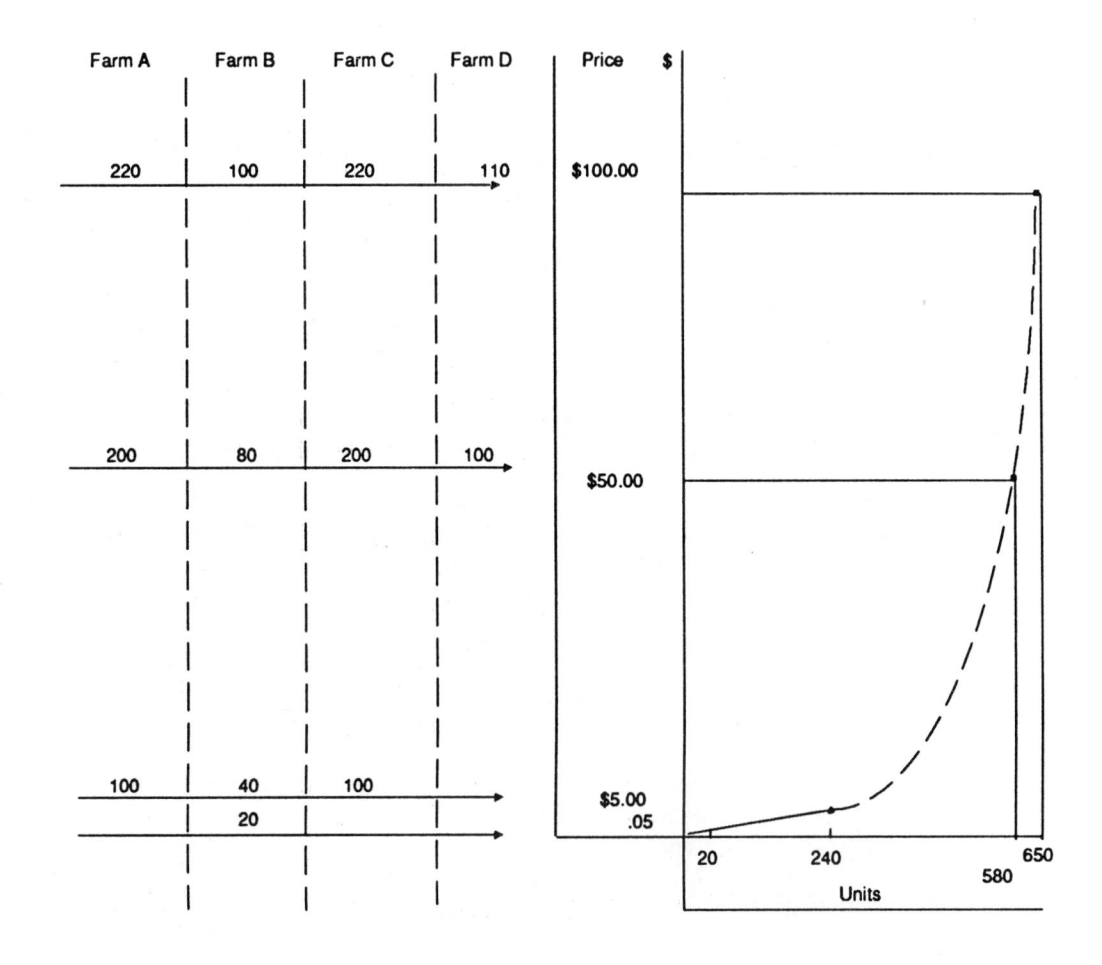

the reactions of individuals to the changing level of price. Both understandings were developed using the axes of price and units, so it is no logical problem to place the curves on the same graph. Figure 30 depicts this.

This figure may be used to demonstrate several important points concerning basic supply and demand in a free and competitive market. First, the two lines intersect at point e (equilibrium) which translates on the price axis as Pe (Equilibrium price) and on the quantity axis as Qe (equilibrium quantity). The *Equilibrium point* is the point at which the horizontal summation of the many individual decisions to demand results in the same number of units as the horizontal summation of the many individual decisions to supply. Stated differently, *the quantity willingly demanded equals the quantity willingly supplied at the equilibrium point.*

This has important *social implications*. As markets work themselves toward equilibrium, a social compromise is being voluntarily worked out. Supply is being *matched* with demand. The questions of who provides what for whom are being worked out by free individuals, each making choices according to his or her own perspectives and values. As with any social compromise not everyone gets exactly what is desired at a desired price. But everyone remains free to select according to his or her individual values.

The *price system* plays an important role in this matching process. The price system, or the set of prices in a society's markets, provides signals to individuals who would demand or supply. The price system signals what the current social compromise value of an item is, thus encouraging or discouraging demand and encouraging or discouraging supply. For example, if the price in figure 30 were at the level Ph (high price), Qa would be demanded and Qb would be supplied. The high price has *signaled* that the social compromise value is high. This has *signaled* people demanding to conserve (consuming only Qa) while *signaling* people supplying to supply a great deal (supplying Qb). Given people's values, this social compromise value appears to be too high, as it has resulted in a surplus. More is being supplied than demanded (the distance between Qa and Qb). However, the *great strength of the price system as a matching device for the allocation of societies resources is that it adjusts the incentives that it provides automatically.* The surplus will have a downward effect upon price. Suppliers will drop the price to obtain sales, forcing the price toward Pe. This adjustment encourages more demand and less supply, adjusting social allocations toward a voluntary match. Should a price be lower than the price which results in a match, then similar automatic adjustments of prices and incentives occur. At a low price (Pl) Qc would be supplied and Qd would be demanded. The low price has *signaled* to people demanding to go ahead and consume, and to people supplying to cut back. Given people's values, the social compromise value now appears to be too low, as it has

Figure 30
Supply and Demand in a Market

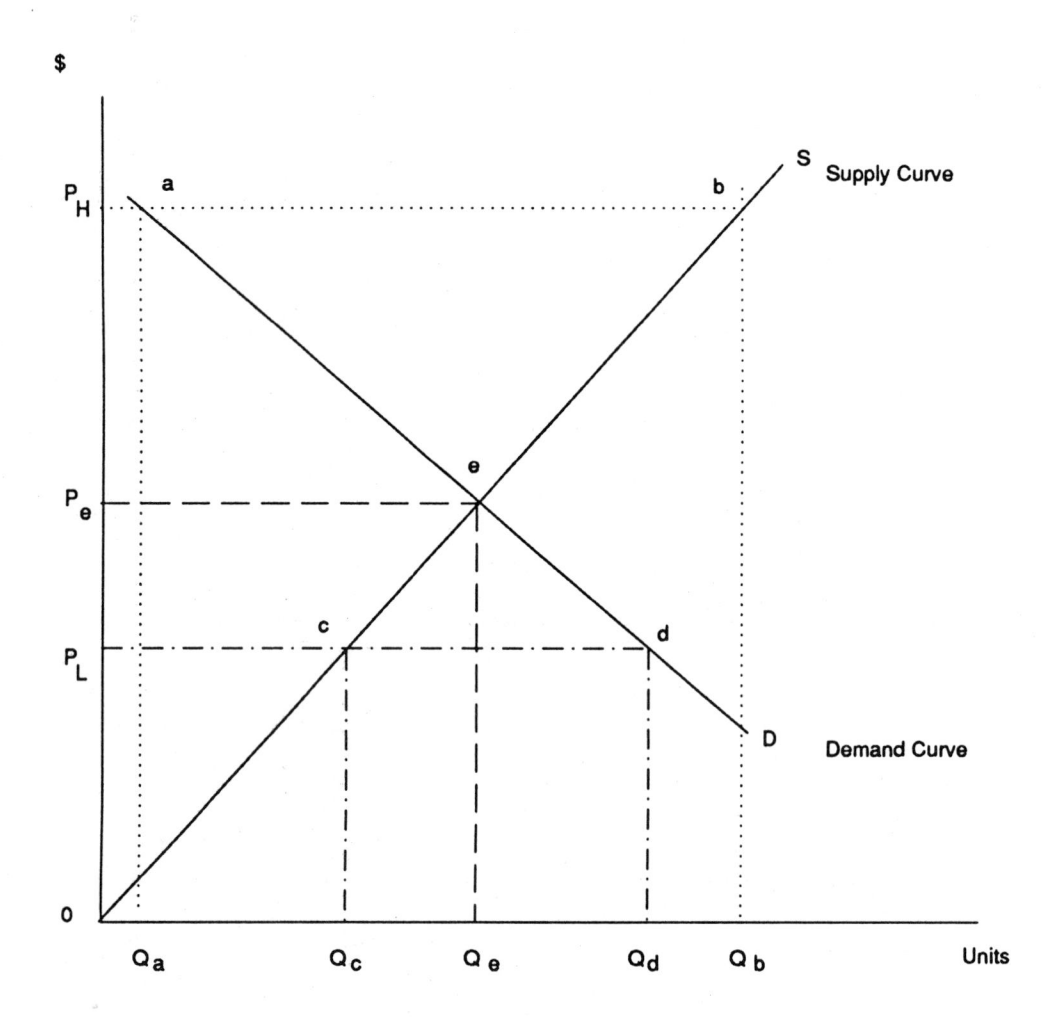

How the price system facilitates the matching of individuals or groups involved in exchange

resulted in a shortage. More is being demanded than supplied (the distance between Qd and Qc). The shortage will have an upward effect on price. Buyers will bid the price up, again forcing it toward Pe.

Markets are rarely if ever seen to be stable at equilibrium price. Constant change in individual attitudes, opinions, perceptions and financial conditions will result in constant changes in the demand curve. Constant changes in the condition of supply; technology, cost of inputs, attractiveness of alternatives, and risk will result in constant changes in the supply curve. Throughout this process of change, the *price system* continues to automatically *signal* for compensating adjustments, continuing to *facilitate* the market *matching* process.

Social compromise is an appropriate term for this process. Sometimes people cannot afford what they want; sometimes they must pay more for it than they would like to. At the same time, it is quite often the case that an individual will receive a product or service for much less than the individual would have been willing to pay had it been necessary. In these cases the individual pays a market price which through the social compromise process, is lower than the price the individual was willing to pay. This phenomenon is known as *consumer surplus* and is illustrated in figure 31.

Pure Competition: A Polar Extreme Case of Market Structure

The level of price in relation to cost and thus the level of *profit* for the firm which results from the interaction of supply and demand *differs greatly with market structure*. Beyond this, *some of the effects of market structure can be created psychologically*. The beginning student and the practical market analyst need not understand all of the nuances of market structure. They do need to understand the substantially different kinds of market niches which are created for the firm by the polar extreme cases of pure competition and monopoly. They should also understand the psychological and economic reasons why any real market under consideration should approximate or deviate from the behavior of one of these polar extreme cases.

The polar extreme case of pure competition has been introduced above as being characterized by a homogeneous or undifferentiated product, by many sellers, by perfect information about the market and by low barriers of entry into the market.[6] This *situation will result* in supplier entry into the market when prices are high enough to yield profits above the normal risk adjusted return. It will result in suppliers departing from the market when prices are so low as to yield less than a normal risk adjusted return.

Figure 31
Consumer Surplus

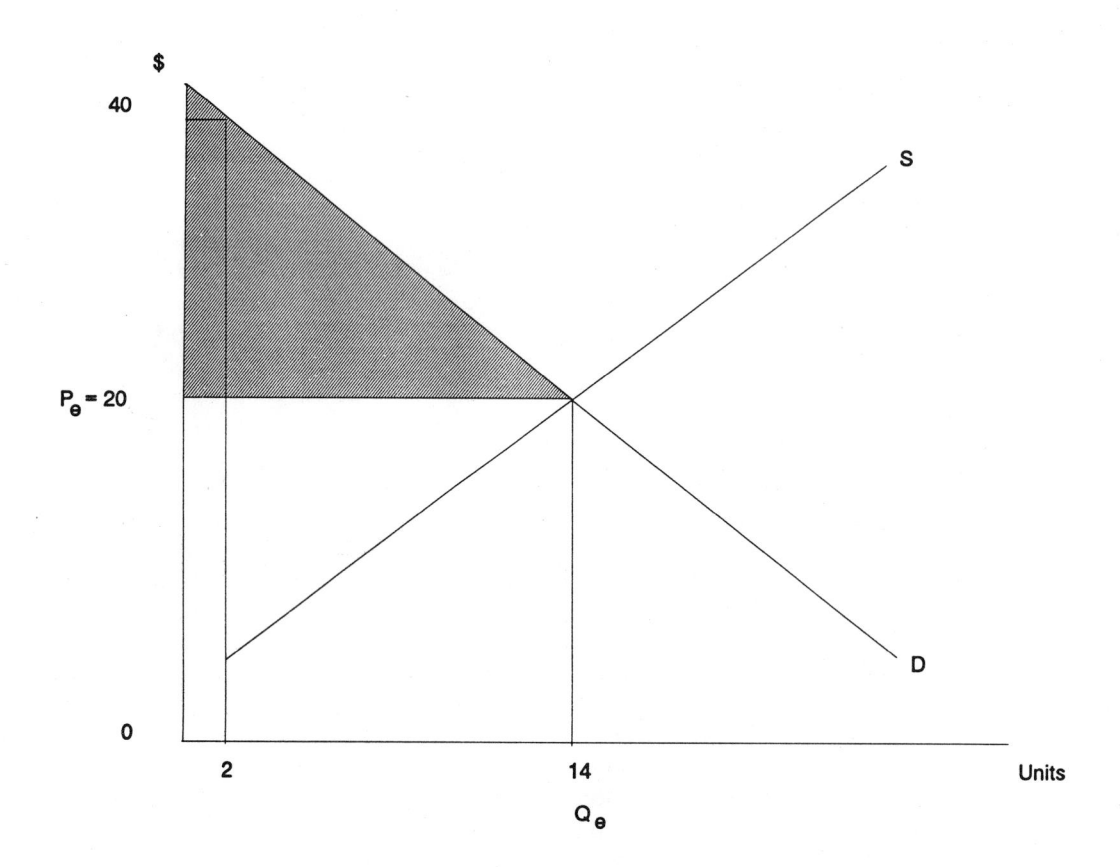

$P_e = 20$

Q_e

The two units which would have been purchased at $40 may be purchased for the market price ($P_e = 20$) resulting in consumer surplus. Units 1-13 each have been purchased with some amount of consumer surplus.

These *results* may be *demonstrated* by placing the graph of the firm next to the graph of supply and demand. This is accomplished in figure 32a. In these two graphs the vertical axes are identical. A dollar of price or unit cost on one is equivalent to a dollar of price or cost on the other. The horizontal axes are not identical but are directly related. The units produced by the representative firm in the left graph are summed up across all such firms to arrive at the total units supplied to the market in the right graph. This is the horizontal summation process that has been discussed earlier as the horizontal summation of individual decisions to supply.

The interaction of the firm and the market can now be illustrated. Market price P = MR = AR may be taken from the market graph directly to the graph of the firm because the vertical axes are identical. Profit maximization or loss minimization is found where MC = MR at Q1 in figure 32a. Here the firm enjoys *economic profit* or a return over and above the risk adjusted return to capital.

The nature of this kind of market niche may now be seen. If an economic profit were solid, sustainable, and defensible, the representative firm would have a desirable market niche indeed. But because of the characteristics of pure competition, this market niche is much less desirable. The product is homogeneous and undifferentiated. Thus no seller is to be preferred to another and all sellers must *take price* from the market. Anyone who tries to sell at a price above the market level will not be able to sell the product at all. In economic terms the demand for the individual vendor's product is *perfectly elastic* regardless of what the elasticity of market demand might be. In pure competition the products are the same, so there is no reason not to prefer a lower price. The many sellers in the pure competition marketplace will insure that the buyer will always have the power that comes with the option of choosing from a large group of vendors. Perfect market information will ensure that everyone knows about the high rate of economic profit (the distance between price and ATC in figure 32a). Many will then want to invest in the industry and this investment will be encouraged by the low barriers to entry which characterize the industry. The economic profit will draw more firms to the industry.

With *more firms*, more is now being supplied at any given level of price. This is interpreted on the graph of the market as a *shift of the supply curve to the right*. This shift is incorporated in figure 32b. Here, Si represents the original supply curve and S2 represents the supply curve after its shift to the right. As there is more competition, the new price which results is much lower and figure 32b now shows the representative firm sustaining an economic loss (the distance between price and ATC in figure 32b). Price is less than average total cost no matter what quantity is produced. With economic losses, investors

84   Part I

Figure 32
Pure Competition

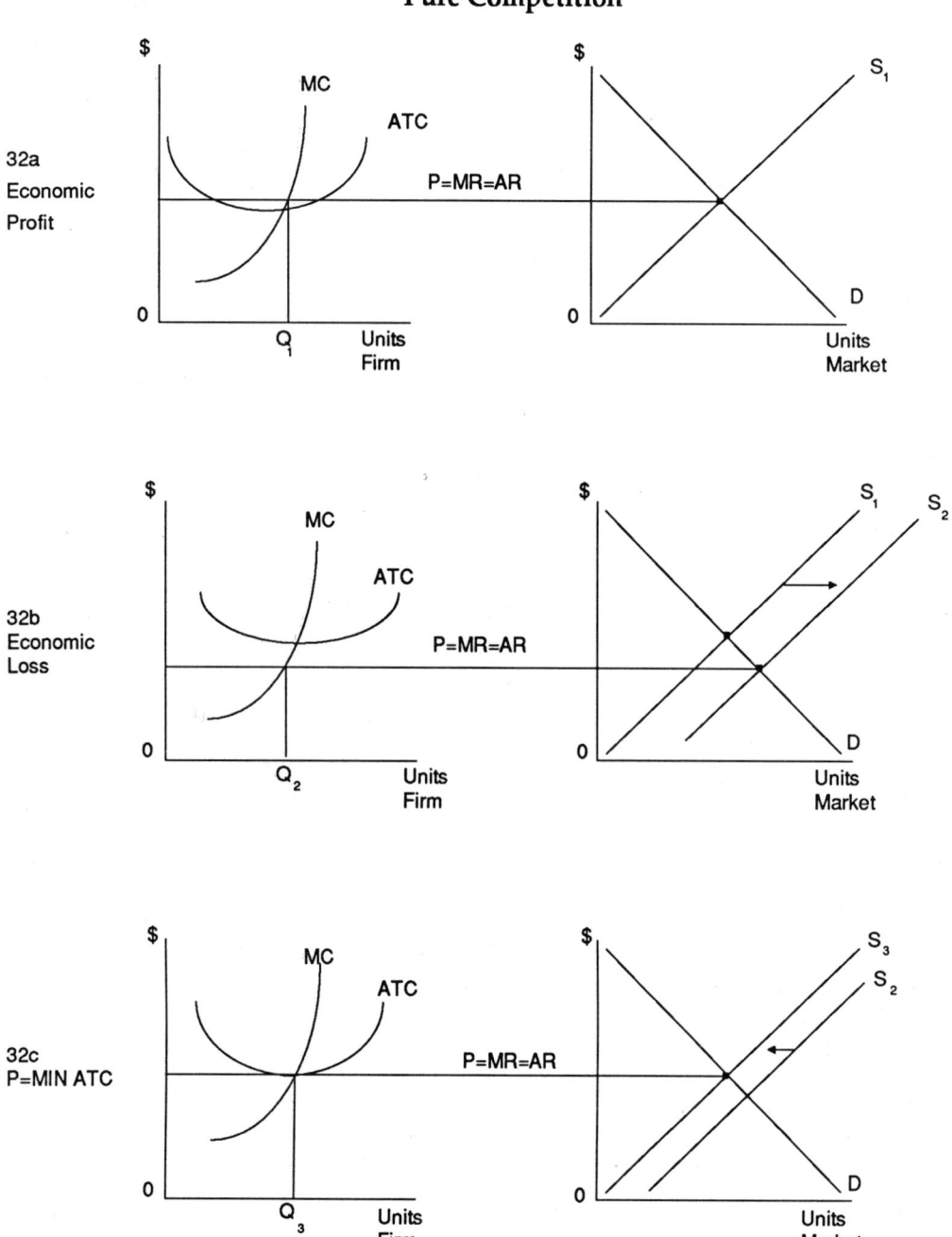

32a Economic Profit

Firm: MC, ATC curves; P=MR=AR horizontal line; quantity Q_1.
Market: Supply S_1 and Demand D.

32b Economic Loss

Firm: MC, ATC curves; P=MR=AR horizontal line; quantity Q_2.
Market: Supply shifts from S_1 to S_2; Demand D.

32c P=MIN ATC

Firm: MC, ATC curves; P=MR=AR horizontal line; quantity Q_3.
Market: Supply shifts from S_3 to S_2; Demand D.

lose heart and firms begin to "exit the market." This means less is supplied at any given price and the supply curve shifts back to the left, allowing the price to rise again.

This *entry and exit process continues until* such time as the *price equals the minimum average total cost*. It is only at this point of no economic profit and no economic loss that there is no incentive to enter or leave this industry. This final condition is demonstrated in figure 32c (price equals minimum ATC in figure 32c).

The result of a price equal to the minimum average total cost of production is desirable from a social point of view, and is often one of the arguments for deregulation when markets are thought to be competitively structured. But, the implications for the market niche of the firm are not so positive. The attainment of some economic profit has resulted in more competition, driving the economic profit from the market and eventually resulting in attrition among the competitors. With homogeneous products, the firm without a cost advantage (the representative firm) has no differential advantage during the attrition process. *Pure competition yields only a difficult and tenuous market niche for the representative firms.*

Monopoly: A Polar Extreme Case of Market Structure

Monopoly may be considered the polar opposite of pure competition. Monopoly market structure is characterized by high barriers to entry, so high as to allow one firm to remain the sole supplier of a product to a market. A monopoly situation can (but need not) stabilize with a *very high level of economic profit*. The high levels of economic profit are attractive to potential competitors, but the barriers to entry simply prevent new competitive entry into the market.

In the economist's graphic analysis of the case of monopoly, only one graph is necessary. This is because the horizontal axes need not be divided into separate segments for the representative firm and the market, as was done in the analysis of pure competition. The units the single monopoly firm supplies are the units the market receives. There is also no need for a supply curve. There is no horizontal summation of individual decisions to supply. There is only the decision of one firm to supply a certain amount, given its evaluation of demand and costs. The economist's graph of this situation is constructed by placing the demand curve on the same set of axes used by the average total cost curve and the marginal cost curve. This is accomplished in figure 33a and very nearly completes the graph of monopoly.

The graph is completed with the addition of a marginal revenue curve. Since this kind of firm enjoys the demand curve all to itself, it makes sense that the appropriate marginal revenue is the marginal revenue derived directly from the demand curve. That is, in order to sell a greater number of units the firm must lower its price according to the dictates of the demand curve. The curve which plots the resulting marginal revenue will fall between the demand curve and the vertical axis. Figure 33b demonstrates this. The addition of this marginal revenue curve to the graph results in the completed picture of monopoly, figure 33c.

In this situation MC = MR at point a. The firm is thus encouraged to produce Qm, monopoly quantity. This quantity is priced in accordance with demand at Pm monopoly price. Note the *powerful, almost impregnable market niche* that this situation produces. The monopolist is in a position to be *a price maker, not a price taker* as the representative firm was in pure competition. Economic profit per unit is designated by the distance d - b, and economic profit for the period is given by the rectangle d, b, c, Pm. This is a *large amount of economic profit relative to costs*, and there are no dynamics intrinsic to this type of market structure whereby this level of profit will be adjusted downward.

The generalization which may be derived here is that *monopoly market structure can and often does result in an extremely powerful market niche* for the firm. It would not be correct to say that monopoly market structure always results in such a niche. Despite the advantage conferred by a lack of competition, the monopolist must still be aware of the nature of the match between demand and the costs of production. Consider for example, the firm which has managed to monopolize the world market for lead lifeboats. These items are extremely expensive to produce and, aside from the gift and collector's market, there is no real demand. The monopoly graph of this money-losing monopoly situation comprises figure 34.

Market Structures between Monopoly and Competition

Economists have developed other models to describe market structures which lie between the polar extremes of monopoly and competition. Monopolistic competition and *oligopoly* are important market structures to understand.[7]

A monopolistically competitive market may be characterized by few or many sellers, and is characterized by heterogeneous or differentiated products.[8] This market structure may be seen as a first step away from pure

Chapter 3   87

**Figure 33
Monopoly**

33a
The Firm and
the Demand
Curve

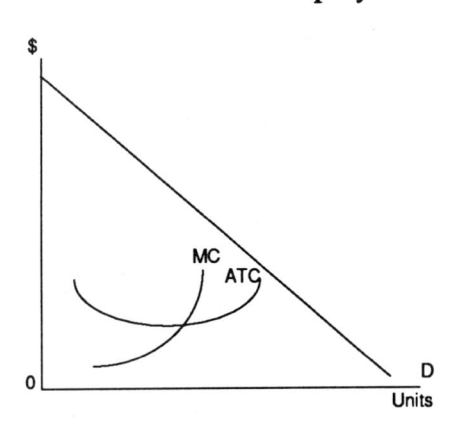

33b
Marginal Revenue
from the Demand
Curve

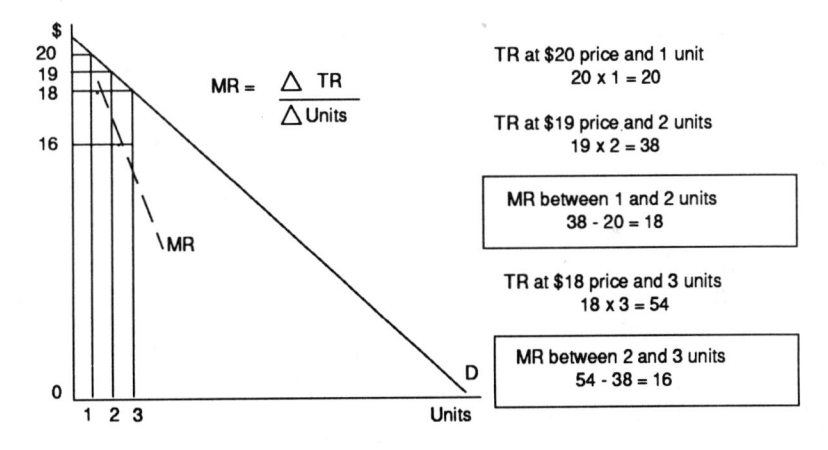

$$MR = \frac{\Delta \, TR}{\Delta \, \text{Units}}$$

TR at $20 price and 1 unit
20 x 1 = 20

TR at $19 price and 2 units
19 x 2 = 38

MR between 1 and 2 units
38 − 20 = 18

TR at $18 price and 3 units
18 x 3 = 54

MR between 2 and 3 units
54 − 38 = 16

33c
Monopoly Pricing
where MC=MR

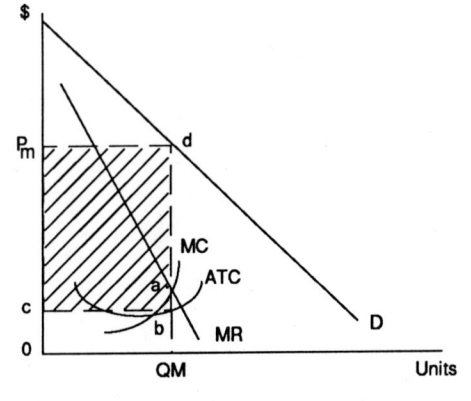

88   Part I

Figure 34
Monopoly of the World Market for Lead Lifeboats

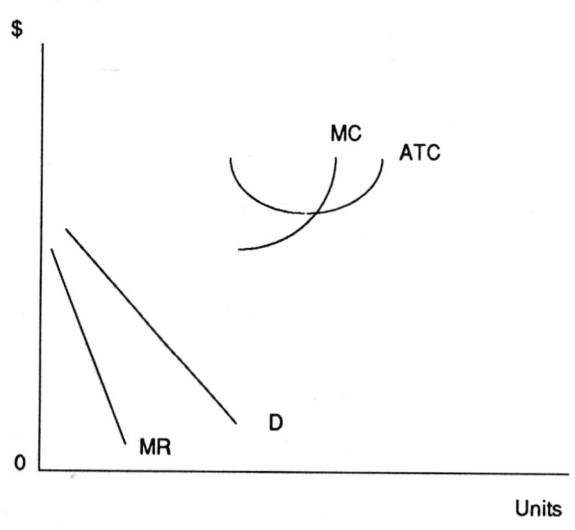

Figure 35
Price Effects of Shifting the Demand Curve

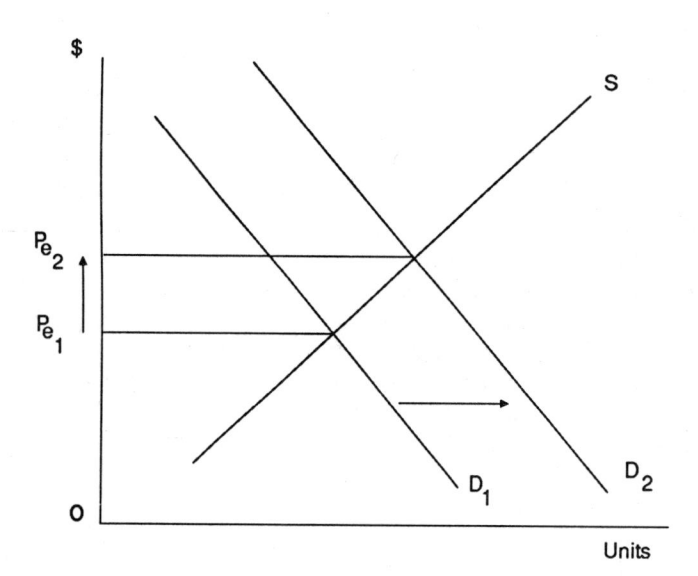

competition in the direction of monopoly. The key to the increased power of this market niche relative to that found in pure competition is *product differentiation*. This means that the *products* or services in the market are *no longer homogeneous*; each vendor will offer a product that is in some sense "different" from those offered by competitors. If this difference resulted in the consumer preferring the product, the product differentiation is termed "successful." Product differentiation does not turn the competitive price taker into a monopolistic price maker, but it does move the situation in that direction. Successful product differentiation delivers some pricing power to the firm. *First* product differentiation may *realign the demand* curve by shifting it to the right or by making it less elastic. As demonstrated in figure 35, this alone can result in an increased price. *Secondly* successful product differentiation simultaneously *reduces the degree of effective competition*. No other vendor offers the identical product as differentiated. If the buyer *prefers* the differentiated product it is then successfully differentiated and the buyer anticipates *greater marginal utility* from its purchase than from the purchase of its competitor. The buyer is therefore willing to pay somewhat more for it. The buyer will select the preferred product so long as the ratio of marginal utility to price $\frac{mu}{p}$ remains greater for the preferred or successfully differentiated product. Because the buyer is viewing both utility and price it is possible for the vendor of the preferred product to price too high and force the buyer to select a second choice.

This can be illustrated with an example. A consumer might be in the market for a European sport sedan. In considering the BMW, Volvo and Saab, this individual consumer may prefer front wheel drive. In this case, and for this individual consumer, the Saab is the successfully differentiated product, being the only offering in this group with front wheel drive. This delivers to Saab a certain small degree of monopoly power. While not the only vendor of European sport sedans, it is after all, the only vendor of the front wheel drive Saab. This delivers pricing power to Saab in the case of this individual customer and in the case of any market segment composed of individuals who view the exchange in the same way. This quasi-monopoly pricing power is limited by the degree to which the product is successfully differentiated. At some price differential the consumer will be satisfied with a second choice.

While the auto industry may be used to demonstrate product differentiation, a key to building a market niche in monopolistic competition, there were periods of history during which the US automobile industry would also serve as an example of *oligopoly*. Oligopoly is a market structure characterized by the existence of high barriers to entry and few sellers.[9] The product may or may not be differentiated.[10] This situation places vendors in a position to engage in pricing, product, promotion and place decisions with some large measure of understanding about how the other vendors might react. In the international arena, where the law substantially differs from that in the United States, a condition of few sellers is likely to result in a *cartel*. A cartel is a formal organization wherein the few sellers coordinate efforts to maximize and share their monopoly power. As a shared monopoly, a cartel will openly meet to decide upon prices and production quotas. The Organization of Petroleum Exporting Countries (OPEC) is an example of this situation and behavior.

In the United States, a long term social commitment to the encouragement of competitive markets and the discouragement of monopoly is reflected in the *anti trust laws*. These laws render cartel-like coordination behavior illegal.

Managers making decisions concerning oligopolistic markets in the United States find themselves in the difficult position of understanding the powerful market niche available to them as a shared monopoly, while understanding the legal expectation that they behave competitively. This managerial quandary may partially explain the difficulty that has been encountered in making generalizations about oligopoly behavior. For years it has been taught that oligopoly behavior resulted in a "kinked" demand curve for the product of the individual firm.[11] This kind of demand curve is illustrated in figure 36. This price and unit movement pattern for the output of the individual oligopolist assumes a set of behaviors on the part of the other oligopolists which may or may not actually be carried out. It is assumed that fellow oligopolists would immediately follow a price cut, but would not follow price rises. Some research has indicated that oligopoly firms are as likely to follow each others price rises as price cuts.[12] In this context, the oligopoly demand curve remains useful in demonstrating the sensitivity of an individual oligopolist's results to the activities of the other oligopolists.

Firms in oligopoly markets may elect to maximize and share the power of their joint monopoly market niche while staying within the letter of the anti trust laws. The term applied to simultaneous or nearly simultaneous price adjustments and the tacit avoidance of overproduction is *conscious parallelism*.[13] Individual instances of consciously parallel behavior may or may not be legal and may place the manager on shaky ethical grounds.

As may occur within the formally organized cartel, discipline or coordination within the oligopoly occasionally fails.[14] The catalyst for such a failure is often a drop in demand for the oligopoly's product. When this occurs, individual oligopolists may begin to compete for *market share* or the percentage of the total market represented by the sales of the individual firm. The motive for this competition is to try to maintain enough unit movement (and thus revenue) to cover fixed costs after covering variable or incremental costs. In these situations oligopolistic firms may engage in aggressive competition. Often, one firm's price cuts are immediately neutralized by another firm's

Figure 36
The Oligopoly Kinked Demand Curve
(Facing the individual firm)

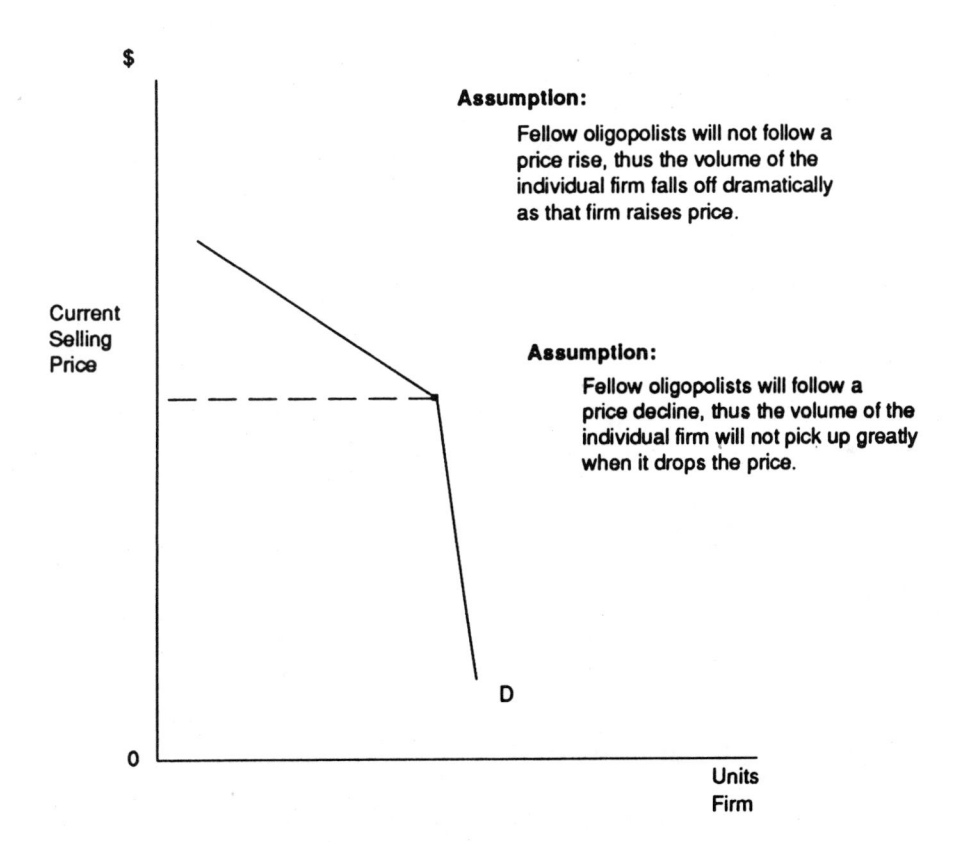

Assumption:
Fellow oligopolists will not follow a price rise, thus the volume of the individual firm falls off dramatically as that firm raises price.

Assumption:
Fellow oligopolists will follow a price decline, thus the volume of the individual firm will not pick up greatly when it drops the price.

price cuts, with the result that no one gains market share and everyone loses revenue.[15]

The oligopoly group may attempt to avoid this scenario by trying to hold back production in the early stages of the drop in demand. But this requires that participants sustain immediate revenue reductions and is hard to enforce.[16]

Oligopolies may be classified as *undifferentiated* if they are vending relatively undifferentiated products such as crude oil, or *differentiated* if they are vending differentiated products such as automobiles. A differentiated oligopoly firm adds the pricing power of product differentiation to the pricing power of an oligopoly participant when creating its market niche.

Market Structure and Pricing Power

Pricing power is the ability to influence the terms of an exchange. In pure competition, the representative firm has no pricing power, but must take whatever price is dictated by the market. In monopoly the firm has a great deal of pricing power. Price in monopoly is not conditioned by competition at all but is constrained by the nature of demand and the firm's costs. Therefore if demand is equivalent, pricing power accrues as competition diminishes. The reduction of competition may be the result of straightforward economic factors. There may be high barriers to entry, economic or technical, there may be a lack of required information, or there may be legal constraints upon competitive entry. Importantly for marketing people, *the reduction of competition as well as the stimulation of demand may be accomplished psychologically*. If a product is differentiated successfully, so that it is preferred by the buyer in question, there is an effective reduction of competition in the mind of that buyer. This psychological effect has measurable economic results in terms of pricing power. The effects of market structure upon pricing power are summarized in figure 37.

Regulation and Market Niche

Government intervention in markets has become so common that an understanding of government intent and government results must become a part of the basic discussion of the firm's market niche. Government regulation creates, destroys, and alters market opportunities. Thus, "working government regulation" to the firms advantage has become an integral part of the establishment and defense of the market niche for many firms. The permutations of such political-market strategies are as numerous as the government regulations themselves. Much government regulation is conditioned by the

Figure 37
Market Structure and Pricing Power

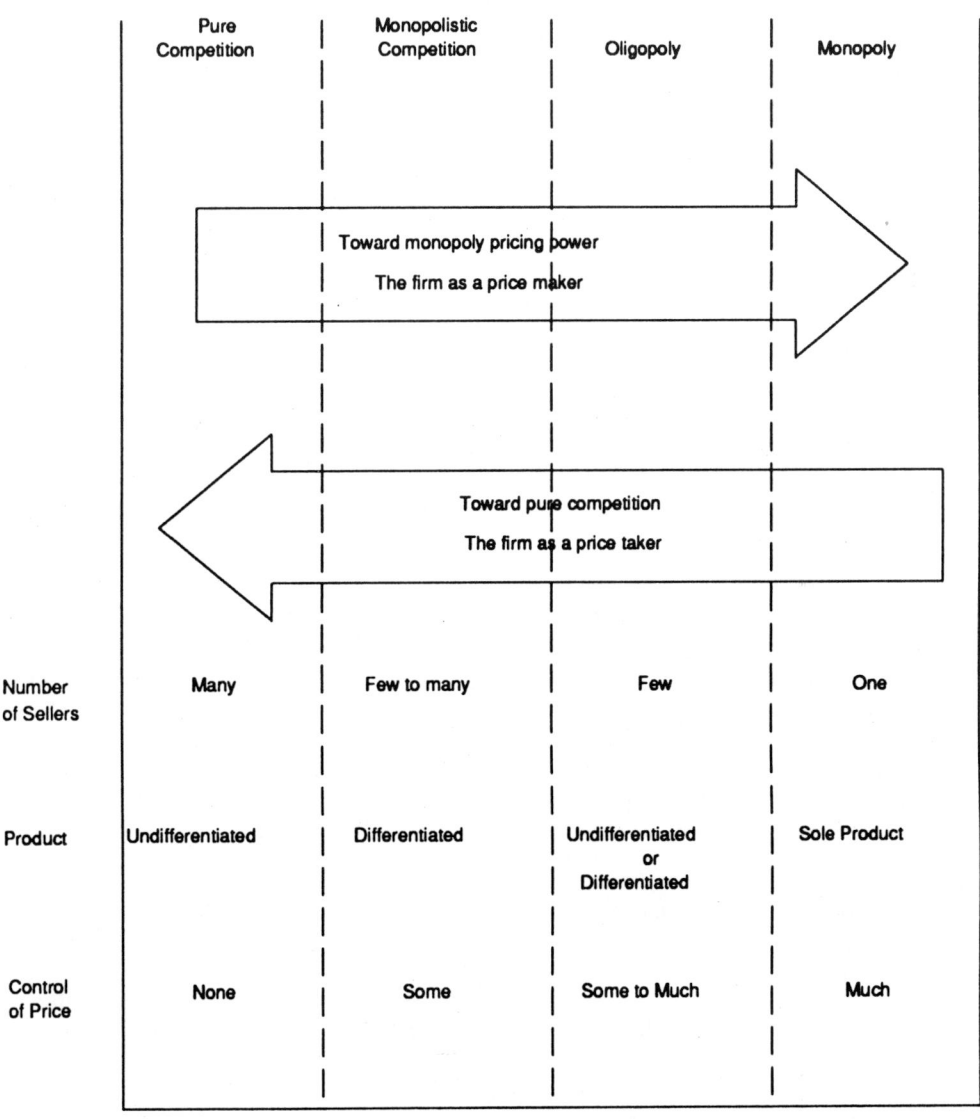

	Pure Competition	Monopolistic Competition	Oligopoly	Monopoly
		Toward monopoly pricing power — The firm as a price maker →		
	← Toward pure competition — The firm as a price taker			
Number of Sellers	Many	Few to many	Few	One
Product	Undifferentiated	Differentiated	Undifferentiated or Differentiated	Sole Product
Control of Price	None	Some	Some to Much	Much

lawmakers assumptions about market structure. This section will introduce common government intent and result using a set of examples organized according to market structure.

Examples in Competitive Markets

In market structures resembling competition, consumer groups may be successful in setting *price controls* or *ceiling prices*. Should such a control be equal to or greater than equilibrium price, it would not be an effective control and would pose little difficulty for the firm. Should such a control comprise a real price constraint, as illustrated by price Pc in figure 38a, the result may be a shortage. The shortage is the difference between the quantity demanded and the quantity supplied in figure 38a.[16] Other results are also possible. The price regulation may be ignored, resulting in an *illegal or "black" market*. The actual exchange price might then vary somewhat from Pe. Demand might be affected by the illegal nature of the exchange. Some people might prefer illegal exchange, others would avoid it. The supply curve would likewise be altered. Some people would refuse to supply, others might incur additional expenses in the supply effort. Another result of price controls might be the *altering of the product*, allowing profitable market exchange at the control price. Firms anticipating this kind of regulation may elect to publish *high list prices* and discount to the level of Pe to gain sales. This strategy provides a higher base from which to calculate should the government consider list prices when setting Pc.

In situations approximating competition, it is also possible that the beleaguered vendors, having suffered in the vice which exists between competitive market price and their minimum average costs, will be able to influence legislators to create *price supports*. These are prices at which the government buys surplus production in order to prevent further price decline.[17] This situation is depicted in figure 38b, where the support price is denoted by Ps. Agricultural markets provide useful examples of regulation in competitive markets.

Examples in Monopoly Markets

In some situations the government will actively control entry into a market. There are various stated reasons for this, to include the idea that, given the size of the market and the nature of production technology, only one or a few companies will be able to achieve substantial economies of scale.[18] In other situations, a monopoly might exist without a government policy to deter entry. In either situation the government will often elect to control the price.

Figure 38
Regulation of Competitive Markets

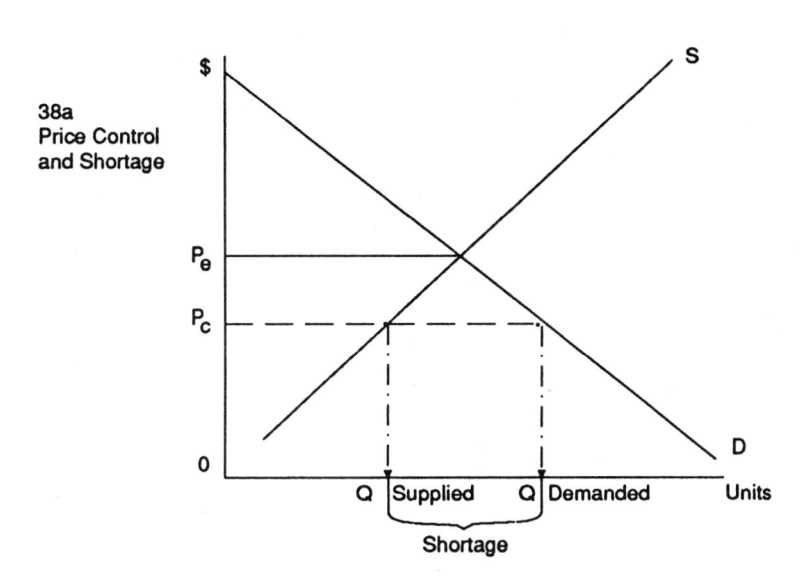

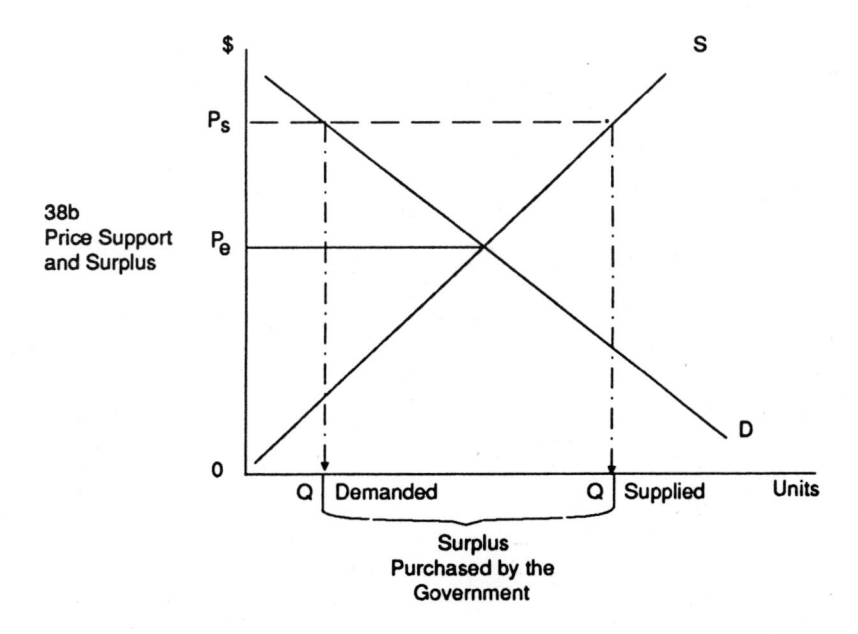

38a
Price Control and Shortage

38b
Price Support and Surplus

The intent is to remove the burden of excess monopoly profit from the consumer.[20] The economic logic of price control in monopoly is set forth in figure 39.

In this situation the regulatory body attempts to squeeze more quantity from the monopoly for a lower price. Where the free monopoly would provide Qm for price Pm, it is theoretically possible to derive Qc for Price Pc. This is because the control price, which is lower than the free monopoly price, becomes the new effective marginal revenue. Since each additional unit is sold at the control price, the change in total revenue with the change in units sold (MR) is equal to the control price. In figure 39, the new MC = MR point is to the right of the old MC = MR point. This indicates that under the new constraint of vending at the control price, the firm will maximize profits by selling most quantity. Armed with this kind of logic, regulators justify price control in monopoly.[21] The economic results will differ depending on the exact level of the control. The price control may be set below minimum ATC or below minimum average variable cost, forcing long run failure or immediate shut down of the business. In figure 39 this has not happened, but profit has been reduced by the regulation. Compare area Pm - a - Qm - O with area Pc - MC = MR - Qc - O.

In this context, the firm may elect one or more of several responses to expand and defend its market niche. It may successfully lobby for a deregulation. It may successfully argue before the regulators that its current rate of profit is insufficient to attract capital, or that the accepted methods of accounting for profit should be changed in its favor.[22] The firm may also succeed in expensing a larger number of items within the accounting system currently accepted by the regulators. In these later two strategies, the real strength of the market niche will not be evidenced by the stated profit alone, but by the stated profit and generous expense policies. Public utilities such as power companies provide useful examples of regulated monopolies.

Examples in Oligopoly Markets

In regulated oligopoly situations, the original intent of the regulation may have been to promote the industry (to allow a new industry to be profitable) or to insure safe operation of the industry.[23] In these cases the government will often regulate the number of operators in the industry in order to prevent "cutthroat" competition and to insure adequate profit for growth and safe operation.[24] Rate levels are often set with other social goals in mind as well. Small businesses may get favorable rates.[25] Devices for the enforcement of oligopoly discipline might also be tolerated in these situations. For example, firms may be allowed to discuss rates among themselves, a practice which is

Chapter 3   97

**Figure 39
Price Control In Monopoly**

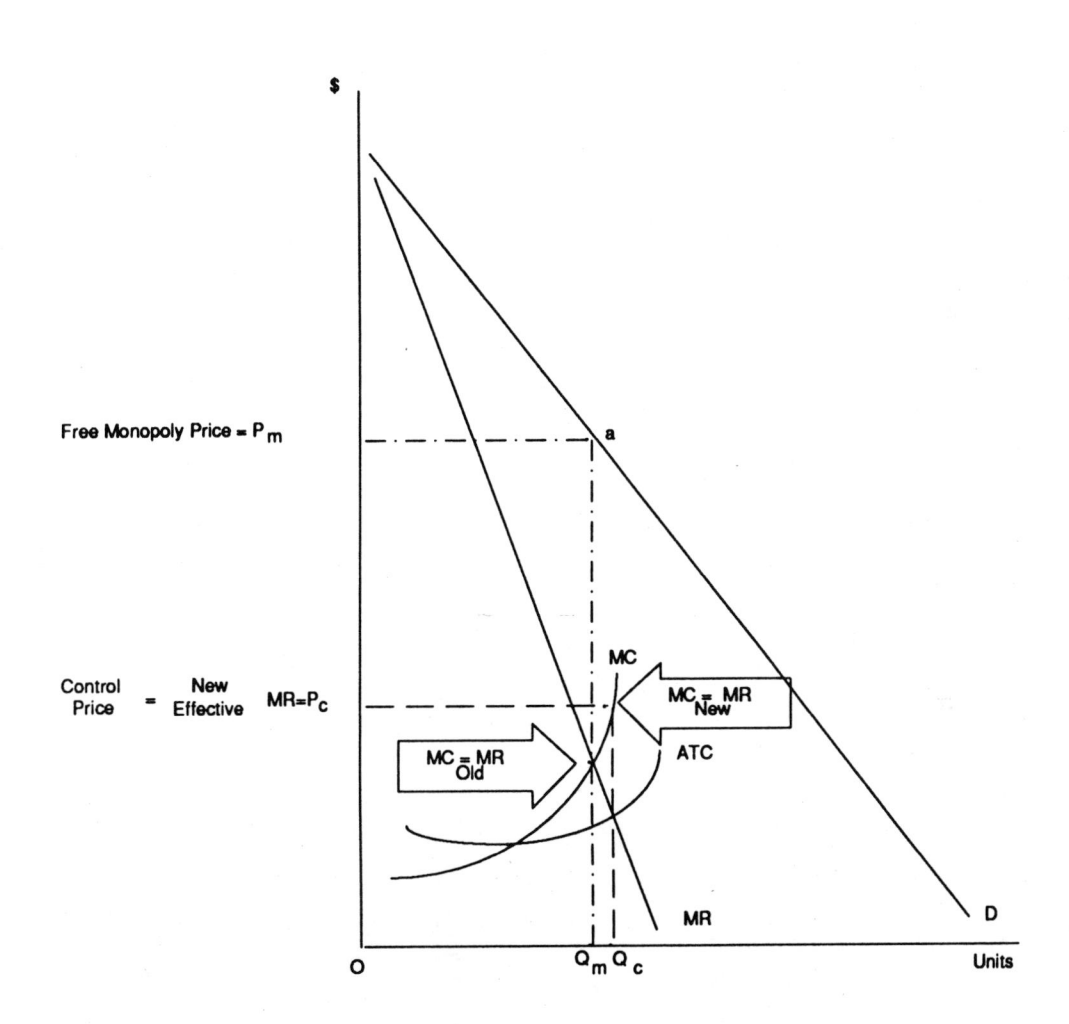

ordinarily in violation of the antitrust acts.[26] In a situation such as this, when the government is actually encouraging oligopoly behavior, firms will often learn to live happily within the regulatory framework. Firms finding themselves protected inside of these markets might lobby for continued regulation, while firms desiring to enter these markets might lobby for *deregulation* in the form of reduced barriers to entry.[27] When such a market is deregulated, it reflects a government judgement that the industry no longer needs protective support, and might benefit from the efficiency and cost discipline of a more competitive market.[28] Transportation industries, particularly air and motor carrier, provide useful examples of this kind of oligopoly regulation and deregulation.

Examples in Monopolistically Competitive Markets

Government regulators appear to respond with regulation according to the ways a market niche is built and defended in the different kinds of market structures. Competitive farmers are aided with price supports, monopoly utilities are disciplined with price controls, and oligopolistic industries are either aided with entry barriers or disciplined with their removal. Such price and entry based regulatory mechanisms are rarely seen in monopolistically competitive industries. Product differentiation is a major key to profitability in these industries and it is the modes of product differentiation that become the focus of government attention. This attention takes the form of the regulation of false and misleading advertising, as well as the prohibitition of unfair and deceptive practices.[29] Industries involved in the marketing of differentiated products and thus particularly subject to this type of regulation would include the mass marketers of consumer goods such as soaps, toothpastes, and cosmetics.

Heterogeneity, Psychology and Ecological Niche

The careful characterization of market niche as it is a function of market structure has been a useful introduction. The beginning student or analyst should now have developed the instincts to ask about costs, information, demand, competition, barriers to entry, and successful product differentiation when trying to characterize a market niche. An understanding of market structure is necessary to market analysis.

But the market structure approach is somewhat mechanical and may have its limits in describing real market situations. Consider, for example, the difficulty of classifying a given situation at the margin between catagories of market structure. Is a large consumer goods marketer, with a one billion dollar per year advertising budget, a monopolistic competitor in the "soap industry"? Or, is the firm a differentiated oligopolist in the "mass media soap marketing industry," an industry which may effectively count large advertising budgets among its barriers to entry? Consider also the problem of finding homogeneous situations to conform to pure competitive assumptions. Are two competitive milk farmers producing a homogenous product if one has a better reputation for equipment cleanliness? Consider logistics; do two competitive farmers producing the same product conform to pure competitive assumptions if one is further away from the market? Consider finally, individual psychology. Even if two market offerings were identical in some absolute sense, would two different people be likely to perceive or evaluate them in identical fashion?

All of these perspectives argue for the *essential heterogeneity of markets*. Each market situation is likely to be somewhat different from others, often rendering clean classification according to market structure difficult. Product differentiation is integral to the establishment and defense of many market niches. Beyond these differences owed to intentional marketing strategy, different conditions of supply, different locations of consumer and vendors, and the essential individuality of human psychology would encourage very different exchange patterns.

An *ecological model* is useful in dealing with this heterogeneity.[30] Imagine the complex natural ecology. In this ecology the various plants and animals may survive and grow if they are able to garner as many or more resources than they need to consume. Garnering more than is necessary for minimum individual survival allows for reproduction, support of families and accumulation for use in leaner times.

Consider the functions that each individual or species provides for the other, sometimes with intention, sometimes without. Consider the complex interactions of competition and cooperation. Consider both the short term and long term dynamics of such an ecology. Individuals are brought forth and die. Whole species may die or proliferate. So it is with individuals, organizations and types of organizations as they interact. They garner and consume resources, surviving, growing, dying. It is due to the complex nature of humans, their institutions and exchanges and the seeming propriety of an ecological model that the term *ecological niche* may be substituted for the term market niche.

The profitability of the firm may be seen in this ecological context. The firm seeks to garner the resources it needs to survive. If more resources can be obtained the firm has a basis for growth. *Profit* is a fair but not always reliable *measure* of this *balance of resources*. Profit is the excess of production over consumption when both are valued by markets. It is not always reliable as a measure of the resources required for survival and growth because a firm may voluntarily elect to reduce its stated profit. The regulated monopoly, seeking permission to raise its allowed rate, a firm reacting to anomalies in the tax laws, a firm which does not wish to enhance investor expectations, or the organization seeking to maintain a tax-free non-profit status would all exemplify voluntary reduction of profit. The careful observer of the individual organization should be able to discern this behavior and adjust estimates of the organization's actual profit potential.

Dynamics

As the birth and death of individual plants and animals provide mechanisms for change in the natural ecology, so such mechanisms are required in the ecology of human exchange. The initiating mechanism is *innovation*. An innovation is something newly invented, a new method, custom, device or change in the way of doing things.[31] A new product, communication or method of distribution would be an important marketing innovation. Real and substantial changes in pricing behavior, might constitute innovations. But, a simple change in the level of price is not usually seen as an innovation. Innovation important to human exchange would include changes in the way of doing things. This would include such innovations as new and more automated modes of manufacture which result in reductions in the cost of the product. While the marketing mix of the firm may not change as the result of such innovation, the market niche of the firm may be greatly enhanced by the reduction of the average total cost curve.

After a period of investment, successful innovation in the marketing mix brings with it a market niche similar to that of monopoly.[32] For the period of time that it takes competition to follow or improve upon the innovation (to neutralize the innovation) the innovating firm enjoys demand without direct competition. As competition eventually enters and more firms begin to sell the innovation, total sales of the innovation will climb. With the entry of more firms, the market structure becomes more nearly competitive and profitability declines. Eventually the innovation, no longer a new idea, may be supplanted by a more recent innovation. Its function may be provided in some other way. When this occurs, the total sales of all suppliers of the item will decline. Sales and profits may eventually disappear altogether.

Thus the first innovation brings market life or a viable market niche for its innovator, while the second innovation may mean market death for the first. In this way railways took traffic from horse drawn wagons and canal barges, and trucks and aircraft took traffic from the railways. This cycle, describing the life and death of an innovation, has been termed the *product life* cycle.[33] Because difficulties can ensue in determining whether a "product" is new enough to have a life cycle of its own, this book will use the term *innovation life cycle*. A successful innovation will begin a new life cycle. This life cycle is pictured in figure 40.

Innovation, especially if a firm is in a position to continually foster a series of innovations, can be excellent strategy for the firm. A series of successful innovations will provide the firm with a series of the profitable growth periods which occur prior to competitive entry. The process of innovation also performs an important social function. Innovation is the mechanism whereby the society rids itself of obsolete or ineffective modes of doing things. As the body cannot survive and grow without the continuing replacement of dying cells, so a society cannot survive and grow with an infrastructure of obsolete and stagnant institutions. Successful innovation often supercedes and destroys previous forms. This process has been termed *creative destruction* and is an important social result of the marketing process.[34]

Crossing National Boundaries

Supply behavior is like demand behavior in the sense that *few* if any of the *generalizations* made in this chapter *will change* when operating across national boundaries. Supply will be forthcoming when there is economic incentive for it and the incentives will vary according to market structure and the individual firms place in the ecology of exchange.

Also paralleling demand behavior, many of the *specifics* of supply behavior *will change* when the firm is involved in international markets. People may not be comfortable working for profit. Some managers may prefer working to satisfy the requirements of debt to the idea of working for profit.[35] People may not understand the social benefits of competition. Only West Germany shares a similar commitment to anti-trust.[36] This would result in more monopoly and oligopoly market structures in other nations. Improving international trade infrastructures such as reduced tariffs and more efficient financial and distribution mechanisms may mitigate these oligopoly situations in individual nations. International markets for any given product may be quite competitive, despite the fact that any given competitor might be the only firm producing the product in that competitors home nation.

The concept of the product life cycle has been adapted to international markets. It is adjusted to account for the differing international locations of production which are reasonable to expect as the product goes through its life cycle. The new innovation might be produced in the nation that inspired or needed the innovation. Production then moves to similar markets. Finally as

102   *Part I*

Figure 40
The Product Life Cycle
or
Innovation Life Cycle

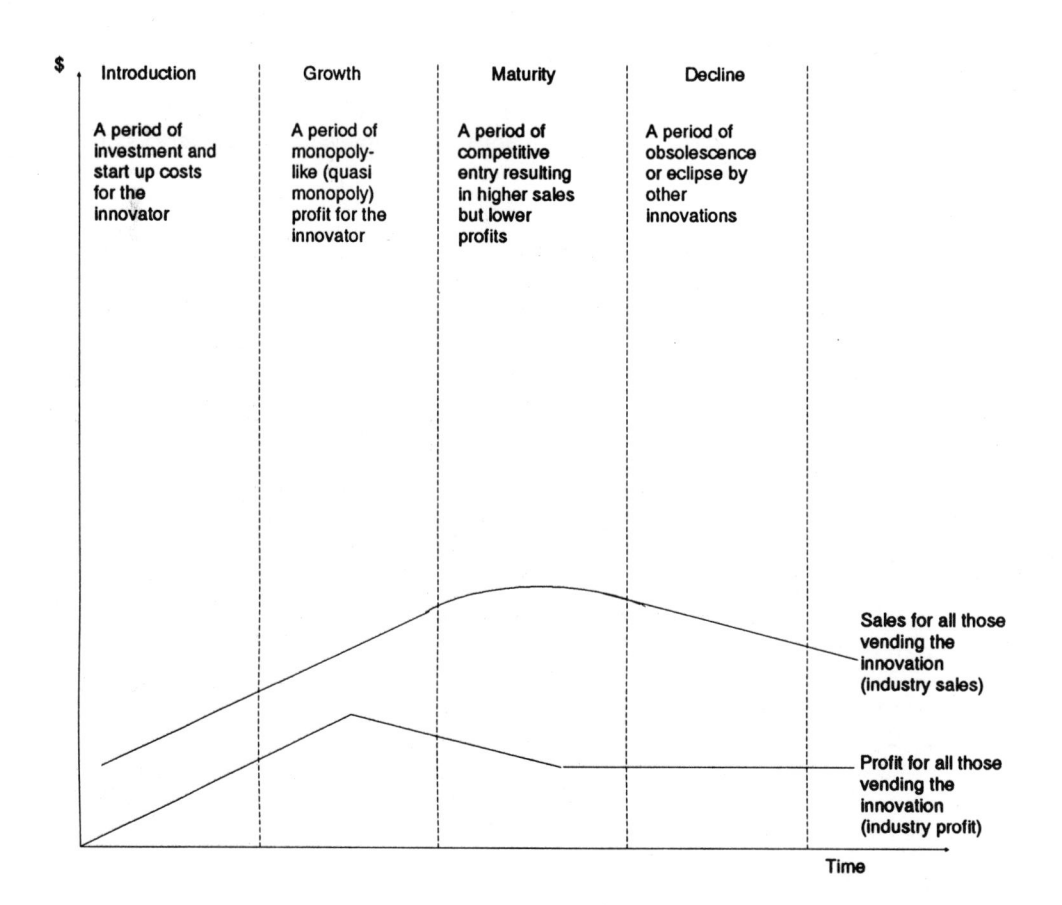

$	Introduction	Growth	Maturity	Decline
	A period of investment and start up costs for the innovator	A period of monopoly-like (quasi monopoly) profit for the innovator	A period of competitive entry resulting in higher sales but lower profits	A period of obsolescence or eclipse by other innovations

Sales for all those vending the innovation (industry sales)

Profit for all those vending the innovation (industry profit)

Time

the market becomes more competitive and the technology more understood, production moves to points of the lowest cost.

Chapter Summary

The market niche is a position in the ecology of human exchange where the firm may survive and grow. It is roughly measured by profit, which results when society values the goods and services that the organization provides more highly than the goods and services that the organization consumes. The society values both the production and the consumption through the mechanism of markets. The nature of the market niche and thus the incentives for supply behavior differ substantially according to the structure of the market considered. Market structure is traditionally analyzed through examination of specific structures such as monopoly, competition, oligopoly and monopolistic competition. The nature of the market niche may be further understood by examining how psychology can create some of the effects of market structure, and by understanding how an ecological model adjusts the ideas of market structure to compensate for the complexity and heterogeneity of markets.

---

[1] Market niche is a popular term understood by practitioners. This chapter develops Alderson's concept of ecological niche, but begins with straightforward microeconomics. See Wroe Alderson, *Marketing Behavior and Executive Action* (Homewood, Ill.: Richard D. Irwin, 1957), pp. 55, 270, 356. Like Alderson but unlike some recent literature, the meaning of the term niche as used here does not necessarily require a low-volume market position.

[2] In the short run (wen the capital input is held constant) the U shape of the cost curve is owed to the particular plant and equipment in use. In the long run (when new plant and equipment may be purchased) the U shape is owed to economies and diseconomies of scale in the industry.

[3] Paul A. Samuelson and William D. Nordhaus, *Economics*, 12th ed. (New York: McGraw-Hill, 1985), p. 25.

[4] See F. M. Sherer, *Industrial Market Structure and Economic Performance*, 2nd ed. (Chicago: Rand McNally College Publishing, 1980).

[5] See C. E. Furguson and J. P. Gould, *Microeconimic Theory*, 4th ed. (Homewood, Ill.: Richard D. Irwin, 1975), pp. 223-225.

[6] Ibid.

[7] Ibid., pp. 312-361.

[8] Ibid., pp. 313-314.

[9] Ibid., pp. 329-331. See also Scherer, p. 11.

[10] Scherer notes that industries characterized by a few large sellers include mining, finance, and retailing. Different degrees of differentiation are available to these industries. See Scherer, p. 151.

[11] See, for example, E. Jerome McCarthy and William D. Perreault, Jr., *Basic Marketing*, 9th ed. (Homewood, Ill.: Richard D. Irwin, 1987), p. 104.

[12] See George J. Stiger, "The Kinky Oligopoly Demand Curve and Rigid Prices," *Journal of Political Economy* 55 (October 1947), pp. 442-44.

[13] See Louis W. Stern and Thomas L. Eovaldi, *Legal Aspects of Marketing Strategy, Antitrust and Consumer Protection Issues* (Englewood Cliffs, N.J.: Prentice-Hall, 1984), pp. 250-255.

[14] This discussion is based on personal observation of the the aluminum industry.

[15] Ibid.

[16] For a more complete treatment see Furguson, pp. 239, 240, 302, 303.

[17] Ibid., pp. 306, 307.

[18] Scherer, p. 482.

[19] Monopoly pricing is seen as inefficient, creating what is termed a "dead-weight welfare loss." See Scherer, pp. 18, 460, 464.

[20] Scherer, pp. 476-480.

[21] As an example of this kind of discussion, see "Comparable Earnings Approach As a Useful Tool in Utility Regulation," *The Public Utilities Fortnightly* 87, No. 5 (March 4, 1971). See also, Hary M. Trebing and Howard R. Hayden, *Rate of Return under Regulation: New Directions and Perspectives* (East Lansing: MSU Public Utilities Studies, Graduate School of Business, Michigan State University, 1969).

[22] For a summary of arguments for and against regulation in a particular industry see James C. Johnson, *Trucking Mergers, a Regulatory Viewpoint* (Lexington, Mass.: Lexington Books, Inc., 1973), pp. 33-36.

[23] See James C. Nelson, "The Effects of Entry Control in Surface Transport," in *Transportation Economics, A Conference of the Universities*, ed. National Bureau Committee for Economic Research (New York: Columbia University Press, 1965), p. 383.

[24] See Merton J. Peck, "Competitive Policy for Transportation?" in *Perspectives in Anti-Trust Policy*, ed. Almanine Phillips (Princeton, N.J.: Princeton University Press, 1965), p. 254.

[25] See for example the discussion of the Reed Budwinkle Act of 1948 in Johnson, pp. 49-50.

[26] See for example Nelson's discussion of the problems of both shippers and carriers in the regulated environment. Specifically note carrier complaints concerning the nature of commission proceedings and limited grants of authority. Nelson, p. 383.

[27] See for example the argument made by Mark Green and Ralph Nader, "Economic Regulation vs. Competition: Uncle Sam the Monopoly Man," *The Yale Law Journal* 82 (April 1973), pp. 871-879.

[28] See Stern, pp. 370-380.

[29] The concepts of the ecological model and the ecological niche are owed to Wroe Alderson. See Alderson, pp. 55, 270, 356.

[30] Ibid.

[31] Webster's definition of innovation is used here.

[32] See McCarthy, pp. 251-263.

[33] Joseph A. Schumpeter, *Capitalism, Socialism and Democracy* (New York: Harper and Row, 1950), pp. 81-86.

[34] Stefan H. Robock, Kenneth Simmonds, and Jack Zwick, *International Business and Multinational Enterprises* (Homewood, Ill.: Richard D. Irwin, 1977), p. 502.

[35] Philip R. Cateora and John M. Hess, *International Marketing*, 4th ed. (Homewood, Ill.: Richard D. Irwin, 1979), p. 206.

[36] Raymond Vernon, "International Investment and International Trade in the Product Cycle," *Quarterly Journal of Economics*, May 1966, pp. 190-207.

Questions for Study, Discussion and Examination

1. Could you define, or explain to a friend who has not studied marketing, each of the following terms? Can you give examples of each?
    a. Market match
    b. Voluntary exchange
    c. Market niche
    d. Social reward structure for suppliers
    e. "U" shaped average total cost curve
    f. Marginal costs
    g. Marginal revenue
    h. Maximum profit or minimum loss point
    i. Market structure
    j. Average total cost
    k. Average variable cost
    l. Economic profit
    m. Supply Curve
    n. The decision to supply
    o. Elasticity of supply
    p. Perfect inelastic supply
    q. Market
    r. Equilibrium point
    s. Price system
    t. Consumer surplus
    u. Pure competition
    v. Monopoly
    w. Shift of the supply curve
    x. Monopolistic competition
    y. Oligopoly
    z. Product differentiation
    aa. Cartel
    ab. Antitrust laws
    ac. Conscious parallelism
    ad. Kinked demand curve
    ae. Market share
    af. Undifferentiated oligopoly
    ag. Differentiated oligopoly
    ah. Pricing power
    ai. Price control

aj. Shortage
ak. Black market
al. Price support
am. Promoting an industry with regulation
an. Deregulation
ao. Ecological model
ap. Ecological niche
aq. Balance of resources
ar. Innovation
as. Product/innovation life cycle
at. Creative destruction

2. Is the study of supply behavior as important to the understanding of markets as the study of buyer behavior or demand behavior? Why or why not?

3. Relate the marketing mix to supply behavior. Is it supply behavior?

4. As a consumer adjusts behavior to improve satisfaction, what is it that a supplier strives to improve when adjusting supply behavior?

5. How is a market niche established?

6. How is a supplier rewarded or punished by the mechanism of markets?

7. In general, what specific kinds of behavior does the market reward? What specific kinds of behavior does it punish or fail to reward?

8. Explain how the economist pictures the producing firm. Draw a picture of the ATC and the MC curves. Why are they shaped the way they are?

9. What is the AVC curve in the economist's picture of the producing firm? Why does it lie below ATC?

10. How does an accountant's concept of cost differ from an economist's concept of cost? How is the economist's concept useful in explaining competitive entry and exit?

11. What is a risk adjusted return to capital? Give an example of an industry in which you would expect the risk adjusted return to capital to be high. In what sense is this amount of profit a cost?

12. What is an economic definition of capital? A social definition? What other definitions of capital are you aware of?

13. How is capital created? How is it allocated?

14. Karl Marx suggested that capital was generated by underpaying workers. Is this possible? Is it always true?
15. Why is maximum profit or minimum loss expected to occur where MC = MR?
16. If firms did not intentionally maximize profit could there be a market mechanism which would deliver a greater chance of survival to those who did? Why or why not? Is there a question of short run versus long run profit and survival involved? Is there a way to deal with this?
17. Why is the understanding of market structure important to the analysis of markets? How is a market characterized by its market structure?
18. What is meant by a polar extreme case of market structure? Which types of market structure are considered to be polar extreme cases? Why is it useful to understand these?
19. What is a supply curve? Characterize the individual competitor's decision to supply. How does this decision relate to the supply curve? In what kind of market structure will supply be characterized by a supply curve? Why?
20. Characterize the situation of a firm when p > ATC, when p = MIN ATC, when p < min ATC but p > AVC, when p < AVC. Use as realistic a set of examples as you can. Each of these situations encourages what kind of supply behavior?
21. Give two basic reasons why supply to the marketplace might be expected to be greater when the price is higher. How is each of these reasons reflected in the shape or the behavior of the supply curve? What market structure assumption underlies this?
22. To what extent do you believe that business decisions about what to supply and whether to supply approximates the economist's model? Why might a decision deviate from the economist's expectations? What does this say about the supply curve?
23. Characterize a situation of perfect inelasticity of supply.
24. What is a market? Why are both supply and demand curves used to characterize a competitive market while both are not used to characterize a monopolistic market? Can you characterize a competitive market with a picture?
25. What is the Equilibrium point? Equilibrium price? Equilibrium quantity? What happens when the price in the competitive market is

higher than equilibrium price or lower than equilibrium price? Can you characterize this with a picture?

26. What are the social implications of a market adjusting itself toward equilibrium?

27. What is the price system? How does it play a role in the market matching process? What kinds of signals does it use to control supply or demand?

28. Marxist societies such as the People's Republic of China and the Soviet Union are experimenting with greater use of markets as an allocation device for society's resources. Why do you suppose they might be attracted to such a mechanism?

29. In what sense is the market price and market quantity a social compromise? How does the market arrive at this compromise? What justice or injustice do you see in this? What is consumer surplus?

30. Characterize pure competition, use words, examples and pictures. What kind of a market niche does it result in for the representative firm? How much pricing power does the representative firm have? If you were the manager of such a firm what ways would you see to improve your situation?

31. Characterize monopoly, use words, examples, and pictures. What kind of a market niche does it result in for the monopolist? Can a monopolist lose money?

32. Characterize monopolistic competition. How is it like monopoly. How is it like pure competition? In what two ways might product differentiation work to improve the market niche of the firm?

33. Will the preferred product always be the one purchased? Why or why not? Are there any systematic ground rules to aid in the understanding of when the preferred product might be selected and when it might not be selected? If so, can you explain them?

34. What is an oligopoly? What is a cartel? What differentiates them? Why might an oligopoly sometimes behave like a shared monopoly and sometimes like competition?

35. What is a kinked demand curve? Is it a curve describing the demand in the marketplace the way an ordinary demand curve does? What assumptions about the other oligopolists' behavior are implicit in its shape? What other assumptions might reasonably be made? What would the shape of the curve be then? What does this demonstrate about the sensitivity of one oligopolist's results to the behavior of the other oligopolists.

36. What is pricing power? What generalizations can be made about pricing power as a function of market structure?
37. Can some of the economic results of a change in market structure be accomplished psychologically? Explain.
38. What are some of the possible results of price regulation in competitive markets? What strategies does this suggest for the enhancement of the market niche for firms involved in these kinds of markets?
39. What are some of the possible results of price regulation in monopoly markets? What strategies does this suggest for the enhancement of the market niche for firms involved in these kinds of markets?
40. What kinds of government regulation might be expected in oligopoly markets, in monopolistically competitive markets? In the context of this, what might the firm do to enhance its market niche?
41. What is an ecological model? How does it enhance our understanding of exchange behaviors? Is it compatible with the economists' ideas of market structure? Why or why not?
42. What is the mechanism for change in the ecology of human exchange? Can you relate this mechanism to the idea of the product life cycle?
43. What changes in market structure might be expected when crossing national boundaries. How might this affect the market niche(s) of the international firm?
44. How has the idea of the product life cycle been altered to describe the life cycle of an innovation in international markets?

CHAPTER 4

QUANTIFYING THE MARKET NICHE: FINANCIAL MEASUREMENT

In the foregoing chapters, the concept of market niche was developed and the ability of the organization to survive and grow was seen to be dependent upon many factors. Profitced as a practical but imperfect measure of the firm's ability to survive and grow; its ability to garner more resources than it needs to consume. Organizations might elect to reduce their stated profitability for several reasons. But astute observers, especially internal observers such as managers, should be able to know when an organization is in a position to realize a higher stated profitability in its current market niche. Despite problems, profitability remains a practical way to measure and evaluate the market niche of an organization.

The market niche of the organization is often extremely sensitive to mismanagement. Most new firms fail, and successful large firms tend to experience an average profit of only about 5% of revenue.[1] Since small miscalculations can destroy a market niche, marketing managers must have a solid understanding of the many financial dimensions of the market niche which they are in a position to control. This section introduces perspectives concerning marketing controllable profit from the disciplines of accounting and finance. This section introduces perspectives from the disciplines of marketing and finance which allow for a better understanding of those components of profit which are affected by marketing decisions.

Breakeven

Breakeven analysis is a very limited technique which is nonetheless a useful stepping stone in the discussion of profit.[2] Its limitations are derived from its nature as a single product analysis. Its strength is derived from its initial separation of fixed costs from variable costs. Separation of costs into those costs which are incremental to the product (variable costs in breakeven analysis) and those which are not incremental to the product (fixed costs in breakeven analysis) will be very important for other, more sophisticated forms of profit evaluation. A *cost incremental to a product* is defined as a cost which appears when the product is added to a firm's group of offerings and disappears when the product is dropped from a firm's group of offerings. Variable costs of production are straightforward examples of *incremental costs*.

Breakeven analysis begins with a separation of incremental costs but later combines costs. In breakeven analysis, the firm is first presumed to start up, incurring fixed costs. Fixed costs are depicted as line "A" in figure 41. The firm is seen as beginning to produce its single product line. The variable costs associated with (or incremental to) this production are depicted as dotted line B in figure 41. Total costs are then derived by adding the variable costs to the fixed costs. This *combination of the two types of costs will not create problems in this single product analysis but could create substantial difficulty in a multiple product analysis.* The total costs are depicted as line C in figure 41. Finally, the revenue incremental to the sale of this product line is plotted as line D. The breakeven point is seen as that point in the growth of the quantity produced and sold, where revenue finally equals total cost. After the firm breaks even, total revenue begins to exceed total cost and profits are realized.

In terms developed earlier, a market niche exists for this firm when producing quantities are greater than the breakeven quantity. These quantities lie to the right of the breakeven point in figure 41, the area marked "profit."

Contribution Margin

Breakeven analysis works well in the single product case sometimes exemplified by "start up" entrepreneurial firms. But breakeven analysis requires that variable costs be added to fixed costs in the analysis. This will not create difficulty in the single-product case. But combining costs directly associated with the product (incremental costs like the variable costs) to other kinds of costs can lead to trouble in the multiple-product case. The problem is best illustrated by demonstrating how a marketing decision can be adversely affected by this practice.

Figure 41
Breakeven Analysis

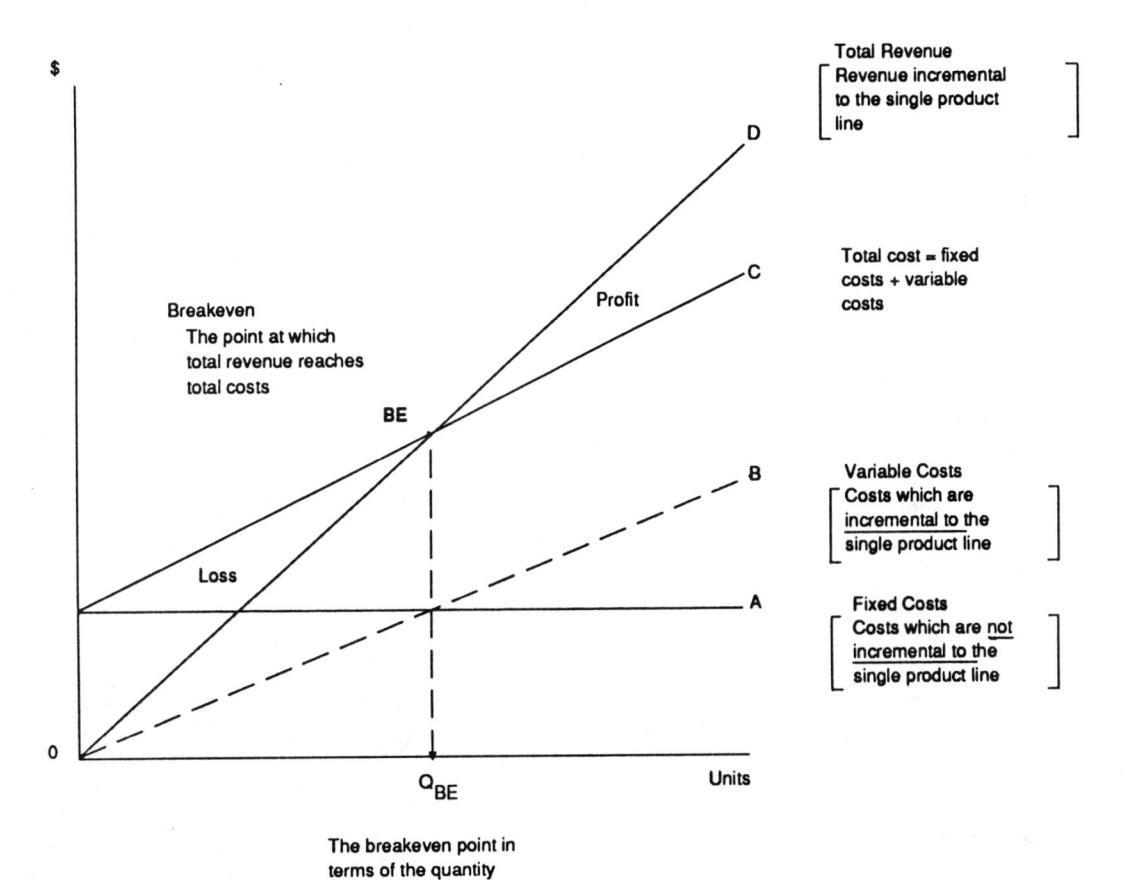

Breakeven
The point at which total revenue reaches total costs

Loss

Profit

BE

Total Revenue
[Revenue incremental to the single product line]

Total cost = fixed costs + variable costs

Variable Costs
[Costs which are incremental to the single product line]

Fixed Costs
[Costs which are not incremental to the single product line]

Q_{BE} Units

The breakeven point in terms of the quantity produced

Consider a two product *example*. For the firm under consideration, last years costs which were not incremental to products totaled 10 million dollars. These were costs which simply allowed the firm to exist and involve itself in the exchange process. They cannot logically be attached to a product or service offering. It is useful to refer to such costs as *overhead*. These costs are shown as component A in figure 42. *Last year, Product #1 cost* the firm 3 million dollars to produce, promote and distribute. These are the incremental costs associated with product #1, and comprise component B in figure 42. The market responded to this offering by exchanging 8 million dollars in *revenue* for examples of product one. This revenue, incremental to product one, comprises component C of figure 42.

Last year, product #2 cost the firm $3 million to produce, promote and distribute. This is coincidentally the same amount that it cost to produce, promote, and distribute product #1. The market responded to this offering with 9 million dollars of revenue in exchange for examples of product #2. Product #2's incremental costs form component D, and product #2's incremental revenues form component E, of figure 42. *Last years results were quite respectable*, with $1 million profit being made on $17 million of revenue. This amounted to a smaller before-tax profit of 5.9% for the firm as a whole.

This years results were substantially worse. Revenues declined to 12 million dollars and the firm suffered a loss of 2 million dollars, a 16.7% loss.

This *example* will now *demonstrate the severe decision making difficulties encouraged when overhead costs are not kept separate from incremental costs. Two decision making approaches will be contrasted.* The first vice president (VP #1) prefers to combine costs, allocating overhead to products in order to derive "product profitability." The second vice president (VP #2) prefers to keep the incremental costs separate from the overhead costs when analyzing the problem. The *logical results of each perspective will now be illustrated.*

The *first vice president* looks at the numbers and feels that overhead must be allocated to the products in order to arrive at "profitability." The allocation formula is one that is commonly used. The *allocation of overhead* to products, *based upon last years sales volume* is 8/17 of the overhead to product #1 and 9/17 of the overhead to product #2. The resulting "product profitability" analysis for this year comprises figure 43a.

This *product profitability analysis leads VP #1 to believe that product #2 is losing money. Both* the manager of product #2 *and* the manager of product #1 are competing for the firm's capital by promising that 1 million dollars in advertising will return 5 million dollars in new product revenue for their respective product. After a time of political competition, the managers are informed that the *investment will go to* the manager of *product #1*. The manager

Chapter 4 115

Figure 42
Overhead, Incremental Costs and Incremental Revenues

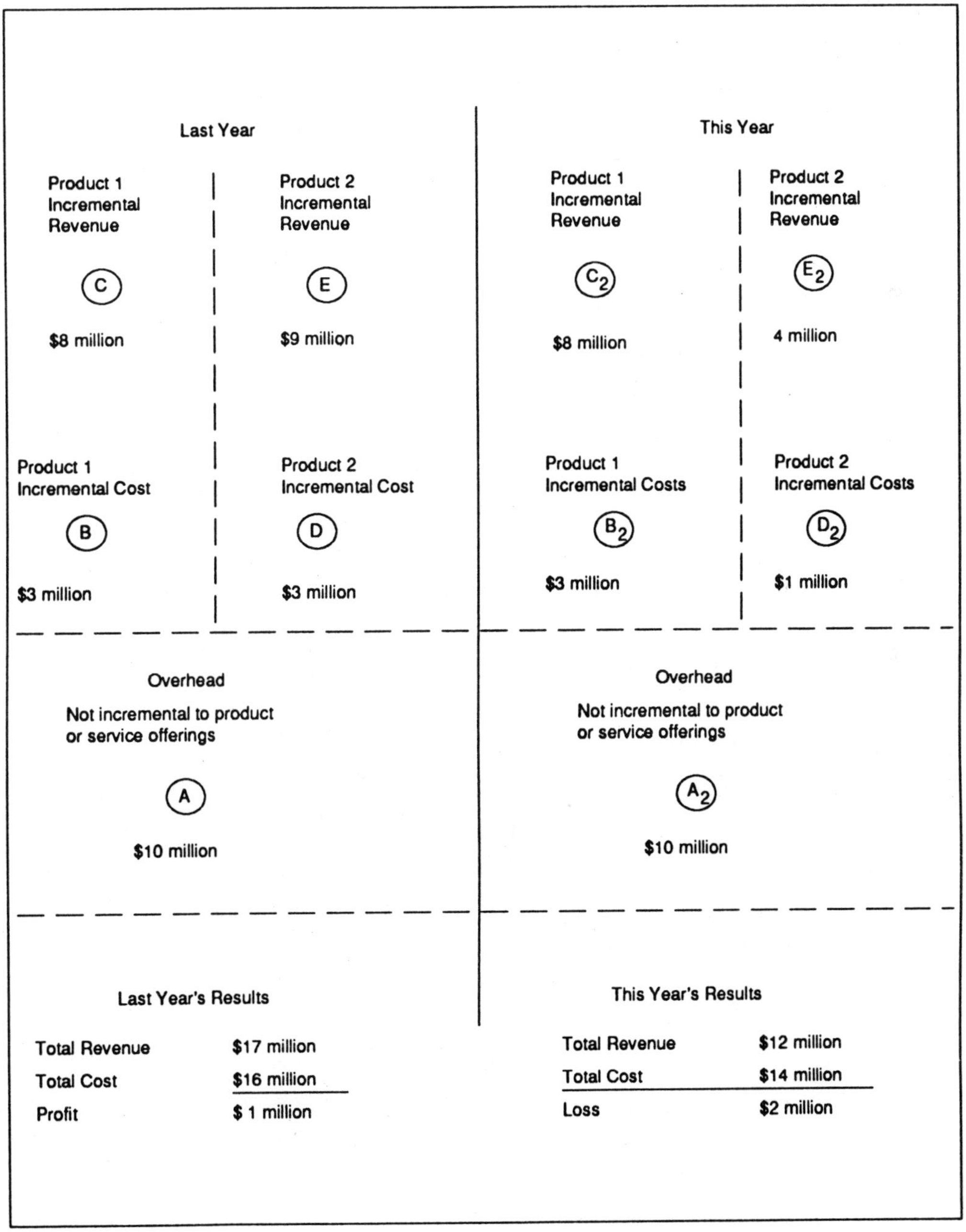

Last Year

Product 1 Incremental Revenue
(C)
$8 million

Product 2 Incremental Revenue
(E)
$9 million

Product 1 Incremental Cost
(B)
$3 million

Product 2 Incremental Cost
(D)
$3 million

This Year

Product 1 Incremental Revenue
(C_2)
$8 million

Product 2 Incremental Revenue
(E_2)
4 million

Product 1 Incremental Costs
(B_2)
$3 million

Product 2 Incremental Costs
(D_2)
$1 million

Overhead
Not incremental to product or service offerings
(A)
$10 million

Overhead
Not incremental to product or service offerings
(A_2)
$10 million

Last Year's Results

Total Revenue	$17 million
Total Cost	$16 million
Profit	$ 1 million

This Year's Results

Total Revenue	$12 million
Total Cost	$14 million
Loss	$2 million

Figure 43a
Product Profitability Analysis

a. Product profitability analysis this year for VP #1

Product #1	Product #2
Revenue $8 million	Revenue $4 million
Total costs $7.7 million	Total costs $6.3 million
$\begin{bmatrix} \text{Total costs} = \\ \text{Inc. cost 3m} \\ \text{\& 8/17 x 10m} \end{bmatrix}$	$\begin{bmatrix} \text{Total costs} = \\ \text{Inc. cost 1m} \\ \text{\& 9/17 x 10m} \end{bmatrix}$
$.3 million profit	$(2.3) million loss

b. Next year's results VP #1

Product #1	Product #2
Revenue $13 million	Revenue $4 million
Inc. cost $4.9 million	Inc. cost $1 million
+ 1 million in new advertising expense	

Overhead = $10 million

Total revenue   #17 million
Total cost   16.9 million

.1 million profit
or about 1/2 of 1%
before tax

of product #1 has promised 5 million dollars in new (product #1) revenues for a 1 million dollar advertising investment. This promise has been supported with capital, and the equivalent promise on behalf of product #2 has been rejected. According to the "product profitability" analysis, product #1 is more profitable, and so the decision seems straightforward. The *result* of this decision is a *very low level of profit*, illustrated in figure 43a.

The *second vice president* has a greatly different perspective and *does not trust the allocation of overhead to products*. This vice president keeps incremental costs separate from overhead costs and *is* particularly *interested in the amount of money a product contributes to the organization after its incremental costs have been paid*. This person likes to have the figure expressed both in dollars and as a percentage of a products incremental revenue. The percentage allows an analysis of profitability which is not biased against small-volume products. The *analysis of* product contribution to the firm (*contribution to overhead and earnings*) is duplicated as figure 44a.

This analysis allows the second vice president to see that while *product #2* has lost revenue, it remains a *"higher contribution" product* as a percentage of its revenue. Vice president #2 reverses the decision of vice president #1, *investing in product #2*. The second vice president's *results* for next year show considerably *more profit*. They are displayed in figure 44a.

Vice president #2's results show 7.5 times the profit made by vice president #1. *This improved decision making was facilitated by carefully separating incremental costs from those costs which were not incremental. In formal terms, the second vice president used "contribution margin" or contribution to overhead and earnings* in the analysis. This idea is often referred to using the abbreviation C.O.E.

The accounting concepts used to arrive at C.O.E. are straightforward. The firm isolates *revenues which are incremental* to the product. This is usually just those sales associated with the product less returns and allowances. But, adjustments may be required if these sales have caused lost sales elsewhere. The firm then isolates and *subtracts* the *costs which are incremental* to the product. This is usually more than just the variable cost of production. It would include promotion and distribution costs which are incremental to the product. It would also include fixed costs which are controllable and assignable to the product. An example of this kind of a fixed cost would be a warehouse which is used for the product and which could be disposed of should the product be discontinued. The accounting concept of C.O.E. is depicted in figure 43b.[3]

Figure 43b
Contribution to Overhead and Earnings [C.O.E.]

Sources: Donald J. Boweresox, M. Bixby Cooper, Douglas M. Lambert, and Donald A. Taylor, *Management in Marketing Channels* (New York: McGraw-Hill, 1980), p. 305. Reproduced with permission of McGraw-Hill Inc. See also Douglas M. Lambert, *The Distribution Channel Decision* (New York: The National Association for Accountants; and Hamilton, Ontario: The Society of Management Accountants of Canada, 1978), p. 122. Reproduced with permission of McGraw Hill Inc.

CONTRIBUTION TO OVERHEAD
AND EARNINGS
C.O.E.

A useful summary

A more detailed development

Incremental revenue

Less: Incremental costs

C.O.E.

Incremental revenue

Less: Incremental costs of production

Manufacturing contribution

Less: Offering specific costs of promotion and physical distribution

Offering contribution margin

Less: Fixed costs assignable to the offering and incremental

Controllable margin of the offering

Figure 44a
C.O.E. Analysis

a. Contribution to overhead and earning analysis this year for V.P. #2

Product #1		Product #2	
Revenue	$8 million	Revenue	$4 million
-Incremental costs	$3 million	-Incremental costs	$1 million
C.O.E. =	$5 million	C.O.E. =	$3 million
C.O.E. =	5/8 = 62.5%	C.O.E. =	3/4 = 75%

Product #1's contribution to
1. Overhead
2. Earnings once the overhead has been paid

Product #2's contribution to
1. Overhead
2. Earnings once the overhead has been paid

b. Next year's results V.P. #2

Product #1		Product #2	
Revenue	8	Revenue	9
Inc. cost	3	Inc. cost	2.25
		+ 1 million in new advertising expense	
C.O.E.	5	C.O.E.	5.75
	62.5%		63.9%

Overhead = $10 million

Total Revenue	17 million
Total Inc. Cost	(6.25) million
Total C.O.E.	10.75 million
Total Overhead	(10.00) million
Earnings	.75 million
About 4.4% before tax	

Figure 44b
Three Dimensions of Contribution Margin

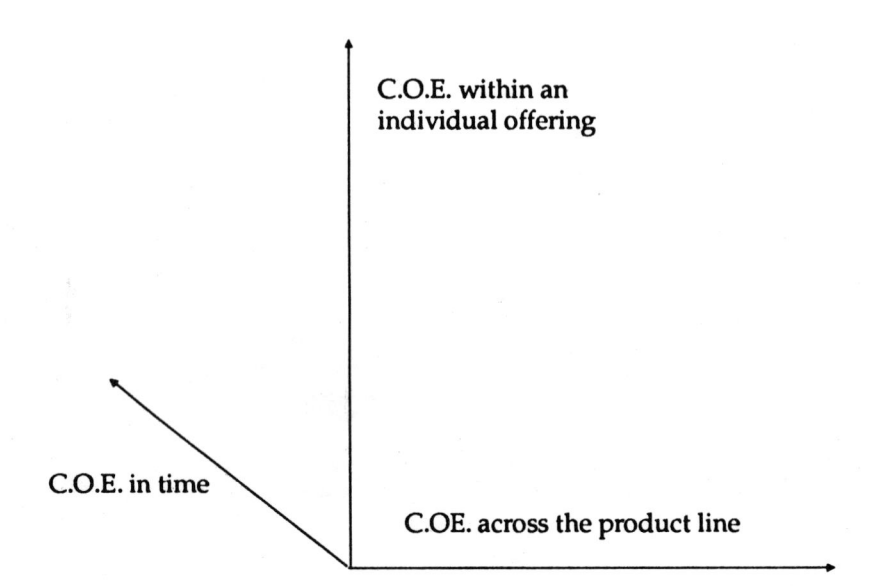

C.O.E. within an individual offering

C.O.E. in time

C.OE. across the product line

Three Dimensions of Marketing Controllable Profit

Contribution margin may be thought of as the component of profit which is *controlled by marketing decisions*. It may be thought of as "marketing controllable" because the vice president of marketing will have a great deal of control over which products are offered, and how they are priced, promoted, and distributed. These decisions are reflected in C.O.E. In contrast, decisions made by the vice president of marketing will have little direct effect upon the level of general corporate overhead.

Contribution margin, the aspect of the market niche which is controllable through marketing decisions, may be thought of as having *three dimensions*. The *first dimension* is affected as the four managerial variables, product, price, promotion and place, are adjusted by marketing management for *each individual offering*. The market then responds with differing levels of unit movement and revenue. As the four managerial variables are adjusted, each new combination will imply not only differing levels of revenue, but differing levels of incremental cost. In this way marketing management adjusts the *contribution margin of the individual offering*, the first of the three dimensions of marketing controllable profit.

Marketing management may also elect to add or delete individual offerings, or to emphasize some offerings at the expense of others. This kind of decision making was demonstrated in the example of the two vice presidents, detailed above. One vice president emphasized one product while the other vice president emphasized the other. They experienced very different results. As marketing management makes these kinds of decisions, they will affect the contribution margin derived from the product line as a whole. This is because individual products have different contribution margins, and successfully emphasizing the higher C.O.E. products will have the effect of bringing the average C.O.E. of the product line up. In this way marketing management adjusts the *contribution margin across the product line*, the second of the three dimensions of marketing controllable profit.

The third dimension of marketing controllable profitability was also illustrated in the earlier example of the two vice presidents. Each vice president made an investment in order to reap the benefits of improved sales and profitability in the next year. Thus marketing controllable profitability has a time dimension. Investments are made now in order to improve contribution margin in the future. *Contribution margin in time* is the third dimension of marketing controllable profit. The three dimensions of marketing controllable profit are illustrated in figure 44b. The three dimensional space may be thought of as *contribution margin space*, although few practitioners would recognize the term. For any given time period considered, such as a given year, the dollar amount of C.O.E. described by this space (so many dollars from product one plus so many dollars from product two, etc.) *must exceed the dollar amount of corporate overhead if the firm is to have a stated profit for that time period.*

Exploring C.O.E. Within an Individual Offering

The *concept of C.O.E.* which was developed earlier and detailed in figure 43b, is *placed in the context of the three dimensions* of marketing controllable profit in *figure 45*. The C.O.E. within the individual offering appears as component A-1. It represents the amount of C.O.E. generated by offering A in year 1. If offering A were to generate incremental revenue which did not cover incremental cost, it would appear as a negative component, descending below the zero point at the intersection of the three axes. *It is important that this financial picture be seen in the context of the important ideas presented in earlier chapters.*

The *incremental revenues* are a function of price (revenue/unit) and the number of units sold. Higher incremental revenue could be the result of high unit movement and low price or high price and low unit movement. Buyers will perceive and evaluate the offering, and will anticipate the satisfaction or utility which they expect to derive from the offering. Depending upon their budget constraints and the nature of competitive offerings, they will enter into exchanges, resulting in unit movement and incremental revenues for offering A in year 1.

Incremental costs of production will be a function of the cost curves of the firm. The cost curves are not only affected by the technology of production and the resulting economies of scale, but are themselves functions of numerous market evaluations. Costs of production would thus include the market prices of such things as raw materials, component parts, and labor. *Costs* of production *may also be* seen as potential investments in the creation of greater revenue. For example, investment in a better product may generate greater incremental revenue than incremental cost. There may therefore be important interactions between cost and revenue.

Incremental costs of promotion and distribution may also interact with revenue and affect revenue and C.O.E. in complex ways. C.O.E. may be improved by keeping these costs down. On the other hand, C.O.E. may also be improved by increasing production costs, promotion costs or distribution costs. These investments can result in an improved product, an altered perception of the product or an increased availability of the product. Any of these

Chapter 4   123

Figure 45
C.O.E. in the Individual Offering

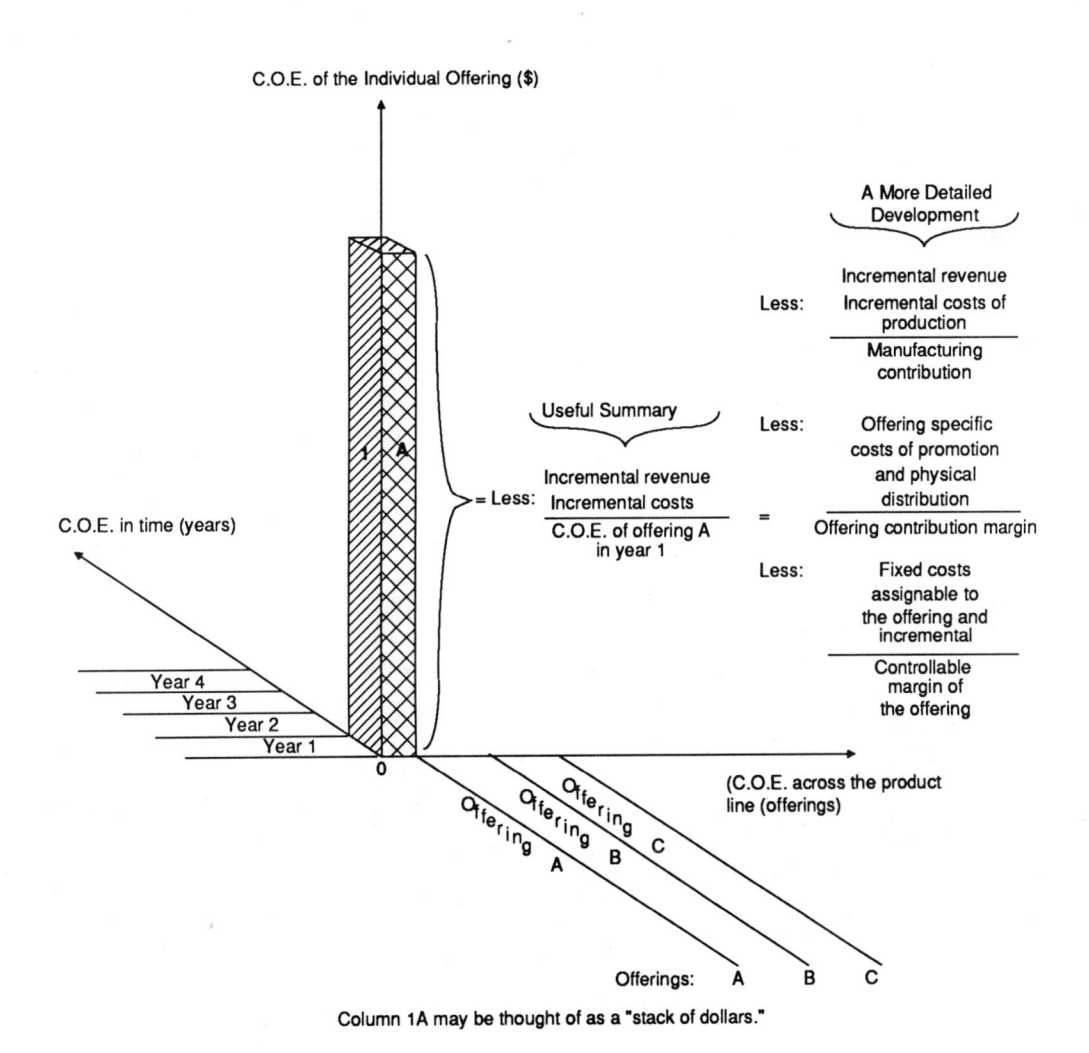

C.O.E. of the Individual Offering ($)

A More Detailed Development

Less: Incremental revenue
Incremental costs of production

Manufacturing contribution

Less: Offering specific costs of promotion and physical distribution

= Offering contribution margin

Less: Fixed costs assignable to the offering and incremental

Controllable margin of the offering

Useful Summary

= Less: Incremental revenue
Incremental costs

C.O.E. of offering A in year 1

C.O.E. in time (years)

Year 4
Year 3
Year 2
Year 1

Offering A
Offering B
Offering C

(C.O.E. across the product line (offerings))

Offerings: A   B   C

Column 1A may be thought of as a "stack of dollars."

improvements might be evaluated in the marketplace as being worth more than what it cost to create them.

Some *fixed costs* should be viewed in the same context. If a cost can be assigned to an offering and may be eliminated if the offering is eliminated, it should be viewed as the other incremental costs are viewed, despite the fact that it may be carried as a fixed cost by the firm's accountants.

Contribution Margin in Time: The Future Pattern of C.O.E., Without Investment and with Investment

The great social job of marketing is matching heterogeneous supply with heterogeneous demand.[4] It is in essence a job of resource allocation. It should come as no surprise therefore that the day to day chore of marketing management is also resource allocation. No matter how small the marketing decision, a pay raise for a salesperson, an advertisement in a paper, an addition to the product line or a deletion from the line, it is a resource allocation. Usually the benefits of an intelligent resource allocation are not immediately seen but accrue over time. A group which successfully allocates resources to uses that the market will reward, will enjoy a market niche in the future.

Components A-1, A-2, A-3, and A-4 in figure 46a demonstrates how the future market niche may be seen. Figure 46a demonstrates a pattern of constant C.O.E. for offering A in years 1, 2, 3, and 4. But the product life cycle indicates that the market is likely to be too dynamic for an unchanged product to simply continue generating constant C.O.E. A much more likely pattern in figure 46a would be a gradual attenuation or diminishing of C.O.E.

To prevent a loss of C.O.E., marketing management may wish to *invest* in offering A. Two forms of investment in offering A are demonstrated in figure 46b. In year one, the firm has elected to improve the product, increasing the incremental costs of production. This is reflected in reduced C.O.E. and is shown as an "investment in reduced C.O.E." At the same time the firm is installing new capital equipment to allow more efficient production of the improved product. This is shown as a "capital investment associated with offering A." Figure 46b supposes that these investments have been successful, recovering an "incremental or extra C.O.E. received in years 2, 3, and 4." It is incremental or extra because it is over and above what the firm might legitimately have expected without the investment. Given the nature of product life cycles, the firm might have made a more realistic assumption about the incremental C.O.E. than the assumption reflected in figure 46b. The

Chapter 4 125

**Figure 46a
C.O.E. in Time: No Investment**

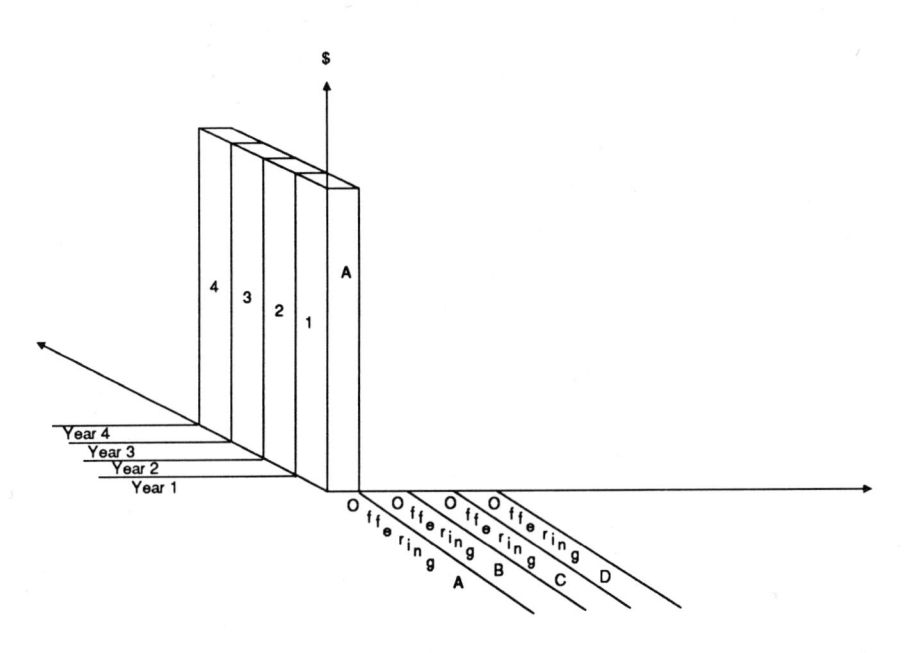

**Figure 46b
C.O.E. in Time: Investment**

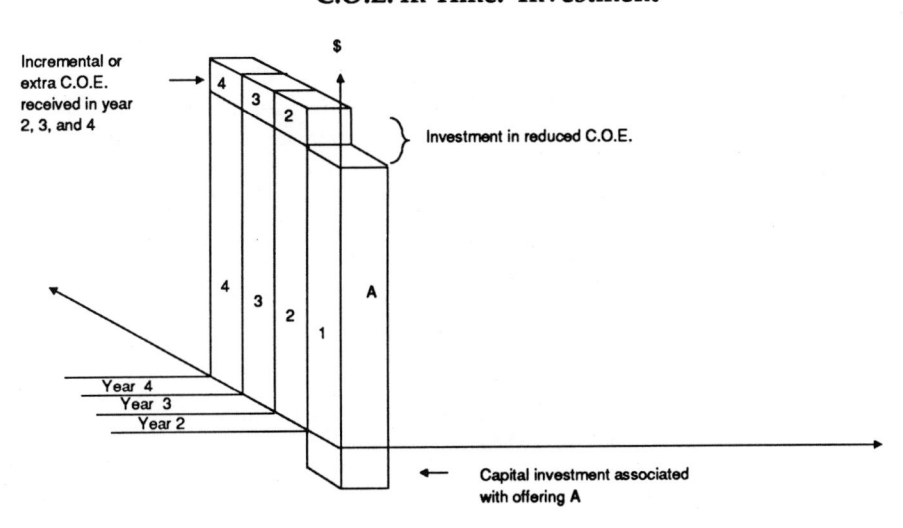

incremental amount should increase in year three and four reflecting the assumption that the product would be dying without the investment.

Financial people have developed ways of calculating and evaluating the desirability of these kinds of investments. *Marketing people should be thoroughly familiar with these calculations and able to propose and defend their resource allocations in these financial terms. The important calculations are the net present value of the investment, the internal rate of return of the investment and the payback period of the investment.* The net present value calculation adjusts the comparison of today's costs with future benefits for the time value of money (a dollar today is worth more than a dollar next year) and for tax effects. The *internal rate of return* is the result of converting the net present value, which is a dollar figure, into a percentage. This allows the comparison and ranking of projects without a bias toward large dollar products. The *payback* provides an index of liquidity or an understanding of how quickly the investment funds are returned. These and other calculations are *detailed in Appendix A*—"Important Calculations and Perspectives for Marketing Managers."

C.O.E. Across the Product Line: Solving the Problem in Year One

Investment theory, with its net present value, internal rate of return and payback calculations, address the resource allocation problem in the long run. *In the short run*, the problem becomes a question of giving the immediate production, promotion and distribution priority to those offerings capable of generating the higher percentage C.O.E. This is done in order that the higher percentage C.O.E., when multiplied by the enhanced unit movement which results from the new priority, will generate greater total C.O.E. for the firm. This is the problem of improving profitability across the product line.

There are limits to the shifting of priorities. The firm is committed to certain physical facilities, to conformity with the law, to ethical mandates and to long run strategies which may require some sacrifice of immediate short term profit. The problem thus becomes one of *maximizing contribution margin across the product line subject to constraints (or limits)*. This problem is illustrated in two ways. The nature of differing C.O.E. across the product line is illustrated in figure 47. The nature of maximization of C.O.E. subject to constraints is illustrated by the linear programming approach in figure 48. In this approach the short term profitability of the product line is maximized subject to various *short term* operating *constraints*, such as the productive capacity of existing plants. Real problems may be too complex to describe with a linear program, but a linear program provides an excellent example of a useful philosophy, maximization subject to constraint.

Chapter 4 127

Figure 47
C.O.E. Across the Product Line

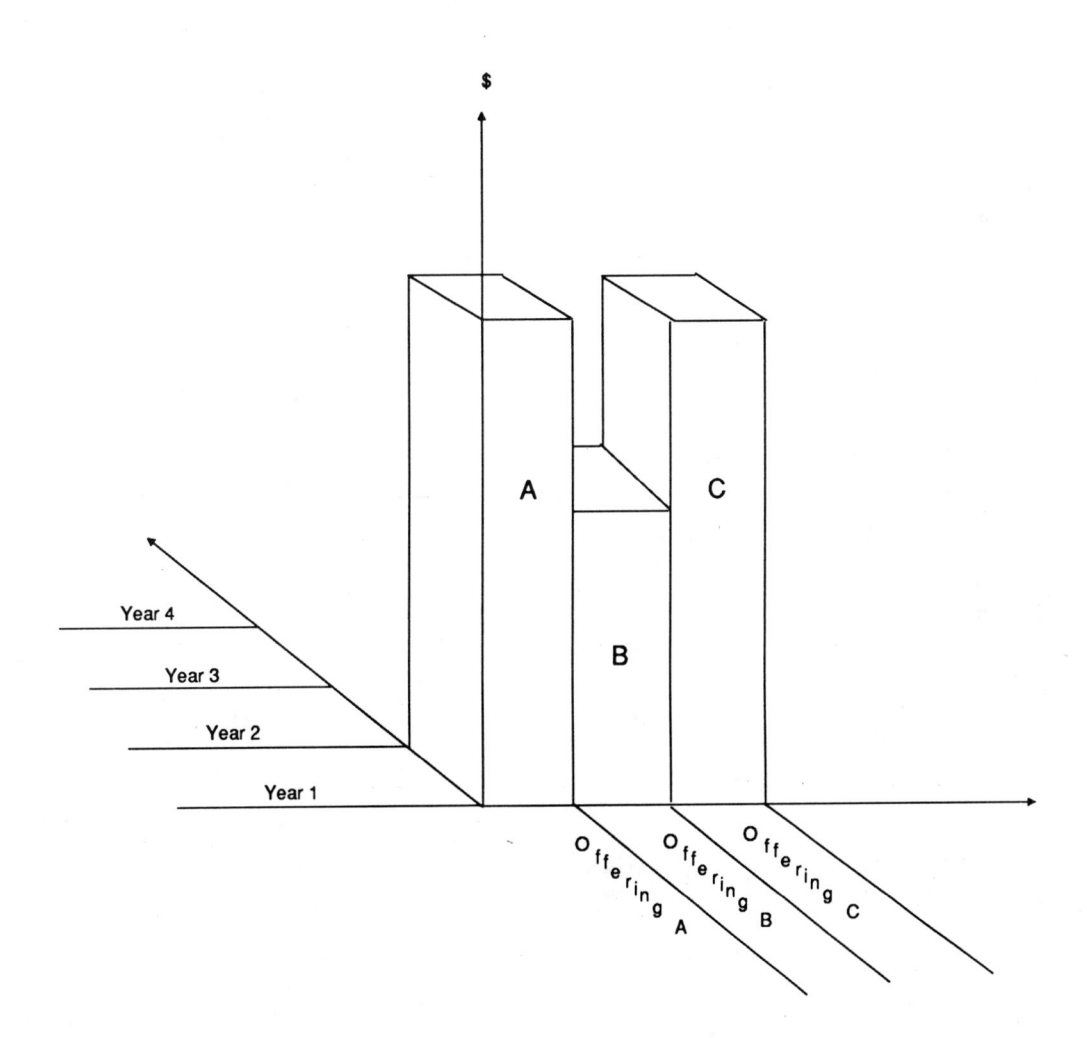

Figure 48
Example of a Linear Programming Approach to Short-Term Profit Maximization Across the Product Line

Problem:

Max π when:
$\pi = 2p + 3c$
Subject to labor constraint:
$5p + 2c \leq 100$
Machine constraint:
$p + 10c \leq 90$

Logic:

The objective function is given by the relative profitability of the two products $\pi = 2p + 3c$. Product p contributes $2.00 of profit ($2.00 C.O.E.) per unit while product c contributes $3.00. The problem is constrained by what is possible given the labor available ($5p + 2c \leq 100$) and what is possible given the machines available ($p + 10c \leq 90$). The problem is approached by finding corner points A, B, and C of the feasible range (the shaded area bounded by constraints) and comparing the profitability of those points

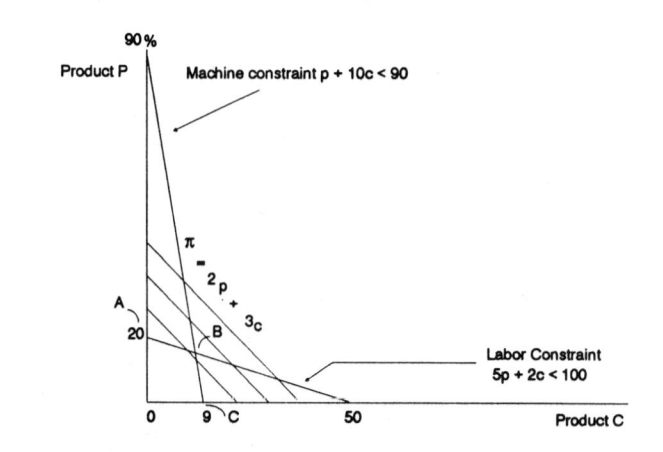

Calculation:

Point A is found by maximizing production of product p to the exclusion of product c as constrained by the most constraining equation

$5p + 2c \leq 100$
$5p \leq 100$ Profit $\pi = 20 \times 2 = 40$
$p \leq 20$

Point c is found by maximizing production of product c to the exclusion of product p using the most constraining equation

$p + 10c \leq 90$
$10c \leq 90$ Profit $\pi = 9 \times 3 = 27$
$c \leq 9$

Point B is found by solving for the intersection of the two constraining equations, using a slack variable to make the inequalities into equations.

$5p + 2c + S_1 = 100$
$p + 10c + S_2 = 90$
Solve for c   Solve for p
$5p + 2c = 100$ $p + 10c = 90$
$p + 10c = 90$ $p + 73 = 90$ Profit = 34 + 21.9 = 55.9
$5p + 2c = 100$ $p = 17$
$-5p - 50c = -450$ (Best solution)
$c = 7.29$

Longer Term Constraint: Society and Capital

In the longer term it is unlikely that such problems as labor or machine availability will constrain the firm's activities. If they pose a short term problem they will be seen as candidates for investment, to be viewed through the lens of the net present value, internal rate of return and payback calculations. In the longer term a competition for capital allocation is likely to resolve the product mix problem. *The product mix may thus be viewed as a portfolio of investments.* New products may be added or old products may be dropped, based on investment analysis. Without strategic, legal or ethical arguments to the contrary, investment opportunities might be ranked in declining order according to their internal rate of return.

At this point, society places subtle but powerful constraints on the investment activities of the firm. Society evaluates what the firm is doing and rates the firm itself as an investment. The real *long term constraint* upon the firm then becomes the firms ability to attract capital at rates which allow profitable investment. As the firm proceeds down its list of ranked investments toward those of lower attractiveness, the capital markets will sense the situation. Sensing lower returns and higher risks the capital market will raise the cost of capital to the firm. Declining investment profitability and increasing capital cost will eventually combine to create a socially imposed constraint on the firm.

The Capital Market

The mechanism whereby society encourages or discourages a group's activities through adjustment of the cost and availability of capital should be well understood by marketing decision makers. Marketing decisions control contribution margin, both in the present and in the future. Contribution margin minus overhead yields profit, and the capital market responds to profits and expected future profits.

Capital may be thought of as a store of value which is created when production as valued by markets exceeds consumption as valued by markets. It is therefore created when an individual saves or when a corporation makes a profit. This store of value is allocated to society's uses in the capital market where it is bought, sold and loaned using financial instruments such as stocks and bonds. The price of capital is the effective yield of these instruments, expressed as a percentage.

Capital markets, such as stock markets and bond markets will demand higher yields on stocks or bonds from a given firm if they see that firm as risky, as having a lower potential for survival and growth. The logic is that an investor may be willing to take a chance on such a firm, but will demand remuneration for the increased risk. Such a company must pay more for capital by creating stock or bond offerings which yield more to the investor. In this way marketing managers making decisions which decrease the profitability of the product/service portfolio are subjected to double punishment. First, the contribution margin space itself is smaller, but secondly the cost of capital to the firm is likely to go up. In terms of the kinds of costs that have been discussed in this chapter, a given capital instrument is not usually associated with one product in an incremental way. The cost of capital is associated with the firm as a whole, an overhead cost. Thus poor marketing decisions not only result in a reduction of contribution margin but can in this indirect way result in an increase in overhead.

Capital Allocation

Marketing management may constructively view their decision making as capital allocation. Capital may be drawn from the pool of capital available to the firm as a whole. In this case, marketing managers often must argue for the allocations in front of top management. In other cases, marketing managers may be able to allocate capital from one product to another without as much top management involvement. These perspectives are illustrated in figure 49, where arrows represent sources and use of capital. Here, arrow one represents a transfer of capital from one product to another, a behavior sometimes termed *cross subsidy*. Arrow two represents a reinvestment in the same product. Arrows three and four represent allocations to products from the general capital pool of the firm.

Aids to Conceptualization: Models of Capital Allocation

Due to the complexity of the capital allocation problem, the marketing community has developed various conceptual models to aid the capital allocation decision. These models simplify the problem, making certain aspects easier to grasp. *Product portfolio models* are examples of this kind of conceptual aid. The Boston Consulting Group or BCG model, depicted in figure 50 is such a portfolio model. The BCG model or grid evaluates the desirability of investment in products by forcing the decision maker to classify the products according to their relative market share and the rate of growth

Chapter 4 131

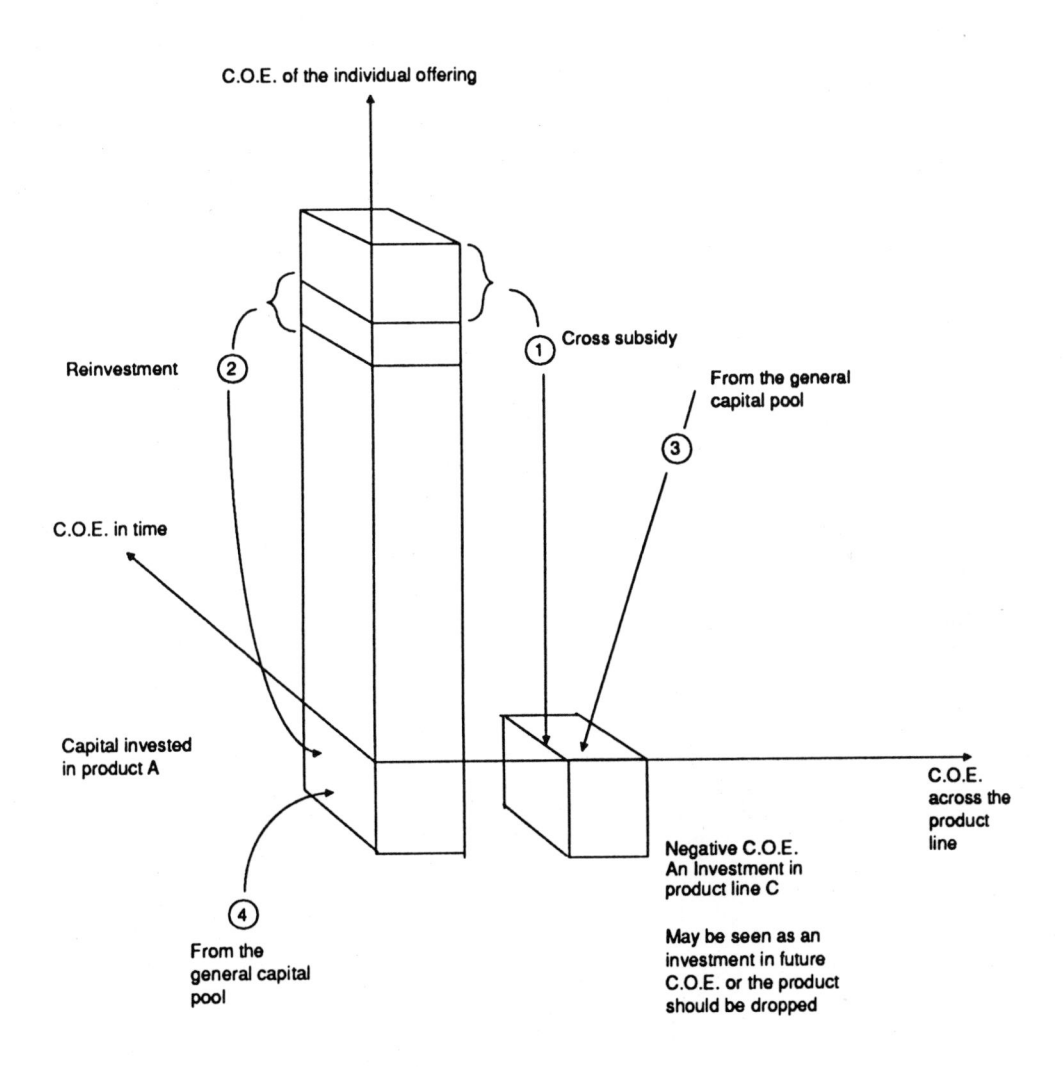

Figure 49
Marketing Decisions as Capital Allocations

C.O.E. of the individual offering

Reinvestment ②

① Cross subsidy

From the general capital pool

③

C.O.E. in time

Capital invested in product A

C.O.E. across the product line

Negative C.O.E. An Investment in product line C

④
From the general capital pool

May be seen as an investment in future C.O.E. or the product should be dropped

132   Part I

**Figure 50
Marketing Decisions as Capital Allocations: The BCG Model**
Source: George S. Day, "A Strategic Perspective on Product Planning," *Journal of Contemporary Business*, 1975, pp. 1-34. Used by permission.

Market Growth

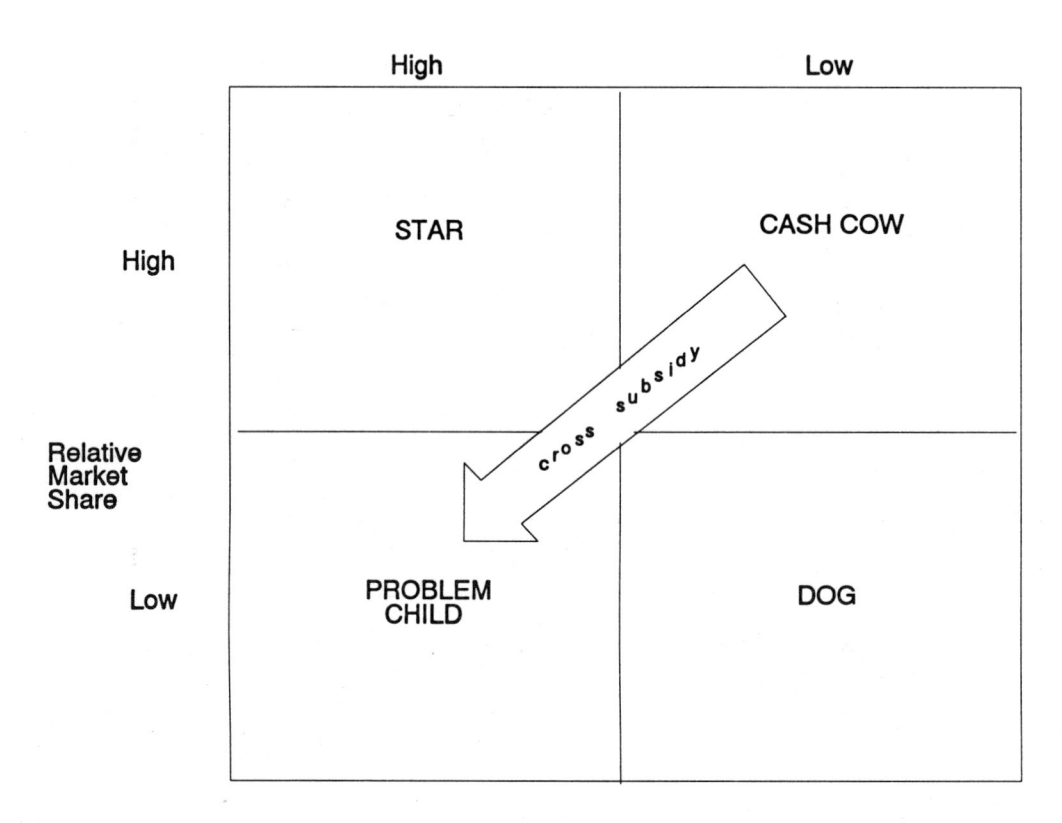

	High	Low
High Relative Market Share	STAR	CASH COW
Low	PROBLEM CHILD	DOG

cross subsidy

of the market they participate in.[5] The model suggests cross subsidy of one product by another in order to move the company's capital out of low growth markets into investments which build market share in high growth markets. As with any conceptual aid which greatly simplifies a problem, models such as these can be misleading. For example, many successful market niches exist in low market share, low growth situations. But, portfolio models such as the BCG grid are common conceptual aids in marketing and can be well used if used in the context of an awareness of the real complexity of the capital allocation problem. Portfolio models will be discussed in greater depth in chapter nine.

Adjustments: Non Profit Organizations

While the model used in this chapter is most straightforwardly applied to represent the for profit firm, some small adjustments will allow it to describe the market niche of any organization. The concept of overhead will remain unchanged as all organizations incur such costs. The concept of contribution to overhead and earnings will remain largely unchanged. Enough C.O.E. must be generated to cover overhead even if no earnings are intended or anticipated. As the average profit of an American business is only about 5% of revenue, the large majority of C.O.E. dollars will be used to cover overhead, even in the "for profit" organization.

The results of offering products and services for exchange with others will not be changed. C.O.E. will be generated with the same dimensionality that was described in this chapter. The non profit organization might expect to generate a larger proportion of its C.O.E. in ways other than offering things for sale, however, and these may be straightforwardly described.

A contribution is entirely contribution margin after deductions are made for administrative costs incremental to handling the contribution. If the contribution is associated with an individual product or service by the donor or granting agency, the contribution should be seen as adding to the C.O.E. of that item. Otherwise it should be seen as a separate block of C.O.E. Tax subsidies and grants may be dealt with in the same way. The expectations of donors and granting agencies may be evaluated as the expectations of normal exchange customers are evaluated.

Crossing National Boundaries

The evaluation of the market niche using financial measurement and perspectives is complicated considerably by currency fluctuations. In the international environment, revenues may be in one currency, some costs in a second currency and other costs in a third. At the same time, some products may be produced and sold entirely within the boundaries of a fourth nation with all costs and revenues in the fourth currency. Investments may be made in dollars to retrieve benefits in yen. The understanding of C.O.E. must be expanded in order to effectively deal with these complications.

Figure 51 represents an expanded understanding of C.O.E. when revenues and costs are being realized in both dollars and yen. In this example, a product manufactured in Japan and marketed in the United States, the company engages in many dollar exchanges, many yen exchanges and some exchanges involving both. When all is completed and the net figures are assembled, the company has gained 1,700 dollars and expended 350 yen. The big question then becomes, what does this constitute in terms of C.O.E.? Two decisions must be made in order to approach the question of C.O.E.

First it must be decided whether to state C.O.E. in terms of dollars, yen or some third currency. This is called selecting the *reference currency* to be used.[6] The instinctive response of a U.S. based company might be to use the U.S. dollar. In that case, all currencies would be *translated* to (or restated as) U.S. dollars. The instinctive selection of the home currency as a reference currency may or may not be wise. The selection of reference currencies should be an intentional strategic choice of the firm, as there will be a natural tendency among the managers to try to improve the firm's position in terms of the reference currency that was chosen. The reference currency might decline sharply in value. In that case, it might have been better strategy to have selected another reference currency and to have improved the company's position in terms of that currency.

Secondly, it must be decided when to translate one currency into another. This decision is necessary because currency values fluctuate in terms of one another on a minute by minute basis. It may be appropriate to translate as of the date of *conversion,* or actual exchange of one currency for another.[7] Alternatively, it may be appropriate to translate based on the relative values at the end of the fiscal year or according to other generally accepted accounting principles.

Figure 52 illustrates how *exchange rate fluctuations may substantially alter the real economic value of the mixed currency exchange*. In this illustration, part A shows the results translated to a U.S. dollar reference currency when the exchange rate of dollars for yen is 1:1. Part B illustrates an exchange rate of 2:1, and part C illustrates an exchange rate of 4:1. As the value of the dollar declines in relation to the yen, the real economic gain represented by the exchange is diminished substantially.

Figure 51
Marketing a Japanese Manufactured Product in the United States: Results in Dollars and Yen

Incremental revenue		2000 dollars
Less: Incremental costs of production	(300 yen)	
Manufacturing contribution	(300 yen)	and 2000 dollars
Less: Incremental costs of promotion and distribution	(50 yen)	and (200 dollars)
Offering contribution margin	(350 yen)	and 1800 dollars
Less: Fixed costs assignable to the offering and incremental		(100 dollars)
Controllable margin of the offering	(350 yen)	and 1700 dollars

When a firm's market niche becomes international, the economic effects of constantly fluctuating exchange rates can become a part of every component of C.O.E. Contribution margin within an individual offering, across the product line and out in time can all be affected.

Overhead costs can be affected as well. For international firms, the three dimensional financial representation of the market niche will remain unchanged, with the important exception that the dollar values involved would now be seen as the result of a translation to dollars. This is illustrated in figure 53. As discussed earlier, international managers may also wish to select a

Figure 52
Translated to C.O.E. in U.S. Dollars

Part A   Exchange rate, dollars for yen, 1:1

    Before   After translation to dollars
    $1700-350 yen ⎯⎯⎯⎯ $1700-$350 = $1350 C.O.E. in U.S. Dollars

Part B   Exchange rate, dollars for yen, 2:1

    Before   After translation to dollars

    $1700-350 yen ⎯⎯⎯⎯ $1700-$700 = $1000 C.O.E. in U.S. dollars

$$\begin{bmatrix} 350 \\ \times 2 \end{bmatrix}$$

Part C   Exchange rate, dollars for yen, 4:1

    Before   After translation to dollars
    $1700-350 yen ⎯⎯⎯⎯ $1700-$1400 = $300 C.O.E. in U.S. Dollars

$$\begin{bmatrix} 350 \\ \times 4 \end{bmatrix}$$

---

reference currency other than the U.S. dollar. Again the three dimensional financial representation of the market niche will remain unchanged, with the exception that the stated currency values involved are now a result of a translation to that reference currency.

Substantial currency fluctuation may occur during one year and cause the C.O.E. across the product line to vary as is illustrated in figure 53. Often firms have short run contractual obligations which will mitigate these kinds of results. But, the problem of currency fluctuation becomes particularly acute when trying to plan for the future. Thinking about long term international investments now must involve assumptions about future exchange rates. Future benefits should still be discounted to their present value, but future

Figure 53
Currency Fluctuations and Results in the Reference Currency

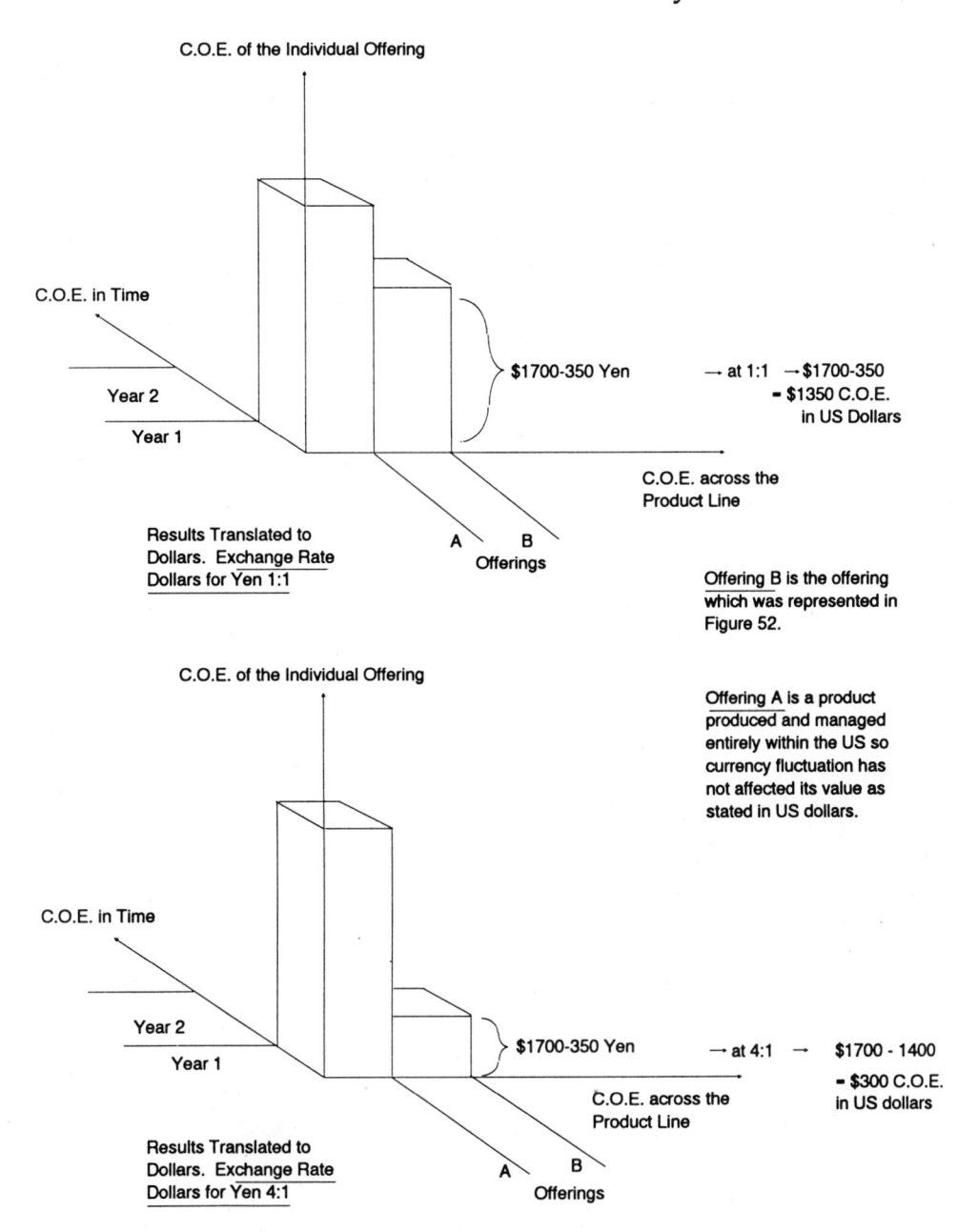

C.O.E. of the Individual Offering

C.O.E. in Time

Year 2

Year 1

Results Translated to Dollars. Exchange Rate Dollars for Yen 1:1

A B
Offerings

$1700-350 Yen

C.O.E. across the Product Line

→ at 1:1 → $1700-350
= $1350 C.O.E. in US Dollars

Offering B is the offering which was represented in Figure 52.

Offering A is a product produced and managed entirely within the US so currency fluctuation has not affected its value as stated in US dollars.

C.O.E. of the Individual Offering

C.O.E. in Time

Year 2

Year 1

Results Translated to Dollars. Exchange Rate Dollars for Yen 4:1

A B
Offerings

$1700-350 Yen

C.O.E. across the Product Line

→ at 4:1 → $1700 - 1400
= $300 C.O.E. in US dollars

benefits should also be understood in terms of the various currencies involved and how they might fluctuate. People involved in market planning for international environments should be prepared to make some estimate of future exchange rates. This will be necessary in order to translate the expected currency flows into a reference currency for discounting to the present value. The logic of predicting exchange rate fluctuation is presented in Appendix A.

Chapter Summary

This chapter has introduced three dimensions of contribution margin which are created by the product service line. These are seen as a fair if not perfect quantitative representation of the firm's market niche. If the amount of dollars represented by contribution margin exceeds the dollar amount of overhead, the firm enjoys a profit, and profit allows the firm to survive and grow. The perspective is adaptable to the analysis of non profit organizations. Contribution margin of some kind or another, perhaps simple contributions, must equal overhead if the organization is to survive without cutbacks. Contribution margin must exceed overhead if the organization is to invest and grow. Contribution margin must be adjusted for currency fluctuations when the firm is crossing international boundaries.

APPENDIX A

Important Calculations and Perspectives for Marketing Managers

Perspectives and Calculations for Evaluating C.O.E. in Time

Net Present Value

A calculation may be performed in order to estimate the value of future revenues and costs which result from current investments. The calculation is more complex than a simple comparison of the dollar volume of the investment with the dollar volume of the C.O.E. received. This is for two reasons.

First, there are *tax effects*. When a capital investment is made, the firm is allowed to take a depreciation expense over the life of the investment. Since the cost of the investment may actually be paid out in the first year, annual depreciation over the next several years is a "non cash" expense. This non cash expense has an important effect on cash flows. It affects the amount of tax paid in each year. For this reason the discounted cash flow or net present value analysis uses a *cash flow benefit*, which incorporates the revenues and costs that C.O.E. incorporates, instead of using C.O.E. itself. A cash flow benefit is derived in figure A-1.

Simple calculation of the cash flow benefit is the appropriate approach when the benefits are to be associated with a new product. But, when the benefits are to be associated with the improvement of or replacement of a product or productive facility which already exists, a new calculation must be made. This calculation develops the extra or incremental cash flow benefit, since some benefit would flow in without the investment. Calculation of the incremental or extra cash flow benefit is also illustrated in figure A-1.

Beyond depreciation and its tax effects, the second major problem that must be dealt with in the net present value calculation is the simple fact that a dollar received next year is worth less than a dollar received this year. Even without the effect of inflation, this years dollar is worth more because it can be invested, retrieving interest by the time the other dollar would have been received next year. This effect is called the *time value of money*.

In order to *compare* future benefits, benefits received in years 2, 3, and 4, with an investment which goes out now, in year 1, the value of the future benefits must be adjusted. They must be adjusted downward because of the time value of money. They must be adjusted all the way back to their equivalent value in the year of the investment so that they may be fairly compared with the investment. The logic of discounting to present value (the current or year 1 value), is fairly straightforward.

Figure A-1
Cash Flow Benefits

Sales		11,000
Less: Operating Costs		-5,000
Less: Depreciation	(D)	-1,000
Taxable Income		5,000
Less: Income Tax		-2,500
Profit after Tax (P)		2,500
Plus Depreciation (D)		1,000
Cash Flow Benefit (B = P + D)		+ 3,500

} Cash flow benefit with a new machine which improves the product and reduces production costs.

Calculation of increment cash flow benefit of the new machine

	Without	With New Machine
Sales	10,000	11,000
Less: Operating Costs	-7,000	-5,000
Less: Depreciation	-500	-1,000
Taxable Income	2,500	5,000
Less: Income Tax	-1,250	-2,500
Profit after Tax (P)	1,250	-2,500
Plus Depreciation (D)	+ 500	+ 1,000
Cash Flow (P + D)	1,750	3,500

Incremental cash flow benefit $3,500 - 1,750 = $1,750 = B

Consider the dollar received today, in year 1. If it were invested at 10% interest, its value would compound as depicted in figure A-2. To return this compounded dollar to its present value, one simply divides each years compounded figure by the factor that was used to arrive at the compounded figure. Figure A-2 depicts both the compounding and the discounting of the results to present value. In order to create a general formula from this specific example, simply replace the example interest rate of 10% or .1 with the general term r, denoting the interest rate. Thus (1.1) becomes (1+r). With these understandings, the net present value calculation itself may be developed. This is accomplished in figure A-3. The calculation allows marketing management to estimate for any given investment considered, how far ahead it is likely to be in terms of todays dollars. This dollar figure is referred to as the *net present value of the investment*. The practical computation of net present value is facilitated by the use of present value tables. An interest factor (I.F.) is selected for the present value of an annuity for R (interest rate) and N (number of years). this factor is then multiplied by B (cash flow benefit), and the result is compared to C (the capital investment). Thus:

$$B\ (I.F.) - C = NPV$$

Ranking Investments: Internal Rate of Return

As useful as the net present value calculation is, it can be misleading when attempting to rank investments. This is because the N.P.V. is a dollar figure and is therefore biased toward large projects when it is used to rank alternative investments. Should management wish to adjust the net present value to a percentage figure for purposes of ranking investments, NPV may be converted to *internal rate of return (IRR)*. This procedure is illustrated in figure A-4.

Payback

The net present value and internal rate of return calculations neglect the question of how fast the investment funds are returned. The payback calculation provides this needed information. The payback period in years is calculated as:

$$\frac{\text{Payback period}}{\text{in years}} = \frac{\text{Capital investment}}{\text{Benefit}} = \frac{C}{B}$$

Chapter 4   143

Figure A-2
Compounding of $1.00 at 10%

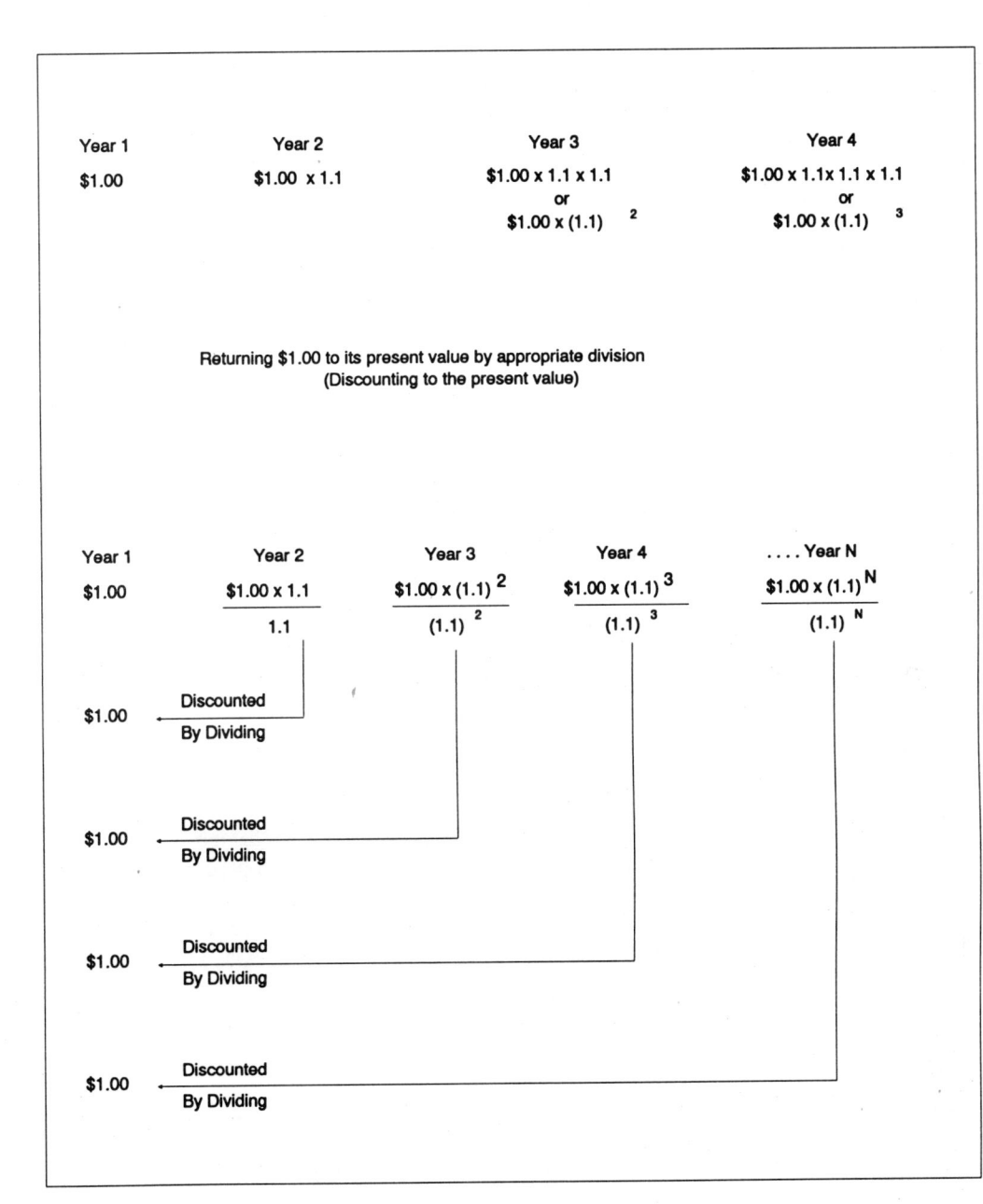

Year 1	Year 2	Year 3	Year 4
$1.00	$1.00 × 1.1	$1.00 × 1.1 × 1.1 or $1.00 × (1.1)^2	$1.00 × 1.1 × 1.1 × 1.1 or $1.00 × (1.1)^3

Returning $1.00 to its present value by appropriate division
(Discounting to the present value)

Year 1	Year 2	Year 3	Year 4	.... Year N
$1.00	$\dfrac{\$1.00 \times 1.1}{1.1}$	$\dfrac{\$1.00 \times (1.1)^2}{(1.1)^2}$	$\dfrac{\$1.00 \times (1.1)^3}{(1.1)^3}$	$\dfrac{\$1.00 \times (1.1)^N}{(1.1)^N}$

$1.00 ← Discounted By Dividing

$1.00 ← Discounted By Dividing

$1.00 ← Discounted By Dividing

$1.00 ← Discounted By Dividing

Figure A-3
A Logical Development of the Net Present Value Calculation

Step 1. The net investment (net of immediate tax credits, etc.)
C for capital investment

Step 2 Calculate the incremental cash flow benefit
B calculated as in Figure A-1

Step 3 The "net value" of an investment is the benefit minus the cost

NV = B - C
or equivalently
NV = - C + B

Step 4 Extend the benefit stream over the estimated life of the project in years "N"

NV = - C + B + B + B + B + ... B

Step 5 Discount the benefit stream to its present value so that the comparison with the capital investment is a fair comparison, a comparison of net present value.

$$NPV = -C + \frac{B}{1+r} + \frac{B}{(1+r)^1} + \frac{B}{(1+r)^3} + \frac{B}{(1+r)^4} + ...\frac{B}{(1+r)^n}$$

Figure A-4
Converting NPV to IRR

$$NPV = -C + \frac{B}{1+r} + \frac{B}{(1+r)^2} + \frac{B}{(1+r)^3} + \cdots \frac{B}{(1+r)^N}$$

1. Set NPV = ZERO

2. Insert the dollar value of the investment, -C

3. Insert the dollar value of the cash flow benefit, B.

4. Solve for the value of r:

> This is accomplished using present value tables. Using the appropriate table for investment life (N), values for r are selected on a trial and error basis. Each value for r has an associated interest factor (I.F.) which is taken from the table. Interest factors are used in the equation B (I.F.) -C = NPV until the equation solves to equal ZERO.

Return on Investment and Associated Calculations

Return on investment or ROI is commonly used to evaluate the relative profitability of subordinate divisions in a firm. Return on investment is calculated as:

$$\text{Return on Investment (ROI)} = \frac{\text{Net Profit after Tax}}{\text{Investment}}$$

Similar logic is used to develop return on assets and return on assets managed. These calculations are:

$$\text{Return on Assets} = \frac{\text{Net Profit after Tax}}{\text{Assets}}$$

$$\text{Return on Assets Managed} = \frac{\text{Profit or C.O.E. attributable to a manager}}{\text{Assets Managed}}$$

Understanding Currency Fluctuations

An understanding of the nature of currency fluctuations contributes in an essential way to the understanding of the firms international market niche. A marketing manager's decision may result in a flow of currency which is worth only a small fraction of what had been planned. So, international market planning must be accompanied by careful judgement concerning anticipated currency values.

Some currencies have a stated value in terms of gold, or another commodity. Such currencies are said to be "pegged" to that commodity. In the cases of these currencies, the analyst's chore is to predict the value of the commodity and to predict the political probabilities of the country removing the stated value and substituting another, or allowing the currency to "float" (find its own value) in currency markets.

Most currencies are not pegged to any commodity or to any other currency. They derive their value, not from any guaranteed relationship to a commodity, but from the simple fact that they are legal tender in their nation of origin. This means that the currency must be accepted as payment of debts and obligations within that country. Thus a person holding the currency of a nation has a claim on the assets, goods and services of that nation. The real value of such a claim will depend upon the quantity and quality of those assets, goods and services and the number of claims outstanding. Thus with

Chapter 4 147

Figure A-5
A Balance of Trade Deficit and Its Effect upon the Value of Currency

U.S. Dollar Example
$

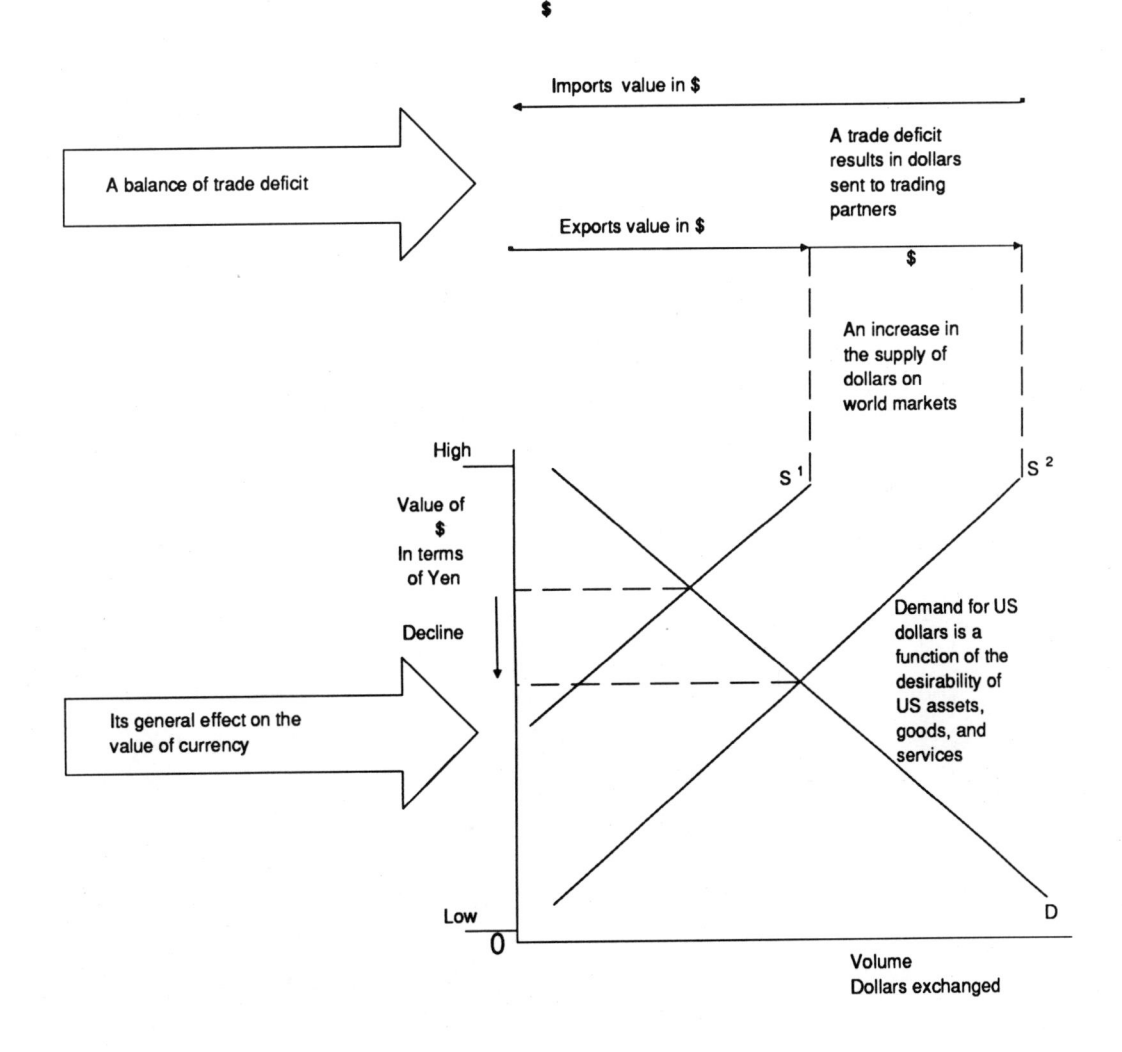

Imports value in $

A balance of trade deficit

A trade deficit results in dollars sent to trading partners

Exports value in $

An increase in the supply of dollars on world markets

High

Value of $ In terms of Yen

Decline

Its general effect on the value of currency

Low
0

S^1 S^2

Demand for US dollars is a function of the desirability of US assets, goods, and services

D

Volume
Dollars exchanged

a given level of assets, goods and services, an increase in the supply of money is likely to reduce the value of the money. This relationship tends to be true in international markets as well as within a domestic economy.

As countries engage in international exchange, the exchanges will sometimes become unbalanced. That is, a nation may import more than it exports, creating a *balance of trade deficit* or export more than it imports, creating a *balance of trade surplus*. When this occurs, the nation whose imports exceed its exports (the deficit nation) must compensate for this by sending some of its currency overseas to its trading partners. Thus, the quantity of the deficit nation's currency which is held by its international trading partners increases. This set of relationships is illustrated in figure A-5.

In the example shown in figure A-5, the trading partners have not found the (US) exports, as they are currently constructed, priced promoted and distributed, to be sufficiently attractive to completely balance the imports the (US) has taken from the trading partners. The result is the (US) has had to compensate with dollars or general claims on assets, goods and services of the United States. In this way, the number of such claims held in the international community is increased.

As the number of claims increases, the supply of the currency in world exchanges increases. If the demand for the currency does not change this will result in a decline in the value of the currency.

The demand for general claims on a nation's goods, services and assets depends on the desirability of those goods, services and assets as it is perceived by the international community. This in turn is a function of both the quantity and the quality of goods, services and assets. In this sense, the natural resource endowment and the productivity of the economy as reflected in the quantity, quality and cost of its outputs are critical to the value of a nations currency.

Therefore, when evaluating the future value of a currency, the analyst should expect a *currency* to *decline in value when*:

1. The domestic money supply is expanding more rapidly than the output of goods and services.
2. There is a balance of trade deficit.
3. There are small resource and asset bases.
4. There is low productivity resulting in goods and services which are expensive and inferior.
5. There is general pessimism about the future of the nation and its economy.

Currencies may be expected to *rise in value when* economies are characterized by:

1. Money supply growth not in excess of the growth in the output of goods and services.
2. Balanced or surplus trade situations.
3. Large resource and asset bases.
4. High and growing economic productivity resulting in superior goods and services at low economic costs.
5. General optimism about the future of the nation and its economy.

When the market niche becomes international, such evaluations must become a part of the organization's evaluation of future overhead costs and future contributions to overhead and earnings.

---

[1]According to Dun and Bradstreet, *Business Failure Record*, 1986 (Murray Hill, New York: Dun and Bradstreet 1989), 13.1% of firms one year old or less had failed, and 54.5% of firms five years old or less had failed. Manufacturing firms in the USA showed after tax profit expressed as a percentage of sales of 4.4%, 5.3%, 5.6%, 4.2%, and 6.0% for each of the four quarters of 1987 and the first quarter of 1988 respectively, according to the U.S. Census Bureau, *Quarterly Financial Report*, manufacturing companies (Washington D.C., U.S. Census Bureau, 1988).

[2]For an introduction to breakeven analysis see J. Fred Weston and Eugene F. Brigham, *Essentials of Managerial Finance*, 2nd ed. (New York: Holt, Rinehart and Winston Inc., 1971), pp. 69-80.

[3]The two-dimensional understanding of contribution margin which is used in this text is owed to Frank H. Mossman and Douglas M. Lambert. See, for example, Frank H. Mossman, W. J. E. Crissy, and Paul M. Fischer, *Financial Dimensions of Marketing Management* (New York: John Wiley and Sons, 1973). See also Donald J. Bowersox, M. Bixby Cooper, Douglas M. Lambert, and Donald A. Taylor, *Management in Marketing Channels* (New York: McGraw-Hill, 1980), p. 305. The three-dimensional understanding, to the best of my knowledge, are original.

[4]Wroe Alderson, *Marketing Behavior and Executive Action* (Homewood, Illinois: Richard D. Irwin, 1957), pp. 195-227.

[5]George S. Day, "A Strategic Perspective on Product Planning," *Journal of Contemporary Business*, 1975, pp. 1-34.

[6]This is also called a "yardstick" currency. See Stefan H. Robock, Kenneth Simmonds and Jack Zwick, *International Business and Multinational Enterprises* (Homewood, Illinois: Richard D. Irwin, 1977), p. 492.

[7]Ibid., p. 487.

Questions for Study, Discussion and Examination

1. Could you define, or explain to a friend who has not studied marketing, each of the following terms? Can you give examples of each?
    a. Breakeven analysis
    b. Incremental cost
    c. Breakeven point
    d. Overhead
    e. Allocation of overhead to products
    f. Product profitability
    g. Contribution to overhead and earnings (C.O.E.)
    h. Incremental revenue
    i. Profit controlled by marketing decisions
    j. Contribution margin of the individual offering
    k. Contribution margin across the product line
    l. Contribution margin in time
    m. Incremental costs of production
    n. Incremental costs of promotion and distribution
    o. Fixed costs which may be incremental
    p. Marketing as resource allocation
    q. Investment in an offering
    r. Net present value
    s. Internal rate of return
    t. Payback
    u. Maximizing contribution margin across the product line
    v. Constraint
    w. Linear program
    x. Short term constraint
    y. Long term constraint
    z. Capital market
    aa. Product portfolio model
    ab. Reinvestment
    ac. Cross subsidy
    ad. Contribution margin in a nonprofit organization
    ae. Reference currency
    af. Translation
    ag. Conversion
    ah. Balance of trade deficit
    ai. Balance of trade surplus

2. What are the advantages and disadvantages of using profit as a measure of market niche? Can the disadvantages be overcome? What are the advantages and disadvantages of using contribution margin as a measure of market niche? How can this approach be adjusted for the evaluation of non profit organizations?

3. What is meant by the statement that "the market niche of the organization is very sensitive to mismanagement"?

4. Demonstrate your understanding of breakeven analysis with a fully labeled drawing. What are the strengths and weaknesses of this approach?

5. How can the attachment of costs which are not incremental to costs which are incremental lead to decision making difficulties? What is meant be "allocation of overhead to products"?

6. What is the difference between a product profitability analysis and a contribution to overhead and earnings analysis?

7. What kinds of decisions do marketing people make that will affect profit? What component of profit is controlled by marketing decisions? Demonstrate your full understanding by discussing the dimensions of marketing controllable profit. Can profit be a misleading term here? Would there be a better term?

8. How is the C.O.E. within the individual offering affected by ideas presented in chapters 1, 2 and 3?

9. What is the great societal job of marketing and how is that reflected in the day-to-day job of marketing managers?

10. How are the understanding of investments and means of evaluating the desirability of investments important to marketing managers?

11. What is the net present value calculation? What exactly does it do? Demonstrate your understanding by writing out the equation, labeling all of its components and explaining each of the components in the context of a marketing decision. (See appendix A for help.)

12. What is the relationship between net present value and the internal rate of return? Under what circumstances might the internal rate of return be preferred? How would you actually go about solving one of these complex looking equations? How would you go about solving the real marketing problem represented by these equations? (See appendix A for some of these.)

13. What does the payback tell us that the internal rate of return and net present value equations do not?

14. How does linear programming illustrate a philosophy of decision making? What problem does it address? What do you think the strengths and weaknesses of this philosophy might be in practice?

15. How does the society impose constraint on a company's marketing decision making through the mechanism of the capital market? Explain how this constraint functions and how its effects are seen in the company's costs.

16. How is the BCG grid, a portfolio model, also a capital allocation model? What are the strengths and weaknesses of viewing capital allocation in this way?

17. Why, from an internal political point of view, might marketing management find it easier to engage in reinvestment and cross subsidy than to draw capital from the general capital pool of the firm?

18. Explain the survival and growth of a "for profit" company in terms of contribution margin and overhead. Explain the survival and growth of a non profit organization using the same terms.

19. How does currency fluctuation affect contribution margin and overhead for firms involved in international marketing? What is the strategic importance of the selection of a reference currency?

20. Why would it be important for an international marketer to be able to predict currency fluctuation? When is it reasonable to expect that a particular currency will drop in value? When is it reasonable to expect that it will rise in value? (See appendix A for help.)

21. What is the mechanism of a rise or drop in the value of a currency? How should this understanding aid market planning? (See appendix A for help.)

PART II

THE MANAGERIAL VARIABLES AND THE MARKET NICHE

The first part of the book developed an understanding of the voluntary exchange process and the resulting market niche of the firm. The second part examines how management can adjust the exchange by working with the controllable variables of product, price, promotion and place. The relationship of product and price is examined first. The exchange is in essence, an exchange of a product or a service for a price. The exchange can be adjusted by adjusting the product or service design, adjusting the price, adjusting what is communicated, or adjusting when and where the product or service is available.

CHAPTER 5

ADJUSTING THE EXCHANGE: THE INTERACTION OF APPROPRIATE PRICE AND PRODUCT DESIGN

The first four chapters of this book introduced those factors which combine to create the market niche of an organization and some ways in which that niche might be understood and measured. *This chapter begins the discussion of what management can do to adjust the exchange, and thus adjust the market niche of the organization.* The traditional variables which are thought to define the responsibility of marketing management, the *product, price, promotion and place*, will be considered in the next three chapters. *Focusing on the exchange, wherein a product or service (as promoted and placed) is exchanged for a price, the product-price interaction is considered first.* It is termed *an interaction because* price should be considered to be a decision separate from product design only in the case of homogeneous, undifferentiated products. In other cases, product design and appropriate prices are inextricably intertwined. In the common case of differentiated products, the appropriate price is a function of the nature of the differentiation vis-a-vis competition, as well as other factors which will be introduced in this chapter.

Promotion and place or physical distribution activities are *ways of adjusting this product-price interaction.* Often promotion efforts or changes in distribution will be *used to enhance the buyers' perception of the product.* This will have the *economic effect of increasing the marginal utility* which the buyer anticipates with the purchase. If these kinds of *product differentiation activities* are successful, the firm might be able to retrieve a higher price without sacrificing unit movement, expand unit movement at the original price, or hold onto market share in the face of increased competition.

Sometimes promotion efforts or changes in distribution will be used to adjust the price component of the product-price interaction. A new price level or policy might be communicated to a target market. Distribution activities might be made more efficient, resulting in cost savings which will give management the option of reducing prices.

Pricing the Homogeneous Product

The unusual case of the perfectly homogeneous product (agricultural commodities, etc.) will be considered first. *Pricing the homogeneous product is somewhat more straightforward than pricing the differentiated product.* However, the *principles* of market structure and competitive behavior *which govern* the pricing of the *homogeneous product* will *also have great influence on the pricing of differentiated products.* Thus, an understanding of this pricing situation forms the groundwork for an understanding of appropriate pricing for differentiated products.

Perfectly homogeneous products exist only in the market structures of pure competition and undifferentiated oligopoly. In *pure competition* the *firm is a price taker*; the market dictates price to individual vendors. In pure competition, the product will be sold "at market" because the individual vendor faces perfectly elastic demand. If the vendor prices at a penny per unit below market that individual can sell all that he or she can produce. But there is no point in doing that, no incentive, because the same quantity could be sold at market price, a penny per unit higher. On the other hand, should the vendor try to sell a perfectly homogeneous product at a penny per unit above market, nothing will be sold. This situation is termed *perfect elasticity* of demand for the products of an individual vendor, and was introduced using these economic terms in chapter three.

A more complete understanding can now be developed if perfect elasticity is also characterized using the relationship of economics to psychology which was introduced in chapter two. This relationship was summarized in figure 10 and is duplicated as figure 54. It will help to illustrate pricing of the homogeneous product and will be very useful in pricing the differentiated product.

In figure 54, it can be seen that the *buyer makes a choice by weighing marginal utility against price*. The way the consumer views *marginal utility* and *price* is a function of the buyer's individual perception and cognition. In the case of the "perfectly homogeneous" product, the psychological assumption is that the product is perceived and thought by all buyers to be homogeneous, regardless of which vendor is used. In other words, each buyer may perceive the product differently than another buyer does, as discussed when the demand curve was developed, but there is no perceived difference in the products of different vendors. Therefore the marginal utility enjoyed by any given buyer would be the same, regardless of that buyer's choice of vendors. In accordance with the rules of buyer choice (1-3 in figure 54) the choice among vendors of homogeneous products would be made based upon which vendor had the lowest price. *When marginal utility is constant, the ratio of $\frac{mu}{p}$ can only be improved by reducing price.* Using these ideas, the economic phenomenon of perfect elasticity may be more clearly understood. The vendor raising prices above the market level has suddenly created the lowest or worst ratio of $\frac{mu}{p}$. All buyers now shun this vendor, resulting in perfect elasticity of demand. *The integration of psychology* into the economic understanding enriches the comprehension of this simple homogeneous product case, and *will be necessary to the understanding of the case of differentiated products.*

As the buyer selection of a truly homogeneous product is a price game, where the ratio $\frac{mu}{p}$ can only be adjusted by adjusting P, *pricing strategy for homogeneous products largely involves the understanding of competitive effects* on the level of price. In the case of *pure competition*, and as introduced in chapter three, price in excess of minimum average total cost (ATC) attracts new competitors, driving the price back down to minimum ATC. When price falls below this level, competitors will exit, allowing the price to move back up to minimum average total cost. Homogeneous products produced in industries where there are low barriers to entry will be priced according to these market dictates. Price will approximate minimum average total cost in the long run, with fluctuations as demand changes and competitors enter and exit. Only particularly efficient or low cost producers will have a long run advantage in this situation.

In the second homogeneous product situation, the case of *undifferentiated oligopoly, buyers will continue to choose vendors based upon price.* This is because it is another case of the marginal utility to an individual being the same, regardless of which supplier is used. Here the competitive effects that govern price are those resulting from the sometimes successful and sometimes unsuccessful attempts to obtain the economic results of a shared monopoly. This idea was introduced in chapter three. High barriers to entry will substantially reduce the price fluctuations which are due to entry of new competitors. However, price fluctuations will still occur as a result of changes in demand.

Figure 54
Buyer's Choice—The Consumer Behavior and Micro-Economic Perspectives Related

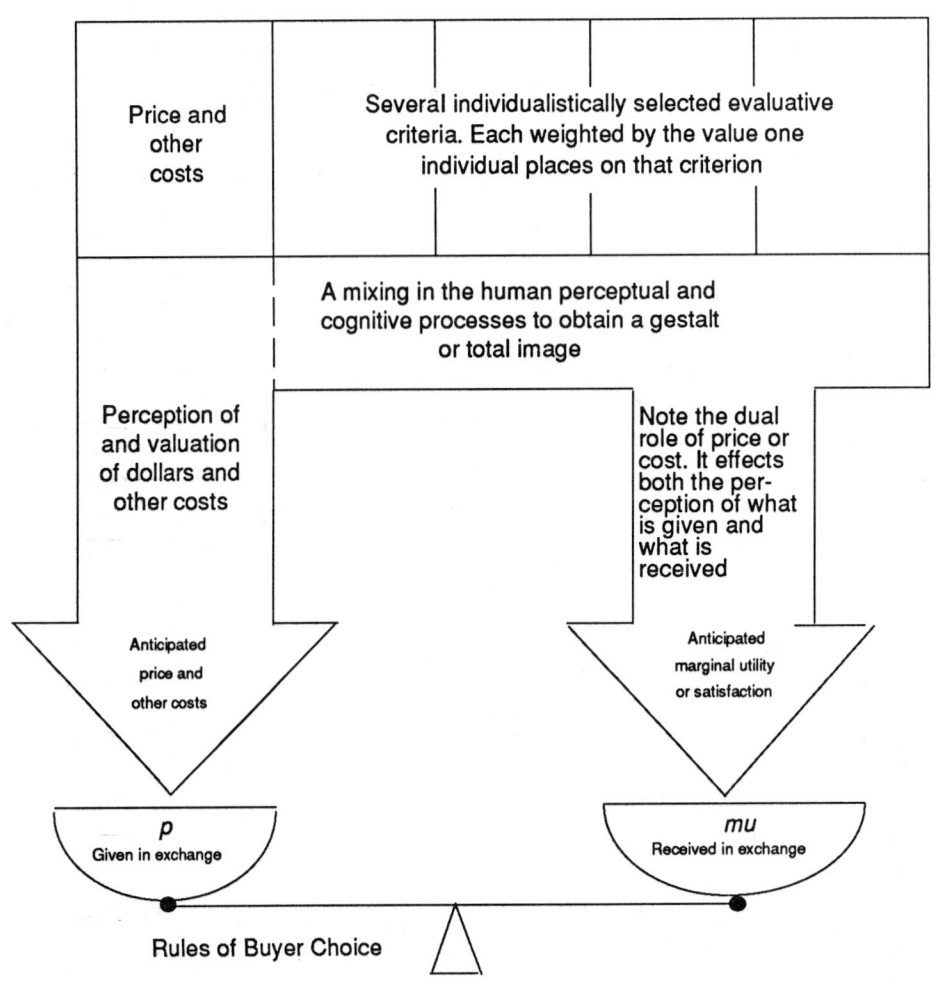

```
┌─────────────┬──────────────────────────────────────┐
│             │                                      │
│ Price and   │ Several individualistically selected │
│ other       │ evaluative criteria. Each weighted   │
│ costs       │ by the value one individual places   │
│             │ on that criterion                    │
├─────────────┼──────────────────────────────────────┤
│             │  A mixing in the human perceptual    │
│             │  and cognitive processes to obtain   │
│             │  a gestalt or total image            │
│ Perception  │                                      │
│ of and      ├──────────────────┬───────────────────┤
│ valuation   │                  │ Note the dual     │
│ of dollars  │                  │ role of price or  │
│ and other   │                  │ cost. It effects  │
│ costs       │                  │ both the per-     │
│             │                  │ ception of what   │
│             │                  │ is given and      │
│             │                  │ what is           │
│             │                  │ received          │
└─────────────┴──────────────────┴───────────────────┘
```

Anticipated price and other costs ↓   Anticipated marginal utility or satisfaction ↓

⏝ p Given in exchange   ⏝ mu Received in exchange

Rules of Buyer Choice

1. The purchase of an alternative will not be considered unless $mu > p$
2. The choice of alternative 1 will be preferred to alternative 2 when $\frac{mu_1}{p_1} > \frac{mu_2}{p_2}$
3. The buyer is indifferent between alternative 1 or alternative 2 (could choose either) when $\frac{mu_1}{p_1} = \frac{mu_2}{p_2}$

As demand expands, individual oligopolists will find it easier to be profitable without competing for the market share of other oligopolists. Shared monopoly conditions may then be easy to attain, although this might entail legal and ethical problems. In this situation, a common price which is well above costs might be expected. As demand collapses, oligopolists may elect to compete for market share. This situation would result in pricing behaviors resembling those in pure competition. Oligopolists could drive prices close to costs. Assumptions about oligopolists choosing to compete for market share versus electing to behave in parallel are illustrated in the kinked oligopoly demand curve, which was reviewed in chapter three. Oligopolists are often involved in major industries providing basic commodities such as fuels and metals. Demand fluctuations in these industries can be expected with general upturns and downturns in the economy.

Pricing the Differentiated Product

The differentiated product lies between the homogeneous product found in pure competition or undifferentiated oligopoly and the unique product found in monopoly. As discussed, buyers of the truly *homogeneous product* will prefer the vendor with the lowest price. Therefore, pricing the homogeneous product is a question of what the "going price" or market level of price is going to be. Pricing for the individual firm is determined by the nature of competition as it responds to demand.

At the opposite extreme, the *monopolist* has no competition. As discussed in chapter three and as will be briefly reviewed below, the monopolist prices according to demand and according to the costs of the monopoly firm. The way the product is perceived and thought of by potential buyers and the way that translates to demand largely determines monopoly price.

In the middle, the vendor of the *differentiated product* has a degree of uniqueness but also some degree of competition. The vendor of the differentiated product, found in monopolistic competition and differentiated oligopoly, does not have to "take price" as the vendor of the undifferentiated product must. Nor can the vendor of differentiated products "make price" the way the monopolist does. Instead the vendor of the differentiated product enjoys some degree of *pricing power*, more than the pure competitor and less than the monopolist.

To know that the possession of a successful differentiated product, one perceived and thought to be better because of its differences, delivers some pricing power is useful. *Pricing power* gives the vendor the option of charging a higher price. However, a more precise understanding of the nature of pricing power can be developed using figure 54 in the way that it was used to understand perfectly elastic demand. Careful development of a more precise understanding can allow marketing planners to predict unit movements for different product designs at different levels of price. Because this kind of prediction carries with it both revenue and incremental cost implications, contribution margin can then be projected.

Pricing and Designing the Differentiated Product: Understanding the Differentiation

Understanding the differentiation of a product allows management to see where the product can be priced in relation to competition, just as understanding market structure allows management to see where the product can be priced in relation to costs. Possession of a *successfully differentiated product delivers pricing power relative to the competition* in accordance with the rules of buyer choice which are summarized in figure 54. These rules describe an individual buyers choice behavior in economic terms. Consider rule number two. Rule number two states that the choice of alternative one will be preferred by the individual buyer to the choice of alternative number two when the ratio of marginal utility to price for alternative one is greater than the same ratio for alternative two. This is formulated as $\frac{mu_1}{p_1} > \frac{mu_2}{p_2}$. For this individual buyer, offering one is preferred to offering two.

To understand the extent of the pricing power which product one has in relation to product two, begin by holding the prices equal; $p_1 = p_2$. When prices are held equal, the inequality $\frac{mu_1}{p_1} > \frac{mu_2}{p_2}$ implies that this individual consumer, through the perceptual and cognitive processes, anticipates greater marginal utility or satisfaction from the selection of offering one. In quantitative terms $p_1 = p_2$ when $\frac{mu_1}{p_1} > \frac{mu_2}{p_2}$ implies $mu_1 > mu_2$. The pricing power that product one has in relation to product two in the mind of this buyer can now be approximated by raising p_1 until the condition described in buyer choice rule number three is reached. When this condition is reached, the buyer is indifferent between alternative one and alternative two; $\frac{mu_1}{p_1} = \frac{mu_2}{p_2}$. The percentage price increase that was necessary to move the initial situation of $\frac{mu_1}{p_1} > \frac{mu_2}{p_2}$ when $p_1 = p_2$ to the situation of indifference, $\frac{mu_1}{p_1} = \frac{mu_2}{p_2}$ is a useful approximation of the pricing power that has been delivered by the product differentiation when this individual consumer is considered.

Three important adjustments should be made to improve management's understanding of the nature of the differentiation before marketing planners can choose product and price strategy and project results in terms of C.O.E. *First, it is necessary to translate individual reaction into market or market segment reaction.* The individual understanding that was just outlined does not allow the projection of unit movement. Unit movement in a market or market segment may be projected by conducting market research or a market experiment which varies the price in accordance with the logic above, and observes changes in unit movement. If this is done with a large enough group which is representative of the market, unit movement can be projected. For example, a 200 person group might be used to conduct research which simulates decision making at different levels of price. Alternatively, a real test market might be used. In these situations a 50% loss of unit movement might be found to result from a 30% increase in price. This kind of result, expressed in percentages, can be expected because the individuals who comprise the market perceive the product and the competition differently. They thus become indifferent and eventually switch preference at different levels of price. As price moves by a certain percent, a percent of the representative experimental group will change their minds and make a different choice. These percentages can then be applied to estimates of total market size and market share to derive estimates of unit movement, revenue, incremental cost and C.O.E.

Secondly, it is desirable to explore the psychological dynamics which result in the buyer's anticipated marginal utility, perception of price, and choice. This exploration *can suggest new ways of product differentiation which might further increase pricing power.* Figure 54 uses summary statements which indicate that an individual's evaluation of the offering is a function of anticipated marginal utility (or satisfaction) weighed against anticipated price and other costs. Marginal utility and price are functions of the individual's perception and cognitions. The marginal utility of any specific offering which is being considered is thus a function of individualistically selected and weighted evaluative criteria. At a *minimum* it would be advisable to *know what the evaluative criteria are* for the product choice and the target market involved. At a *more sophisticated level*, it may be possible to understand how these criteria are weighted, how they interact to create gestalt or total image effects, and the extent to which the alternative evaluation process is conscious and explicit, versus unconscious. Investigations of the alternative evaluation process may be aided by *linear models of the process* such as the Fishbein and Rosenburg models.[1] These models and their relationship to the Engle Blackwell Model which was introduced in chapter two, are illustrated in figure 55. The investigation may also be aided by a measurement technique called *conjoint measurement.* This technique attempts to quantify utility, using the results of field research to assign "part worths" or increments of utility to the attributes of a product.[2]

Figure 55
Linear Models and the Engle Blackwell Model

Rosenburg Model, Source: Milton J. Rosenburg, "Cognitive Structure and Attitudinal Effect," Journal of Abnormal and Social Psychology" 53 (November, 1967), pp. 367-72. Copyright 1967 by the American Psychological Association. Reprinted by permission.

$$A_o = \sum_{i=1}^{N} (Vl_i)(Pl_i)$$

Where:

A_o = The overall evaluation of the attractiveness of Alternative O
Vl_i = The importance of the ith value
Pl_i = The perceived instrumentality of Alternative O with respect to value i
N = The number of pertinent or salient values

Fishbein Model, Source: Martin Fishbein, "An Investigation of the Relationships between Beliefs about an Object and the Attitude toward that Object," *Human Relations* 16 (August 1963), 233-240. Reprinted by permission.

$$A_b = \sum_{i=1}^{n} (b_i)(e_i)$$

Where:

A_B = Attitude toward the behavior
b_i = The belief that performing Behavior B leads to consequence i
e_i = The evaluation of Consequence i
n = The number of salient consequences

Place in the Engle Kollat Blackwell Model (Complete Model on p. 26)

Place in the Engle Blackwell Model (Complete Model on p. 27)

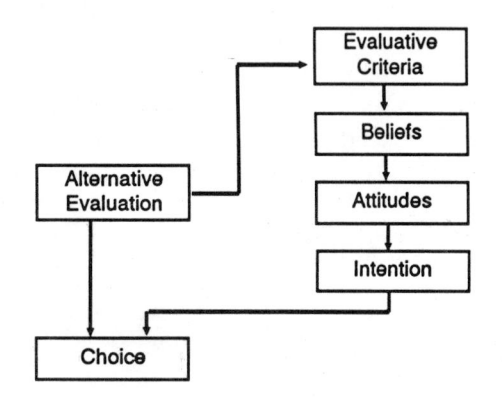

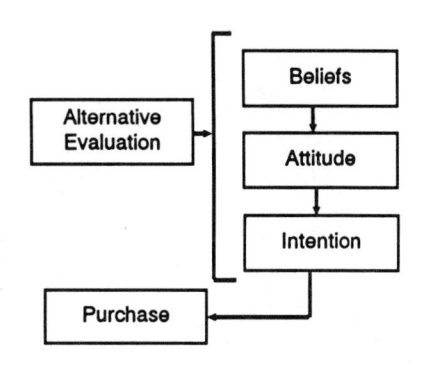

The *results* of this kind of investigation into the psychological dynamics of the choice process are likely to include *guidance for intelligent redesign of the product* as well as guidance for *pricing, promotion and physical* distribution changes. For example, the firm may discover that the product includes expensive components which are not valued by the consumer. Alternatively, the firm may discover that the consumer would greatly value a change in the product that would cost the company little or nothing to make. C.O.E. could be greatly improved by altering the product, and pricing power could be increased.

The *third and final adjustment* in the understanding of the differentiation is the question of *possible change in competitive offerings*. The discussion of product differentiation and appropriate pricing has thus far proceeded in the context of the established competitive offerings. In all probability, the multiple competitive offerings will change. Product differentiation and pricing decisions should be undertaken in the context of the competitive offerings which can be expected by the time the results of management's work come to market.

The *process of product differentiation and product pricing* may be *best understood as logical parts of the greater social job of marketing management*. Marketing managers are involved in *resource allocation*. They are rewarded when they make market matches which combine resources in such a way that society places a higher market value on the new combination than it placed on the sum of the components which were utilized.[3] Fine tuned adjustment of this allocation process within individual product design and pricing conforms to the same logic. The marketing manager may be rewarded with higher C.O.E. for including attributes in the product which are highly valued by the consumer. These deliver pricing power which might be exercised by marketing management in a number of ways. In the context of the terms used in figure 44, this means that the successfully differentiated product has attributes which appropriately address the consumer's evaluative criteria, especially those criteria which are particularly important to the consumer or "heavily weighted." The marketing manager is further rewarded when the resource allocation is also the allocation of a resource or component which is not highly valued when taken by itself in society's markets. In similar fashion, the manager is punished with reduced C.O.E. when using expensive resources to create product attributes which are not valued by the consumer.

Pricing and Designing the Differentiated Product: Other Factors Affecting Price

Understanding the nature of the differentiation results in guidance for product design, promotion, physical distribution and pricing with respect to competition. At the same time, there are other factors which affect price. For example, understanding market structure provides guidance for pricing with respect to costs. Marketing managers should also consider the options they have for management initiative, the ways the market niche as measured financially is likely to respond, the general strategic direction they want to take, and legal or ethical guidelines. Market structure, management options, response of the niche and general strategic direction are considered below. Legal and ethical guidelines comprise chapter ten.

Market Structure

The nature of the product differentiation, and the pricing power it delivers allow management to see where they might price with respect to competition. Management might for example, be able to calculate that they could price product number one at 130% of competitive product number two's price without losing market share. But management is also interested in how prices might relate to the level of costs and for this, the understanding of market structure can help.[4]

The product differentiation itself can be seen in terms of market structure. The act of successful product differentiation delivers a degree of monopoly power. The product is made more unique and the effective competition is reduced. However, underlying the differentiated product and the pricing power it delivers with respect to competition is the question of the actual number of competitors in the market, the economic market structure. This will help to determine the appropriate level of price with respect to cost. In general, the more competitors there are the more the prices of all competitors will be forced toward their costs in the manner of pure competition. In this context, the price of a successfully differentiated product, set at 130% of the competitor's price, might be a price which equals 300% of cost when there are few competitors or only 130% of cost when there are many.

Differentiated products may be found in the market structures of monopolistic competition and differentiated oligopoly. In the case of monopolistic competition, there may be relatively low barriers to entry and many sellers. In this case, the market structure is similar to pure competition with the exception of the differentiated product. The pricing power in this situation may have to come largely from the differentiated product, as the entry of many sellers will press the general price level toward costs. In the case of differentiated oligopoly, the high barriers to entry can prevent this type of downward pressure on price. Oligopolists might therefore expect a general price level well above costs, so long as demand is adequate.

Options for Management Initiative

Pricing is conditioned by the options which are open to management. Some options may be available and others unavailable. For example, management may be able to afford some product improvements and not others, some promotion and distribution options but not others. Mass media advertising may be too expensive for the firm, or management may feel that it is unethical to cater to some evaluative criteria used by consumers.

Marketing management should view their chief options as potential *investments* in products and potential investments in promotion and physical distribution. These investments can help *to create the product* in the eyes of the buyer and *thus condition the price*. This relationship is presented in figure 56.

With this extension, the price product interaction remains essentially the same. Recognition has simply been given to the fact that buyer perception of the product and thus the price he or she is willing to pay is a function of the other options which management may have exercisedp—options for investment in the product, promotion and distribution.

The Response of the Market Niche

For each combination of product, price, promotion and place that management is seriously considering, an attempt should be made to estimate or simulate the effect that strategy would have upon the three dimensional market niche. Estimates should be made of contribution margin within the offering, across the offerings and in the future. Market research or market testing can be expected to provide estimates of unit movement for each strategy considered. This in turn may be translated to revenue and, in consultation with production people, costs can be attached and contribution margin derived.

The results of these simulations or estimates can be most enlightening. A pricing strategy can have surprising results and more impact than management is likely to realize without careful consideration, simulation or estimation. Figure 57 can begin to demonstrate this. Figure 57 illustrates that two very different pricing strategies can generate the same C.O.E. This comes as a result of the economies of scale in production that are realized when the lower price causes larger numbers to be sold. While identical C.O.E. figures would be unusual, this is a fairly realistic kind of choice for management. Suppose the differentiated product has delivered some pricing power. Perhaps it has been determined that market share can be held constant with a price that is 30% above that of competitor "A." This is good information, but it does not determine the appropriate price to be 130% of competitor "A's"

Figure 56
Options for Management Initiative and the Place of Price

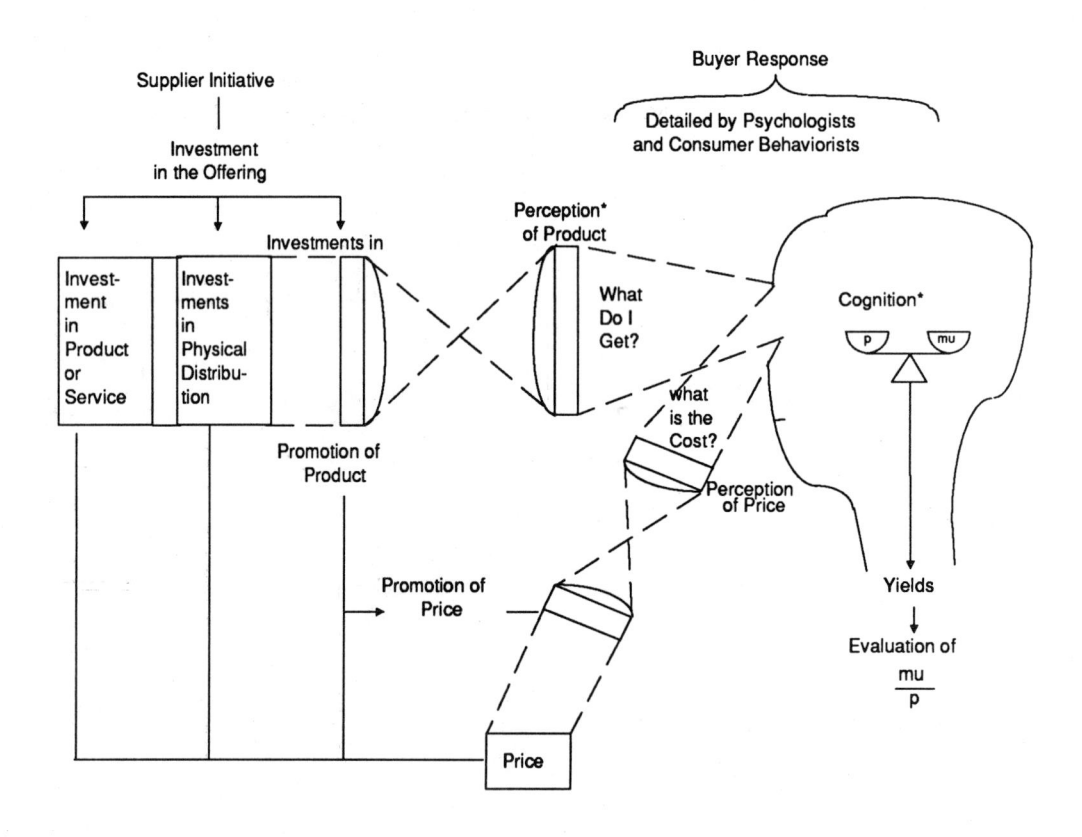

Rules of Buyer Choice

1. The purchase of an alternative will not be cosidered unless mu>p

2. The choice of alternative one will be preferred to alternative two when $\dfrac{mu_1}{p} > \dfrac{mu_2}{p_2}$

3. The buyer is indifferent between alternative one and alternative two (could choose either) when $\dfrac{mu_1}{p_1} = \dfrac{mu_2}{p_2}$

*Price sometimes affects perception of product resulting in the phenomenon of prestige pricing described in Chapter Two.

Chapter 5   169

Figure 57
Contribution Margin of the Individual Offering

High price and low price strategies can result in the same C.O.E.

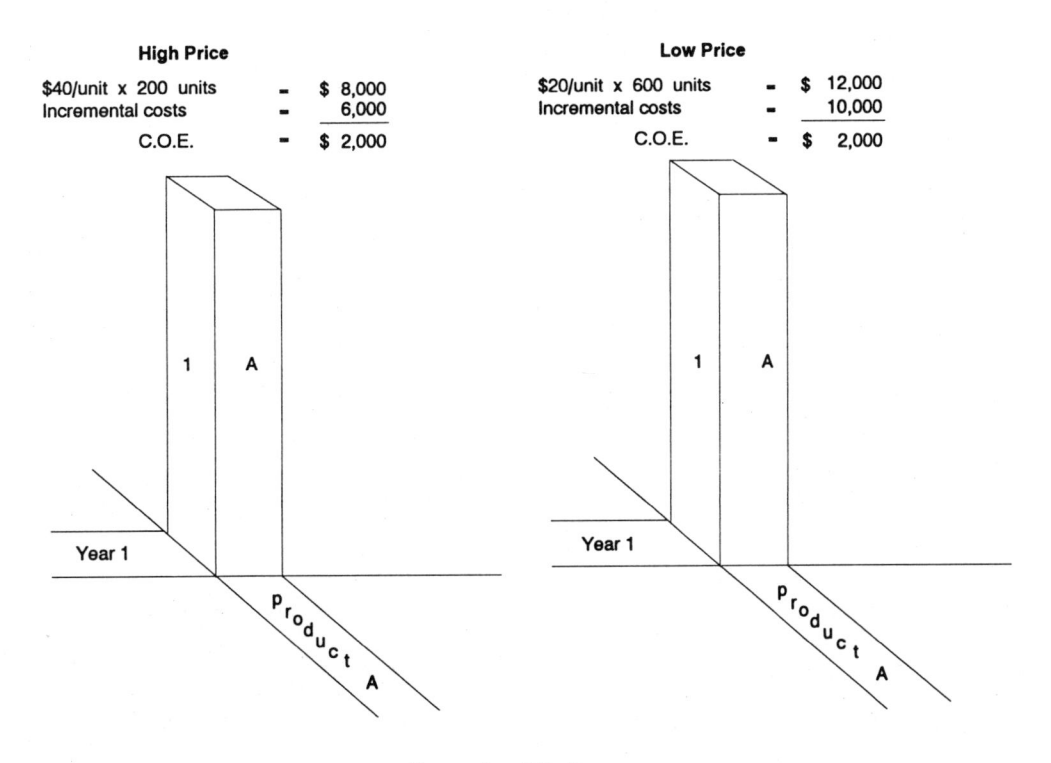

High Price

$40/unit x 200 units	=	$ 8,000
Incremental costs	=	6,000
C.O.E.	=	$ 2,000

Low Price

$20/unit x 600 units	=	$ 12,000
Incremental costs	=	10,000
C.O.E.	=	$ 2,000

Economies of Scale

$$\frac{\$6,000}{200 \text{ units}} = \$30.00/\text{unit}$$

$$\frac{\$10,000}{600 \text{ units}} = \$16.67/\text{unit}$$

price. It simply estimates that market share will probably remain constant when pricing at 130% of competitor A's price. Management may elect a high price, low market share strategy, or may elect to price at or below competitor A, intending to pick up market share.

The probable results of these kinds of choices should be examined before committing to the strategy. After examining the effect upon the contribution margin of the individual offering, as has been illustrated in figure 57, effects across the product line and in time should be considered. Figure 58 illustrates this expanded perspective. Even in the unusual case when the high price strategy yields the same C.O.E. for offering A in year 1 (A-1) as the low price strategy does, the two strategies are likely to have very different effects on the other products and on future C.O.E. If "A-1" is priced at a low level it might stimulate sales of the other products, perhaps because it is often sold to complement them. For example A-1 may be a sought after set of hiking boots and low prices on A-1 might encourage sales of the tents, attire and equipment that comprise the other offerings. On the other hand, it might be a high price on A-1 that best aids the sale of the other offerings. For example A-1 may be the prestige leader of the offerings and the others are thought to be more affordable versions of the same kind of product. In this case, a low price on A-1 could destroy the set of perceptions that encourages sales of the prestige leader as well as its more affordable versions.

Thinking about effects in the future is equally important. Taking a high price and a low market share might encourage the competition. The low share might guarantee the firm high costs of production at the same time the competition is gaining economies of scale and reducing costs. The competition might then be in a position to price so far below the firm that the pricing power of the firm's differentiated product is more than compensated. The firm may thus be trapped between high unit costs and downward pressure on price. Alternatively, the competition could refrain from placing downward pressure on price while it reinvests the resulting C.O.E. in a new generation differentiated product. The new product might give the competition pricing power at the same time its higher market share gives it lower costs. Future implications of today's pricing strategy should always be considered.

General Strategic Direction

The appropriate price and product should also be conditioned by the strategic direction of the firm. The strategy for an individual offering should logically support a cohesive marketing strategy which itself should be a component designed to fit the total organizational strategy. For example, it might be that a firm's long run strategy involves getting into a market,

Chapter 5 171

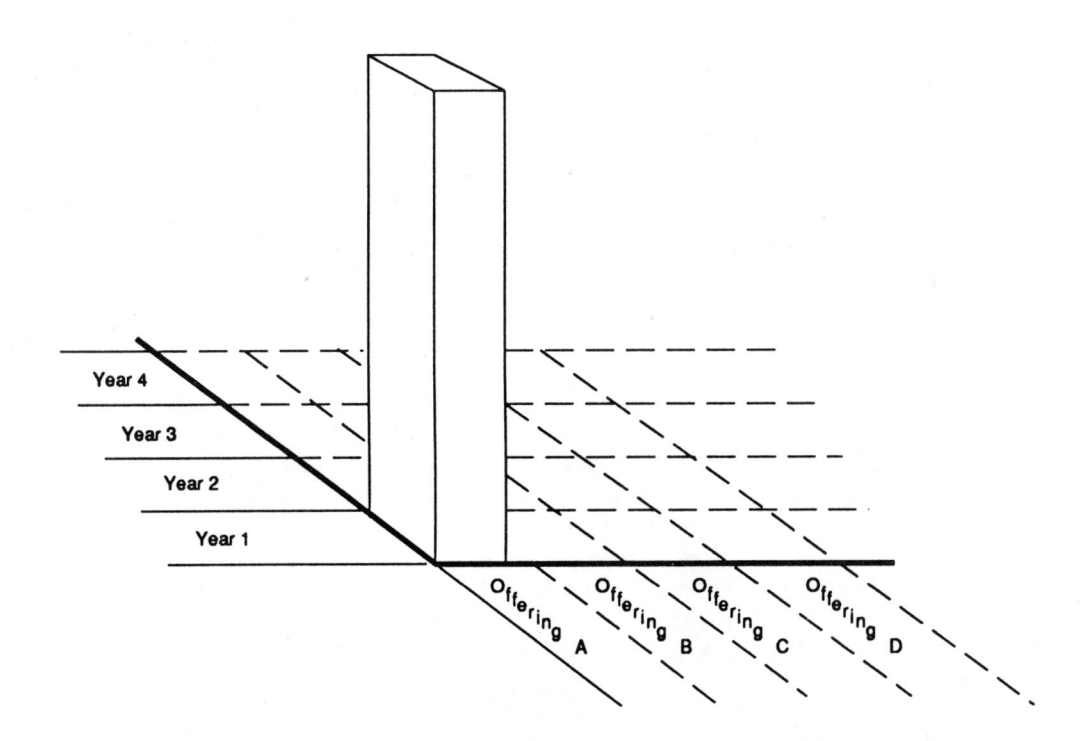

**Figure 58
Effects to Consider when Pricing**

How will pricing for a C.O.E. effect
in A-1 affect others: B-1, 2, 3, 4, 5, etc.
C-1, 2, 3, 4, 5, etc.
D-1, 2, 3, 4, 5, etc.

New Product: E-4, 5, 6, 7, etc.

Future of A: A 2, 3, 4, 5, 6, etc.

establishing itself, building an image and building market share. Aggressively maximizing the contribution margin of product lines in that target market might not support the long run objectives. In such a case, it might be better to forego some C.O.E. and view that sacrifice as an investment in attaining the market objectives. In markets where the firm has no long run ambitions, C.O.E. might be maximized. Strategic directions for the firm are discussed in detail in chapter nine.

Pricing the Monopoly Product

Marketing practitioners will have little opportunity to price true monopoly products. In those circumstances where a genuine monopoly exists, it is often regulated. In such cases, management will price by making arguments before rate making boards. These arguments are usually based upon the need to provide an adequate return to investors. In other cases there may be many substitutes for the product which is monopolized, making the pricing problem similar to the pricing of a differentiated product. For example, should public utility rates be high enough, people would buy solar panels and woodburning stoves. In these cases demand for the monopoly product will be more elastic than it would be without the substitutes.

When unregulated monopoly conditions exist, management evaluates the unit movement at various levels of price, evaluates costs at different levels of unit movement and picks the most profitable price. This procedure was illustrated in detail in chapter three. Monopolists should consider the effects of the pricing of one product upon the others and upon future market opportunities much as the vendors of differentiated products should.

Typical Pricing Objectives

Few functioning firms will view the pricing decision in the way that has just been described. They are likely to take a somewhat narrower view. They may involve themselves in *profit maximization* where this year's results are maximized without a view toward the future. They may respond to investor expectations by making pricing and product decisions so as to achieve an expected *target return*, or the return on investment which is expected in a given period. (Return on investment is detailed in appendix A.) They might pursue a *sales oriented objective*, focusing on revenues instead of contribution margin and profit. This could be motivated by the intelligent choice to pursue market share, or it could be encouraged by the possession of accounting and report systems which report revenue but do not isolate contribution margin. A firm might use an implicit *status quo objective* where change is avoided. This could be due to management lethargy or it may be due to an intelligent awareness that they do not know enough about the market to risk making a noticeable change.[5]

The Specialized Terminology of Pricing

The basic perspectives which should govern the product-price decision have been outlined. But numerous terms exist in the academic and practicing market communities which the reader should be aware of. In general, these terms are used to *describe pricing behaviors* or to *express prices*. These terms are summarized in Appendix B.

Perspectives in Product Design

There are several ways of viewing the product which are useful in planning successful product differentiation. These include the concepts of *product classes, branding and packaging*.

Product Classes

Both goods intended for consumer use and those intended for industrial use have been *classified according to the way the buyer views them*. From the point of view of the creative marketer, such classification schemes can be either good or bad. They can be good in the sense that they facilitate examination of the way a buyer views and purchases products. They can be bad because they can encourage a rigidity of thought, a tendency to think of a certain kind of product as always belonging to a certain product class. The creative marketer should view product classes as describing the way buyers ordinarily view and purchase an item. Moving an item from one classification to another constitutes an option available to those who would *innovate*, and innovation, as discussed in chapter three, can be excellent marketing strategy. Typical consumer goods classes are illustrated in figure 59, while typical industrial goods classes are illustrated in figure 60.[6]

Branding

Branding a product is selecting the name by which it will be promoted and known in the marketplace. The brand should be an efficient communication vehicle which conveys the desired product image through the buyer's perceptual and cognitive processes and lodges it in the buyer's memory. The presence of efficient communication is useful to both buyer and seller. From

Figure 59
Consumer Goods Classes

The list of consumer goods classifications is reprinted with permission from E. Jerome McCarthy and William D. Perrault, Jr., *Basic Marketing*, 9th ed. (Homewood, Illinois: Richard D. Irwin, 1987), p. 223. Definitions are original.

Classification	Definition—Example
Convenience Goods:	Goods which are successfully differentiated by making their purchase easier for the consumer
Staple	A convenience good which is routinely purchased (bread, milk)
Impulse	A convenience good which the consumer does not intend to purchase but which is given immediate consideration because of its ready availability (tabloid magazines)
Emergency	A convenience good which is immediately required and therefore purchased from the most convenient source (ambulance)
Shopping Goods:	Goods which are carefully compared (shopped) by the consumer before purchase
Homogeneous	Identical shopping goods such that $MU^1 = MU^2$. Thus purchase is made at the lowest price because only a price difference can result in $\frac{mu_1}{p_1} > \frac{mu_2}{p_2}$ (identical tool set found at several stores)
Heterogeneous	Substantially different shopping goods such that MU^1 / MU^2 (most automobiles)
Specialty Products::	Substantially differentiated products, resulting in clear product preference and little consideration of the competition (Mercedes Benz)
Creative Marketing Strategy:	In the late 1970's SAAB, a Swedish vendor of 2500-pound front drive sedans, sees General Motors planning to enter the same market. SAAB moves their car from a shopping good to a specialty good with the introduction of the sport specialty SAAB Turbo.

Figure 60
Industrial Goods Classes

The list of industrial goods classifications is reprinted with permission from E. Jerome McCarthy and William D. Perreault, Jr., *Basic Marketing*, 9th ed. (Homewood, Illinois: Richard D. Irwin, 1987), p. 228. Definitions are original.

Classification	Definition—Example
Capital Item:	A major capital investment (a new factory)
Expense item:	Something consumed during the year and charged off to the year's expenses (components of the product)
Installation:	A mechanical apparatus fixed in position for use (a heating system)
Accessory Equipment:	Equipment which is readily demountable and replacable (desktop computers)
Raw materials:	An input to the productive process which has not yet been processed (iron ore)
Component Parts & Materials:	Fabricated or partially processed items or materials which are to become a part of the product (axles, sheet steel)
Supplies:	Materials or provisions required for the ongoing maintenance and day-to-day operation of the business (paper, pencils, floorwax)
Professional Services:	A component of the work, research, or analysis that the firm must perform which is provided by an outside vendor (CPA services, legal advice, marketing consulting)
Creative Marketing Strategy:	The data analysis needs of firms have been supplied as installations and capital items (mainframes sold), expense items (lease of mainframes), accessory equipment (desktop computers), and professional services (computer payroll and accounting services marketing consulting services)

the buyers point of view it is a form of shorthand. The buyer learns to associate a brand with performance according to certain evaluative criteria. This eliminates much of the shopping task. For example the brand "Toyota" might effectively convey an image which reflects high scores according to the evaluative criteria of reliability, durability and economy. In this way the brand can aid the consumer in the shopping process, shortening the task. From the seller's point of view an image such as this is an efficient vehicle for product differentiation, which can then deliver a measure of pricing power.

The branding decision usually includes the selection of a *brand name* which is a word or set of words, and often includes the selection of a *trademark* as well, which is a unique visual image.[7] Examples of such images would include shapes or names in certain kinds of script. The brand name itself may be involved in the trademark.

A *successful brand* is often easy to spell and remember and is suggestive of the product image that it wishes to convey.[8] Examples of this would include the "Tuff-Coat" auto rustproofing and "Git Rot" rot treatment for wood. Both brand names and trademarks must be legally available for use. The *Lanham Act* provides legal protection for those using brands and also provides registration procedures.[9]

Diagnosing the level of *brand familarity* in the target market is a useful way of determining which market chores have been accomplished and which remain to be done.[10] For example, if research were to find brand *rejection*, the market would be communicating that the brand is known, but believed to be of poor quality. This indicates a major marketing problem. It is possible that the situation cannot be retrieved without a new product and/or a new brand. If research were to find *non recognition* a clean slate exists, the brand is unknown. *Recognition* indicates that the brand has been heard of. While this does not constitute a ringing positive affirmation of the brand, it is likely that a buyer will prefer a brand which is recognized to an unknown brand. With recognition, the marketing chore becomes one of building positive associations with the brand. If this effort is more effective than the similar efforts of the competitors, the result will be brand *preference*. Preference reflects successful product differentiation and delivers pricing power. When prices are equal, the preferred brand will always be selected. Thus the preferred brand will be priced at a higher level than the competitor's brand when the buyer becomes indifferent. The marketing chore may now be viewed as complete if management is satisfied with the results of having achieved brand preference. Alternatively, management may wish to invest in the achievement of brand *insistence*. In this situation, the competitors are not viewed as satisfactory substitutes. This clearly delivers a measure of pricing power approaching that of monopoly. Brand insistence may be quite difficult and expensive to achieve.

Competition Among Brands

Almost anyone can brand a product. Manufacturers, wholesalers and retailers have brands. Products may carry an individual brand name or a broader "family" brand name which expresses a relationship to other products. Also, *brand names may not directly reflect the origin of the product.* They may be licensed by their owners to others who wish to use them. Management may wish to take a low profile and offer products as unbranded or *generic* products. Management may also wish to keep the identity of the firm from being too closely associated with any given brand, thus reducing the company's risk of failure should an individual brand fail.

This profusion of brands results in a *substantial degree of competition* among them. Each is attempting to build associations in the consumer's mind which will successfully differentiate a product. Not all will be successful at this. The competition among brands is usually resolved in favor of the vendor whose brand comes to be viewed by the buyer as the best guarantee of quality and performance as tested by the buyer's important evaluative criteria.

Packaging

The package is important to the product image. The consumer perceives the offering as a subjective "whole." The buyer often perceives the packaging as an integral part of the total offering. First class products always seem to appear in first class packages, and package design can affect buyer feelings about the product. For example a menthol cigarette which is differentiated as smoking "cooler" than its competition might appeal in a cool blue and white package. Packaging has other *strategic implications* as well.[11] The size and color of a package can command shelf space and consumer attention in retail outlets.

Packaging also has *physical implications.*[12] Those making the packaging decision must weigh the cost of damaged merchandise against the cost of the packaging itself. A packaging system which allowed no damage whatsoever is likely to involve more packaging cost than is necessary. On the other hand, a packaging system which allowed damage to half of the inventory shipped is also likely to be too costly. Packaging costs must be carefully weighed against costs due to damage in shipment.

Modern packaging often uses *unit pricing* or the price per pound or other standard unit. It is also likely to be marked with the *universal product code*

(UPC) which is a series of computer readable marks which allow retailers to use computer operated inventory control systems. Packaging and labeling must conform to the Federal Fair Packaging and Labeling Act of 1966 which discourages misleading packaging. Other laws which will be outlined in chapter 10 will also affect packaging strategy.

Crossing National Boundaries

When entering a different culture the results of the equation for appropriate price and product design will change. New perceptual sets, new cultural expectations, new patterns of thought or cognition, and new evaluative criteria will substantially change the way in which a product offering creates marginal utility. The utility that a person places on money will also be different, due to substantial differences in personal values and income. Thus, the buyer decision processes leading to an evaluation of $\frac{mu}{p}$ will be greatly different.

Once these differences are understood, appropriate pricing and product design may proceed according to the general approaches set forth in this chapter. The general principles of pricing in different market structures, product differentiation and pricing power should not change, and the general rules of buyer choice should not change.

All of this might suggest that the firm should develop entirely new products for each foreign market. If sensitively done, this approach would certainly improve the marginal utility of the offerings. But, entirely new products for different markets might result in smaller unit movement per product than would be experienced with the export of existing products. This smaller unit movement could then result in such poor economies of scale that prices would have to be quite high. Prices might be so high for individualized products that the ratio $\frac{mu}{p}$ would look more attractive for the exported product; a standardized product with a lower price. These realities have brought forth *several product and communication strategies* to resolve what has come to be called the *standardization, differentiation problem* in international marketing.[13]

To deal with this problem, the same product might be exported, but promoted differently in the new country. This approach is called "product extension, communications adaptation." Alternatively the product might be altered and the general thrust of the communication kept; thus "product adaptation, communications extension." Both product and communication might be altered, thus "dual adaptation." Finally the expensive alternative of creating a new product for the overseas market might be selected, this strategy is called "product invention."[14]

The changing relationship of marginal utility to price as a product is innovated, grows, matures and declines is reflected in the international product life cycle.[15] A new innovation is often manufactured in the nation where the innovation took place. A successful innovation will have high marginal utility and little if any competition. The level of production costs and thus the lowest level of price that can be achieved would not be critical to market success at this early point. Much later in the international life cycle of a product, production can be expected to shift to points in the world where costs are much lower, thus giving management the option of offering lower prices. The innovation is now old and the marginal utility it generates may have declined, or it may have been eclipsed by the marginal utility associated with more recent offerings. Price now becomes critical to keeping the ratio of $\frac{mu}{p}$ attractive, and production moves to places in the world where low costs can be achieved.

The international environment creates many administrative difficulties for the marketing organization. The chief cause of these is currency fluctuation. Firms may be tempted to set a price by simply translating the domestic price into the overseas currency at the time the pricing decision is made. This is a convenient solution, but demonstrates an insensitivity to the nature of marginal utility, price, and buyer choice in the overseas market. A price too high or too low for the overseas market situation could logically result.

The fact that currency fluctuations are constantly occurring creates another administrative problem. Even if the price had been set with great sensitivity at the time of the original decision, the fluctuation in exchange rates can result in *constant price fluctuation*. This would occur if the price had been set in terms of the home currency and held constant in those terms. This constant value would translate to different prices in the overseas currency on a continuous basis. On the other hand holding the price as stated in the overseas currency constant will result in *fluctuations in C.O.E.* when the results of the exchanges are translated into the home currency. These kinds of problems can be approached using administrative systems for price indexing or price review. International marketers will have to remain sensitive to changes in their real economic price in overseas markets, as well as to the effects of currency fluctuation on contribution margin.

Finally, international pricing decisions may have important tax effects. When a good, service, component part or material is transferred from one international division of a firm to another, a price is often set for accounting purposes. This price, which is attached to such "intra-corporate international transfers" is referred to as the *transfer price*.[16] Adjustment of the transfer price allows the firm to move stated profit from one nation to another. This can result in a reduction of tax liabilities, because different nations have different tax rates. For example, a firm might want to show more profit in a low tax nation and less profit in a high tax nation. Transfers from the low tax nation should be priced high and transfers to the low tax nation should be priced low. This will encourage high stated profit in the low tax nation. Legal difficulties can arise from this practice however. Section 482 of the US internal revenue code institutes regulations which have as their goal transfer pricing at the market price of the item.[17] Managerial difficulties may also result from transfer prices which deviate from market price. Managers whose performance is evaluated by stated profit are sure to complain if that stated profit is artificially reduced.

Chapter Summary

Pricing and product design may be approached as separate managerial decisions. This is most appropriate in the case of homogeneous or undifferentiated products. In the case of differentiated products, the nature and degree of differentiation from the competition may deliver a measure of pricing power, or ability to charge higher prices. In this way pricing and design of differentiated products are inextricably intertwined. Promotion and physical distribution may be seen as extensions or alterations of the product and so should also be considered when pricing.

The appropriate combination of price and product design is conditioned by the nature of the product differentiation if any, the market structure, the options open to management, the way in which the market niche can be expected to respond, general strategic direction, law and ethics.

Successful product differentiation may be achieved in many ways. These include differentiating with an understanding of the buyer's evaluative criteria, vending the product in a new class or category, creative branding and creative packaging.

Crossing international boundaries brings special problems in pricing and product design. These include the effects differing cultures will have upon the buyers evaluation of marginal utilities and prices, the problems which come as a result of currency fluctuation and the choice of intra-corporate transfer prices.

[1]Martin Fishbein, "An Investigation of the Relationships between Beliefs about an Object and the Attitude toward that Object," *Human Relations* 16 (August 1963), pp. 233-240. See also Milton J. Rosenburg, "Cognitive Structure and Attitudinal Effect," *Journal of Abnormal and Social Psychology* 53 (November 1956), pp. 367-72. An article reviewing issues in the use of such models is provided by William L. Wilkie and Edgar A. Pessemier, "Issues in Marketing's Use of Multi-Attribute Attitude Models," in *Journal of Marketing*, 10 (November 1973), pp. 428-441.

[2]For a discussion of conjoint analysis see David S. Aaker and George S. Day, *Marketing Research*, 3rd ed. (New York: John Wiley and Sons, 1986), pp. 491-505.

[3]Market matches as used here should be seen in the context of Wroe Alderson, *Marketing Behavior and Executive Action* (Homewood, Illinois: Richard D. Irwin, 1957), pp. 195-227.

[4]A complete discussion of market structure and the resulting price-cost relationships is available in F. M. Scherer, *Industrial Market Structure and Economic Performance*, 2nd ed. (Chicago: Rand McNally College Publishing, 1980).

[5]The profit maximization assumption is criticized and other hypotheses discussed in William J. Baumol, *Business Behavior, Value and Growth* (New York: The Macmillan Co., 1959). The list of pricing objectives is reprinted with permission from E. Jerome McCarthy and William D. Perreault, Jr., *Basic Marketing*, 9th ed. (Homewood, Illinois: Richard D. Irwin, 1987), pp. 448-451.

[6]Goods classifications have been useful in marketing analysis for some time. See, for example, Richard H. Holton, "The Distinction between Convenience Goods, Shopping Goods and Specialty Goods," *Journal of Marketing* 22 (July 1958), pp. 53-56. The lists appearing here as figures 59 and 60 are essentially those appearing in E. Jerome McCarthy and William D. Perreault, Jr., *Basic Marketing*, 9th ed. (Homewood, Illinois: Richard D. Irwin, 1987), pp. 223, 228.

[7]Trademark Act of 1946, 45, U.S.C. & 1127 (1976). As cited in Louis W. Stern and Thomas L. Eovaldi, *Legal Aspects of Marketing Strategy* (Englewood Cliffs, N.J.: Prentice Hall, 1984), p. 43.

[8]McCarthy, p. 239.

[9]Stern, pp. 50-61.

[10]McCarthy, p. 238. See also Kent B. Monroe, "The Influence of Price Differences and Brand Familiarity on Brand Preferences," *Consumer Research* (June 1976), pp. 42-49.

[11]McCarthy, p. 243. See also Douglas M. Lambert and James R. Stock, *Strategic Physical Distribution Management* (Homewood, Illinois: Richard D. Irwin, 1982), p. 198. See also Joan F. Spencer, "A Picture of Packaging in the Context of Physical Distribution," *Handling and Shipping*, 18 No. 10 (October 1977), p. 47.

[12]Ibid.

[13] See S. Tamer Cavusgil and John R. Nevin, "State of the Art in International Marketing an Assessment," in *Review of Marketing 1981*, eds. Ben M. Enis and Kenneth J. Roering (Chicago: American Marketing Association 1981), p. 200 for an introduction to the literature in this area.

[14] This classification of strategy is from Warren J. Keegan, "Multinational Product Planning: Strategic Alternatives," *Journal of Marketing* 33 (January 1969), pp. 58-62. Reprinted with permission of the American Marketing Association, Chicago, IL.

[15] Raymond Vernon, "International Investment and International Trade in the Product Cycle," *Quarterly Journal of Economics* (May 1966), pp. 190-207. Copyright 1966 by John Wiley and Sons, Inc. Reprinted by permission of John Wiley and Sons, Inc.

[16] Maurice Levi, *International Finance, Financial Management and the International Economy* (New York: McGraw-Hill, 1983), pp. 256-258.

[17] Stefan H. Robock, Kenneth Simmonds, and Jack Zwick, *International Business and Multinational Enterprises* (Homewood, Illinois: Richard D. Irwin, 1977), p. 467.

APPENDIX B

Commonly Used Terms to Describe Pricing Behavior and Express Price

Allowance Allowable:	A reduction of price in exchange for something of value.
Allowance, Advertising:	A reduction of price in exchange for the buyer's commitment to advertise the product.
Allowance, trade in:	A reduction of price in exchange for something traded in.
Average cost pricing:	Calculating historical average costs, adding a profit margin and obtaining price. (This 1. ignores market demand, 2. relies upon a cost structure which varies with the number of units sold.)
Bait pricing:	Unethically and illegally using the philosophy of the price leader (defined below) when in fact the leader is not available for sale.
Bid pricing:	Submitting competitive offers to vend goods or services.
Complementary product pricing:	Pricing products which complement each other, such as table and chairs, with an awareness of how the pricing of one might affect the sales of the other.
Demand backward pricing:	Evaluating market reaction to various prices prior to setting the price.
Discount:	A reduction of price.
Experience curve pricing:	Pricing in recognition of expected cost improvements based upon further experience in the production process. This can result in prices which are below historical costs.
Flexible price policy:	A willingness to enter into individual negotiations resulting in price adjustments.

F.O.B.:	Freight on board or free on board. The F.O.B. point designates the geographic location where title of the item is transferred and the transport costs become the responsibility of the new owner (e.g., $100 f.o.b. Detroit).
Freight absorption pricing:	Choosing not to include transportation costs in the price, thus absorbing particularly expensive transportation with reduced C.O.E.
Full line pricing:	Pricing different products in relation to one another so as to recognize the position of each in the total product line. For example pricing to keep Chevrolet products at lower prices than Cadillac products in the General Motors line.
Introductory price dealing:	Special low price to spur the market entry of a new offering.
List:	The official published price.
Markdown:	An amount or percentage subtracted from the list price to arrive at selling price.
Markup:	A percentage of cost which is added to cost to arrive at selling price. (It is sometimes used to mean a percentage of list price which describes the difference between price and cost.)
Non price competition:	Defending or increasing market share by adjusting product promotion or physical distribution and avoiding any reduction of price.
Odd-Even pricing:	Choosing an exact price level which encourages the perception of price as being low, thus improving the ratio $\frac{mu}{p}$. For example $5.95 might be perceived as five dollars and change, or as an even $6.00, rather than the $6.19 it would come to with 4% sales tax.
One price policy:	Avoiding special deals for individual customers or groups of customers.
Penetration price policy:	A low price high unit movement strategy.
PMS:	Special incentives for sales people to promote specific offerings.

Prestige pricing:	Choosing a high level of price in hopes that the high price will communicate quality or exclusivity. When this is unusually successful, the high price affects MU more than it affects P and more is demanded at the higher price.
Price leader:	An offering at an attractively low price which may encourage interest in other offerings in the product or service line.
Psychological Pricing:	Pricing with recognition of the buyers evaluative criteria and how they affect marginal utility and thus the ratio of marginal utility to price $\frac{mu}{p}$.
Quantity discount:	A reduction of price for buyers purchasing a certain quantity. This often reflects economies of scale.
Quantity discount, cumulative:	A reduction of price for buyers purchasing a certain quantity, when the quantity is allowed to add up or accumulate over a period of time.
Quantity discount; non-cumulative:	A reduction of price for buyers purchasing a certain quantity at one time.
Rebate:	A cash payment from vendor to buyer which may be used to reduce the net price of the offering.
Seasonal discount:	A reduction of price for buyers purchasing an item during a particular season (often a season of low demand).
Skimming price policy:	A high price low unit movement strategy.
Terms, 1%10 net 30:	One percent may be deducted from the invoiced or billed amount if paid within ten days. If not, the total invoiced amount is due in thirty days. Note: This means that the buyer pays 1% to use the money 20 days, and effective annual interest rate of 18.25%.
Terms, cash discount:	A reduction of price for buyers purchasing with cash instead of credit.
Terms, net:	The net or full amount is due immediately upon purchase.

Trade or functional discount:	A reduction of price for intermediate or wholesale buyers who agree to perform a function such as storage.
Trading stamp:	Stamps which when accumulated in sufficient number, may be used to reduce the net price of products. Often given in lieu of cash discounts as they are only redeemable with the same vendor.
Uniform delivered pricing:	Including transportation costs in the price by including a freight change which does not discriminate between long and short distances.
Value in use pricing:	Pricing in the context of an understanding of the economic advantage the offering will deliver to the buyer.
Zone pricing:	Including transportation costs in the price by dividing up the delivery area into zones and charging transportation costs according to the costs of serving the zone to which the delivery is made.

Question for Study, Discussion and Examination

1. Could you define, or explain to a friend who has not studied marketing, each of the following terms? Can you give examples of each?
    a. Managerial variables which are the responsibility of marketing management (the marketing "mix")
    b. Homogeneous product
    c. Differentiated product
    d. Product-price interaction
    e. Promotion and place as adjusting product-price interaction
    f. Price taker
    g. $\frac{mu}{p}$ in economic terms, in psychological terms
    h. Perfect elasticity of demand in terms of $\frac{mu}{p}$
    i. Pricing power
    j. Pricing power in relation to costs
    k. Pricing power in relation to competition
    l. Evaluative criteria as affecting MU
    m. Linear model of the alternative evaluation process
    n. Conjoint measurement
    o. Product design and pricing as resource allocation
    p. Options for management initiative and their effects on product and price
    q. Response of the market niche and its effect on product and price
    r. General strategic direction and its effect on product and price
    s. Profit maximization objective
    t. Target return objective
    u. Sales oriented objective
    v. Status quo objective
    w. Terms in appendix B
    x. Product classes
    y. Innovative marketing strategy using product classes
    z. Terms in figure 59
    aa. Terms in figure 60
    ab. Branding
    ac. Brand name
    ad. Trademark
    ae. Lanham Act
    af. Brand familiarity (5 levels)

ag. competition among brands
ah. Strategic implications of packaging
ai. Physical implications of packaging
aj. Effect on $\frac{mu}{p}$ when crossing national boundaries
ak. Effect on buyer choice rules when crossing national boundaries
al. International product strategies; product extension-communications adaption, product adaptation-communications extension, dual adaption, product invention
am. Each international product strategy in terms of $\frac{mu}{p}$ and economies of scale
an. International product life cycle in terms of $\frac{mu}{p}$
ao. Transfer price

2. When does it make sense to see the pricing decision as one separate from the decision of which product to offer? When does it make sense to see product design and price to be "inextricably intertwined," a product-price interaction?

3. How do promotion and physical distribution affect the product price relationship? How can "MU" be affected? How can "P" be affected?

4. Discuss the perfectly elastic demand that faces the price taking supplier in pure competition. Describe the phenomenon of perfect elasticity in economic terms and in psychological terms. Use the construct $\frac{mu}{p}$ to describe what is happening.

5. "Pricing strategy for homogeneous products largely involves the understanding of competitive effects on the level of price." Explain this statement in the context of pure competition and undifferentiated oligopoly. Is there any pricing power with respect to costs available to vendors in these situations? Is there any pricing power with respect to competition available in these situations?

6. Explain how the pricing power that offering one has with respect to offering two in the mind of an individual consumer can be approximated. Use the construct $\frac{mu}{p}$.

7. How can pricing power be translated from individual buyer reaction to market or market segment reaction? How can this be used to develop estimates of C.O.E.?

8. Can pricing power be approximated without understanding the psychological dynamics behind a consumer's evaluation of marginal

utility? Why study these psychological dynamics? How might linear models of alternative evaluation or the technique of conjoint measurement fit into this process?

9. Should product design and price be evaluated in the context of the current competition? Why or why not?

10. In what sense is product design, product differentiation and pricing an exercise in resource allocation? What is encouraged and what is discouraged in this process? How would you evaluate this process from a social point of view?

11. What other factors affect or condition price beyond the product differentiation? How does each work?

12. In what sense is management making investment decisions when deciding upon product, price, promotion and place? What are the objectives of these investments?

13. Which develops more C.O.E., a high price low unit movement strategy or a low price high unit movement strategy? Will there be other C.O.E. effects besides the effect upon the C.O.E. of the offerings in question? Why or why not? Do the pricing alternatives mentioned above have specific names? What should influence the choice of an alternative beyond the C.O.E. calculations suggested?

14. What is the objective when choosing a brand? What kinds of brands tend to be successful?

15. How is the competition which exists among brands often resolved?

16. How should packaging money be invested? How can this be decided?

17. Explain the logic of the several product and communication strategies useful in resolving the standardization differentiation problem in international marketing. Explain how each related to $\frac{mu}{P}$ and how each might generate contribution margin.

18. Describe possible problems when currency fluctuations occur and:

    18a: Price is set by simply translating the domestic price to overseas currency

    18b: Price is set in terms of a sensitive understanding of $\frac{mu}{P}$ in the overseas market, but price is set and held constant in terms of the overseas currency.

18c: Price is set in terms of a sensitive understanding of $\frac{mu}{P}$ in the overseas market, but price is set and held constant in terms of the home currency.

How might problems such as these be avoided?

19. How does the transfer price affect the international location of profit? Why should the firm be concerned about this? What are the goals of the US internal revenue service (IRS) with respect to transfer pricing?

CHAPTER 6

ADJUSTING THE EXCHANGE: ALTERING THE PRICE— PRODUCT INTERACTION WITH PROMOTION

The buyer's perception of the product and its price can be adjusted by saying things about them. Marginal utility can be altered and perception of price can be changed. Investments in communication activities may thus be financially justified when the communications successfully defend or enhance the market niche of the organization. Communications may be *inbound*, providing information to management about the environment, or *outbound*, reflecting management's initiatives. This chapter focuses on outbound communication. Inbound communication, exemplified by market research and other information gathering approaches, will be treated in chapter eight.

Communications efforts can be *expensive*. Keeping a salesperson on the road can cost well over $80,000 per year, while some companies have advertising budgets which exceed $1,000,000,000.00 a year. With these kinds of costs it is easy to see how *communications efforts can result in a reduction of contribution margin* even when they have been "effective" in achieving communication goals. For this reason marketing management must be aware of the characteristics of the many communications options that they have. In this way they might be able to select "cost-effective" communications which contribute more to incremental revenue than to incremental cost. Management may elect to emphasize one type of communication almost to the exclusion of others, but most organizations select a balanced *blend* of communications, designed to work in harmony.

The General Problem

The general problem is to improve contribution margin by communicating with a target audience so as to improve demand, reduce costs, reduce competition or achieve a more favorable business environment. Traditional *promotion* activity interprets this mandate as requiring communication with a target market about the firm and its offerings. But other forms of corporate communications, such as *public relations* interpret the mandate to include broader communications activities such as press relations and lobbying.

The Options

There are many communications options open to management. Each will be examined in terms of its particular strengths and weaknesses in generating contribution margin.

Sales Promotion

Sales promotion involves the creation of short term communication and incentive packages. These may be directed at the firm's sales force, to stimulate excitement, to motivate, or to boost morale. Special contests and trips might be used. Sales promotion may be directed at individuals and businesses in the trade, using special allowances or contests for dealers and distributors. It can also be directed toward the consumer, using such interest generating offers as free samples, rebates and contests. The idea of this kind of communication is to peak interest by offering something different and exciting. In order to achieve this, the sales promotion is often expensive. Because such efforts tend to be expensive and because they are designed to be different and exciting they are rarely designed to last more than a short period of time.

Public Relations

Public Relations people are concerned with enhancing the organization's image. They are well paid, with salaries ranging to over $65,000.[1] They involve themselves with the press, with government and with other important groups who may influence the firm's environment. They develop relations with the press so as to be able to convince members of the press that positive aspects of the organization and its offerings are newsworthy and that the negative aspects are not. This is referred to as managing *publicity*. This can be a particularly cost effective investment when the organization is not expected to engage in much advertising and sales, as might be the case with hospitals or colleges and universities. It can also be particularly cost effective when there are aspects of the organization's activities which are apt to be viewed negatively. Relations with government take the form of *lobbying* which has as its goal the modification of government activities so as to create a more favorable business environment. Lobbyists are cost effective investments when government activity has a great effect on the organization's market niche. The government has substantial effects on the market niche when price subsidies or controls are involved, when barriers to entry are involved, when government regulation affects the content of the offering or the cost of production, and when government constitutes an important customer. Lobbyists are particularly cost effective when any of these government policies may be in the process of reevaluation or change. Public relations people may also communicate with *other important target audiences* both inside and outside the organization when the goal is improvement of the organization's image or modification of the organization's environment.

Advertising

Advertising is a communication aimed at a group, without the personal, interactive nature of the salesperson or lobbyist communications. Advertising can be extremely expensive and creates a substantial barrier to entry in those industries which require large amounts of it. Since advertising is expensive and does not employ the interactive human sensitivity of the individual lobbyist or salesperson, it is important that advertising be designed with great awareness of consumer psychology. Otherwise large amounts of money might be wasted.

For this reason a consumer behavior model is useful in designing advertising strategy. The Engle Blackwell Model, reproduced as figure 61 would guide advertisers to ask the following kinds of *diagnostic questions* when designing an advertising campaign:

1. What have we done to insure that the proper target market is *exposed* to this advertisement? Is it in the appropriate magazine? Is it on the appropriate TV channel or radio station in accordance with the target market's *media habits*? How do we fit into their *search behavior*? What research should be run on this?

2. What have we done to ensure that once exposed, the target audience will pay *attention* to this advertisement? Have we done what we can with color, contrast, music, visual images? What research should we run on this?

Figure 61
Consumer Behavior Perspectives Are Useful in Advertising

Above: The Engle-Blackwell High Involvement Model (Figure 2.7 from *Consumer Behavior*, Fifth Edition, by James F. Engle, Roger D. Blackwell, and Paul W. Miniard. Copyright 1986). Below: The Engle-Kollat-Blackwell Model (Figure 20.4 from *Consumer Behavior*, Third Edition, by James F. Engle, Roger D. Blackwell, David T. Kollat). Reprinted by permission of the Dryden Press, a Division of Holt, Rinehart and Winston Inc.

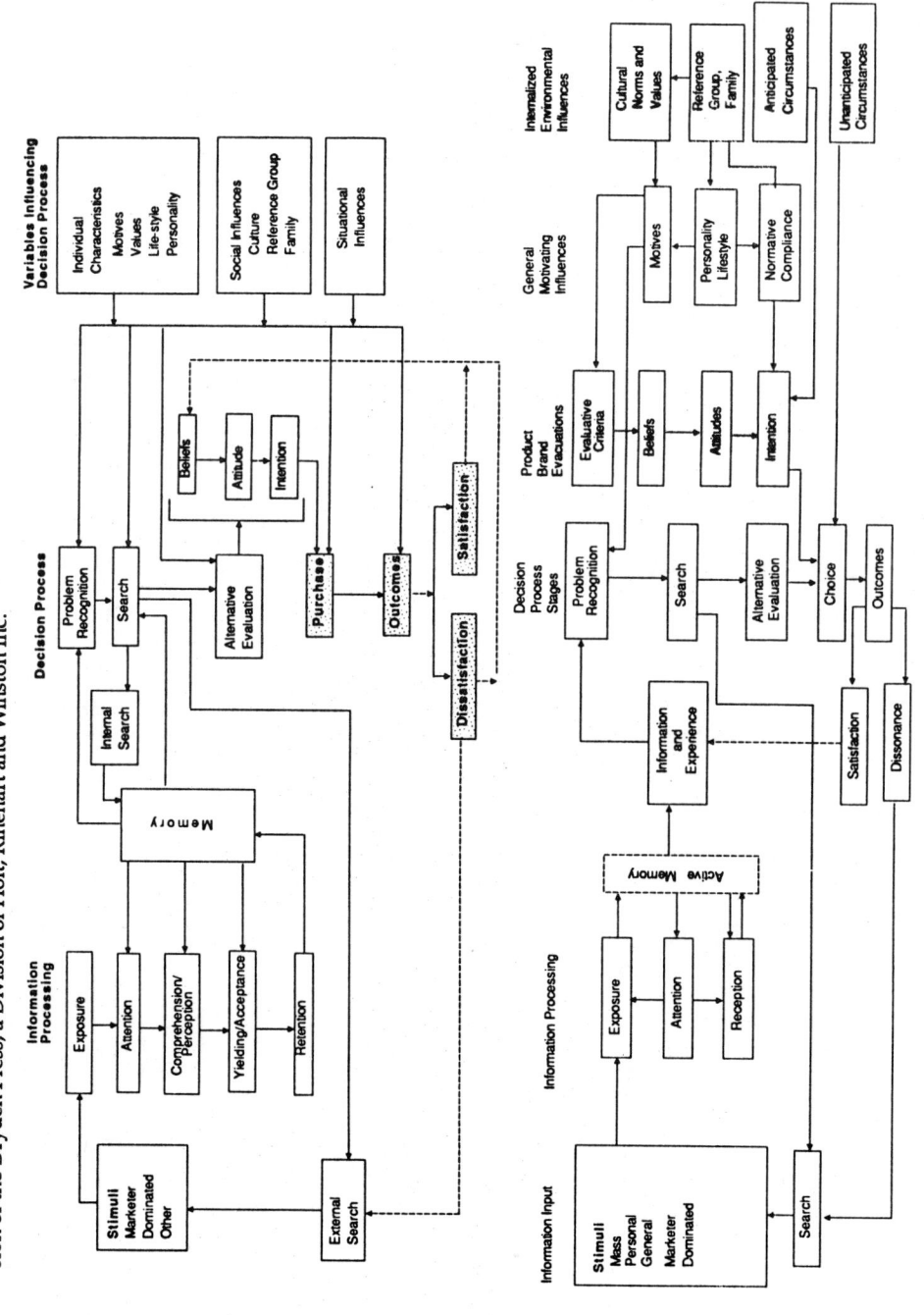

3. Will they understand or *comprehend* this advertisement the way we want them to? Should we research what they understand about the ad and make necessary modifications before running the ad in a full scale way?
4. Are they yielding and *accepting* the message or posing *counter arguments* to it? What are the counter arguments and how might the ad be redesigned to deal with them?
5. Are they *retaining the message in memory* the way we want them to? Is our product a member of the "evoked set" of alternatives called forth when memory is searched for alternatives?
6. Does the consumer *recognize the problem* that we are attempting to solve? Should we, strategically and ethically, be involved in creating or aiding problem recognition?
7. What are the *alternatives being evaluated*? What are the *buyers beliefs* about how the alternatives perform in light of his or her *evaluative criteria*? What are the evaluative criteria and their *relative importance*? Given this, does the advertisement *differentiate* the product in a successful way?
8. Should we be advertising to confirm satisfaction or reduce dissonance (or dissatisfaction) in buyers who have already purchased our product?
9. Should the advertisement be aimed toward reference groups or opinion leaders or toward individual family members?

Gestalt or total image effects become extremely important in advertising. An advertisement may attract only a few seconds of the consumer's attention. In this time it must convey its message about the vendor, the product attributes and how they address the consumer's evaluative criteria. For this reason, *great emphasis is placed on the ability to develop messages and visual images which efficiently wrap the offering in appropriate associations and lodge the entire package in memory. This is a very involved chore to be accomplished during a few seconds.*

As a first step, it is critical that the appropriate media channel be selected so that the target market is *exposed* to the advertisement. Media vendors price their services according to the *demographics* that they "deliver." This means that they keep track of who reads their paper or watches their program. They characterize this audience with statistics called demographics and sell the media time or space based upon how many of what types of people are being reached. Once the appropriate people are exposed, *attention must be gained*. Achieving attention has become a high art. Automobiles have been lifted to the tops of mountains, giant replicas of watches have been sunk in the sea, sound levels of advertisements have been raised, celebrities have been employed and intentionally irritating ads designed.

Once attention is captured, the ad must still be *understood*. Advertisers have come to realize that people will organize, interpret and attach meaning to stimuli according to what they already expect and understand. This is due to perception being a function of previously established perceptual sets (as introduced in chapter one) and to the fact that people do not tolerate ambiguity well. Comprehension will therefore be a result of a person's attempt to organize ideas and fill in missing parts, forming a complete and relatively unambiguous understanding of the situation. Such principles invite the marketing communicator to be sensitive to what consumers already perceive and believe, as well as to how messages can be made more understandable using bright or somber colors, nuances communicated by music, and appearances of actors. Powerful generalizations may be drawn from very modest sets of clues.

Acceptance, or receiving a message with approval, is also dependent upon existing beliefs and understandings. Cognitive dissonance, introduced in chapter one, may prevent the acceptance of a message. Cognitive dissonance is the state of psychic discomfort which an individual experiences when there is conflict between thoughts and behaviors. For example, a person who believes that smoking causes cancer may continue to smoke. Such a person is likely to experience *cognitive dissonance*. Because dissonance is uncomfortable, the individual will try to adjust either thought or behavior to reduce the dissonance. This usually takes the form of an adjustment to whichever is easiest to adjust. If the belief or attitude is held strongly, it may be the behavior that changes. If, on the other hand, the behavior has the tenacity of a genuine nicotine addiction, the beliefs and attitudes may change.

Into this potentially tension charged environment, the communication which is *not* consistent with current beliefs, attitudes and behaviors enters as a "*dissonant element*." Rejection of such an element reduces or avoids psychic tension and discomfort. Acceptance of such an element creates or exacerbates psychic tension and discomfort. The psychology of the consumer protects itself by rejecting dissonant elements or by exercising *perceptual defense*; erecting barriers to their very perception. Perceptual defense, introduced in chapter one, may prevent a message from being attended to or comprehended, to say nothing of being accepted. Using similar logic, messages which serve to reduce dissonance are more likely to be accepted, as they reduce psychic discomfort.

Occasionally a communication which is a dissonant element will overcome these barriers and be accepted. It may simply be powerful and irrefutable. The news that Pearl Harbor was bombed invades the mind and must be accepted. If on the day previous, the individual felt secure in a perfectly *stable* system of beliefs which included the belief that such an event was impossible, the message still cannot be avoided. It is simple, straightforward, powerful and irrefutable. It overwhelms psychic defenses. It cannot be rejected and the dissonance its acceptance then brings must be born. Previous beliefs and attitudes must yield and adjust. Seldom can marketers muster this kind of overwhelming psychological power.

It is more likely that dissonant elements can be lodged if other dissonant elements are already present. In these cases the mind is already experiencing some amount of cognitive dissonance. In *unstable* cases such as these, the new element may join a constellation of allied elements and "tip the balance" or cause the belief and attitude structure to yield or adjust.

When marketers are confronted with *stable* belief and attitude systems they may be well advised to avoid the direct assault and try to further their ends by playing upon beliefs and attitudes which already exist. If stable beliefs and attitudes must be changed, and an overwhelming "Pearl Harbor" style message cannot be designed, then marketers might formulate the communication process in *multiple stages*. In this procedure, the first stage is to destabilize a belief and attitude system with the introduction of small, seemingly trivial but irrefutable pieces of information which, when accepted become dissonant elements. For example, an auto salesperson may be confronted with a potential customer to whom safety is an important evaluative criterion. This person has a stable belief and attitude system which holds that the competitor's car is safer. The salesman might then gently pass on a copy of an irrefutable government crash test or insurance safety statistic wherein the salesperson's vehicle outperforms competition. Once lodged, the dissonant element awaits opportunities to form alliances with other communications to eventually cause belief, attitude and behavioral change.

All of these activities would have little net effect if they needed to occur just as the consumer was making a choice. The process is difficult enough without demanding that kind of timing from the communicator. But, people routinely store information in *memory* for later retrieval when recognition of a problem triggers a search for information. The nature of human memory is a mystery which is slowly being unraveled by psychologists, but a few principles are useful to marketers in the current state of knowledge. First, retention in memory appears to be facilitated when information is grouped into a *chunk*. A chunk is a grouping of information familiar to the person which can be processed as a unit.[2] Thus, a brand name may operate as a "chunk." Alternatively, a *visual image personality* (VIP) such as the Pillsbury Doughboy may operate as a chunk. A chunk may also be an easily remembered symbol which carries the grouped information into memory with it.

The chunk is effective because of all of the information that is readily associated with it. *Association* means a union or connection of ideas.[3] Associations determine the placement of something in memory, in the sense of the other ideas it may be connected with. When something is retrieved from memory or recalled, it is generally recalled in the context of the other things associated with it. When a group of ideas or memories are commonly recalled together, that set of ideas or memories may be referred to as the *evoked set*. The concept of the evoked set is useful to marketers in that marketers may want to choose symbols, brand names and visual images with the motive of evoking certain sets of associated ideas. For example the name "Accura" may have been chosen for a Honda automobile because it suggests accuracy and would thus be "evocative" of such ideas as precision engineering and accuracy in design and manufacture. The name of the parent company, Honda, may still evoke ideas about motorcycles in the minds of many consumers.

How long an item is retained in memory may be a function of how important it seems to the customer when it is first perceived. If it is seen as important to achieving goals or solving problems it appears to be more likely that it will be retained.[4] For this and other reasons marketing communicators may wish to stimulate *problem recognition* as a part of their communications strategy. Problem recognition has been defined by Engle and Blackwell as the distance between the ideal state and the actual state. Problem recognition may be stimulated if the ideal state is elevated, as when an individual first sees a desirable new car. Alternatively it may be stimulated when the actual state deteriorates, as when the individual's current car fails by the side of the road. Problem recognition initiates the consumer decision making process, and facilitates the transfer of ideas into long term memory.

The foregoing has served to introduce the psychological complexity of the advertising chore; the problem of wrapping the offering in appropriate associations and lodging it in memory. It is only an introduction. The many psychological nuances and the many possible strategic objectives of organizations guarantee that there will be many more useful perspectives from which psychology and the process of communication may be viewed. Advertising may for example be intended to stimulate classical conditioning, encouraging the association of appropriate feelings with their product or service. This perspective was introduced in chapter two.

The *traditional advertising response to this* daunting *psychological challenge* has been *creativity*. Creative people, artists who appreciate the subtlety of perception, have initiated the "big ideas", the "message appeals" and the artistic execution of ad campaigns.[5] Strategic direction has been provided by those who must approve and pay for the campaign. Quite often the creative people are employees of *advertising agencies*, firms specializing in adverting, while those approving and paying for the campaign are employees of the firm offering the product or service being advertised. The firm purchasing the advertising is referred to as an *account*.

As scientific understanding of the advertising communication process has advanced, the efforts of creative artistic people have been supplemented by the efforts of more scientifically oriented people. But nothing has become so scientific that the spark of creative initiative has not been required. Artistic initiative may now be researched, analyzed, coaxed and evaluated scientifically, but the complexity and subtlety of the chore is such that it is unlikely that science will soon replace art in advertising.

Advertisements may employ *various types of message appeals*. A message appeal is the specific approach the communicator takes in addressing the buyer's needs. They may appeal to rationality or emotion; they may be focused upon product attributes and benefits or upon the consumer and the lifestyle facilitated by the product.[6] They may appeal to any level on Maslow's Hierarchy of Needs (figure 62). The message appeal may be neatly encapsulated in a *big idea*.[7] A big idea is a communication which serves as a "chunk"; efficiently suggesting associations. For example "the Marlboro Man" was a big idea which suggested associations with rugged individualism. "The friendly skies of United" was a chunk which communicated associations which would relax an individual about the idea of flying. Supporting the big idea in an advertisement is the *copy thrust*. The copy thrust is a statement which summarizes the concepts that the advertisement intends to communicate. The big idea and the copy thrust may be communicated to the account using a *story board* or a set of drawings showing the proposed advertisement in proper sequence. Any aspect of advertising design, from media choice through understanding of consumer evaluative criteria, the big idea, the message appeal, and creative execution may be scientifically researched. In general the research can give some idea about the communications effectiveness of the advertising approach.

But executives must be worried about more than communications effectiveness. Executives must be worried about the *cost effectiveness* or efficiency of the communication. And so the psychological, creative and scientific perspectives must in the end be governed by the economic and financial perspectives that the executive can bring to bear.

Beyond choices in the areas already discussed, the executive must make decisions concerning the *general types of advertising*.[8] These types include *product advertising*, which communicates aspects of the individual product, and *institutional advertising*, which communicates aspects of the organization

Figure 62
A Message Appeal May Appeal to Any Level
of Maslow's Hierarchy of Needs

Maslow's *Heirarchy from Motivation and Personality*, Second Edition, by Abraham H. Maslow. Copyright 1954 by Harper and Row Publishers Inc. Copyright 1970 by Abraham H. Maslow. Reprinted by permission of the publisher.

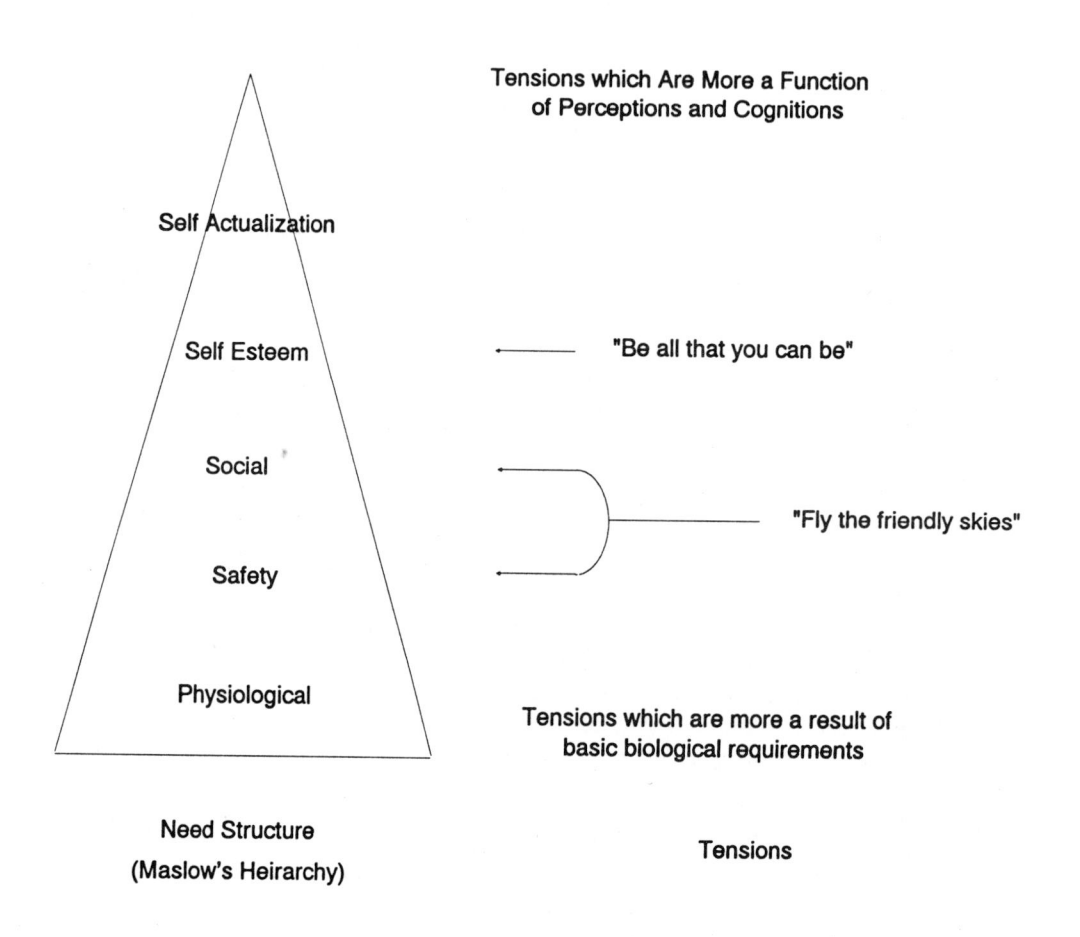

Tensions which Are More a Function of Perceptions and Cognitions

Self Actualization

Self Esteem ← "Be all that you can be"

Social

Safety

"Fly the friendly skies"

Physiological

Tensions which are more a result of basic biological requirements

Need Structure
(Maslow's Heirarchy)

Tensions

or its activities. *Pioneering advertising* creates primary demand or demand for the general product category. For example the ad may be designed to stimulate demand for "microwave ovens", not a specific brand or model. *Competitive advertising* generates *selective demand* or demand for a specific brand or model. *Comparative advertising* compares products which are named. The Federal Trade Commission (FTC) has guidelines which specify that any such comparison be backed by research evidence.[9] *Reminder advertising* is intended to keep a product name in front of the public, reminding them of previous communications.

In addition to selecting the advertising agency, the executive must exercise judgement in making a *media* choice. *Media options* for advertising would include newspaper, television, direct mail, radio, magazines and outdoor advertising such as billboards. Each will differ according to the *demographics* of the group which it *exposes* to its advertising, *how many* people are exposed, *how often* they are exposed, and the *way* the particular medium *affects them*. Common media terms to describe these concepts are *reach*, for how many people are exposed, *frequency* for how many times people are exposed, and *impact* for the effectiveness of the ad upon exposure.[10] Media choices are rapidly changing. Technological advances in printing have allowed profitable magazine operations at lower circulation volume. This has resulted in numerous small volume *special interest magazines*. The advent of *cable television* has resulted in the parallel phenomenon of more specialized television programming aimed at narrower markets. The advent of *modern data base technology* coupled to the increasing use of credit cards has resulted in large data bases containing information about an individual shopper's behavior. In some cases, data bases have been built which geographically locate consumers. Such *geodemographic information* allows more precise understanding of individual consumers and favors the choice of media capable of precise targeting of individual consumers or small consumer groups.

Precise targeting may take the form of *telemarketing*, a technique which, depending on its format, could be considered advertising or personal sales. Telemarketing uses direct telephone calls to targeted consumers. *Direct mail* advertising sends communications direct to a target customer by mail. If a form of marketing communication allows the consumer to respond directly to the communicator, it is referred to as *direct response* marketing. Telemarketing, direct mail, advertisements or shopping formats using toll free "800" phone numbers, and some experimental computerized shopping formats typify direct response marketing.[11]

Executives must translate such choices into their *financial implication*. For example, the choice of a large target market might favor the choice of mass media advertising. A large investment in radio or television advertising may be appropriate. This relatively expensive approach to communication may be justified if it successfully influences a large number of individuals in the target market. A firm may spend ten million dollars for a six-week television advertising campaign, but it may successfully influence fifty million individuals. This would result in a cost per individual influence of only $.20. This is less than the postage cost of sending that individual a first class letter. If such a campaign were successful in stimulating demand, economies of scale might also be realized in production and physical distribution. Mass media advertising of common household items exemplifies this kind of mass selling, mass production, mass distribution situation.

The choice of a narrow target market also carries with it a set of financial implications. Mass media advertising is unlikely to make sense if one is trying to reach a select target market of twenty-five hundred individuals. A six-week television advertising campaign would still cost ten million dollars, but even if twenty-five hundred individuals were successfully reached, the cost per individual would be four thousand dollars. In these cases, specialized media make sense. A small magazine catering to this special interest group would not have high enough circulation to command too high an advertising rate. In this situation, economies of scale are unlikely to be reached in production, physical distribution or communication. But, the design of the product as amplified by appropriate communication might be so specialized as to be of great interest to the target audience. This could result in high marginal utility, which could translate into relatively high prices and adequate revenue.

Any communications investment to include advertising should be subjected to the same kind of *competitive capital investment analysis* that all major corporate allocations of funds are subjected to. This should be placed in the *context of the strategic direction of the organization*. There will be difficulties encountered in this attempt. There is much that is subjective, creative and artistic in the design of communications. Results can be measured but are difficult to isolate as results of a specific communication investment. This should constitute an argument for the tolerance of some imprecision and a careful use of probabilities in the calculations. It should not justify decisions without investment analysis. Executives should have a good idea of just what is being purchased. Costs should be associated with the accomplishment of specific tasks and measurable *objectives*. Creativity should be guided.

Knowledge of the business can allow executives to *seek value* in the purchase of communication efforts. For example, media pricing is based on historical ratings and demographics. By purchasing media time, the executive buys the opportunity to approach a certain number of people (estimated by media ratings) who have certain lifestyles and incomes (estimated by demographics). Media vendors price their services based upon these historical ratings and demographics. Executives may "seek value" by noting those instances where changes in format or programming might be expected to raise ratings or improve demographics. This can result in obtaining better ratings and demographics than the price had been based upon.

Media budgets may also be based upon *competitive parity* or matching the expenditures of competition, and constrained by *affordability*, the simple question of financial constraint.

Personal Selling

The most advanced mass communications systems yet devised do not compare with individual human beings as sensitive, flexible and empathetic communicators. For this reason, personal selling remains a popular and effective mode of marketing communication. *Personal selling* is marketing communication performed by an individual in such a way that feedback is immediate and the communication can be readily modified based upon the feedback. Buyer and seller may be face to face or may be connected by telephone lines. At the margin, personal selling can be distinguished from advertising by the question of immediate feedback. Lee Iacocca uses television advertising wherein he communicates to the audience as an individual salesperson, but there is no immediate feedback, and the advertisement could not be immediately modified if there were.

Personal selling is a very common entry level position in marketing and is a common background of top level corporate executives. This may be due to the fact that some of the same social and communication skills developed in personal selling can be used to advocate one's positions, ideas and capabilities within the corporate hierarchy. Sales positions are well paid, but can be risky as one's job may be in jeopardy if the competition becomes too effective. But, the dollar rewards and the rewards of personal freedom found in many sales jobs have kept large numbers of people in the profession. About one person of every ten persons in the labor force is involved in sales.[12]

The organization decides on the use of personal sales by evaluating the *investment* of sales costs and the *market coverage* it returns. Respectable pay levels translate into high costs when the organization employs direct sales as a communication mode. A top industrial salesperson may make $65,000 (1988 dollars) and average five personal calls on customers in a day. Adding $30,000 per year for fringe benefits, travel and entertainment expense (T&E) and company car, this individual might cost the firm $95,000 per year. Given a two-week vacation the cost per call would be $76.00. Dropping to three calls per day and taking four weeks of vacation the cost per call would come to $131.94. As it makes no financial sense to invest this kind of money without an adequate return, such a salesperson would be expected to be responsible for very large dollar volumes. $100,000 in sales costs would translate to only 1% of revenue in a moderately sized $10,000,000 industrial sales territory. The cost per call can be substantially reduced when the salesperson makes greater use of the telephone, but the personal nature of the communication erodes as well. Personal sales costs may be further reduced by having the sales people assume some of the marketing risk. Sales people may be independent agents or employees who are remunerated on a commission basis. When this translates into underemuneration, the firm can be expected to sustain the *costs of turnover*. Salespeople will leave, and others must be attracted, hired and trained.

Once the decision to use personal sales has been made, the organization must decide *what the nature of the sales approach should be* given the nature of the offering and the nature of the target audience. *Once this is decided, it will logically guide the day to day questions* concerning how many and what kind of sales persons are needed, the sales presentation they will use, how they should be selected, trained, organized, compensated and motivated.[13]

Consider for example the differences in the nature of the offering and the nature of the target audience in three industries which commonly make great use of personal sales. The pharmaceutical industry uses personal sales people to call on medical doctors, hospitals and other individuals and institutions which make decisions concerning the use of pharmaceuticals. The mills which produce great quantities of metals such as steel and aluminum use representatives to communicate with producers who use these metals as component materials. The direct sales or door-to-door vendors of consumer goods use representatives to call on individual households. Very different offerings exist, and very different target audiences exist. Therefore very different sales approaches are used. The pharmaceutical salesperson must be professional and highly trained, able to differentiate extremely complex products in the eyes of professionals. The aluminum sales person must be an aggressive territory manager, selling products that are hard to differentiate by differentiating the vendor and by understanding the economic situations wherein profitable price cost relationships can be found. The door-to-door vendor of consumer goods sells relatively small ticket (small dollar amount) items to householders. This often precludes the use of expensive salaried employees as salespeople. Often these firms use independent distributors who sell on a part time basis to achieve extra income. These broad understandings must guide the day-to-day decisions.

In the choice of *how many salespersons* to use, the firm again *invests* the costs of salespeople and *derives* coverage of the market. This investment decision may be substantially constrained; a small firm cannot afford to employ as many salespeople as a large firm can. If the small firm tries to cover the same market, each sales person from the small firm must compete with several representatives of the larger firm. This situation might be compatible with a corporate strategy which included a price, distribution or product advantage for the small firm. At least one of these advantages would be necessary because the situation amounts to the small firm ceding the promotion and service advantages of personal sales to the larger competitor. In cases such as this, the small firm may elect to concentrate its effort, using its small sales force to outpromote the larger firm in certain targeted market segments.

The choice of *what kind of salesperson* to employ depends upon the type of offering, nature of the competition, and the nature of the target audience. Stereotypes of the "supersalesperson" can be misleading. Some sales positions require great sensitivity and thoughtfulness. Some salespeople should enjoy travel. A salesperson who is expected to make new or "cold" calls will differ from one who answers the telephone. A sales person who must memorize a sales presentation might be a very different kind of individual from the person who is expected to evaluate a situation and generate an individualistic sales presentation. Just as the matching process is heterogeneous in nature so is its component communication process. Good salespeople are by necessity as well as by nature heterogeneous.

A sales position may be characterized according to the *type of sales task* that must be accomplished. Management must decide which positions accomplish which tasks. Often a sales position will include elements of two or more of these basic sales tasks. *Order getting* is the task of seeking and acquiring orders while *order taking* is more passive. Salespeople who are held responsible for the level and profitability of sales in a territory or a product line are often order getters. These positions are often referred to as *field sales* or *outside sales*. Salespersons who respond to telephone calls (inside sales) exemplify the more passive *order taker*. Some sales tasks involve *supporting* the sales efforts of others. *Missionary sales people* communicate with buyers but do not seek the order themselves. Some sales people are always involved in this kind of work. The pharmaceutical "detailer" informs doctors of the details of the product but waits for the doctor to write a prescription. The pharmacist will fill the prescription and it is the pharmacist who actually orders the drug. Other salespeople may occasionally engage in "missionary work or prospecting" when making calls well before it is reasonable to expect an order.

Technical representatives are also *supporting* salespeople. They help the field sales people by providing the technical information needed in unusual applications. When technical representatives work with other salespersons in this way it is also an example of *team selling*. Team selling involves joint communication efforts where two or more individuals represent the vendor.

The *nature of the sales presentation* varies substantially. In cases where the firm must hire less skilled people, or where the strategy is to present the offering to a great number of customers, hoping to convince a small percentage, a *prepared sales presentation* may be appropriate. This is simply a memorized presentation which is developed by the firm.

To achieve a little more flexibility and opportunity for feedback while retaining a large measure of control over what is said, a *selling formula* may be used. In this approach, the salesperson leads the customer through logical steps which allow the salesperson to diagnose customer needs and offer a predesigned response.

The *need satisfaction approach* is the most free form approach to selling. Sensitivity, skill and experience are required of the salesperson. The salesperson must first engage in a diagnostic procedure, asking questions to ascertain what the customer's needs are. The salesperson then may propose a match by translating the features of the product into benefit statements which are relevant to the individual consumer's needs. Sales presentations of all kinds may be analyzed and described using the *common terms and concepts* included in figure sixty-three.

Selection and training of salespersons differs widely. Some firms simply advertise for experienced sales help and make selections based upon resumes, interviews and references. Training might consist of showing the person the product line and assigning the person a sales territory. Other firms, generally larger operations, develop elaborate selection criteria and procedures. They might put a person through several months of formal sales training and several years in a job designed to develop their product knowledge and sales skills. "Inside" or "desk" sales jobs, where the individual responds to consumer inquiries, takes orders, and adjusts orders would be typical of such developmental jobs. Few generalizations about selection and training can be made given the great differences in organizational situations. It might be possible to say that in general, sales people should be sensitive, astute, aggressive, and possessed of a resilient self concept.

There are *several organizational options* from which the firm may select when setting up administrative structures for sales. The salespersons may each be given a geographic territory, with responsibility for all accounts in the area. This is called a *geographic territory structure*. If the firm offers a diverse product line and substantial product knowledge is necessary, it may be desirable to organize *a product specialist sales force*, or a sales force structured by product. In this situation, individuals specialize in selling different products within the line. Any given geographic area might then be covered by three or four salespeople from one firm, each specializing in the sales of a different kind of product.

Figure 63
Common Terms and Concepts to Describe Sales Presentations

Listening Skills:	Salesperson's ability to use human sensitivity in discerning consumer needs.
Need:	State of tension or dissatisfaction in the consumer.
Feature:	Any identifiable aspect of a product or service.
Benefit:	An advantage from the consumer's point of view.
Benefit Statement:	Features of a product translated into advantages from the consumer's point of view.
Handling Objections:	Salesperson's creative response in identifying new needs and benefits or reformulating and restating previously introduced benefits when confronted with consumer objections.
Probe:	Salesperson's questions designed to developed more information about the customer's needs, evaluative criteria, attitudes and objections.
Proof Statement:	Statement which supports a benefit statement with relevant facts.
Supporting Statement:	Salesperson's statement of agreement with a customer statement which is positive about the product.
Closing Statement:	Summarizing benefits which are relevant to the customer and requesting a commitment. (The commitment is not always the order or the sale. Sometimes the appropriate commitment is an appointment for further discussion.)
Assumptive Close:	Closing statements and behaviors wherein the salesperson assumes the next commitment has been made.

Substantial differences in types of customers might justify organizing along these lines with a *market specialist sales force*. For example, differences in product requirements and purchasing styles between pharmacies and hospitals might encourage a pharmaceutical firm to use different sales groups to call on these customers. Focus on the type of customer is also manifested in the *national accounts sales force*. This kind of sales force specializes in selling to large national firms such as General Motors or IBM. The size and complexity of these big accounts would overwhelm the attempts of an individual salesperson. The national accounts sales force is often an elite cadre, composed of experienced and successful salespeople who have worked their way up through the ranks.

Many sales forces evolve into *complex systems* where elements from each form of organization mentioned above might be present. For example, the firm might start with a geographic territory form of organization. Then, without dismantling the territory system, it might superimpose some combination of product specialized, market specialized and national account salespersons. This kind of complexity can be difficult to manage. A *matrix* form of organization might be used, which facilitates reporting to multiple managers. Under a matrix form, the territory salesperson might be free to call on any account in the assigned territory, under the authority of a *regional or district sales manager*. However, when calling on certain accounts the territory sales person may be obliged to coordinate activities with a *product manager*, a *market manager* or a *national accounts manager*. These concepts are further examined in chapter nine.

Marketing management must also make decisions concerning the *compensation and motivation* of salespeople. Decisions must be made concerning both the *level* of compensation and the *formula* used to calculate compensation. A high level of pay encourages a greater number of applicants and may attract higher quality applicants. It will also reduce turnover and other associated costs. A low level of pay can obtain market coverage at low costs, but can result in low quality people and high turnover. Both will create a poor image with buyers. This is an aspect of communication with the customer which is quite powerful and which cannot be easily counterbalanced by *what* the "unending chain of unreliable salespeople" might have to say. Who is willing to sell for the firm, and how much of their lives they are comfortable committing to it are very important aspects of a firm's communication with its customers.

Decisions concerning the level of compensation must be coupled with decisions concerning the *formula* of compensation. The formula will be very important to the motivation of the salespeople, so management must carefully consider the *system of rewards and punishments* which they are creating. For example, a salesperson working on straight *salary* would be sensitive to the wishes of superiors, as they control salary. Straight salary remuneration plans for salespeople allow the firm to enter and exit accounts as broad strategy concerns dictate without encountering a great deal of resistance from the salespeople. The salespeople respond to those who control rewards.

Salary might be combined with some amount of *commission,* or reward based on some measure of performance. These *salary plus commission* plans allow for some degree of management control plus some degree of motivation derived from the commission structure. If the commission were to be based on sales or dollar revenue, salespersons would be motivated to maximize performance as measured that way. If in such situations the salesperson were to have any control over the selling price, the results could be large sales volume with low contribution margin. For this reason, commission structures have been designed to reward sales behavior which is more congruent with corporate goals. *Commissions* might be paid *based upon the C.O.E.* developed in a sales territory. This could encourage sales people to be aware of the profitability of every transaction. Some firms have experimented with compensation based upon *return on assets managed* (R.O.A.M.).[14] In these plans, the C.O.E. in a sales territory would be compared with the assets the sales person uses to manage the territory. Thus, a salesperson generating a given C.O.E. would see greater remuneration if the C.O.E. were generated using a company car and a home office, than if the same C.O.E. were generated using a company car and an expensive office facility belonging to the company.

Using the philosophy of designing commission structures to reward specific behaviors, firms have generated *complex commission formulae.* For example, a salesperson in a woman's wear store might receive extra money if she encourages the buyer to purchase complementary items. In such a situation, the commission structure would be designed to reward "multiple item sales."[15]

In many circumstances it may make sense to operate a sales force on *straight commission* or commission only. A straight commission might be based upon any of the formulae discussed: commission on sales, C.O.E., R.O.A.M., complex commission formulae or others designed to meet a company's goals. The choice of a commission structure might be severely limited by the capabilities of the company's accounting system. Some accounting systems simply cannot separate incremental costs to allow the creation of accurate C.O.E. figures. In these cases, commission plans might be based on figures which only approximate the figures the company really wants to use. In general, straight commission plans are attractive to experienced salespeople who do not need the security of a salary.

The organization might obtain salespeople and provide compensation and motivation through the use of *agency or distributorship plans.* In such plans, the salesperson is not an employee of the firm, but is an independent agent or distributor. For example, the manufacturers representative or "rep" is often an independent agent. Such plans often provide compensation by allowing the independent business person to keep the difference between the wholesale and retail price of the item. Other compensation and motivation plans might also be used and could include commissions, quantity discounts applied to the wholesale price, the use of company cars and performance bonus prizes such as trips to desirable vacation resorts. The latter approach constitutes the use of *sales promotion* as a method of sales force motivation. Sales promotion, discussed in an earlier section, may be used in conjunction with any other form of compensation and motivation.

Communication Feedback

Communication efforts should be both designed and implemented using *feedback* from the target individuals. This is information concerning the way people are responding to the communication. It may be gained with face-to-face human sensitivity or with market research which will be discussed in detail in chapter eight. Judicious use of feedback can guide communications design. Different "big ideas" or specific executions can be tried on individuals who are representative of the target group. Their responses can be used to adjust the communication. In the final stages, feedback from the target group can be obtained in order to determine whether the desired effect has been had. For example, the attitudes toward a product which people held before a communication can be compared with the attitudes that they held after the communication. Such measurements allow management to evaluate the effects of communications and to compare these effects with their costs. If the research is designed in such a way that the effects of communication can be translated into changes in units demanded at different prices, management is in a position to perform a complete financial analysis.

Useful Diagnostic Models

This discussion has evaluated communications using the understanding of C.O.E. and the market niche, as well as insights from psychology and consumer behavior. There are many other useful models of the communication process. The skillful marketing practitioner is well advised to *consult several models* as the communication approach is being designed and evaluated. Each model will provide a unique insight, stimulate new questions and provide an important increment of guidance for those involved in marketing communications. Useful diagnostic models of the communication process comprise appendix C.

Crossing National Boundaries

Communications efforts must undergo substantial adjustment when crossing national boundaries. These adjustments will involve:

1. Strategic adjustments to tune the product price relationship for the new environment
2. Translation
3. Brand name modifications
4. New product functions
5. Differences in media capabilities
6. Different institutional arrangements
7. Different advertising law
8. Lack of market data
9. A different cultural place for marketing
10. Different cultural expectations concerning influence on the legislative process
11. Selection of appropriate salespeople

The *strategic adjustments* which must be made to communications when crossing national boundaries have been introduced in chapter four. Different cultures will create different evaluations of marginal utility (MU) for any given product and any given promotion or communication. Different cultures and different economic conditions will also affect people's reactions to different levels of price (P). Thus the ratio $\frac{mu}{p}$ for a given offering will change in other nations and cultures. The general strategic approaches to this problem and the ways in which *product and communications combinations are altered* were discussed in chapter four.[16]

Translation can create difficulties which are not solved by simply hiring an individual competent in two languages to translate a communication from the home language to the language used in the new market. Languages are so complex and the correct interpretation so filled with subtle nuance, that the effective communication can change substantially in simple translation. This problem can be dealt with through the use of *back translation*.[17] Back translation involves getting a second individual competent in both languages to translate the results of the first translation back into the original language. This form of cross check can often discover unintended interpretations before the target audience is offended or confused. For example, a possible back translation of the phrase "the spirit is willing but the flesh is weak" might be rendered as "the wine is good but the meat is rotten."

Related to translation difficulties are problems with the communications which are implicit in the *brand name*. The brand name may need to be changed to avoid unfortunate translations in other cultures. A classic example of this kind of problem would be the logical Spanish translation of the Chevrolet "Nova" as no va or no go.

Communications people should also be aware that a given product may not serve its original purpose or perform its initial *function* in another society. This may be a result of intentional organizational strategy, as outlined in chapter four, or the change of function may be initiated in the target market. In either case, sensitivity is required to insure that marketing communications stress appropriate functions. It may be better to sell bicycles based upon their function as reliable, economical commuter vehicles for workers than as recreational vehicles for physical conditioning.

Media capabilities will differ greatly in other cultures. A firm should not become too attached to ideas about "the proper way" to communicate about certain products. For example, in the United States toothpaste is often sold through mass television advertising. In another culture, it might be that television stations are so weak and unreliable, and the number of television sets so small that television would not be as cost-effective a way to sell toothpaste as personal sales.

The *institutions* used for marketing communication might also differ greatly. Advertising agencies may be arms of the government. Private advertising agencies may differ greatly in nature and capability from those the organization is used to working with in the domestic environment. Large international advertising agencies exist which may be very effective in some regions and not as effective as local competitors in other regions.

Advertising and *communications law can be expected to differ*. The United States provides a relatively permissive environment for marketing communication. Other nations may regulate the number of advertisements that can be run in a period of time or confine advertisements to one period of time during the day.[18] Some nations provide penalties for creating a false impression as well as for making explicitly false statements.

Market data may be lacking. The United States provides an unusual amount of data concerning demographics, lifestyles and media habits of individuals. Few countries will match this data availability and managers who have become accustomed to the use of substantial amounts of research when designing and evaluating communications may find the overseas experience frustrating.

The place of marketing may be different in other societies. The United States is relatively unusual in the high degree of freedom and respectability given to marketing activities. Other societies will differ and in many cases marketing people will not be highly respected. This may result in less influence and more constraint for marketing people. In the resurgent entrepreneurial societies of the Pacific rim, marketing may be held in higher regard than in the United States. In Japan, Taiwan, South Korea, Hong Kong and Singapore marketing and entrepreneurial activities are well respected as vehicles for national economic improvement.

The activities known as *lobbying* in the U.S. will be different in other cultures. In some cultures, exchanges of favors are expected, although such favors might be seen as bribery in the United States. Sensitivity to this issue should not entail a compromise of personal ethics, but understanding of the way in which this affects the business environment is desirable.

The *appropriate type of salesperson* is likely to *differ* from culture to culture. U.S. businesses have traditionally favored hard driving individuals who "get right down to business" and negotiate aggressively. This type of individual is likely to be offensive in many cultures, where the careful development of a friendship is expected before one trusts another in a business deal.

Chapter Summary

The price product relationship can be adjusted by saying things about the offering. Marginal utility can be changed and the perception of price can be changed. The general problem facing management is to improve contribution margin by communicating with a target audience so as to improve demand, reduce costs, reduce competition or achieve a more favorable business environment. Traditional promotion communicates with a target market about the organization or its offerings. Other forms of communication engage in more broadly defined activities which affect the business environment. The basic communications options are sales promotion, public relations, advertising and personal sales. The effectiveness of these forms can be evaluated through the financial and psychological perspectives used in this chapter. They can also be evaluated using the diagnostic models which comprise appendix C. Substantial alteration of communications will be required when crossing national boundaries.

Appendix C

Useful Diagnostic Models for Marketing Communications

Chapter 6   215

Above: The Engle Blackwell Model of Consumer Behavior[19]—High Involvement (Source: Figure 2.7 from *Consumer Behavior*, Fifth Edition, by James F. Engle, Roger D. Blackwell, Paul W. Miniard. Copyright 1986). Below: The Engle-Kollat-Blackwell Model (Source: Figure 20.4 from *Consumer Behavior*, Third Edition, by James F. Engle, Roger D. Blackwell, David T. Kollat. Copyright 1978). Reprinted by permission of the Dryden Press, a Division of Holt, Rinehart and Winston, Inc.

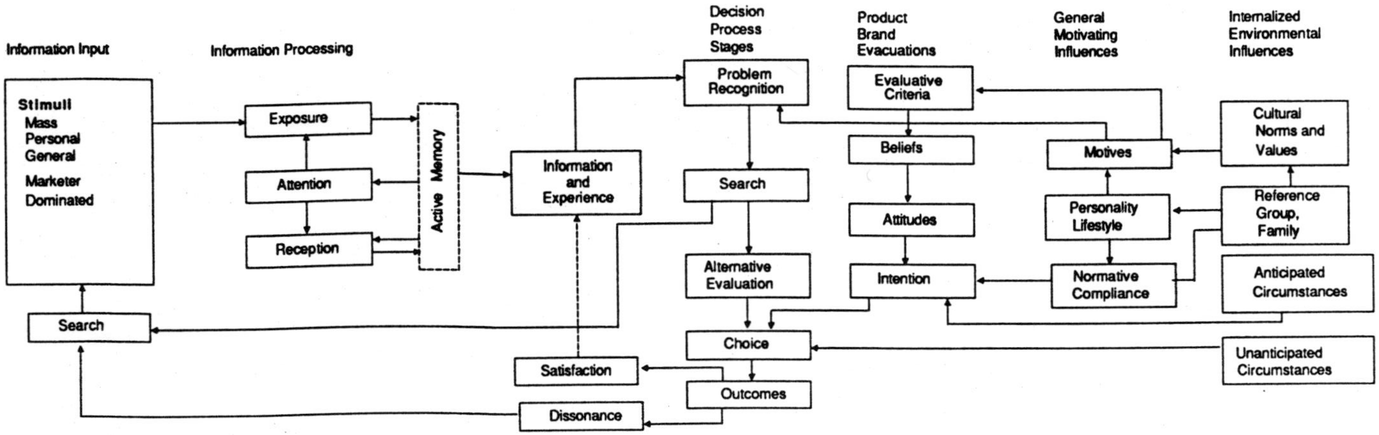

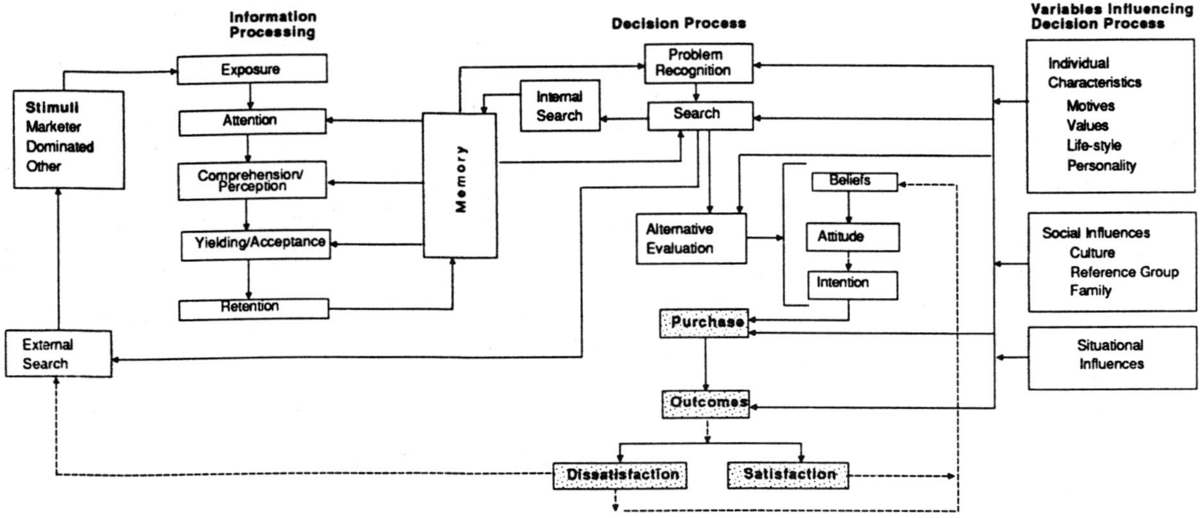

216   Part II

The Engle Blackwell Model of Consumer Behavior[20]
Low Involvement

Source: Figure 2.10 from *Consumer Behavior*, Fourth Edition, by James F. Engle, Roger D. Blackwell. Copyright 1982 by The Dryden Press, a Division of Holt, Rinehart, and Winston, Inc. Reprinted by permission of the publisher.

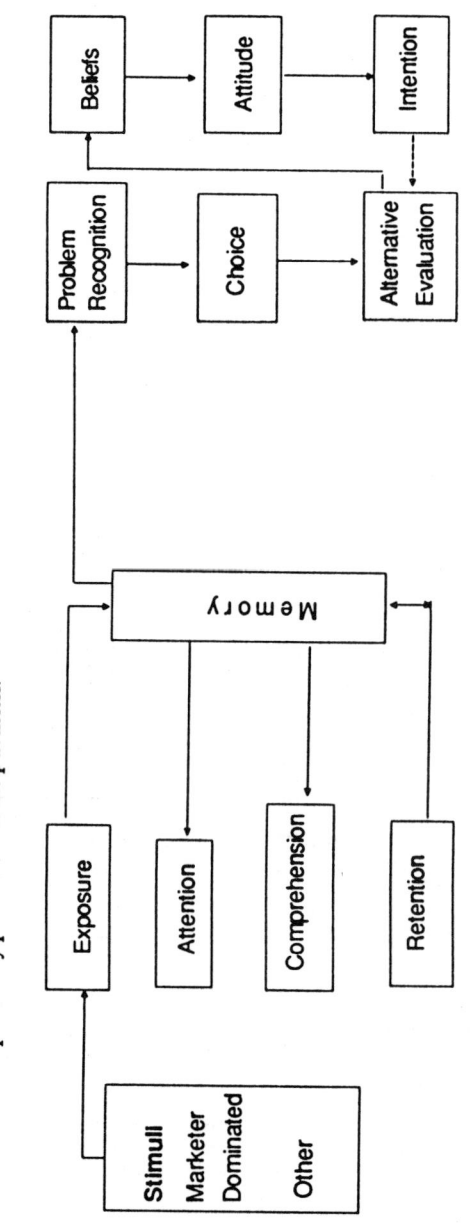

Chapter 6   217

Information Loop Concept

Information Loop Concept

The Organization   →Outbound Communication→   The Environment

                     ←Inbound Communication←

This model stimulates the question:

    Does your organization have sufficient communication linkages with its environment to allow survival?

A General Model of Communications[21]

Source: E. Jerome McCarthy and William D. Perreault, Jr. *Basic Marketing*, Ninth Edition (Homewood, Illinois: Richard D. Irwin, 1987), pp. 373-374. Reprinted by permission.

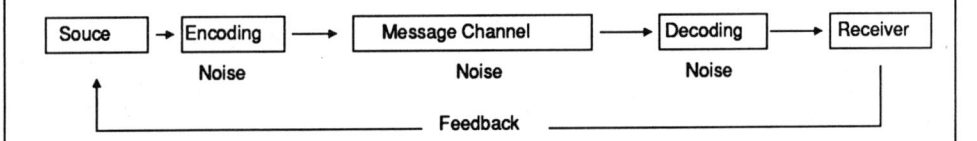

Souce → Encoding → Message Channel → Decoding → Receiver

Noise   Noise   Noise

————— Feedback —————

This model stimulates the questions:

1. Are you encoding properly (putting your communication together in a way that the target audience will understand it)?

2. Are you selecting the proper medium for communication?

3. Are they decoding the message the way you want them to (understanding your message the way you want them to)?

4. Do you understand their perceptual and cognitive processes (understand the receiver)?

5. Are you getting feedback?

6. Are you competing adequately with other thoughts and communications (noise)?

Microeconomic Models[22]

Communications to Alter Demand

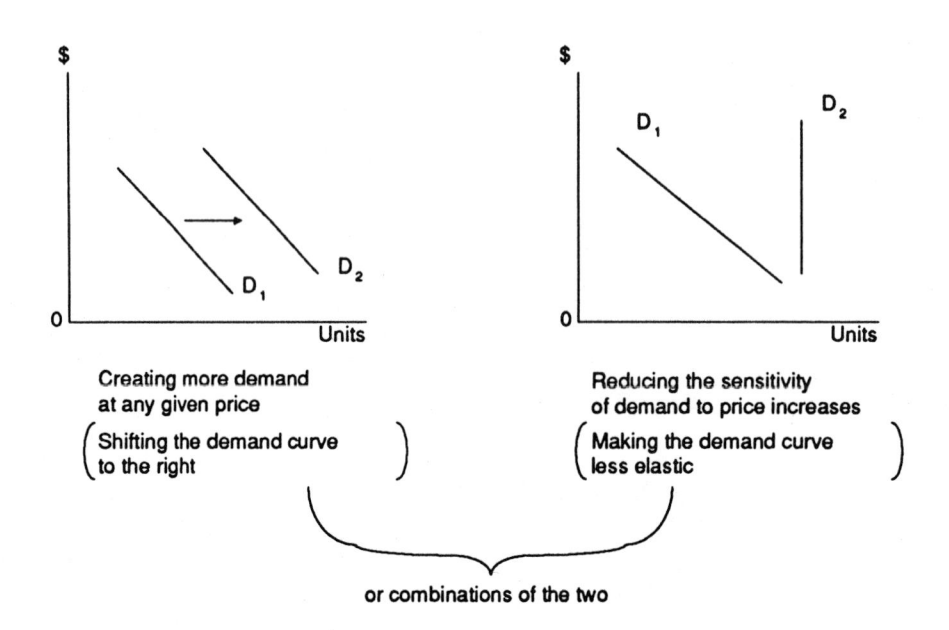

Creating more demand
at any given price

(Shifting the demand curve
to the right)

Reducing the sensitivity
of demand to price increases

(Making the demand curve
less elastic)

or combinations of the two

Communications to Lower Cost

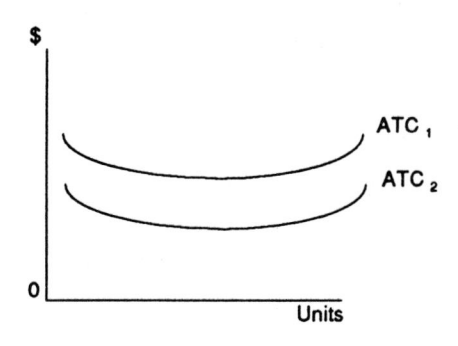

Communication may reduce
costs of inputs or influence
government to alter regulations
on production (OHSA)

Communications Which Reduce Competition

Communications which reduce competition
1. Product differentiation reduces direct competition
2. Barriers to entry can be affected through communication

[Communication as a barrier to entry or lobbying for barriers to entry]

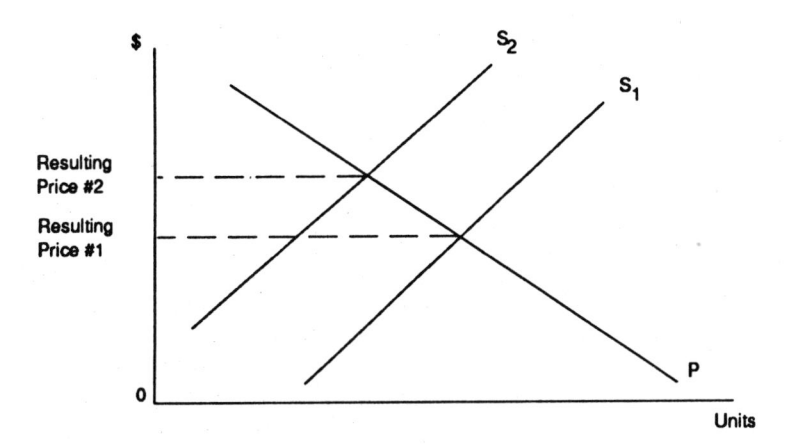

Communications which affect the business environment

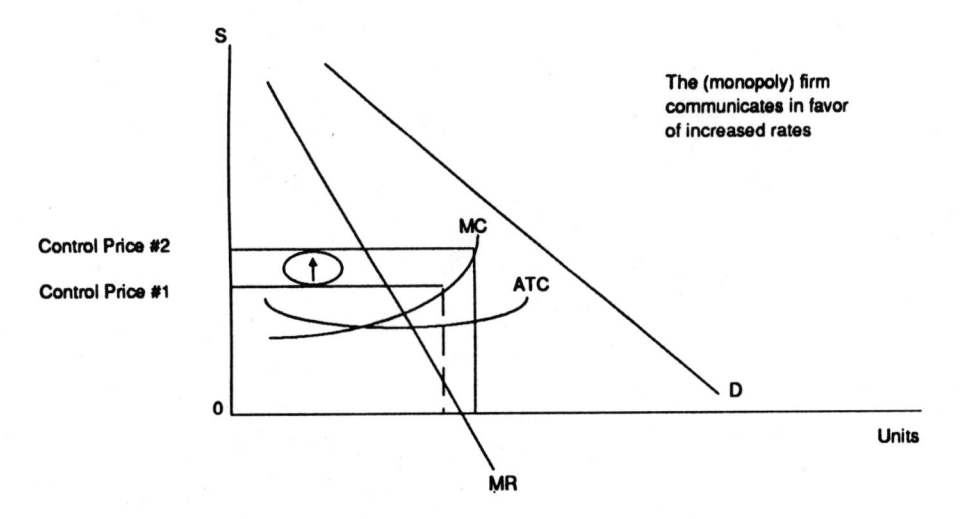

The (monopoly) firm communicates in favor of increased rates

220 Part II

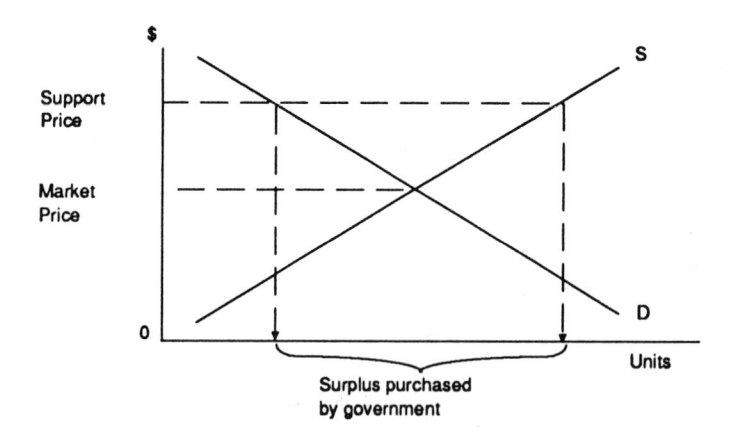

The competitive firm lobbys for price supports in the competitive market

Surplus purchased by government

The pricing power of pure monopoly

1. Approached in very succesful attempts to differentiate product
2. Approached when competition is very substantially reduced by product differentiation or lobbying

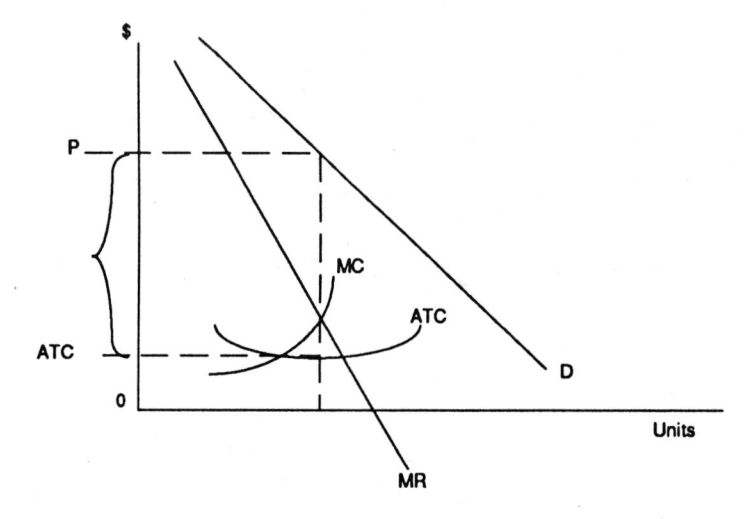

Adoption Process Model[23]

Consumers go through these stages, not always taking them in the same order:
1. Awareness of the product
2. Interest in the product
3. Evaluation of the product
4. Trial of the product
5. Decision confirmation

Effective communication depends on *understanding the proper order for a given product* (a low involvement product such as napkins may be tried as the sole means of evaluation). It *also depends on understanding where consumers are in the adoption process* and *communicating to facilitate* the consumer *at the appropriate stage*. For example, a firm with a brand new product may communicate simply to establish awareness of the product.

The Adoption Curve Model[24]

Consumers may be categorized according to the probability of their adopting a *new idea*. Marketers should identify target markets which have a greater probability of accepting their offering, and communicate with them using their preferred channels of communication.

1. Innovators (3-5% of consumers)

    Are young, well educated, mobile, rely on impersonal and scientific information sources.

2. Early Adopters (10-15% of consumers)

    Are well respected and may be opinion leaders. They are younger and better educated than all groups except innovators. They use sales people and mass media as information sources.

3. Early Majority (34% of consumers)

    Await news of product success with others, are not usually opinion leaders. They use mass media, sales people and opinion leaders as information sources.

4. Late Majority (34% of consumers)

    Cautious older consumers who may need pressure to adopt new ideas. They do not trust outside sources of information but rely upon others in the same group for product information.

5. Laggards or Non-Adopters (5-16% of consumers)
    Older and less well educated consumers who are suspicious of new ideas and rely upon those in their own group for new ideas.

The AIDA Model[25]

The AIDA Model is a simple diagnostic. It simply asks does your communication:

Get	**A**ttention?
Develop	**I**nterest?
Stimulate	**D**esire?
Get	**A**ction?

The Multistage Flow Model[26]

Simply points out that effective communication may go through thought leaders or opinion leaders before affecting end consumers.

Source ⟶ Opinion Leaders ⟶ Consumer

This implies that identifying and targeting those who lead opinion concerning a particular product may be an appropriate communication strategy.

---

[1] E. Jerome McCarthy and William D. Perreault, Jr., *Basic Marketing*, 9th ed. (Homewood, Illinois: Richard D. Irwin, 1987), p. 626.

[2] Herbert A. Simon, "How Big Is a Chunk?" *Science* 183 (February 1974), pp. 482-488. See also James F. Engle and Roger D. Blackwell, *Consumer Behavior*, 4th ed. (Chicago: The Dryden Press, 1982), p. 268.

[3] Webster's definition.

[4] Engle, p. 271. See also Ulrich Nesser, *Cognitive Psychology* (New York: Appleton, 1966).

[5] For a discussion of "The Big Idea" see Michael L. Rothschild, *Advertising* (Lexington, Massachusetts: D. C. Heath and Company, 1987), p. 216. See also David Ogilvy, *Ogilvy on Advertising* (New York: Crown Publishers, 1983), p. 16.

[5]For a discussion of "The Big Idea" see Michael L. Rothschild, *Advertising* (Lexington, Massachusetts: D. C. Heath and Company, 1987), p. 216. See also David Ogilvy, *Ogilvy on Advertising* (New York: Crown Publishers, 1983), p. 16.

[6]For a discussion of message appeals see Rothschild, pp. 218-234.

[7]Ibid., p. 216.

[8]Advertising types are from McCarthy, pp. 425-430. Reprinted by permission.

[9]Ibid., p. 427. See also Louis W. Stern and Thomas L. Eovaldi, *Legal Aspects of Marketing Strategy* (Englewood Cliffs, N.J.; Prentice-Hall, 1984), pp. 57-59, 403-409.

[10]The definitions of reach, frequency, and impact are taken from Philip Kotler and Gary Armstrong, *Marketing: an Introduction* (Englewood Cliffs, N.J.: Prentice Hall, 1987), pp. 426-427.

[11]Ibid., pp. 430-431.

[12]McCarthy, p. 396. The original data were Census Bureau statistics.

[13]Ibid., p. 396. The classification of sales activities is reprinted by permission.

[14]Martin Marietta Corp. was investigating the use of this technique during the author's time with that firm.

[15]Derived from a student report on such a commission structure.

[16]Warren J. Kegan, "Five Strategies for Multinational Marketing," *European Business* (January 1970), pp. 35-40.

[17]Philip R. Cateora and John M. Hess, *International Marketing*, 4th ed. (Homewood, Illinois: Richard D. Irwin, 1979), p. 270. See also Lee Adler and Charles S. Mayer, "Meeting the Challenge of Multinational Marketing Research," *Multinational Product Management Proceedings* (Cambridge, Mass.: American Marketing Association/Management Science Research Institute Workshop, August 1976, Report #76-110), pp. xvi-13.

[18]Cateora, p. 431.

[19]Engle, p. 500.

[20]Ibid., p. 38.

[21]McCarthy, pp. 373-374. Reprinted by permission.

[22]The models shown are straightforward applications of macroeconomics. See, for example, C. E. Furguson and J. P. Gould, *Microeconomic Theory*, 4th ed. (Homewood, Illinois: Richard D. Irwin, 1975).

[23]From *Diffusion of Innovations*, Third Edition, by Everett M. Rogers. Copyright 1962, 1971, 1983 by the Free Press, a Division of Macmillan Inc. Reprinted by permission of the publisher.

[24] McCarthy, p. 376. See also Everett M. Rogers, "New Product Adoption and Diffusion," *Journal of Consumer Research* (March 1976), pp. 290-301.

[25] McCarthy, pp. 374-375. Reprinted by permission.

[26] E. Jerome McCarthy, *Basic Marketing*, 7th ed. (Homewood, Illinois: Richard D. Irwin, 1981), p. 443. Adapted by permission.

Questions for Study, Discussion and Examination

1. Could you define, or explain to a friend who has not studied marketing, each of the following terms or ideas?
    a. Inbound communication
    b. Outbound communication
    c. The general problem addressed by communication
    d. Promotion
    e. Sales promotion
    f. Public relations
    g. Publicity
    h. Lobbying
    i. Advertising
    j. Diagnostic questions
    k. The involved chore which advertising must accomplish
    l. Exposure
    m. Attention
    n. Understanding
    o. Yielding/accepting
    p. Cognitive dissonance (see chapter two as well)
    q. Dissonant element
    r. Perceptual defense
    s. Multiple stage communication process
    t. Chunk
    u. Association
    v. Placement in memory
    w. Retrieval from memory
    x. Evoked set
    y. Problem recognition
    z. Creativity
    aa. Advertising agency
    ab. Account
    ac. Message appeal
    ad. Big idea
    ae. Story board
    af. Cost effectiveness (contrast with effectiveness)
    ag. General types of advertising
    ah. Media options
    ai. Geodemographic information

aj. Telemarketing
ak. Direct mail
al. Direct response marketing
am. Financial implications of advertising
an. Seeking value in the purchase of communications
ao. Competitive parity
ap. Affordability
aq. Personal selling
ar. Decision on the use of personal sales
as. Decision on the nature of the sales approach
at. Day-to-day questions concerning sales
au. Sales tasks (several plus examples)
av. Field or outside sales
aw. Inside sales
ax. Types of sales presentations
ay. Terms in figure 63 (describing sales presentations)
az. Organization options for sales (several plus examples)
ba. Complex systems of sales organizations
bb. Matrix organization
bc. Regional or district sales manager
bd. Level of compensation
be. Formula of compensation (several options)
bf. Agency or distributorship plan
bg. Communication feedback
bh. Engle Blackwell High Involvement Model
bi. Engle Blackwell Low Involvement Model
bj. Information Loop Concept
bk. A general model of communications
bl. The general problem addressed by communications expressed as microeconomics
bm. Adoption Process Model
bn. Adoption Curve Model
bo. AIDA Model
bp. Multistage flow model
bq. Adjustments to communication when crossing national boundaries

2. What does marketing communication attempt to do in terms of $\frac{mu}{p}$?
How does this adjust the product price relationship or interaction?
How can marketing communication be financially justified?

3. In what way can a marketing communication be "effective" and still result in a reduction of contribution margin?

4. What is the general problem of communication in economic and financial terms? How do traditional promotion and other forms of corporate communication address this general problem? How could one judge cost-effectiveness of communications efforts? Would traditional financial tools such as NPV, IRR and payback be useful? If so under what circumstances?

5. What is sales promotion? Give some examples of sales promotion. Under what circumstances do you think sales promotion is likely to be cost effective? How might it justify its costs?

6. What constitutes public relations? Give examples. Under what circumstances might public relations activities be "cost-effective"? How would you evaluate these activities financially?

7. Respond to questions 5 and 6 for advertising and personal sales.

8. In what sense is advertising a "barrier to entry". Evaluate the economics of high advertising costs, from the points of view of a large established firm, a small new firm, the society.

9. What diagnostic questions for advertising are suggested by the Engle Blackwell model of consumer behavior? Why is it so important to study consumer behavior before designing an advertisement? Isn't such an understanding just as important for the salesperson or lobbyist?

10. Think of an advertising communication, one you have experienced or are aware of. Describe in detail how this advertisement does or does not communicate with its target audience successfully. Perform this exercise for an "ad" which you believe is a dissonant element, and one which is not. How do the dynamics differ?

11. Describe a multiple stage communication in the manner suggested by question ten.

12. What do we know about memory? (You may wish to review parts of chapter two.) How are the principles that we understand useful in designing marketing communications. What are the roles of chunks, associations, VIPs, evoked sets, and problem recognition.

13. Describe a marketing communication that stimulates problem recognition. How does it do this? Why does it make sense to do this from a consumer behavior perspective? (At least two reasons.) How do you evaluate stimulation of problem recognition, from the consumers

point of view, from the advertisers point of view, from a social or ethical point of view?

14. How does creativity respond to the challenge of advertising communication? Experience some advertising creativity by creating an advertisement and presenting it to the class on a storyboard. Be prepared to defend it. Select something you are interested in such as why you should be hired, or why someone should choose your college. Use the principles presented in the chapter.

15. Find some advertisements in a magazine. Bring them to class and use them to demonstrate the concepts of the "big idea", "message appeal," "copy thrust", and "AIDA" (appendix C). Illustrate any other principles or ideas that these ads use.

16. Bring in and/or describe examples of each of the general types of advertising.

17. Expand the exercise in question 14 by getting classmates to act the role of people in the "account" to whom you are trying to sell the advertisement. Be sure they ask realistic questions.

18. Consider each of the mass media options, how do they differ? Under what kind of circumstances would you consider each to be particularly cost-effective.

19. Evaluate the changes in marketing communications being brought about by such advances as desk top publishing software, cable television, modern data base technology, increasing use of credit cards, wide area telephone service (WATS lines), increasing use of home computers.

20. Imagine you are responsible for the financial evaluation of all of your organization's marketing communications. How would you go about it?

21. Evaluate the targeting of narrow markets versus broader markets in terms of economics and finance.

22. How do you see the relationship of communications creativity to management decision making in the organization? What is the place of strategy? Of financial analysis?

23. Evaluate the use of the following criteria in communications budgeting: NPV, IRR, payback, competitive parity, affordability. When would you prefer one to another?

24. Give a detailed example of the use of each of the above criteria in budgeting for sales promotion, public relations, advertising and personal sales. Assume numbers in your example if you believe those

numbers might be available in a real situation. Use probabilities where appropriate. What kinds of difficulties might you expect with these procedures in practice?

25. What distinguishes the personal sales communication from the advertising communication?
26. What do you think the probabilities are that you will become involved in sales work? If you choose to become a CPA, will that involve sales? Why or why not?
27. In what sense are sales jobs "risky"? How does that provide training for marketing?
28. If you paid a salesperson $40,000, and associated expenses totalled $20,000, how would you evaluate your investment?
29. What are the costs of "turnover" in sales?
30. Give examples of how the nature of the sales approach might be different in different situations and different industries. How does this guide the questions of how many and what kind of salespersons are needed, the sales presentation they use, and how they should be selected, trained, organized, compensated and motivated?
31. Evaluate the situation of a small firm, which can only afford a few salespeople, when competing with a larger firm with many more salespeople.
32. Think of a realistic sales situation such as recruiting for your college or selling for your employer. List and evaluate the sales tasks that should be accomplished. Design positions to accomplish these tasks. Compare and contrast your approach to that suggested in the text.
33. Consider the various types of sales presentations. When do you think each type might be appropriate?
34. Study the terms and concepts which describe sales presentations in figure sixty-three. Then choose something to sell and a classmate to be the buyer you want to convince. Set up an audio or video tape to record your activities as you play these roles. Then go back and try to identify your use of the ideas in figure sixty-three. If you have time, play the roles again and try to improve the salesperson's performance. Share your tapes with the class.
35. Consider a realistic sales situation as you did for question thirty-two above. How would you organize the people? Why did you choose this organizational form over the other options?

36. In the situation described above, how would you select, train, compensate and motivate your people? Be as specific as you can. Why did you choose these approaches over the other options?
37. Suppose your company has been successful domestically and you have been chosen to head up the new international divisions communications operation. What kind of things will you have to consider in order to be successful?
38. Give examples of communications feedback as it might occur in sales promotion, public relations, advertising and sales.
39. What is meant by a balanced blend of communications, designed to work in harmony? Can you give an example of this? Reviewing the specific communications situations discussed in the foregoing questions can you see how a blend is functioning? Can you see how it could be improved? (See questions 32, 35, 36, 37.)

CHAPTER 7

ADJUSTING THE EXCHANGE: ALTERING THE PRICE-PRODUCT INTERACTION WITH PLACE

As discussed in the last chapter, the buyers' perception of the value of an offering can be adjusted by what is said about it. In like fashion, the value perceived in an offering has much to do with *where* and *when* it is available. The buyer is more likely to enter into a voluntary exchange if the rewards are perceived as being available *here* and *now*. Recognizing this, marketing executives must consider the way they get things to the buyer to be an important part of their marketing strategy. Thus, *place* belongs to the set of managerial variables traditionally seen as comprising marketing.

Channels

Place decisions involve several kinds of choices for marketing executives. To begin with, decisions must be made concerning who is to help in the distribution process. Will the firm use the services of other companies and if so whose services will be used? These decisions involve legal relationships among the firms concerned and may involve exchange of title to the goods being distributed. Such decisions are referred to as *channel decisions*. A *channel of distribution* is the series of organizational entities which is used to transfer the offering from its originator to its end customer. The individual organizations which are involved are referred to as *channel members*.

Forms of Channel Organization

The legal and economic relationships among channel members may take one of several forms. These are referred to as *forms of channel organization*.

A very common form of channel organization is the *traditional channel*. In the traditional channel system, it is the straightforward economics of self interest which keeps the channel organized. There are few formal relationships among channel members. The originator of an offering sells it where it is profitable to sell it. Other channel members then buy and sell, furthering their own profitability, until the offering eventually reaches the end customer. The end customer may or may not be understood by most of the channel members. As haphazard as this may sound, it is often amazingly efficient. Because there are few formal ties among channel members, new firms are quite free to compete for channel membership. In this way, if one channel member is providing the marketing function of storage, and a new firm feels that it can provide storage more efficiently, the new firm is *free to compete for the business*. Thus, traditional channel systems are constantly forming new relationships and restructuring themselves for greater efficiency.

While the traditional channel system can deliver economic efficiency, it often gives the originator of the offering *little control* over what is happening to the offering. The originating firm may feel that it could be more successful if it could influence more of the promotion, physical distribution and pricing activities in the channel.

When the firm begins to feel this need for control, it may be willing to sacrifice some of the natural economic efficiency of the traditional channel system for the control derived from the use of a *vertical marketing system*. Vertical marketing systems are distribution channels which use some form of coordination to focus channel attention and activities on the end consumer. The term "vertical" is used in the context of the standard depiction of a marketing channel, as shown in figure 64. Here, the raw materials and manufactures are at the top and the retailers and consumers are at the bottom of the drawing. Products will logically have to travel along the "vertical" axis to reach the consumer.

Chapter 7   233

Figure 64
The Terms Vertical and Horizontal as Used in Distribution

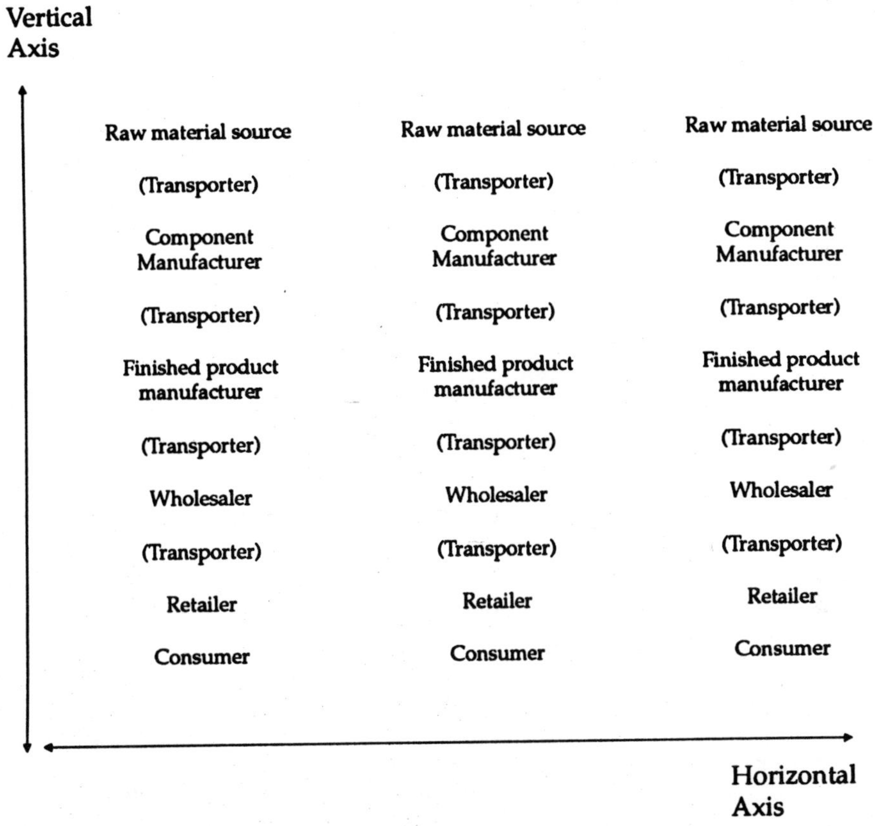

Vertical Axis

Raw material source	Raw material source	Raw material source
(Transporter)	(Transporter)	(Transporter)
Component Manufacturer	Component Manufacturer	Component Manufacturer
(Transporter)	(Transporter)	(Transporter)
Finished product manufacturer	Finished product manufacturer	Finished product manufacturer
(Transporter)	(Transporter)	(Transporter)
Wholesaler	Wholesaler	Wholesaler
(Transporter)	(Transporter)	(Transporter)
Retailer	Retailer	Retailer
Consumer	Consumer	Consumer

Horizontal Axis

Vertical marketing systems may be classified according to the form of coordination which is used. If the originating firm uses its various forms of power to *lead* the others, the system is referred to as an *administered system*. If such leadership is augmented with contracts which specify relationships in the channel, the system is referred to as a *contractual system*. If control is established simply through ownership of the other channel members, the system is referred to as a *corporate system*.

Entities and Their Typical Functions

The functions comprising the marketing process were introduced in the beginning of the book as:

1. Buying and Selling
2. Transportation and Storage
3. Standardizing and Grading
4. Financing
5. Risk Taking
6. Market Information

It is important to understand that *any* member or any combination of members of a channel of distribution may perform *any or all* of these functions. Therefore, *creative flexibility* is the best principle to use when trying to understand who does what in a channel of distribution. In the traditional channel, who does what is decided largely by economic competition. In vertical marketing systems who does what may be decided by a *channel leader*, who may be a manufacturer, wholesaler, or retailer. The channel leader is the channel member who successfully takes control of the channel and focuses its activities on providing a well coordinated offering to the end consumer. *The power to do this* may come from one or more of many sources, such as those illustrated in figure 65. In a marketing context, the most important source of power may be *consumer trust*. In the long run, consumer trust tends to be placed in that channel member who comes to be seen as *guaranteeing the quality of the offering*. Therefore, the retailer may have the consumers' trust in one channel of distribution, and be in the best position to make the other members behave. In another channel, the wholesaler or the manufacturer may have this kind of power. Sears is a retailer with this kind of power because consumers have come to trust the "Sears," "Kenmore," and "Craftsman" brand names as guarantees of quality. Toyota is a manufacturer with this kind of power. Midas Muffler shops began as a wholesaling operation and now have this kind of power. When the consumer places trust in a brand name, that trust delivers great channel power to the owner of the name. Creative flexibility should determine which channel member performs which function, and

Figure 65
Sources of Power

Adapted from J. R. P. French and B. Raven. "The Bases of Social Power," in *Studies in Social Power*, ed. D. Cartwright (Ann Arbor: University of Michigan, 1959). Adapted with permission from J. R. P. French and B. Raven.

Legitimate power

    Formal authority and position

Rewards

    Control of reward

Expertise

    Knowledge relevant to the problem at hand

Referent

    Subordinate identification with leader

Coercive

    Control of punishment

consumer trust will often give direction to this flexibility. However some channel members have become so well associated with the performance of certain functions that awareness of these typical associations is required in marketing. For this reason, wholesalers, retailers, and their subcategories should be understood in terms of the typical functions which they provide.

Wholesalers and Their Typical Functions

The *wholesaler* is a channel member who does not ordinarily deal with the end consumer. The wholesaler is thus a "middle person" in the channel. The existence of such a middle person can be justified if the wholesaler performs needed functions in a more cost effective way than any available alternative. The way a wholesaler might accomplish this can be understood by studying the functions that might be performed.

1. Buying and Selling

Wholesalers often buy from one channel member and sell to another, typically buying from manufacturers and selling to retailers. This eliminates the worry and cost of selling for the manufacturers, performing a function which has economic value to them. This value is partially reflected in the difference between the price level at which the wholesaler can buy from the manufacturer, and the price level at which the wholesaler can sell to the retailer. In similar fashion, buying from the manufacturer and selling to the retailer provides a buying function for the retailer. The retailer need not worry about contacting various distant manufacturers directly, nor invest in purchasing the large quantities that manufacturers prefer to sell. Performance of this buying function has economic value to the retailer. This value is also partially reflected in the difference between the price at which the wholesaler can buy and the price at which the wholesaler can sell.

Not all wholesalers actually buy and take title to the items involved. Those who take title are termed *merchant* wholesalers; those who do not are termed *agent* middle persons. By arranging transactions between other channel members, agent middle persons such as auction companies can perform buying and selling functions without actually taking title themselves.

2. Transportation and Storage

A wholesaler may improve a market niche by providing transportation and storage. Transportation is costly. It reflects an investment in machinery, people, fuel, taxes, insurance and maintenance. Storage is also costly because it represents investments such as floor space, insurance, utilities, working capital in inventory, inventory accounting costs, and materials handling systems. It also represents the risks of product deterioration and market obsolescence. A firm in the channel may be happy to shift some of these costs and management responsibilities to a wholesaler. The difference between the price at which the wholesaler buys and the price at which the wholesaler sells may seem reasonable in comparison to these costs, risks and responsibilities.

3. *Standardizing and Grading*

A wholesaler may elect to perform the function of standardizing and grading, becoming responsible for quality standards. This often involves costly inspections and difficult negotiations with suppliers. If standardization and grading does not become the responsibility of a channel member, the responsibility for it will fall upon the consumer. The consumer will have no one to trust as a guarantor of quality and so must engage in more shopping and evaluation prior to purchase. Standardization and grading may take the form of inspections. For example, a farmer's co-op grain elevator inspects and grades wheat as it comes in off the farm. Standardizing and grading may take the form of extensive comparison shopping and the stocking of only those brands and models that the wholesaler approves of and is willing to stand behind. It could also take the form of creating design specifications and contracting with manufacturers to build the items according to those specifications. The wholesaler might acquire a manufacturing facility and build the items. In any case, the wholesaler may elect to create a unique brand name or trade name, placing it on items manufactured by others or on those manufactured by the wholesaler. In these ways, a wholesaler may survive in the channel by providing a quality control function that competes cost effectively with the other options that are available to consumers and channel members.

4. *Financing*

Without someone in the channel who is willing to invest capital on the chance that someone will repay a greater amount at a later date, the consumer would have to advance the funds to get everything done. The consumer would, for example, have to advance the auto manufacturer the funds it needed to purchase the materials and hire the labor to build and deliver an auto. The fact that this strikes us as ridiculous in our modern economy illustrates how common it is that someone in the channel of distribution is willing to advance the funds to facilitate the process. Often that person is the wholesaler. Consumers are rarely in a position to advance funds prior to purchase. In fact they often expect funds to be advanced to them in the form of a loan. Manufacturers are often short of cash as well, requiring money as soon as an item is manufactured so that they can pay suppliers and write checks for their employees. Given these kinds of cash shortages, the wholesaler can build a niche in the channel by providing capital. The wholesaler advances cash to both suppliers and customers, and is repaid by the margin between the buying and selling price. When the provision of capital is the only function of a wholesaler, that individual or firm may be referred to as a *factor*.

5. Risk Taking

Part of the matching of heterogeneous demand with heterogeneous supply is bearing the cost of the mismatches that sometimes occur. Occasionally something is produced which is not demanded, or which is so little in demand that price must be set below cost before the item will sell. The consumer takes this kind of risk when purchasing an item "on the chance that it might be needed". Channel members take this kind of risk when they produce, buy or decide to keep in inventory, any item "on the chance that it will sell". The wholesaler, especially the merchant wholesaler, assumes a great deal of risk in the channel when holding items in inventory. The wholesaler's contribution margin on items that sell must be sufficient to cover the costs of items that do not sell or items that sell below cost.

6. Market Information

Often it is hard to understand why some wholesalers can exist in a channel if they do not buy, sell, transport, store, finance, or take risks. In these cases, an explanation may be found in what the wholesaler is in a position to know and who the wholesaler is in a position to contact and influence. In other words, wholesalers may exist in the channel by serving as a conduit for marketing information. The wholesaler may for example know who may want to buy something and who is in a position to sell that item. Yet the two parties to this potential exchange might not know each other. Putting knowledge of consumers and knowledge of suppliers together to identify potential matches is a logical and important part of the matching process. The wholesaler might therefore logically become involved in market research activities and advertising or sales activities. Market information may be a part of the mix of functions provided by any wholesaler. When the information function is the primary function provided by a wholesaler, that individual may be referred to as a *broker*.

Specific Wholesaler Types

There are many names that have come to denote wholesalers who perform given sets of functions. Unfortunately, these terms often differ from industry to industry and differ across time as a given industry changes. In keeping with the idea of creative flexibility in understanding channel relationships, it is suggested that, as one comes to know a particular industry, certain functions will come to be associated with certain names. Committing wholesaler names to memory may be premature before deciding which industry one wishes to pursue. Despite this, there are some terms in sufficiently common usage to warrant study. These appear in figure 66.

Retailers and Their Typical Functions

A *retailer* is a channel member who deals with the final consumer of a good or service. While conforming to this definition, a retailer may also elect to perform any or all of the functions discussed above in the context of wholesalers. The logic of such a decision would be the same as it would be for any channel member. If the retailer can perform the function in a way that is profitable to the retailer and which comprises a cost effective or desirable option for other channel members, then the retailer should perform the function. Like wholesalers, retailers may manufacture what they sell.

Therefore, the distinguishing function of a retailer is to sell directly to the end consumer. This places the retailer in a particularly powerful position to alter the nature of the exchange. The retailer may alter the price-product relationship by affecting the ratio of marginal utility to price $\left(\frac{mu}{p}\right)$. Thus, the retailer requires a substantial understanding of consumer psychology. While other channel members are likely to view their functions, and the shifting and sharing of their functions within the channel, from a rather businesslike and economic perspective, the end consumer is quite different. The end consumer is likely to prefer one store to another on the basis of "ambiance" or "image". In other words, the end consumer reacts to whether or not the store "feels right." Understanding what underlies these subjective consumer evaluations becomes the business of the retailer. For example, an exclusive men's store might "feel right" to the target customers under certain conditions of lighting, color, service, background music, and location. It is the retailer's business to understand these things and to artistically mix or combine them so as to create the proper gestalt or total image. The need to understand this consumer choice process encourages an ever more sophisticated study of psychology and consumer behavior. Nonetheless, a preliminary understanding of a retailer's strategy may be gained by understanding the basic axes along which a consumer might evaluate a retailer. Such a set of axes might include:

1. Time convenience (time for entire shopping experience)
2. Distance convenience (cost of transportation and parking)
3. Width of selection (how many different broad categories of item are being offered)

Figure 66
Common Terms Describing Wholesalers

Common Term	Type of Wholesaler					
	B+S Buying Selling	T+S Transport Store	S+G Standard Grade	F Finance	R Assume Risk	MI Market Information
Merchant Wholesalers (All hold title)	Own the products: Subdivisions are service wholesaler and limited function wholesaler					
Service Wholesaler	Provides all functions: 3 types below					
General Merchandise Wholesaler		Much inventory				
Single Line Wholesaler or General Line Wholesaler		Inventory one line				
Specialty Wholesaler		Narrow Inventory				
Limited Function Wholesaler	Provide some functions: 8 types below					
Drop Shipper	✔		✔	✔	✔	✔
Mail Order Wholesaler	✔	✔	✔	Sometimes	✔	✔
Producers Cooperative	✔	✔	✔	Sometimes	✔	✔
Manufacturer's Sales Branch	Selling	✔		Sometimes		✔
Rack Jobber	✔	✔	✔		✔	✔
Factor				✔	✔	
Sales Finance Co.				✔		
Floor Planner				✔		
Agent Middlepersons (None hold title)	Do not own the product: Provide few functions: 5 types below					
Manufacturer's Agent	Selling	Sometimes	✔			✔
Broker	Selling					✔
Commission Merchant	Selling					
Selling Agent	Marketing					✔
Auction Company	✔					✔

4. Depth of selection (how many individual items are available within a given brand category)
5. Quality of products
6. Help from salespeople
7. Quality of salespeople
8. Reputation for integrity
9. Credit availability
10. Service (delivery, returned goods, etc.)
11. Price level
12. Attractiveness of image
13. Perceived value $\left(\frac{mu}{p}\right)$

Insights from consumer behavior would suggest that not all consumers would use the same list, or attribute the same relative importance to each item on such a list. Furthermore, different individuals will have different ways of putting the components together to form a gestalt or total image of the store. These individual differences can become a basis for *segmentation* of retail markets.

A set of axes such as this can also be used to characterize the strategy of retailers. An individual store's strategy, or the typical strategy of a given "type" of retailer, could be characterized using a grid such as that comprising figure 67. In the case of some of the axes in the grid, the placement of a particular store would be fairly straightforward. Viewed from the perspective of an individual consumer or from the perspective of an identified target market, the store is either easy to get to or it is not. By contrast, placement of an individual store or store type on some of the axes (such as "attractive image" or "perceived value") might require substantial consumer research. The research may have to be fairly sophisticated in deriving this kind of information from the consumer, as the consumer might have difficulty articulating his or her feelings.

This set of axes can be used to illustrate the major types of retailers. For example, a *convenience store* focuses on the ease of doing business. It would rate high on the first two axes. *Shopping stores* allow consumers to evaluate competing items under one roof. Therefore they are likely to rate high on both width and depth of offering. These and other common retailer types are listed in figure 68 together with a code number. The code numbers in figure 68 may be used to trace important components of strategy for several representative

Figure 67
Axes to Characterize Retail Strategy

	High	Medium	Low	
Time Convenience				Time Convenience
Distance Convenience				Distance Convenience
Width of Offering				Width of Offering
Depth of Offering				Depth of Offering
Quality of Products				Quality of Products
Help from Salespersons				Help from Salespersons
Quality of Salespersons				Quality of Salespersons
Reputation for Integrity				Reputation for Integrity
Credit Availability				Credit Availability
Service				Service
Price Level				Price Level
Attractive Image				Attractive Image
Perceived Value				Perceived Value
	High	Medium	Low	

Figure 68
Common Terms for Retailer Types

Type of Retailer (and Definition)	Code Number for Figure 69
Convenience Store	1
Shopping Store	2
General Store	3
Single Line Store	4
Limited Line Store	5
Specialty Shop	6
Department Store	7
Supermarket	8
Catalogue Showroom Retailer	9
Discount House	10
Mass Merchandiser	11
Super Store	12
Convenience Food Store	13
Automatic Vending Machine	14
Telephone Direct Response	15
Mail Direct Response	16
Television Home Shopping	17
Door to Door Selling	18
Shopping Center	19

Chapter 7 243

retailer types in figure 69, a reproduction of the axes used to characterize retail strategy.

Management in retail operations must make decisions beyond just placing their operation on axes such a those in figures 67 and 69. A retailing operation must decide whether or not it wants to become involved in a *chain* of retail stores. A chain is a group of retail outlets which have been brought together for purposes of achieving economies of scale. These economies of scale would be reflected in such activities as mass media communications efforts, buying larger quantities and greater efficiencies in such channel activities as transportation and storage.

A chain of retail outlets may be organized in any of several ways. One firm may own all of them. This would be referred to as a *corporate chain*. Sears stores exemplify corporate chains.[1] Alternatively, independent retailers may band together to form a chain. These are referred to as *cooperative chains*. True Value Hardware stores are organized as a cooperative chain.[2] *Wholesalers may also create retail chains.* When wholesalers organize a chain of independent retailers, it is referred to as a *voluntary chain*. Ace Hardware is a voluntary chain.[3] A *franchise operation* is a chain similar in nature to both the cooperative and voluntary chains in that each retailer is an independent business. It is different in the sense that the franchise operation generally recruits new owners and facilitates the establishment of new retail outlets. These must then conform to the established strategies and standards of the franchise operation. McDonalds is a franchise operation.

The Market Niche of the Retailer and Retail Types

Retailer strategy may be characterized by the marketing functions the retailer chooses to perform. It may also be characterized by the special way in which the retailer elects to perform its unique function, that of selling directly to the consumer. These choices will in turn reflect and be reflected in the way the retailer generates contribution margin.

Contribution margin may be generated using various combinations of contribution margin per unit and unit movement, and retail strategy may be thought of in this way. A *specialty shop*, such as a hobby shop or camera shop may successfully adopt a low unit movement strategy. Operating with low overhead and therefore not usually seen in shopping mall operations where the rent is often high, such stores can survive by selling a modest quantity of items at relatively high price levels. This strategy can succeed because there

Figure 69
Aspects of Retail Strategies for Representative Types

	High	Medium	Low
Time Convenience	1 3 13 14 15 16 17	2 18	
Distance Convenience	1 3 13 14 15 16 17 18	2	
Width of Offering	2 7 9 12 19	1 3 8 10 13 18	4 5 6 14 15 16 17
Depth of Offering	2 4 6 8 9 19	7 10 18	1 3 13 14 15 16 17
Quality of Products	Depends on Individual Retailer		
Help from Sales-persons	1 3 6 13 15 18	2 8 9 17	10 14 16
Quality of Salespersons	6	1 2 3 8 9 13 15 18	
Reputation for Integrity	Depends on Individual Retailer		
Credit Availability	2	3 15 16 17 18	1 8 13 14
Service	6	1 2 3 8 18	14
Price Level	1 6 13 14 15 16 17 18	2 3	8 10 11
Attractive Image	6	1 2 3 8	
Perceived Value = $\dfrac{mu}{p}$	Depends on individual buyer perception of $\dfrac{mu}{p}$ as discussed earlier. mu and p will be some function of the above items. Choice is made according to rules of buyer choice per figure 10.		

High Medium Low

is high C.O.E. per unit. High C.O.E. per unit in turn is possible because such stores generally offer high quality items and a high level of service.

At the other end of the spectrum, supermarkets, superstores and discount houses generally adopt low C.O.E. per unit, high unit movement strategies. In adopting this kind of strategy, the *supermarket* has been a key contributor to a high consumer standard of living. Supermarkets specialize in moving high quantities of grocery items through the store at minimum margins. This is a particularly successful strategy in food retailing because food inventories will be fresher and more attractive to consumers as unit movement increases. The *superstore* has adapted the supermarket philosophy to a broader product line, selling more than just food items. The *discount house* has adapted the strategy to the sale of "hard goods" such as cameras, electronics and appliances.

Any retailer adopting a high unit movement strategy may be referred to as a *mass merchandiser*. Hardware chains, lumber and home improvement chains, and chains moving large volumes of diversified product offerings as Sears and K-Mart might, can be seen as mass merchandisers. The high unit movement strategy need not always be accompanied by low C.O.E. per unit. Some mass merchandisers have discovered that their reputation for quality has allowed them to charge higher prices. Others have discovered that pricing need not be uniformly low. They price their product line so as to achieve high C.O.E. per unit in some items while maintaining an image of having low or reasonable prices across most of the product line. The high volume mass merchandising strategy has encouraged firms adopting the strategy to grow. This in turn has allowed the firms to support larger overhead investments in analytical data processing and associated staff. When carefully managed, this kind of capability enhances the firm's understanding of product cost and demand patterns, and improves marketing strategy. It can also create a substantial barrier to entry for new retailers.

The choice of a high unit movement versus a low unit movement strategy does not necessarily follow directly from the choice of the product line. Food has been characterized as particularly well suited to high volume strategies. Yet several retailer types profitably vend low volumes of food products. Convenience food stores, general stores and automatic vending machines sell a limited offering of foodstuffs at high C.O.E. per unit. This is possible because they are successfully addressing important consumer evaluative criteria. They are providing food when and where it would not otherwise be available. The convenience food store often stays open when the supermarkets are closed. The general store is often located in rural areas far from competing supermarkets and the vending machine is usually "just down the hall."

In a similar fashion, choice of product line does not dictate the appropriate type of retailing. Door-to-door sales, television home shopping and telephone or mail direct response retailers address evaluative criteria in different ways than the retail stores do. Stressing the differentiation that is available to them, such firms are often successful in selling items similar to those found in the retail stores.

Technological Change in Retailing

The creative retailer must continue to respond to technological change. The development of modern *data base systems*, which allow the efficient organization, storage and retrieval of information, as well as more cost effective *software for the analysis of information*, will continue to have a substantial effect on retailing. Inventory can now be tracked with greater accuracy. Improved invoicing or billing systems and accounts payable systems allow more efficient cash management. The effects upon unit movement as prices are altered can be known more quickly. Contribution margin on individual products can be more accurately understood, and the effects of advertising and pricing specials can be evaluated more rapidly.

Transportation, storage, and packaging will continue to evolve, delivering cost advantages to large retailers able to develop *"just in time" delivery systems* which use well planned transport operations to reduce inventory costs. Cost advantages will also accrue to retailers using more modern *material handling* equipment. Understanding of the ecological effects of some packaging options may force change in the use of some kinds of disposable packaging.

Changes in the banking and credit industry have accompanied technological change and regulatory change. *Credit strategy* on the part of retailers may involve adaptation to more modern credit systems or the establishment of credit systems controlled by the retailers. Sears, for example, has established a financial corporation and its own "Discover" credit card. In order to compete with the more established bank credit cards, Sears financial division is promoting the Discover card, hoping for increased acceptance by both consumers and other retailers.

Channel Dynamics

Retailers and other channel members are subject to the same innovation life cycle which affects most marketing efforts. A successful new idea yields monopoly gain which then attracts competition. This in turn lowers price and puts participants in the market under severe profit pressure. When a firm wishes to enter the retailing business without a clear, attractive and exclusive innovation, profitability is slower in coming. Such retailers may have to enter the competition as low status, low price operators and gradually build client trust to the point where the offering is viewed as being worth increased prices and profits. When such a firm is successful and eventually increases prices and profits, the market situation would again be attractive to new low status, low price operators. This continuing cycle is referred to as the *Wheel of Retailing*.

The Innovation Life Cycle and the Wheel of Retailing are only two models of the dynamic activities that can be expected in channels. Creative flexibility is again the key concept in understanding channel dynamics, and the question of who performs which function will be under constant review. As the answer to this question changes, channel members will find themselves to be *shifting and sharing functions*. Changes in the channel might require that one member take over a storage function that another member has provided in the past. The storage function has thus been "shifted." Channel changes might require that two channel members combine their efforts to provide storage, thus "sharing" a function.

From a broad social perspective, all of this activity may be seen as *cooperation* in order to effectively *match* heterogeneous demand with heterogeneous supply. The channel members themselves may view it differently. They are likely to see the process as either competitive or cooperative depending on the form of channel organization. In the traditional channel, the mechanism of change is economic competition. The individual channel member seeks to build and defend a market niche in competition with other potential providers of the same marketing functions. In vertical marketing systems the mechanism of change is the decision making and leadership of the channel leader. Here, economic competition enters in to the extent that the decisions and activities of the channel as a whole are disciplined by the competitive efforts of other vertical marketing systems and traditional channels. Thus, social cooperation is brought about in the traditional channel system by economic competition to perform functions. In vertical marketing systems social cooperation is guided by channel leadership and conditioned by economic competition from other channels.

Channel change may be accomplished through mergers or acquisitions. Such activity may take the form of *horizontal integration*. Horizontal integration is the merger with or acquisition of firms on the *same level* of channel activity. The term "same level" refers to the same horizontal level in the standard depiction of a channel system as introduced in figure 64, and as shown again in figure 70. In this depiction, wholesalers are on the same horizontal level as other wholesalers, and retailers are on the same horizontal level as other retailers and so forth. Thus when one wholesaler acquires another as depicted in figure 70a, the acquisition appears to be "horizontal."

The problem with horizontal integration from a social point of view is that it reduces competition. There were four wholesalers in the channel prior to the acquisition depicted in figure 70a, now there are three. The reduction of competition will take some price pressure off of the remaining wholesalers and it is therefore desirable from the point of view of those individual organizations. But the market has moved away from competition in the direction of monopoly and the resulting loss of economic efficiency, as prices no longer closely approximate costs, will hurt consumers. The result is that horizontal integration, while not illegal per-se, is nevertheless subject to the antitrust laws which protect competition in the United States. Thus, managers considering horizontal acquisitions are advised that a particular merger or acquisition may be disallowed if it is found to substantially inhibit competition. The antitrust laws are further discussed in chapter ten.

In figure 70b, a finished products manufacturer, a wholesaler and a retailer have consolidated. This form of consolidation, which proceeds parallel to the flow of the products from manufacturer to consumer is termed *vertical integration*. If one firm acquires another which lies in the direction of the raw materials in figure 70, the action is termed a *backward integration* (a form of vertical integration). If a firm acquires another which lies in the direction of the consumer, the activity is termed *forward integration* (also a form of vertical integration). Thus a wholesaler merging with or acquiring a retailer is involved in forward (vertical) integration. If the same wholesaler were to acquire a manufacturer it would be considered a backward (vertical) integration.

Physical Exchange: Transportation and Storage

The foregoing sections have discussed the various parties to the distribution process. As the offering moves through the channel from manufacturer to consumer, the channel members relate to each other in ways that are both legal and economic. As the situation changes, relationships may change, resulting in changing opportunities for the individual firm to establish and defend a market niche.

What the channel discussion thus far lacks is an understanding of the mechanical functions which are being performed as the product moves from manufacturer to consumer. The mechanical functions of *transportation* and *storage* must be well understood because these functions contribute to:

Figure 70
Integration in Channels

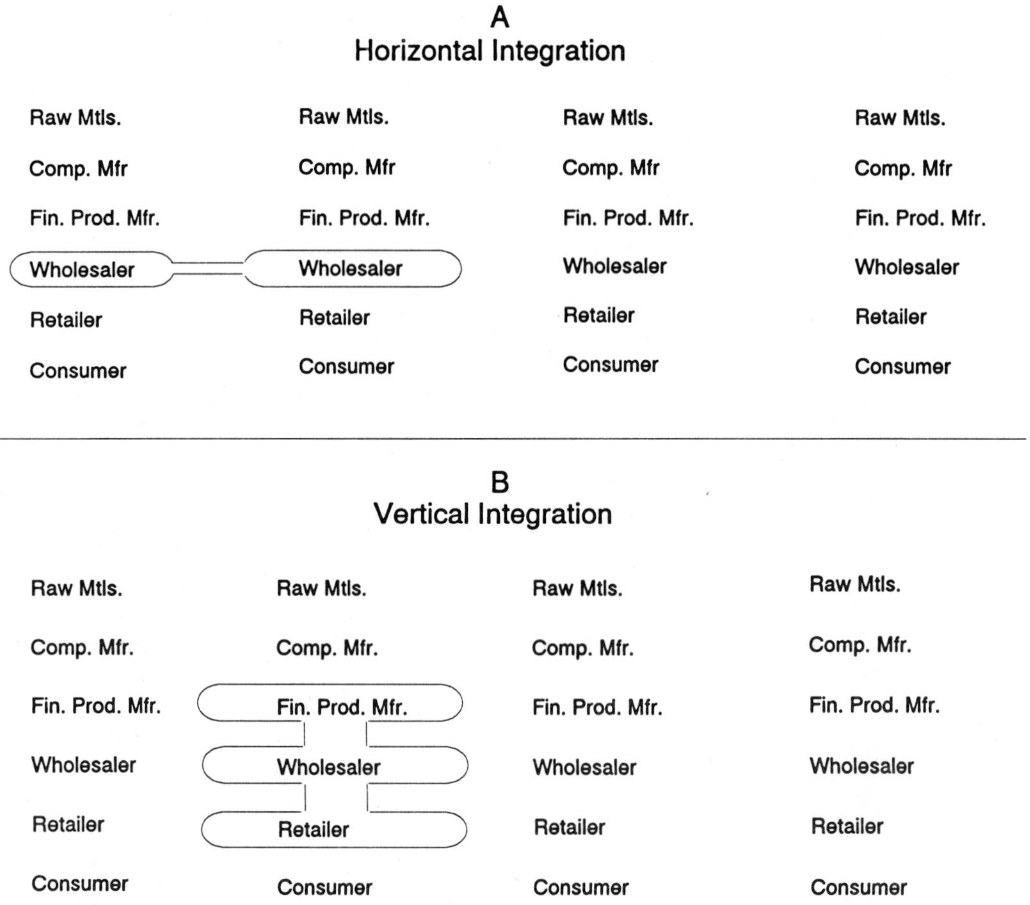

A
Horizontal Integration

Raw Mtls.	Raw Mtls.	Raw Mtls.	Raw Mtls.
Comp. Mfr	Comp. Mfr	Comp. Mfr	Comp. Mfr
Fin. Prod. Mfr.	Fin. Prod. Mfr.	Fin. Prod. Mfr.	Fin. Prod. Mfr.
Wholesaler —	— Wholesaler	Wholesaler	Wholesaler
Retailer	Retailer	Retailer	Retailer
Consumer	Consumer	Consumer	Consumer

B
Vertical Integration

Raw Mtls.	Raw Mtls.	Raw Mtls.	Raw Mtls.
Comp. Mfr.	Comp. Mfr.	Comp. Mfr.	Comp. Mfr.
Fin. Prod. Mfr.	Fin. Prod. Mfr.	Fin. Prod. Mfr.	Fin. Prod. Mfr.
Wholesaler	Wholesaler	Wholesaler	Wholesaler
Retailer	Retailer	Retailer	Retailer
Consumer	Consumer	Consumer	Consumer

1. The offering itself, as viewed by the customer. (When and where is it available? What condition is it in? How reliable is its availability?)
2. (Therefore) revenue
3. The costs incremental to the offering (incremental costs of transportation and storage)
4. (Therefore) C.O.E.

When translating what goes on in distribution into its effect upon contribution margin (C.O.E.), the incremental costs of the distribution service must be identified and the effects the distribution effort has upon revenue must be estimated. Just who among the channel members will derive which portion of the contribution margin attributable to their shared distribution effort will depend upon the negotiating wisdom and power of the individual channel member, and upon the choices of the channel leader.

Transportation and storage together comprise physical distribution. The outputs of a physical distribution effort include: *When* the product is available, *where* it is available, what *condition* it is in, and the *reliability* of these results. These outputs are collectively referred to as the *customer service level*. The customer service level should be viewed in the same way that other attributes of the offering are viewed. Customer service characteristics must successfully address the evaluative criteria of the buyer. The offering can be successfully differentiated and contribution margin created when investments are made in transportation and storage activities. If the buyer values the customer service characteristic more than society's markets have valued the labor and materials needed to create that characteristic, then contribution margin can be improved by making the investment. Industrial buyers as well as consumers differ substantially concerning which customer service characteristics are important to them.[4] For this reason research and sensitivity are required when selecting the customer service goals of a distribution effort.

Transportation Options: Their Costs and Customer Service Capabilities

When making decisions about which transportation mode to place into the distribution plan, the marketing manager must weigh the costs of the mode against its *contributions to customer service*. *Costs* in transportation are generally measured per *ton-mile*. This unit of measure is equivalent to one ton transported one mile. Thus, carriage of a two thousand pound (one ton) compact auto for two miles would be two ton-miles of transportation. Similarly, carriage of a two-ton load for four miles would be eight-ton miles of transportation. The *average costs* of providing ton-miles of transportation can be divided into *fixed* and *variable components*.

In return for the investment of these costs, the firm receives transportation services which can be seen in terms of their contribution to customer service. The *contributions to customer service* which are sensitive to differences in the mode of transportation used are:

1. Door-to-door delivery speed
2. Number of locations served
3. Ability to handle a variety of goods
4. Frequency of scheduled shipments
5. Dependability in meeting schedules

Due to basic differences in the technology of the modes of transportation, they can be expected to perform differently in these contributions to customer service. Also due to basic differences in their technology, they can be expected to have very different cost patterns. The complex pattern of costs and capabilities is best learned in the context of an understanding of the technology which characterizes each mode. These relationships are summarized in figure 71 and are discussed below.

Water

Water transportation, ocean shipping and river barge operations, are the *least expensive* forms on a ton-mile basis. *Transportation is expensive when* the process involves *overcoming* a great deal of *friction and/or gravity*. While water can generate a great deal of friction or drag at high speed, commercial ships and barges do not travel at these kinds of speeds. Water transportation also remains at water level, meaning that there is little energy expended in moving the load against the force of gravity. Some small amount of energy is expended in this way, as when ships or barges work upstream or against tides, or pay fees to pass through locks. But it does not amount to a great percentage of the energy used. Water forms of transport are also inexpensive because ships and barges can be simply constructed, as the water will hold them up and they will require no suspensions, trackways or elaborate guidance systems.

Delivery speeds are *slow* using these modes because the transit speed must be slow enough to avoid the creation of costly friction with the water. The *number of locations served is low* because domestic water transport is limited to coastal routes, the Great Lakes and the inland waterways. Viewed *in an international context* the number of *locations served would be much higher*, as two thirds of the earth's surface is covered by the worlds oceans and many of the

Figure 71
Costs Versus Contribution to Customer Service by Mode

The five contributions to customer service used here are adapted with permission from E. Jerome McCarthy and William D. Perreault, Jr., *Basic Marketing*, 9th ed. (Homewood, Illinois: Richard D. Irwin, 1987), p. 352.

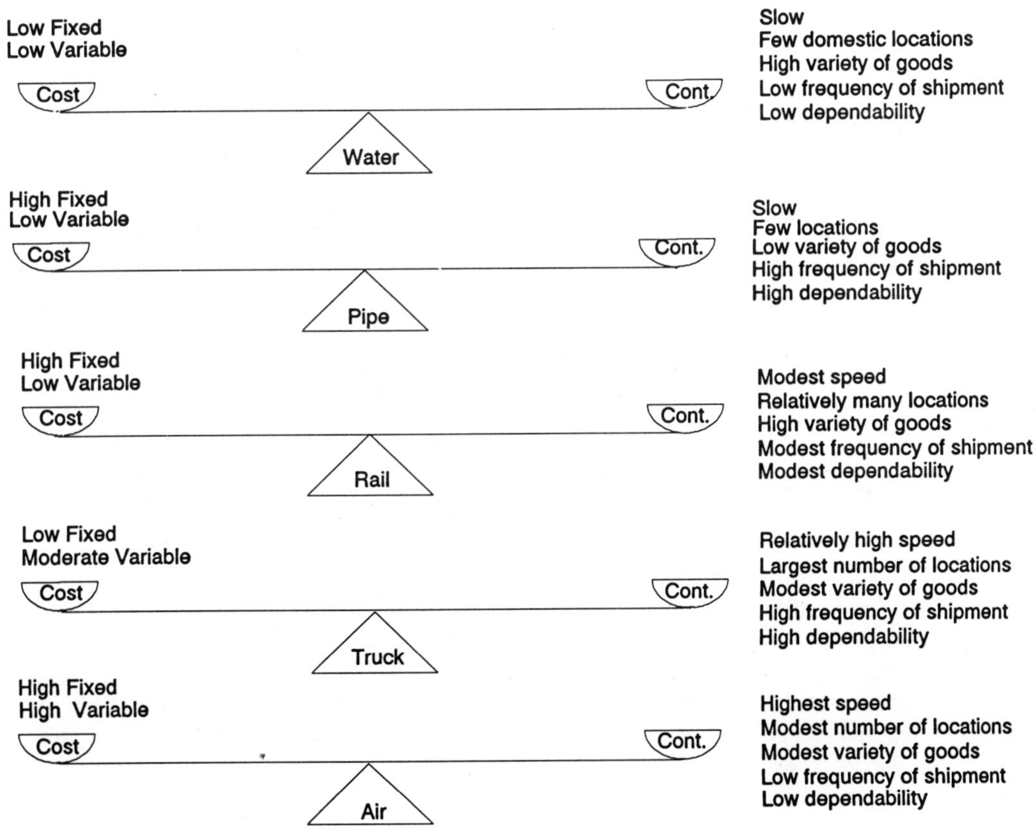

Water

Low Fixed
Low Variable
Cost — Cont.

Slow
Few domestic locations
High variety of goods
Low frequency of shipment
Low dependability

Pipe

High Fixed
Low Variable
Cost — Cont.

Slow
Few locations
Low variety of goods
High frequency of shipment
High dependability

Rail

High Fixed
Low Variable
Cost — Cont.

Modest speed
Relatively many locations
High variety of goods
Modest frequency of shipment
Modest dependability

Truck

Low Fixed
Moderate Variable
Cost — Cont.

Relatively high speed
Largest number of locations
Modest variety of goods
High frequency of shipment
High dependability

Air

High Fixed
High Variable
Cost — Cont.

Highest speed
Modest number of locations
Modest variety of goods
Low frequency of shipment
Low dependability

world's great trade centers are ocean ports. *The ability* of these modes *to handle a variety of goods is high* because the size of a ship or a barge is only limited by the size of the waterway. Oceangoing tankers of five hundred thousand ton capacity are not uncommon. The *frequency of scheduled shipments is low* because the great capacity of "barge trains" (a group of barges with a tug) and ocean-going ships means that each scheduled shipment will move a great quantity. This in turn means that many smaller individual shipments may have to be grouped to await the next sailing. *Dependability in meeting schedules is low* due to problems with weather and to the practice of using flexible sailing times to await a full cargo load.

Pipeline

Pipelines have the *next lowest average cost per ton-mile*. A pipeline requires the high fixed cost investment of establishing real estate rights, welding pipe across the country, and establishing pumping and monitoring stations. Once this has been accomplished, the variable costs associated with moving fluids through the pipeline are quite low. The friction which must be overcome depends upon the viscosity of the fluid, the nature and size of the pipeline, as well as other engineering considerations. The gravity which must be overcome depends upon the nature of the fluid and the route of the pipe. In general, the transport mode of pumping something through a pipeline is so efficient that its costs can only be beaten by putting something in a container and allowing it to float to its destination.

Door-to-door delivery speeds are slow because of the low pumping speeds used to avoid excessive friction. The *number of locations served is low* because traffic density must be high enough to justify the investment in the pipeline. In the United States this means that high volume petroleum producing and refining areas such as Texas might justify investments in pipelines. Pipelines might also be justified in carrying natural gas from fields in the southwest to a major consuming area such as Chicago. The ability to handle a *variety of goods is low* because pipelines can only handle fluids and a given pipeline is limited to the specific fluids it is designed to handle. Both *frequency of scheduled shipments and dependability in meeting schedules are high* because the shipments are continuous. In contrast with the nature of ship or barge traffic, one pipeline shipment is followed immediately by the next, and the pipe is in nearly constant operation.

Rail

Railroads have the next lowest average cost. Like pipelines, railroads invest high fixed costs in order to recover low variable costs. Unlike pipelines or water transport, rail systems must solve the relatively high friction problem of dragging something over land, a problem it shares with trucking or motor carriage. When compared to motor carriers, railroads invest higher fixed costs in the solution to this problem, and this investment results in the recovery of low variable costs. The rail system's elaborate network of carefully designed steel pathways results in modest gradients or "grades" for the locomotives to overcome when pulling their loads. The maximum grade used on a major railroad is about 1.5% or one and a half feet of vertical gain in one hundred feet of horizontal travel. These steel pathways also result in relatively low friction as steel wheels are in contact with steel rails. Railroads also invest in elaborate switching yards. These allow trains of more than one hundred cars to be quickly assembled and disassembled. A one hundred car freight train represents a capacity of roughly five thousand tons.

Door-to-door delivery speed is modest. While modern freight trains may travel at sixty to seventy-five miles per hour, the time that cars spend at sidings and involved in switch yard operations substantially reduces door-to-door delivery speed. The *number of locations served in the U.S. is relatively high* because rail was the vastly superior mode of overland transport in the late 1800s when the U.S. was undergoing rapid geographic and economic expansion. Real estate was easily obtainable, and rail reduced the cost of overland (wagon) shipments by an amazing 95%, greatly facilitating specialization and exchange.[5] The result was a vast web of railroads in the United States, with remarkable density east of the Mississippi river. Modern transportation competition has forced the abandonment of many lines, but the remaining infrastructure is still very substantial. *The ability to handle a variety of goods* is second only to water because rail uses specialized cars designed to handle everything from the fluids that pipelines handle, to the manufactured items, produce, livestock and refrigerated goods often handled by trucks. Rail's ability to handle heavy or bulky individual items is exceeded only by the water modes. Rail is particularly well suited to the carriage of large quantities of bulk commodities such as grain and coal. *Frequency of scheduled shipments and dependability in meeting schedules are modest* because, like water transport, the rail system waits while full shipments are gathered. Rail cars wait at sidings until the company shipping the product has filled them. They then wait until the railroad judges that there are enough cars waiting at sidings to justify sending a switch engine to bring the cars to a switching yard. Another wait is experienced in the yard while a long distance train is made up. In this way the rail system realizes the economies of scale of which it is capable. Switch engines do not move one car when by waiting they could move ten. Long distance trains will not depart with fifty cars if a short wait will allow the accumulation of one hundred cars for the train. Expedited shipments are available from rail companies, but their higher prices often reflect the loss of economies of scale. *Unit trains,* an entire train committed to one cargo, can be used to gain economies of scale while reducing switching costs.

Motor Carriers or Trucks

Motor carriage has the second highest average cost per ton-mile. Trucks share with rail the high friction problem of dragging a shipment over land. Despite the high fixed cost that the government has placed in the highway system (often recognized as a variable cost highway use tax by individual truckers) the highway freight system does not realize as low a set of variable costs as the rail system does. Truckers climb steeper grades, paying more to cope with gravity. They use rubber tires on concrete surfaces, creating more friction than the rail systems' steel-to-steel contract. In some states, truckers are limited to one van or trailer with a capacity of 40-50,000 pounds (20-25 tons). At most, truckers are allowed two such trailers. This results in more horsepower being used to move a pound of payload than would be used by the rail system. It also means that more labor costs might be incurred, as one truck driver can at most move about 50 tons by truck while a two-person freight train crew can move 5,000 tons. But, these are examples of variable costs. Truckers can sometimes beat rail shipment rates, because rail shipments must either be large enough or expensive enough to cover the high fixed costs of the rail system. Having greater overhead, railroads require more C.O.E. than trucking companies.

Despite high variable costs, trucks justify themselves, and their share of intercity ton-mileage has been growing. Their *door-to-door speed is second only to air* because they have transit speeds roughly equivalent to rail without much of the waiting. Once a van is filled, it often departs immediately and directly for its final destination. In cases where less than truckload (LTL) shipments are involved, some waiting is necessary. These small shipments often must be handled at a terminal, and wait there for a van to be filled. Despite this, the waits are not usually as lengthy as those experienced in rail or water transportation. It is only a forty thousand pound shipment that is needed to fill a van. *Trucks serve the largest number of locations in the U.S.* because the U.S. has made such a significant commitment to the construction and maintenance of roads. Highways serve more locations than railways. The country has been virtually "paved over", and there are very few places which are not accessible to commercial trucks. These facts would also explain the observation that shipments using the other modes of transportation often begin and end with some mileage by truck. *The ability to handle a variety of goods is modest* because trucks are severely limited in size and weight by the nature of the highway system. Too large a truck is a safety hazard for others using the highway, while too heavy a truck causes damage to the highways themselves. Therefore, state laws limit trucks sizes and weights, preventing truckers from hauling some of the loads which rail and water transport are capable of handling. *Trucks are second only to pipeline in frequency and dependability* because, almost like a pipeline, truck shipments are departing and arriving in nearly continuous fashion. The nation's highways bear a constant stream of trucks, day and night, weekday and weekend.

Air

Air is the most expensive form of transport. Fixed costs are high. Airports and air traffic control costs are expensive although largely born by government. Aircraft are expensive and computerized ticketing and scheduling equipment is expensive. Variable costs are also high. Much gravity must be overcome and friction or drag is substantial at commonly used speeds. Aircraft consume a lot of fuel and must be piloted and cared for by well paid professionals.

The return on all of these invested costs is that air is incredibly fast in comparison with other modes. Commonly used commercial transport aircraft cruise at just under the speed of sound, setting cruising speeds between five hundred and six hundred miles per hour. This results in the *fastest door-to-door delivery speed*. Aircraft speeds are often high enough to make up for the common practice of freight handling and transfer to trucks for final delivery. The *number of locations served is not as high as the number served by truck and rail roads*, due to the number of airports, but pure air freight is often combined with truck transport. This combination can result in high door-to-door delivery speed to a large number of locations. The *ability to handle a variety of goods is limited*. Whatever is being transported must not only fit into the aircraft but must not be so heavy that it is unsafe to try to fly it. Given the capabilities of even the largest and most modern aircraft, particularly bulky or heavy items are often best sent by water, rail or truck. The *frequency of scheduled shipments and the dependability in meeting schedules has historically been low for air freight*. This has been due to the relatively low volume of air freight, the practice of waiting for more complete loads, and the inevitable sensitivity of aircraft to severe weather. Innovation may be in the process of changing this record however. Air courier services such as Federal Express have demonstrated the capacity of the truck-air combination to operate with high frequency and high dependability in small package operations. Should the innovative "hub" operational techniques that have made this possible become technically and economically feasible for air freight, frequency and dependability may improve there as well.[6] In hub operations, the day's flights arrive at a central airport or "hub" by a certain time, allow time for transfer of shipments between flights, and begin departing at a certain time. Air passenger carriers have already followed air courier services in adopting this operational style.

Transportation Ownership: Cost Versus Price

The foregoing discussion has compared the *costs* of various modes of transportation with the performance characteristics that contribute to a level of *customer service*. Costs are the appropriate thing to look at if it has been the firm's decision to own the needed transportation, or if competition among transportation vendors allows the negotiation of prices that are close to costs. Of course, a successful negotiation from a transportation vendor's point of view would culminate with a price substantially above costs. Therefore, when planning physical distribution and the use of transportation vendors, marketing executives are well advised to understand the nature of transportation pricing.

Pricing in Transportation Services

Prior to 1978 most transportation companies were rigidly regulated as to what services they could provide, where they could provide them and where they could be priced. Transportation services were not so much "priced" in a market sense as simply "looked up" in a bureaucratic sense. Elaborate tariff schedules and rate manuals were consulted and the government approved tariffs or rates were found for shipments according to the type of shipment and its volume. Shipments were typed as "class" (merchandise items such as manufactured goods), "commodity" (bulk items such as grain), and "exception" (special rates). Volume was characterized as *carload or less than carload* (CL or LCL) for rail shipments and *truckload or less than truckload* (TL or LTL) for motor carrier shipments. Much of this set of pricing mechanisms remains today, but actual pricing behavior has been much changed by the relaxation of regulation.

Legislators became dissatisfied with the results of regulatory policy and began a series of deregulations in 1978. The transportation companies were not set entirely free from regulation, but an atmosphere was fostered wherein the power of the market was given a grater role in directing their offerings. Two results are important to marketing decision makers. First, the old-fashioned tariff and rate structures have not disappeared. They often describe rates which are well above the market price that a transportation vendor is willing to negotiate. A shipper is of course, welcome to pay those higher prices. Secondly, even when competition in the marketplace results in transport firms operating close to their costs, different shippers may see substantially different prices. This is because transportation operations are characterized by an *outhaul* and a *backhaul*. For most transportation shipments (the outhaul), there is a backhaul when the transportation vehicle must return to its original location. An astute shipper may force a transport firm to operate below costs on one leg of this operation. The transport firm would then be able to operate profitably if a less astute shipper would allow a compensating profit to be made on the remaining leg of the operation. Thus, pricing in transportation services has become quite flexible and market driven. The astute marketer will use market knowledge to negotiate favorable transportation values, thus contributing to lower costs and better customer service in the distribution system.

Innovation and Facilitating Transportation Services

The transportation industry offers several innovations and specific services to facilitate the channel activities of shippers. The market planner evaluating distribution options should understand that this kind of innovation is possible in transportation and should stand ready to adjust distribution activities to take advantage of it.

Intermodal service, wherein the transport effort uses several modes, has become popular. If the costs of changing from one mode to another can be kept down, it makes sense to use each mode where its cost and service capabilities can make the greatest contribution to the total distribution effort. Thus, it is not uncommon to ship goods from Japan to the American midwest using first trucks, then ships, then rail and a final truck shipment. The costs of changing from one mode to another may be kept down by using *containerization*. This method of packaging shipments in sealed metal containers resembling truck vans reduces pilferage or damage and allows the entire cargo to be moved from one mode to the other by simply moving the container. Specially shaped containers have been designed to fit into the compound curved shapes of aircraft, but these are rarely seen in intermodal use.

Another successful transportation innovation is *package express* which is provided by such diverse carriers as Federal Express, Purolator Courier, U.P.S., Burlington Northern, and the U.S. Postal Service. Package express handles letters and small packages, offering fast and frequent shipment. It generally involves a combination of air and truck transport.

Railroads offer specialized services such as a *pool car* which allows several shippers of the same kind of good to use one rail car. A *mixed car* is a similar service which allows the combination of dissimilar shipments. Railroads also provide *diversion in transit* services, which allow the shipper to divert a car which is already in transit to a new destination. This is useful if for example, a California orange grower discovers while the train is in route, that the price of oranges has dropped in St. Louis and risen in Chicago. Such a shipment might be diverted in transit from a destination in St. Louis to one in Chicago.

An important facilitating service in transportation is provided by the *freight forwarder*. A freight forwarder is a special kind of wholesaler who deals in transportation services. Freight forwarders gather small shipments from different shippers and put them together into larger shipments which realize economies of scale.

Storage Options: Their Costs and Customer Service Characteristics

Transportation facilitates the market match by resolving *discrepancies of place* or problems with *where* things are available. *Storage*, the other major component in physical distribution, resolves *discrepancies of time* or problems with *when* things are available. It makes sense for marketing decision makers to invest in the costs of storage when economies of scale in production dictate large production runs at one time, while the consumers prefer to consume the item more slowly, over a longer period of time. Generally consumers are willing to accept the costs of storage which are reflected in prices when they are able to get something exactly when they want it. They may in fact be willing to pay an incremental amount greater than the incremental amount invested in storage. When that is the case, C.O.E. has been created and the investment in storage has improved the market niche by generating higher revenues as well as retrieving the lower costs associated with economies of scale in production.

At first it would seem that storage would have minimal costs associated with it. In fact there are many kinds of costs associated with storage, and they can be quite substantial. Consider the following components of storage cost:[7]

1. *Warehousing Costs*
   The costs of maintaining a warehouse.

2. *Lot Quantity Costs*
   Costs incremental to the storage of a group or "lot" of items, generally the costs of operations associated with their storage (order costs, handling, inspections, expediting).

3. *Inventory Carrying Costs*
   Costs which are incremental to the actual storage of inventory in a warehouse and which vary with the amount stored. This includes:
   a. Capital Costs—Opportunity cost of money tied up in inventory.
   b. Inventory Service Costs—Taxes and insurance.
   c. Storage Space Costs—Costs that can be associated with the amount of space used. Some warehouses will bill the distributing firm this way.
   d. Inventory Risk Costs associated with the chance of obsolescence, damage, pilferage, etc.

Different entities which might be used for storage will allow the distributing firm to *recognize storage costs in different ways*. For example, when using a *private warehouse*, or a warehouse owned by the distributing firm, the firm will invest the high fixed costs of warehouse ownership and will retrieve lower variable costs. If the firm uses a *public warehouse* or a warehouse for hire, the distributing firm will avoid the fixed cost of investing in its own warehouse, but will see higher variable costs as reflected in bills or invoices for the use of storage space. Many of the components of storage cost, as well as market conditions and differential negotiating skills will be reflected in the public warehouse's storage space charges to the distributing firm. This pattern of costs and charges means that *storage costs per unit* are likely to be lower in the private warehouse situation when the volume of inventory stored is high. This is because when the average cost per unit is calculated, the high fixed cost will be more than compensated by the large volume of low variable costs. In similar fashion the storage costs per unit are likely to be lower in the public warehouse situation when volume is low. This is because there will be a relatively high variable cost per unit as reflected in the warehouses charges, but there will be a small number of units and no fixed costs.

Considerations besides average cost levels and patterns of cost will enter into the decision concerning whether to use a private or public warehouse. Their contribution to customer service must be evaluated. *Private warehouses are more easily controlled* by the distributing firm because the distributing firm owns them. This means that the activities of the warehouse are more easily modified to provide appropriate support for a given set of offerings. On the other hand, the use of a *public warehouse* results in great *flexibility*. Should the distributing firm suddenly decide to change the nature of its offering or shift its distribution effort to another location, it is not burdened with the fixed costs of facilities which it owns. It need only decide not to renew any existing storage contracts.

A recent innovation in storage is the *regional distribution center* or RDC. Specialized in design and therefore generally owned by the distributing firm, RDCs focus on high speed "break bulk" activities. While the function of an ordinary warehouse is to store goods over a period of time, the function of the RDC is to provide an efficient linkage between large scale forms of transportation such as carload or truckload shipments and small scale operations. This allows the distributing firm to realize economies of scale in long distance operations, efficiently break the shipment down or "break bulk" at the RDC, and dispatch smaller shipments via other transportation forms for further distribution. These facilities are usually quite modern, making considerable use of automated and computer controlled materials handling and inventory control devices.

Integrated Physical Distribution: Transportation Plus Storage

The *physical distribution system of the organization* consists of the set of commitments and policies which affect *when and where* the product or service is available. For the physical product this means physical distribution, or transportation and storage. For services, "distribution" may not be seen in the same way. In these cases, transportation may mean airline tickets for consultants, and storage may refer to commitments and policies (including storage of materials) which are affected when the services and supporting materials are available. For example, a college might open an extension center in another city, and begin offering night and weekend classes. In this way the college has altered when and where its services are available. In the case of physical products, integrated physical distribution policies will address the following kinds of *decisions in transportation and storage*:

1. Selection of warehouses or Regional Distribution Centers
2. Inventory levels for different products at different warehouses or Regional Distribution Centers
3. Inventory reorder points (inventory level at which a reorder is placed)
4. Conditions under which alternative modes of transport are used
5. Logic for decisions concerning when to ship less-than-carload or less-than-truckload versus car-load or truck-load
6. Differing policies for different types or values of goods.

The output of these kinds of decisions which is relevant to the market is the set of *customer service characteristics*. These characteristics include the *product availability*. This is the percentage of customer requests for a product which is satisfied because the product is actually there and available without a wait. The *product condition* upon delivery is also an element of customer service. Customer service characteristics such as these are only *relevant to the market* to the extent that they successfully address the buyers' evaluative criteria.[8] Some buyers do not mind waiting up to six months for a new car of a special design. Other buyers will not tolerate a vendor who does not deliver bandages to a hospital within one hour of the time the telephone order was placed. It is the *job of management* to enhance the market niche of the organization by putting integrated distribution policies together which successfully address buyers' evaluative criteria in a cost effective manner.

Enhancing the Market Niche with Integrated Distribution Policy

The goal of *integrated physical distribution* is to enhance the market niche or generate C.O.E. Depending upon the nature of demand for the product and depending on the nature of competition, investments in physical distribution might be greeted with almost any kind of revenue response. For example, revenue pattern "A" in figure 72 might illustrate the demand for Volkswagen Rabbit diesels during an oil embargo. It demonstrates that the buyers will still buy if they are forced to wait. Intensive physical distribution effort might be wasted in this extreme example. There would be no incremental revenue associated with it.

An opposite extreme example is given by revenue pattern B in figure 72. This pattern might illustrate the demand faced by a big city hospital supply operation. It shows no revenue at all until physical distribution reaches a very aggressive level. After that level is achieved, further revenue is available to those who can reduce the hospital's wait for key supplies. In figure 72 the components needed to understand C.O.E. are hidden in the two axes of the graph. Hiding in the horizontal axis are the incremental costs of physical distribution. As the level of customer service improves it is probably but not necessarily the result of spending more on physical distribution. The total revenue plotted on the vertical axis may or may not be genuinely incremental to the physical distribution effort. Assuming other factors are held equal, it appears fair in the case of revenue pattern B to say that the revenue is incremental to the physical distribution effort. In the case of revenue pattern A, it appears that revenue is not incremental to any physical distribution effort.

Because they hide so many important underlying factors, graphs are not very useful in planning real distribution systems. Graphs seem to suggest that the choice lies in selecting a level of distribution along a continuum, and that

264 Part II

Figure 72
Customer Service and Revenue

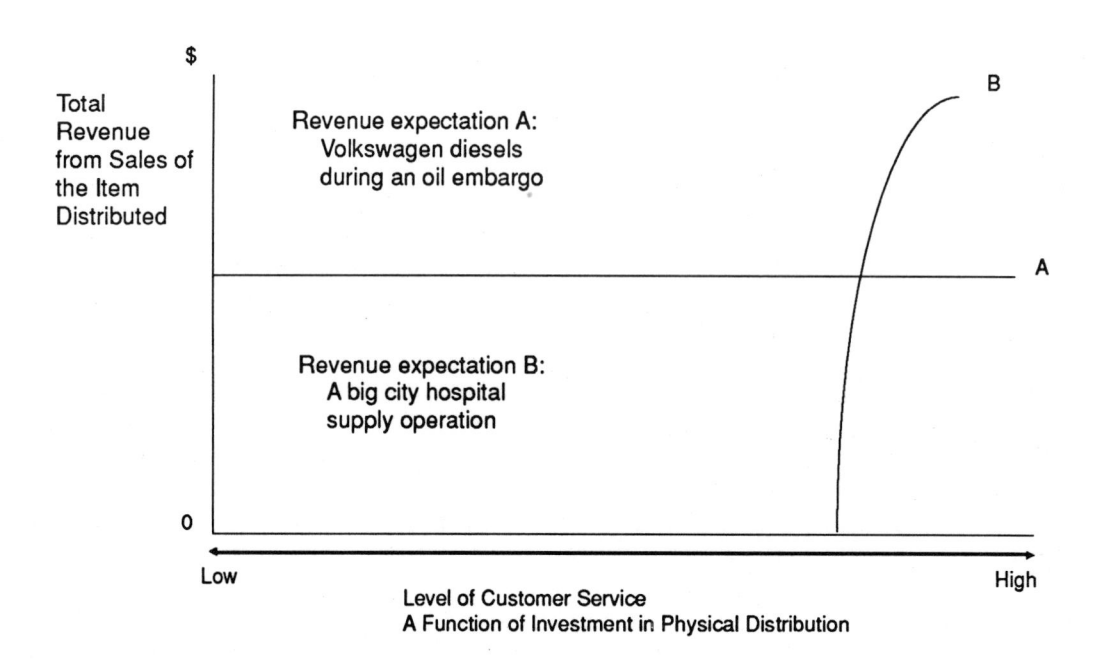

Total Revenue from Sales of the Item Distributed

$

Revenue expectation A:
Volkswagen diesels during an oil embargo

Revenue expectation B:
A big city hospital supply operation

B

A

0

Low ← Level of Customer Service → High
A Function of Investment in Physical Distribution

these choices lie along only one or two axes. In fact, choices tend to be more finite in nature. For example distribution managers must answer such questions as: Do we buy this truck or sign this trucking contract? Do we use this warehouse or that? Do we invest in an RDC in Denver or Atlanta? What should the average inventory of Barbie dolls be in Denver? When should we reorder?

Because of the large number of individual decisions that comprise the establishment of a physical distribution policy, physical distribution planning often takes the form of trying to estimate the financial implications of a specific set of options. For this reason a practical approach is to *simulate* the problem. This simulation may simply take the form of a financial analysis of the expected outcomes for each of several alternatives and it may be done with pencil and paper. Alternatively, a computer model may be constructed to simulate the problem. Some computer models of distribution problems allow the programming of policy details such as average inventory levels and the inventory levels at which an item is reordered (reorder points). Such models record the *costs* of differing levels of customer service, as the transportation and storage policies are adjusted. Market research with customers can then be used to estimate the revenue that might be associated with the differing levels of customer service. Combining these two kinds of research can lead to estimates of C.O.E. under different physical distribution policies.

When a computer model delivers estimates of the implications of particular policies it is termed a *simulation model*. Some computer models of distribution systems are designed to go beyond the evaluation of a given set of alternatives. These models are designed to find a "best" alternative and are termed *optimization models*. Optimization models can be successful to the extent that the relationships between transportation, storage, customer service and revenue can be accurately represented in mathematical form. As this is a difficult task, simulation models remain a practical and much used alternative.

Crossing National Boundaries

The international distribution effort involves new variations on the principle themes presented above. Within the *channel*, there will be *new entities*. Freight forwarders will now deal with *stevedores*, people responsible for putting an ocean load together, and both will deal with large, often intermodal, *international transport companies*. Upon arrival in the new country the shipment must be prepared to pass customs by *customs brokers*. After this preparation, the shipment is reviewed by customs officials. *Customs officials* are representatives of the government of the country receiving the shipment.

They are responsible for valuing, classifying and clearing incoming shipments. International distribution channels often are characterized by *more levels*. That is, a greater number of wholesale entities than would be found in a U.S. channel of distribution would be common. This situation would not be easy for the U.S. distributor to change, as it is often national policy to preserve employment by protecting this kind of inefficient distribution system.

Products going overseas will have to deal with *tariff* and *non tariff barriers*. A tariff is a fee straightforwardly assessed on a product coming into a country. It generally exists for the protection of the local producers and may be assessed in any of a number of ways. Tariffs have been reduced substantially by *GATT*, the General Agreement on Tariffs and Trade. Non tariff barriers are less straightforward barriers to trade such as safety and quality regulations. They often serve the same purpose as tariffs, protecting local producers. Because of their more complex nature they are more difficult to deal with. GATT has been less successful in reducing non tariff barriers.

Financing in the distribution channel will become *more complex* due to currency fluctuations and the need to provide security for the funds transferred between buyers and sellers who are greatly separated by distance, as well as by differences in language, culture and law. International banks have devised *letters of credit* and other financial devices to provide this kind of security.

The *transportation* problem is substantially different when placed in an international context. Industrial development has not provided all of the nations of the world with the kind of dense and well developed infrastructure of highways, railroads and airports that it has provided in the U.S. and Europe. This, combined with the fact that the majority of the earth's surface is covered by ocean, means that water transport will be of great use in international distribution. The protection against weather and pilferage that is available when using containers will make containerized shipment more attractive. Climatic differences will require *different storage approaches* and the availability and reliability of storage options will differ country by country. Beyond this, the *relationship of customer service to demand* will be very different culture by culture. In some cultures, a long wait is expected and may not affect demand.

Chapter Summary

The relationship between product and price in the voluntary exchange can be adjusted by changing *when* and *where* the product or service is available. Management adjusts this by making decisions concerning which other organizations will help in the distribution effort and how the products will be transported and stored.

Members of the channel of distribution may include wholesalers and retailers. Wholesalers exist in the channel by virtue of their ability to perform one or more of the marketing functions in a way that is attractive to other channel members and profitable for themselves. Retailers exist in the channel by virtue of performing the function of selling to the end consumer, among the other functions they may choose to perform.

The channel members will undertake transportation and storage activities to accomplish the physical distribution of their products. They will use the various modes of transportation (air, rail, water, pipeline and motor carriage) in combination with warehousing and regional distribution centers to achieve a level of customer service. If this level of customer service successfully addresses the buyers' evaluative criteria in a cost effective way, contribution margin can be improved through distribution activities.

---

[1] E. Jerome McCarthy and William D. Perreault, Jr., *Basic Marketing*, 9th ed. (Homewood, Illinois: Richard D. Irwin, 1987), p. 317.

[2] Ibid.

[3] Ibid., pp. 317-318.

[4] A complete discussion of customer service characteristics and how they are valued in different industries is available in Bernard J. LaLonde and Paul H. Zinszer, *Customer Service: Meaning and Measurement* (Chicago: National Council of Physical Distribution Management, 1975).

[5] Stanley Shapiro and Alton Doody, *Readings in the History of Marketing; Settlement to the Civil War* (Homewood, Ill.: Richard D. Irwin, 1968), pp. 212-213.

[6] Air Hub operations, where cross crountry transportation is effected by flying first to a central hub, transferring to another aircraft, and then flying to the end destination, have made passenger and small package transportation more efficient in the U.S.

[7] The components of storage cost are owed to Douglas M. Lambert, *The Development of the Inventory Costing Methodology: A Study of the Costs Associated with Holding Inventory* (Chicago, Ill.: National Council of Physical Distribution Management, 1976), p. 7. See also Donald J. Bowersox, M. Bixby Cooper, Douglas M. Lambert, and Donald A. Taylor, *Management in Marketing Channels* (New York: McGraw-Hill, 1980), p. 210. Reprinted with permission, Council of Logistics Management (formerly National Council of Physical Distribution). Copyright 1976.

[8] See LaLonde.

Questions for Study, Discussion and Examination

1. Can you define, or explain to a friend who has not studied marketing, each of the following terms or ideas?
    a. Adjusting the exchange by adjusting when and where something is available
    b. Channel decision
    c. Channel of distribution
    d. Channel member
    e. Form of channel organization
    f. Traditional channel
    g. Vertical marketing system
    h. "Vertical" and "horizontal" dimensions in channels
    i. Administered system
    j. Contractual system
    k. Corporate system
    l. Wholesaler
    m. Creative flexibility
    n. Channel leader
    o. Sources of power
    p. Consumer trust as a source of power
    q. Wholesaler performing functions to survive
    r. Merchant wholesaler
    s. Agent middle person
    t. Retailer
    u. Axes along which consumers might evaluate retailers
    v. Individualistic evaluative criteria in evaluating retailers
    w. The above as a basis for retailing segmentation
    x. "Types" of wholesalers (give some examples)
    y. "Types" of retailers (give some examples)
    z. Convenience store
    aa. Shopping store
    ab. Chain
    ac. Corporate chain

Chapter 7 269

ad. Cooperative chain
ae. Voluntary chain
af. Franchise operation
ag. Specialty shop
ah. Supermarket
ai. Superstore
aj. Discount house
ak. Mass merchandiser
al. High unit movement vs. low unit movement retail strategies
am. Data base systems
an. Software for analysis of information
ao. "Just in time" delivery system
ap. Material handling equipment
aq. Credit strategy
ar. Wheel of retailing
as. Shifting and sharing of functions
at. Horizontal integration
au. Vertical integration
av. Backward integration
aw. Forward integration
ax. Transportation and storage
ay. Physical distribution
az. Customer service level
ba. Ton-mile
bb. Fixed and variable components of transport cost
bc. Contribution to customer service
bd. Modes of transport (5)
be. CL, LCL, TL, LTL
bf. Outhaul
bg. Backhaul
bh. Intermodal service
bi. Containerization
bj. Package Express
bk. Pool car
bl. Mixed car
bm. Diversion in transit

bn. Freight forwarder
bo. Discrepancies of place
bp. Discrepancies of time
bq. Components of storage cost
br. private warehouse
bs. Public warehouse
bt. Regional distribution center
bu. Break bulk
bv. Physical distribution system of the organization (for products, for services)
bw. Decisions in transportation and storage
bx. Product availability
by. Product condition
bz. Customer service characteristics which are relevant to the market
ca. The goal of integrated physical distribution
cb. Simulation in physical distribution
cd. Simulation model
ce. Optimization model
cf. Stevedore
cg. Customs broker
ch. Customs official
ci. Tariff barrier
cj. Non tariff barrier
ck. GATT
cl. Letter of credit
cm. Factor
cn. Broker

2. How can distribution activities affect the product price relationship in voluntary human exchange?

3. How can the market niche of the organization be enhanced by distribution activities?

4. Compare and contrast the forms of channel organization. How is each held together? How is change initiated in each?

5. Evaluate the strengths and weaknesses of the various forms of channel organization.

6. How does the term "creative flexibility" help us understand who is to perform which marketing function in a channel of distribution?

Chapter 7 271

7. What determines who is to be the channel leader?
8. How does consumer trust confer power in a channel? How is the trust gained? Through what mechanisms does it deliver its power to a channel member? How can the power then be exercised?
9. What other sources of power might there be in a distribution channel? Give examples of each and describe how each might function in a channel of distribution.
10. Give an example of how a wholesaler might survive in a channel by performing each of the marketing functions. Which will actually be performed by a given wholesaler and how will that choice be made?
11. Give examples of how specific types of wholesalers might be characterized by the functions they perform.
12. What functional activities characterize a retailer? How is it determined that a retailer will perform certain functions and not others? How is a retailer in a unique position of strength to alter the nature of the exchange?
13. Relate the set of axes along which a consumer might evaluate a retailer (page 240) to the following ideas:
    a. $\frac{mu}{P}$
    b. Consumer behavior or psychology
    c. Individualistic evaluative criteria
    d. Segmentation in retailing
    e. C.O.E.
    f. Retailer strategy
14. Demonstrate how retailer strategy can be characterized using the concepts brought out in the above question (7 concepts) plus the way in which the retailer generates contribution margin in terms of unit movement and margin per unit (8 concepts total).
15. Characterize several specific "types" of retailer using the eight concepts generated in the above question. Illustrate your understanding using examples from the local community.
16. Explain the advantages of a retail "chain" from the perspective of the manager of an individual retail store.
17. Suppose you had the money to start a store in an established franchise chain such as McDonalds. What would you see the advantages and disadvantages of this business proposition to be?

18. In terms of retail strategy and operations, what impact would you see as coming from the evolution of data base systems, analytical software, just in time delivery systems, and any other technological changes you are aware of?

19. Compare and contrast the innovation life cycle and the wheel of retailing.

20. What is meant by shifting and sharing functions in the channel? How does it happen? Can you give specific examples of this?

21. Illustrate examples of cooperation and competition in channels of distribution. How would you view the result of this activity from the point of view of society? How would you view these activities from the point of view of the individual channel member? What is the relationship of competition to cooperation? Does this differ depending upon the form of channel organization?

22. Why would firms wish to involve themselves in horizontal integration activities? In vertical integration activities? As a business person what would you see the advantages and disadvantages of such activities to be? Can you give some examples of each form of integration?

23. How can the functions of transportation and storage add to contribution margin?

24. How is the contribution margin generated by transportation, storage (and other functions performed in the channel) divided up among the channel members?

25. What are the outputs of a physical distribution system? How should the relative importance of these be decided?

26. Evaluate the "water" transportation mode in terms of its: a) costs, b) contributions to customer service.

27-30. Evaluate the pipeline (27), rail (28), truck (29), air (30) transportation mode in terms of its: a) costs, b) contributions to customer service.

31. How does transportation ownership determine whether costs or price of transport service is an appropriate focus for your organization?

32. How should the distribution manager be sure that he or she has negotiated the best possible transportation price with the vendor? What pitfalls should the manager be aware of?

33. Why do you think the following transportation innovations developed?
    a. Intermodal service
    b. Containerization
    c. Package express
    d. Pool car
    e. Mixed car
    f. Diversion in transit

    Based upon your understanding of these, what transportation innovations would you expect next?
34. Explain why marketing planners must consider distribution. How does this relate to the concepts of "discrepancies of place" and "discrepancies of time." Can you relate this discussion to the concept of economies of scale?
35. What does it cost to store something? Can you break these costs down in detail and give examples?
36. Demonstrate what you would have to consider in making the choice between a private and a public warehouse. How would the costs be different? How would the contributions to customer service be different?
37. What is the value of a regional distribution center?
38. What is integrated physical distribution? Give some examples of the kinds of decisions that go to make up physical distribution policies.
39. Are the concepts of distribution useful in the marketing of services? Explain.
40. What is the job of management in physical distribution? The goal of integrated physical distribution? How should management determine the appropriate product availability to set for their distribution system?
41. Does improved physical distribution always "pay off"? Why or why not?
42. Give an example of a simulation approach to distribution costing. How would you turn this into an estimate of C.O.E.? When does it make sense to computerize something like this?
43. If you have the skills, try writing a computer program to simulate distribution costs. Bring the program to class and demonstrate its use.

Alternatively, find a "canned" or preprogrammed package which does the same thing and demonstrate its use to the class.

44. Distinguish between a simulation model and an optimization model. What difficulties might be encountered with the optimization approach?
45. What changes in your distribution activities might you as a manager expect when crossing national boundaries?

PART III

MANAGING THE MARKET EXCHANGE PROCESS

The first part of this book developed an understanding of the voluntary exchange process and the resulting market niche of the firm. The second part examined the effects of the managerially controlled variables of product, price, promotion and place upon that market niche. The third and final part of the book examines the process of marketing management. The understanding of this process is developed in terms of the gathering and analysis of information, information synthesis as it leads to strategic choice, and the legal and ethical guidelines which should inform strategic choice. Some attention is given to direction and control activities such as management by objectives and budgeting, as they are necessarily linked to the strategic choices of the firm, but a detailed discussion of these activities is left to authors in the field of management.

Throughout this discussion, recognition will be given to the fact that organizations differ substantially in size and sophistication. Ideas are therefore discussed both from an entrepreneurial perspective and from a major corporate perspective. Many firms may then be understood by viewing their behavior as lying somewhere in the spectrum between these two styles of marketing behavior. Another distinction in perspective is used in this last section of the book. A differentiation is made between normative managerial ideas, or ideas having to do with the way the process should be managed, and empirical descriptions of how the process may proceed given the natural imperfections in human motivation and behavior. An understanding of this distinction should allow the reader to be creative in dealing with the realities of company politics when pursuing goals.

CHAPTER 8

GAINING AND ANALYZING INFORMATION

The *entrepreneur* is an individual who initiates exchanges, bears the costs, and reaps any reward that might result. This person is an intuitive market matchmaker. The entrepreneur sees a match, an opportunity to solve a problem or make some money, and jumps in. Perhaps the characteristic lack of formal information gathering is part of the reason for the high rate of failure among entrepreneurial firms. The entrepreneur can rarely afford formal information gathering when first starting an enterprise, although the entrepreneur may take in information. The entrepreneur may have been reading and observing for years. It is fair to say that in an informal fashion, the entrepreneur has researched the market match to which so much will be committed.

Environmental Scans

By contrast, the *major firm* is often committed to an extensive and formal process of information gathering and analysis. It may *scan the environment*, routinely picking up and analyzing information concerning the target markets and important publics. This may involve their numbers, ages, incomes, psychology and sociology. The environmental scan is likely to include information about the evolving political, legal, economic, technical and competitive environments.[1] It may include routine image studies concerning how the organization is seen from year to year. *Scan behavior* is routine information gathering for the purpose of maintaining a picture of how the firm's situation is evolving. Scan behavior may be external as just described, or internal as in the case of routine profitability reports or annual audits.

When *scanning target markets*, the firm may wish to begin by understanding the *demographics* of the market. The demographics are the numbers that describe a group of people. The demographics of a group would include how many people there are in the group, the proportion of the group that is male versus female, the ages that characterize the group, and other straightforward measures such as incomes and places of residence. Demographics may be used to characterize existing markets, or a demographic description of a larger group of people such as the U.S. population might be used to identify new potential target markets. For example, demographic understandings of the United States have led to the identification of target markets of "yuppies" (young upwardly mobile urban professionals), "dinks" (double income, no kids), and "baby boomers" (the large group of people born after World War II). Common demographic terms used in marketing comprise figure 73. Scanning target markets may also involve the routine collection of psychological and sociological data concerning how people feel about things and with whom they associate.

This kind of psychological and sociological information is more difficult and expensive to collect than demographic data, and so is more commonly associated with *directed information gathering*. *Directed information gathering* differs from scan behavior in that it is focused on a particular problem or opportunity. A more detailed discussion of this type of information will be a part of a later description of directed information gathering.

When *scanning the political and legal environment*, the firm will want to make use of its lobbyists and other government contacts. The idea here is to try to sense how political feelings are evolving and thus be in a position to anticipate new laws affecting the firm. This will allow time for adjustment of the offering or the initiation of political and communications efforts to change the course of events. The effects of regulation upon the individual firm were introduced in chapter three.

When *scanning the economic environment*, the firm wishes to anticipate general conditions in the economy as well as changes in the markets in which it may participate. Understanding the general condition of the economy is important because it represents the "current within which all firms must swim." For example, a firm that is just holding its own in a competitive sense, and is not losing or gaining market share, might enjoy substantial sales growth if the national economy is enjoying rapid growth. On the other hand, a "winning firm," one which is surpassing its competition and increasing market share, might see a loss in sales if the economy is in a general decline.

Figure 73
Common Demographic Terms Used in Marketing

Age Distribution: The number of people in different age groups

Baby Boomer: One of the large group born after World War II

Birth Rate: The number of babies born per 1,000 people

Dink: A demographic segmentation (double income, no kids)

Disposable Income: That left after tax

Discretionary Income: That left after tax and necessities

Family Life Cycle Stages:
    Singles
    Divorced or separated
    Newly married couples, no children
    Full nest I (youngest child under 6)
    Full nest II (youngest child over 5)
    Full nest III (older couples with dependent children)
    Empty nest (older couples, no children at home. Head of household still working)
    Sole survivor, still working
    Senior Citizen I (older couples, no children at home, head of household retired)
    Senior citizen II (sole survivor not working)

Gross Domestic Product (GDP): The dollar value of all final goods and services produced in a country.

Gross National Product (GNP): GDP adjusted for nationality of ownership

GNP per Capita: GNP divided by population

Household: All persons living in one house, apartment, or dwelling area

Household Income: Income from all earners in a household

Income Distribution: The proportion of income going to different segments of the population

Metropolitan Statistical Area (MSA): An urban region used for statistical summaries

Yuppie: A demographic segmentation (Young upwardly mobile professional)

Even the best economists seem unable to predict the economy with accuracy, but marketing people should have a general idea of where the economy is going if they are to plan for their firm or organization. In general, the economy is seen in terms of the effects of government policy, consumers, and businesses upon the *general level of price* and upon *economic growth*. The general level of price is reflected in the *inflation rate* (rate of increase in the general level of price) or less commonly in the deflation rate (rate of decrease in the general level of price). Either is measured as a percentage for a time period, often a year. Economic growth or decline is measured using *gross national product* or *GNP*. Gross national product is the market value of all final goods and services produced and sold within the time period, usually a year. A national economy is seen as an aggregation (or combination) of all the exchanges within the economy. Thus, it is common to view a national economy as depicted in figure 74. Figure 74 depicts the price level (P) and the gross national product or national income (Y) as the axes. The exact levels of price and GNP or national income (P_a and Y_a in figure 74) are determined by the interaction of aggregate demand (Y_d) with aggregate supply (Y_s). This may be seen in much the same way as demand and supply are seen to interact in individual product or service markets.

For practical market planning purposes, the following generalizations will be useful in most situations. *Aggregate demand will be stimulated* (move to the right in figure 74) when government increases its spending, reduces taxes, increases the money supply, or when other dynamics encourage increases in consumer spending or business investment. Stimulation of aggregate demand can be inflationary unless it is paced by an increase in aggregate supply. *Increases in aggregate supply*, graphed by moving Ys to the right, represent business decisions to supply more to the economy. This may accompany favorable tax policy or other dynamics which increase the return on the investment in supplying larger quantities to the economy. Understanding these basics will provide an idea of what should be monitored in the national economy and why.[2] Marketing planners should be aware of government fiscal policy (taxation and spending), monetary policy, consumer confidence and spending, business investment and other signs of business intent to supply. The prediction of economic direction may also be facilitated using *economic indicators*. These are measures within the economy which have been observed to move before, with, or after moves in GNP. *Leading indicators* are measures within the economy which "lead GNP" by moving in the direction GNP will soon move. *Coincident indicators* move with GNP, while *lagging indicators* follow GNP. A list of leading indicators comprises figure 75. Once an understanding of the general direction of the economy is developed, it should be augmented with an understanding of the evolving nature of the firm's individualistic market niche within that economy.

Chapter 8 281

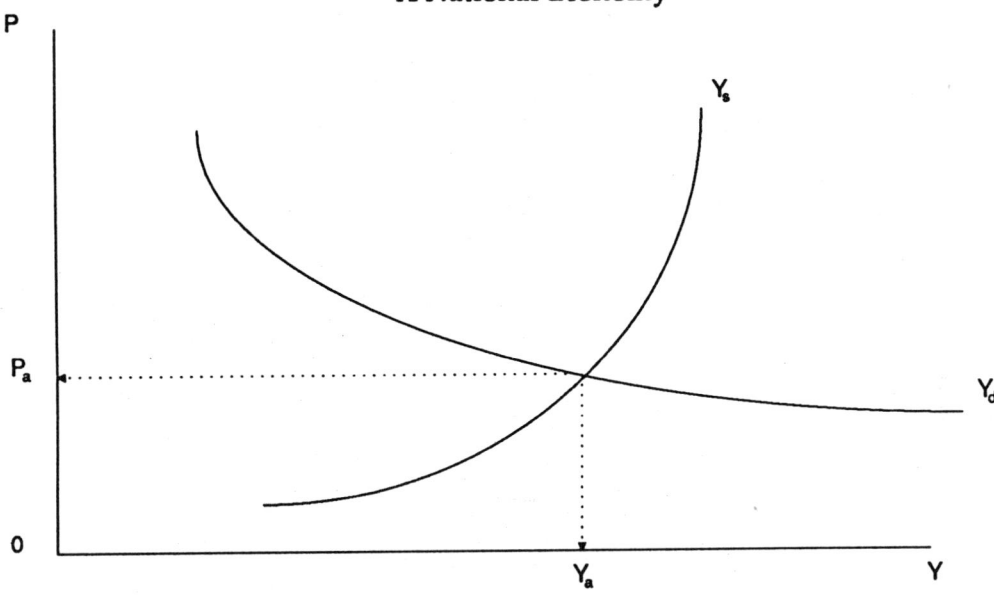

Figure 74
A National Economy

Y	=	Gross National Product (GNP)	=	Market value of all final goods and services in the economy
Y_d	=	Aggregate Demand	=	Demand for all goods and services in the economy
Y_s	=	Aggregate Supply	=	Supply of all goods and services in the economy
Y_a	=	Actual GNP	=	Current year's market value of all final goods and services in the economy
P_a	=	Actual Price Level	=	Current year's general level of prices

Figure 75
Leading Indicators in the U.S. Economy

Reprinted by permission of the publisher, from *The U.S. Economy Demystified* by Albert T. Sommers (Lexington, MASS: Lexington Books, Copyright 1985, D. C. Heath and Company).

Anticipated capital outlays for plant and equipment (from surveys of business)

Automobile sales

Budgetary authorizations from the federal budget

Construction contract awards

Construction starts for residential buildings

Consumer confidence (from surveys of consumers)

Machinery ordering rates

Major household goods sales

Monthly change in business inventories

New incorporations

New orders in manufacturing industries

More defense capital goods orders

Scanning the technical environment is important due to the substantial economic power of successful innovation, as demonstrated by the innovation life cycle. A firm introducing a successful innovation may stand to gain years of quasi monopoly advantage. A firm facing a competitor's successful innovation may have to accept reduced prices and reduced unit movement on its existing line of offerings. The firm keeps abreast of technological developments by investing in its own research and development (R&D) group and by being sure that they attend conferences and mix with other professionals. It also invests in technological journals, newsletters, and other sources of information such as information available through the U.S. patent office.

Scanning the competitive environment is critical because the nature of the competition will determine the market structure. Market structure in turn will say much about the kind of market niche that is available to the firm. These perspectives have been explored in chapter three. In cases where the competition involves differentiated products, the specific offerings of the competition and the way they are viewed by consumers will influence the product, price, promotion and place that are appropriate to offer. These perspectives have been developed in chapters three, five, six and seven. Scanning the competition is also a way to pick up clues concerning other aspects of the environment. Management should always be asking what the behavior of competition says about where the competition thinks that markets, politics, laws, technology and the economy may be going. *The various components of an environmental scan combine to describe one reality.*[3]

For the scan of the external environment, the firm may rely upon a vast and differentiated collection of *information sources*. It may rely upon *syndicated services*. These can include the routine polling of target markets and other important publics concerning the image of firms in the industry. The firm may subscribe to economic and legal *newsletters*. It may employ *econometricians* to generate economic forecasts and lobbyists or other governmental contacts to generate political and legal forecasts. The organization will probably hold *technical journals and bulletins* concerning the industry and may routinely scan information concerning *new patents*. The firm would also subscribe to sources of *competitive information*. These would include audit data provided by outside suppliers which would describe the *market shares* of the firm and its competitors. Audit data can also include *competitive activities*, such as what competitor's salespeople are currently emphasizing. Data such as these can be supplied to the firm in written form as a collection of books. But the evolution of *modern data base technology* has allowed vendors of information to provide an attractive service by simply *selling access to the data base* they have developed. Such data bases, information stored for computers and arranged for efficient access, can be focused on any aspect of the environment. *Information concerning competition* is common, and *information concerning consumers* is becoming so complete that it allows pinpoint targeting of individual consumers. Often the computer terminals used to access such data bases also provide an *analytical capability*. The market analyst might draw information from the data base and perform statistical analyses on the data using the same terminal. To fill gaps which develop between sources of information, firms might subscribe to the services of an *information clearing house*. These operations are usually based in major cities where they have access to libraries and data bases. They also run telephone operations and many are willing to spend a great deal of time on the telephone to find a piece of information. Many modern corporations are not as conscious of security as they might be. *Competitive intelligence* or confidential information about competitive activities can sometimes be derived by simply calling several phones within the company of interest and asking about what's going on.

Internal Scans or Audits

The firm also gains information through internal scans or audits. The development of *modern data base technology* has facilitated this behavior. Many firms are now able to quickly and accurately retrieve internal numbers about sales and costs, and arrange them in several ways. Arrangement and delivery of accounting data in a way that is useful to marketing requires the quick and accurate isolation of revenues and costs incremental to the firm's offerings so as to allow the creation of *C.O.E. reports* as well as the necessary but more routine financial reports. A given firm's accounting procedures, data base design, information system design, and information system staff may or may not facilitate this kind of critical internal scan.

Internal scan behavior also includes accurate and timely *reporting and analyses of marketing activities*. This would include sales call reporting, and information about unit movement and inventory levels on different products. When the product line is large, reporting procedures and designs might use the *report by exception principle*, reporting only those activities which are not within the planned parameters of operation.

Internal scan behavior should also include routine solicitation of marketing ideas, information, and suggestions from any individual in the firm who might wish to contribute. At a minimum, the firm should not fail to seek marketing ideas, information and suggestions from sales people, experienced executives, R&D people, finance and production people. The old idea of the employee suggestion box would not be a bad way to augment this kind of information gathering.

Scan behavior is an ongoing and routine corporate information gathering process. Scan behavior results in the development of formal and informal situation analyses.

These analyses evaluate the organization's evolving fit with its environment and attempt to identify the *problems and opportunities* which are likely to be encountered. Situation analyses may be performed on individual products or services or may focus on the firm as a whole. Individual product or service analyses are likely to be generated by a *marketing services staff*, while analyses for the firm as a whole are likely to be developed by a *marketing planning staff* or a *corporate level strategic planning staff*. While these groups generate formal situation analyses, the formal reports are only as important as they are influential with *top executives and board members*. These top level individuals will have a *situation analysis of their own*, often informal and unwritten. It is this *situation analysis* that *guides the organization*.[4]

Directed Information Gathering: Market Research

Scan behavior is augmented by *directed information gathering*. This is information gathering behavior which is directed toward or focused upon a specific problem or opportunity. This problem or opportunity may have been identified by a situation analysis, or by an individual in the organization. Directed information gathering is project oriented and ad-hoc in nature, designed to develop information for a given situation. In this way it stands in contrast with the ongoing nature of scan behavior.

Directed information gathering may include a re-evaluation of *secondary data*. Secondary data are data which have already been published for another purpose. For example, the firm might re-evaluate the environmental scan data used to develop the situation analysis itself. But directed information gathering is also likely to involve the development of *primary data*. These are data which are generated to address the specific problem or opportunity under study. The gathering of primary data may take the form of a special inquiry using some of the information sources previously discussed as information sources for scan behavior. It is also likely to take the form of a *market research project*.

A Market Research Project

Understanding the nature of a market research project is critical to marketing management. Although the project itself is commonly left to professionals such as the company's market analysts and outside research suppliers, marketing managers must know enough to be able to evaluate the quality of the work. This section will introduce some of the choices which must be made when researching a market.

Market Research: The Management Problem

When engaging in a market research project, one of the first steps is to discuss, and agree upon a careful statement of the *management problem*. This procedure begins to build an understanding of the problem and the resulting statement serves to focus and guide the research procedures that follow. An example of a statement of a management problem might be: "The management problem is to determine whether or not research and development result number 'A-24' is profitably marketable."

A review of secondary data is usually appropriate at this point. Analysis of secondary data might have identified the management problem in the first place, but a second review of the data, in the context of the new, more carefully stated management problem, can provide new pieces for the puzzle. For example, previously overlooked information about costs or competition may now be seen as important. Once this review is accomplished, the places where information is desirable but lacking should become evident. Information to fill these gaps can be obtained by designing and conducting market research.

Market Research: The Research Problem

The next step in research design is to translate the management problem into a statement of the *research problem*. While the management problem reflects management's broad decision making orientation, the research problem is data oriented, providing guidance for the development of new information. An example of a research problem might be, "to determine the extent to which medical doctors (in the specialties specified) would intend to prescribe R&D result 'A-24' for the (specified) indications." At this point perspectives from psychology, consumer behavior, economics and finance as developed in this book should be reviewed. The research problem should be as carefully thought out as possible. Perhaps what you want to know is how something is perceived. Perhaps what you want to know is what the evaluative criteria are. Perhaps what you want to know is price elasticity of demand. Perhaps you want to go directly to C.O.E., combining cost knowledge with knowledge about price elasticity of demand.

Market Research: Research Design

The selection of a research design follows the final formulation of a statement of the research problem. The research design includes the general approach and such specific details as sample size, questionnaire design, method of getting the questionnaire into the field, statistics and analysis approaches.

Several considerations affect the general approach to the project. One is whether or not the project can be conducted as a carefully controlled *experiment*. This approach is desirable but is not always possible. The experimental approach requires that the research design isolate the effects of the variables under study. There are several forms of experimental design. A typical approach is illustrated in figure 76. In the case illustrated in figure 76, the experimental advertisement seems to have had no effect. Since awareness increased by the same percentage in the control group as it did in the experimental group, the increase in product awareness must be due to another factor such as a newspaper story. Experiments such as these are desirable in their ability to isolate results in this way. If no control group had been used, it would appear that the advertisement had increased awareness by ten percent.

Another choice to be made in the general approach of the research design is whether to *observe* behavior or *communicate* with the subjects. If communication is chosen, the *form of communication* (mail, telephone or face to face interview), must also be selected. Each approach will have its positives and negatives. Observation of behavior without the subjects' knowledge may encourage realistic behaviors, but often sacrifices depth of understanding. Depth can be had by communicating, but often at the expense of candor. Each form of communication will also have positives and negatives. For example, mail allows a careful response, but response rates are often low.

Figure 76
An Experimental Design Using a Control Group

R Random Assignment to Experimental Group	O Observation Awareness = 35%	X Experimental Advertisement	O Observation Awareness = 45%
R Random Assignment to Control Group	O Observation: Awareness = 35%		O Observation: Awareness = 45%

The general research approach also reflects decisions concerning the extent to which *qualitative* versus *quantitative techniques* are used. Qualitative techniques can yield in-depth understandings of a few people, while quantitative techniques sacrifice some depth to obtain sample sizes large enough for *statistical inference*. Statistical inference is the process of arriving at estimates of population "parameters" (characteristics) given the sample "statistics" or results. The population is defined as the entire group which is under study.

Qualitative techniques do not allow statistical inferences to be made, but they do allow topic exploration with great depth and sensitivity. A *focus group interview* or "focused" group interview is a commonly used qualitative technique. These interviews are used to explore a topic in some depth with a small (often five to ten person) group. In these situations, a moderator guides the group through points of interest which are set out in the moderator's *discussion guide*. Audio and visual records are made of the conversation and observers may be present, although such observers are usually not visible to the group involved in the discussion. One way glass is often used to facilitate observation. In a *depth interview*, individuals may be interviewed one at a time and attempts made to understand their innermost feelings about the topic. Qualitative techniques such as these are often used to guide or serve as a *pilot study* for a study which uses quantitative techniques.

Quantitative research uses a large enough set of observations, often including hundreds or thousands, to allow statistical inferences to be made about the population from which the sample was drawn. The logic of statistical inference is explored in figure 77. In designing a quantitative study, a *sample frame* must be chosen which is representative of the population to be studied. The sample frame is the list or source of individual names. For example, a telephone book might be used as a sample frame. There will be some difficulties with most sample frames that are chosen. The telephone book will systematically exclude those with unlisted numbers and those with no telephones at all, giving this frame a certain bias toward selection of individuals in the middle of the socioeconomic spectrum.

Once a frame is selected, individuals must then be chosen to participate in the research. For purposes of statistical inference, it is desirable that each individual in the population have an equal chance of being included in the sample. Sampling procedures conforming to this rule are termed *random sampling*. Other forms of sampling include convenience sampling, systematic sampling and stratified random sampling. Sampling procedures are outlined in figure 78.

The size of the sample, the questionnaire design and the statistics used should generally be determined together, as they are quite dependent upon one another. The *questionnaire* may make use of one or several of many types

Chapter 8   289

**Figure 77
Statistical Inference**

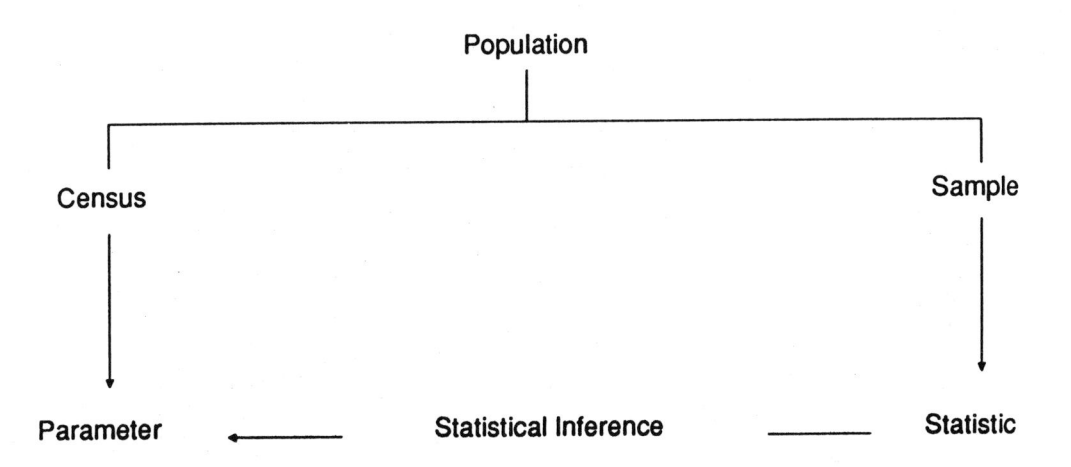

```
                    Population
                   /          \
            Census              Sample
              |                    |
              ↓                    ↓
         Parameter  ←——  Statistical Inference  ——  Statistic
```

Figure 78
Sampling Procedures and Examples

Probability Sample

Every element in the population has a known probability of being in the sample

Random

Numbers given to each element in the population. Random number tables then used to select each element

Systematic

Elements of population numbered as above. The starting point is chosen from one random number table. Then every kth element is chosen.

Stratified Sampling

Population is divided into subgroups. Then random samples are drawn from those.

Non-Probability Sample

Based on researcher's judgment

Convenience

What is available

Purposive

Researcher decides what is representative

Quota

Quotas are established within the sample to encourage representativeness.

of questions. For example, a questionnaire may use *open ended questions*. These questions do not require the respondent to make a selection from a group of responses but allow the respondent to say anything that comes to mind. The questionnaire may also make use of *true-false questions* or *multiple choice questions*.

The output of a questionnaire may thus include data of different kinds. For each kind of data, for different sample sizes and for different kinds of statistical inference, different *statistical tests and procedures* are appropriate. There are hundreds of such tests and procedures available, and the selection of an inappropriate statistic can render the research results useless. People conducting, analyzing, or making use of market research should be familiar with the proper use of statistics. People involved in market research often keep a library of statistical reference books to aid them in selecting and implementing the appropriate procedure.

For any given statistical test, the *size of the sample* will affect the precision of estimates about the population. Larger sample sizes will provide more precise estimates, as illustrated in figure 79. The results of statistical inference may be stated as confidence intervals. A *confidence interval* is an estimate of a population parameter or characteristic such as the percentage of people who intend to vote for a particular candidate or buy a particular product. A confidence interval is stated as a percentage of confidence and a range around the estimate. For example the researcher might be "95% confident that between 40 and 48% of the population described intends to buy product X." Increasing the sample size allows the precision of the estimate to improve. The degree of confidence could be increased and/or the range around the estimate could be decreased. If the sample statistics came from a larger sample we might be able to revise the above estimate to read, the researcher is "98% confident that between 42 and 46% of the population described intends to buy product X."

Once the research design has been hammered out, it should be reviewed for *threats to validity*. Validity is the extent to which we are measuring what we think we are measuring. Imperfections in the research design may constitute threats to validity. *Internal threats to validity* are created by logical problems within the design itself. For example the lack of a control group can constitute an internal *threat to validity*. *External threats to validity* have to do with whether research is representative of the population it is supposed to represent. External threats to validity would include an out of date or non representative sample frame, or an inappropriate sampling procedure.

The design should then be reviewed for *reliability*. Reliability is the degree to which the measurement devices used are consistent in their measurement. A measurement tool is reliable if it always yields the same measurement in a

Figure 79
Level of Confidence, Precision, and Sample Size

Example: Estimating a population proportion; "We are 95% confident that between 45% and 55% of the population prefers taste A to taste B."

A formula for sample size when estimating a population proportion,

$$n = \frac{Z^2 p(1-p)}{d^2}$$

Where Z: is a score for the desired level of precision

p: is the prior estimate of the population proportion. p = .5 is used as it is the most conservative assumption.

d: is the desired precision

Thus 95% confidence, Z = 1.96 and precision d = .1 (± 10%) yields

$$n = \frac{1.96^2 \cdot .5(.5)}{(.1)^2} = 96$$

Increasing precision to d = .05 (± 5%) yields:

$$n = \frac{1.96^2 \cdot .5(.5)}{(.05)^2} = 384$$

Then holding precision at ± 5% while increasing the level of confidence to 99% (Z = 2.58) yields:

$$n = \frac{2.58^2 \cdot .5(.5)}{(.05)^2} = 666$$

given situation. For reasons of reliability, researchers often select *established and tested measurement devices* for use in their research. The *Likert Scale* is such a device, as is the *Edwards Personal Preference Inventory* (EPPI). Some established measurement devices are illustrated in figure 80.

A *statistical package* must be selected in order to implement any statistical procedures which are beyond the scope of hand calculations. A statistical package is a computer software package designed to perform a set of statistical tests and procedures. Use of these packages has resulted in substantial gains in the speed, accuracy, and capability which characterize applied market research. A typical and commonly used package is the *Statistical Package for the Social Sciences* (SPSS).[5] Until recently such packages were for mainframe computer use, which limited their application. But technical advances in desk top computers have allowed versions of these powerful packages to be adapted for use with the personal style computer.

Market Research: Field Work

With these preparations made, the research goes into the field. The focus groups are run, the questionnaires are mailed, the telephone calls are made. This is usually accomplished with the help of a *field research house*. These are specialists in market research who actually mail the questionnaires, make the phone calls, run the focus groups and provide other services. Recent merger activity has resulted in *one source information houses* which combine secondary data services with primary data services. Sami-Burke is an example of this kind of service. Sami provided secondary data concerning sales and market share while Burke offered primary data derived from market research. The newly merged firm provides both kinds of services. Field research houses will generally offer services up to and including final reports and the presentation of results at the buyer's site. The firm dealing with them may also opt for minimum services such as the return of a stack of completed questionnaires.

Market Research: Data Analysis
Interpretation and Communication

Upon receipt of the completed questionnaires, the data will be subjected to analysis. From among the hundreds of statistical procedures some may be used to measure the *statistical significance of differences*. These procedures determine whether it is probable that a difference observed in the sample is representative of a difference existing in the population. Some procedures may be used to measure the degree to which two or more measurements observed might be associated with one another. Perhaps one moves up as the

Figure 80
Established Measurement Devices

The Likert Scale

Statement	Strongly Agree	Agree	Neither Agree Nor Disagree	Disagree	Strongly Disagree
Detergent "X" is Strong	___	✓	___	___	___

Semantic Differential

Score Detergent "X" by placing a mark on one 7-point scale

Strong ___ ___ ✓ ___ ___ ___ ___ Weak

Thurstone Scale

Check the questions you agree with

Detergent X is strong   ✓
Detergent X is weak   ___
Detergent X is very strong   ___

other moves up or perhaps they move in opposite directions in a reliable fashion. *Measures of association* are used to evaluate and describe these kinds of relationships.

When relationships among many variables are to be studied *multivariate statistical techniques* can be used. Some multivariate statistical techniques begin with a matrix which shows the way the several variables associate with one another (a covariance matrix). Matrix algebra is then used to manipulate the matrix and explore relationships in the data. These mathematical operations are performed by the statistical package, but the market analyst should understand what the package is doing.[6]

Statistical analysis should be carefully *guided*, *analyzed* and *interpreted*. The statistical results should be put into the context of the research problem, the management problem and the other information available to the firm. The results should then be *communicated* in such a way that top management will quickly understand it and see its implications for their decisions. These jobs of direction, analysis, interpretation and communication generally fall to a *market analyst*. Market analysts are generally members of the marketing staff. They may be recruited from within the ranks of the firm or the position may be used as an entry level opportunity for M.B.A.s. The analyst usually includes *conclusions and recommendations* when reporting results to the firm's decision makers.[7]

Information About the Future

The tools already described can be combined with some new perspectives to give the organization useful *information about its future environment*. There are two general approaches to developing information about the future: *trend extension* and *modeling*. When using *trend extension*, the organization observes the past in detail and then makes the assumption that the behavior pattern which the variables have demonstrated will continue. The trend may then be extended using approaches ranging from the very simple to the very sophisticated. When *modeling* the organization attempts to identify and understand variables and relationships among variables. Models or representations of situations are then constructed to examine how the variables might relate in new circumstances. As with trend extension, models vary from the simple to the sophisticated; from a drawing on paper to an elaborate mathematical representation programmed into a computer.

Trend Extension

Numerous techniques follow the logical approach of extending past trends. When using *historical analogy*, the analyst identifies past experiences which are seen as being similar, makes adjustments for differences in the current situation and makes an assumption about the future. For example the analyst might note that the last time this particular competitor entered a market, so much market share was lost. This kind of analysis can be facilitated by the use of secondary data describing market shares. After examining such data, the analyst may be able to make a prediction about the share of the market that might be lost when that competitor again enters a market.

Extension of past experience might also take the form of *simple trend extension*. In a simple trend extension, straightforward geometric or mathematical techniques are used to extend the past. The work may be accomplished with drawings. Trend extensions using drawings are demonstrated in figure 81 A and B. Note in figure 81B that the patterns in February and October present a problem for the analyst. The analyst has resolved the problem by choosing a compromise projection; reflecting a compromise between the pattern of year "-1" and the pattern of year "-2."

Simple regression is an example of a simple trend extension using mathematics. Simple regression plots a straight line of the form shown in figure 81A.[8] *Multiple regression* is a multivariate statistical technique which may be used to extend trends in more complex situations. Both procedures follow similar trend extension logic. *In simple regression* the historical data are used to find a line of the mathematical form Y = ax + b which best fits those historical data. Y is the variable being predicted (unit sales in figure 81A) and X is the variable being used to predict "unit sales" (X is the year in figure 81A). The equation that is derived from the historical data has specific numbers for a and b which relate the variable Y to the variable X. This specific equation is then used to predict values for Y (unit sales) in future years. *Multiple regression* uses similar logic in more complex situations.[9] Historical data involving more variables are used to develop a longer equation of the form Y = am + bn + co + z. Here the variables m, n and o are used in combination to predict values for Y. Historical relationships are used to develop an equation which may then be used to predict future values. Figure 82 illustrates a possible use of multiple regression.

More *complex trend lines* can be developed by introducing mathematics beyond the results of regression. For example a simple straight line of the form Y = ax + b might be used as an *underlying trend*, or description of the general direction and pace of growth or decline. Mathematics might then be included which describe the expected *seasonality* of the variable being predicted. For

Figure 81a
Simple Trend Extension by Geometric Projection
(A Simple Pattern)

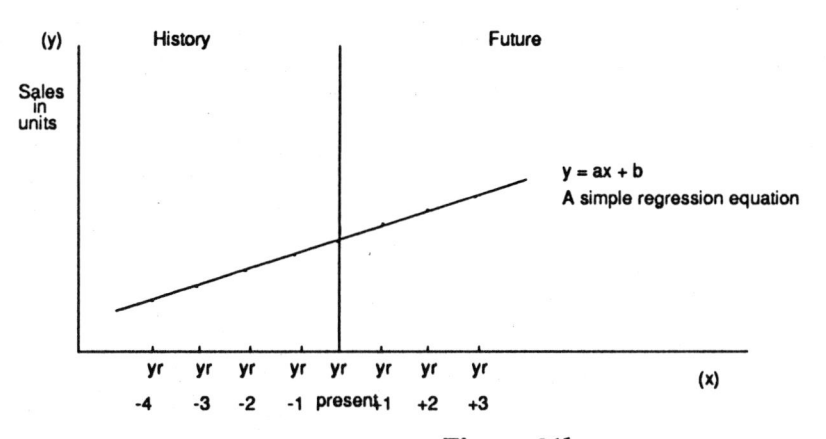

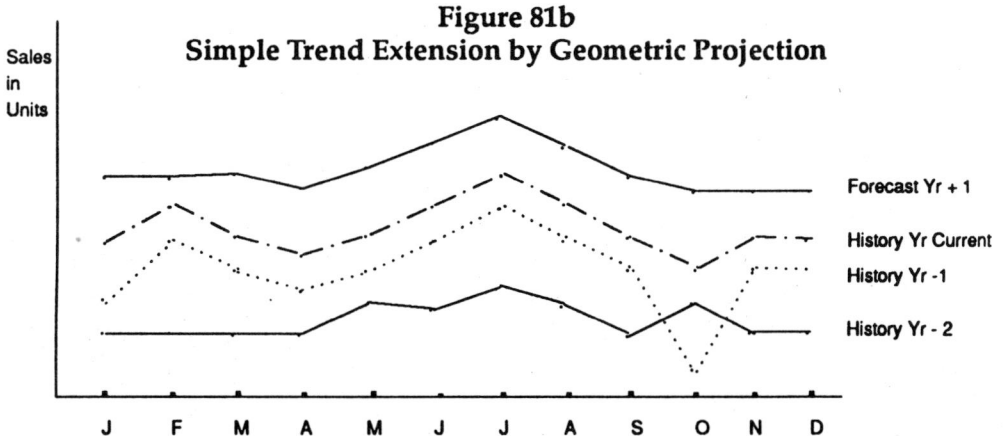

$y = ax + b$
A simple regression equation

Figure 81b
Simple Trend Extension by Geometric Projection

Forecast Yr + 1
History Yr Current
History Yr -1
History Yr - 2

Figure 82
A Possible Use of Multiple Regression

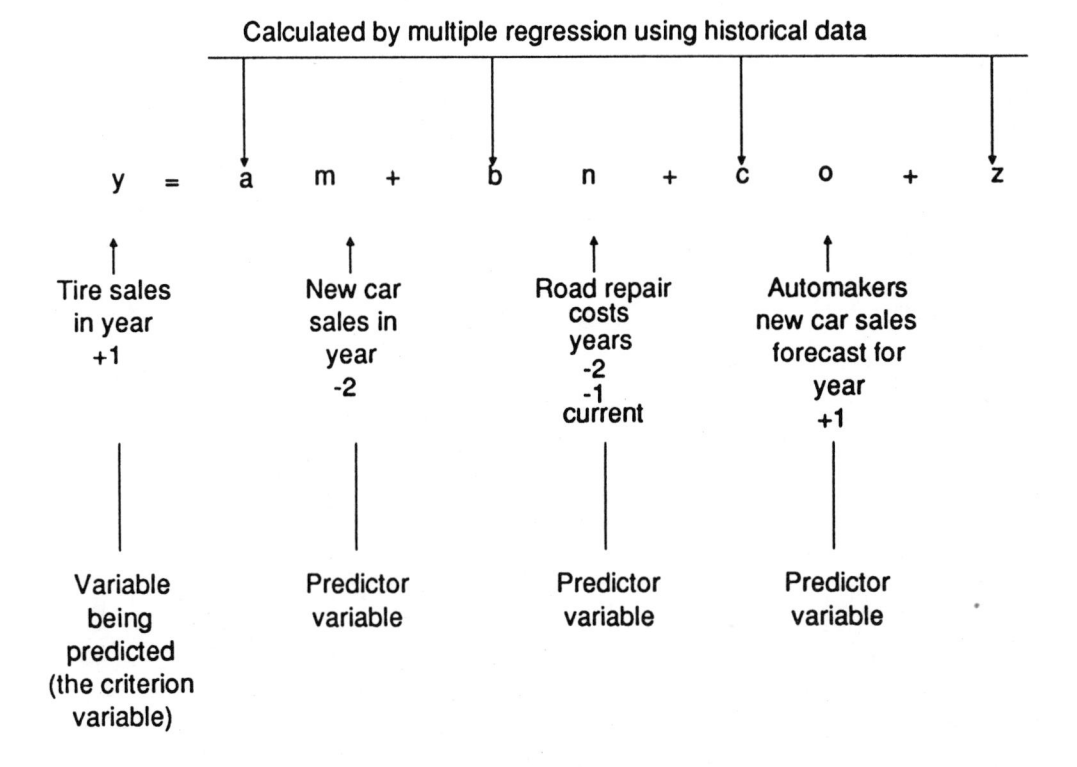

Calculated by multiple regression using historical data

$$y = am + bn + co + z$$

- y: Tire sales in year +1 — Variable being predicted (the criterion variable)
- m: New car sales in year -2 — Predictor variable
- n: Road repair costs years -2, -1, current — Predictor variable
- o: Automakers new car sales forecast for year +1 — Predictor variable

example, the expectation that sales of water skis peak in June and fall off in fall and winter might be included. *Cycles* other than seasonality might be included as well. Regardless of the care that is taken, there will always be a *random component* in the actual sales of a product, a component that could not have been predicted. One test of a good forecast is to observe the nature of the errors. If when the actual sales (or whatever is being predicted) are compared to forecast, the errors themselves are random in nature, it is a good forecast. If the errors display an underlying trend, cycles, or seasonality, it is possible that this could have been corrected in the initial forecast.

Trend Extension and Modeling

There may be some overlap between the methodology of trend extension and the methodology of modeling. When a mathematical model of a problem is developed, some of the relationships within the model may have been developed by using historical data. When this is the case, it can be argued that the model is to some extent an extension of historical trends.

Modeling

If management is unwilling to place a great deal of faith in trend extension, information about the future may be gained by building models. A *model* is a representation of reality. A model may be executed in language form as a story. It may be a physical replica as a 1/100 scale model of a plant or building. It may be a mathematical model where values in equations represent reality. Several approaches to modeling in a future situation will be introduced in this section.

The future may be modeled using *scenario writing*. A scenario is a story which describes a situation. The scenario might describe future strategies, competitive responses and results. It might also describe future environmental trends, company adaptation and the results of these. The strength of this approach, common to most modeling approaches, is that it forces the identification of relevant components of a problem and their likely interactions. It also forces the identification and examination of assumptions. Risk and environmental uncertainty may be taken into this form of future modeling through the use of *alternative scenarios*. An alternative scenario is a story written about the future which assumes one of several possible situations to be the case. For example, a scenario about the future of an organization might be written with the assumption of high priced energy, and another written using the assumption of low priced energy. These two alternative scenarios would then provide a basis for analysis of the company's strategy in these two possible situations. This approach illustrates an important power of modeling approaches in general. That is the capacity to explore "what if" kinds of questions. In this case, what if energy costs are high? What if energy costs are low?

Another approach to modeling the future is to systematically collect the opinions of experts. Such *expert polling* takes several forms, with varying degrees of rigor and sophistication. A less rigorous but often used approach is *brainstorming*. Here a group of experts is put together and their ideas about the future are solicited. The people may be identified within the firm or may be drawn from the greater community. Some rules have been developed to maximize the usefulness of brainstorming. For example, idea generation sessions are often kept free of criticism so that the creativity of the participants is not inhibited.

A more rigorous and systematic form of expert polling is referred to as the *Delphi Technique*. This approach attempts to create a more systematic and rational discussion among experts by providing anonymity for participants and by forcing participants to develop explicit predictions with supporting rationales. When an expert makes a prediction and supports it with a rationale, the results are summarized and sent to the other participating experts. Upon evaluation of this information, the experts adjust their individual predictions and the process goes through another cycle. This recycling (termed a recasting) procedure is repeated until there is a convergence of opinion or until disagreements stabilize.

When specific identifiable alternative strategies are open to a firm, the organization may want to model the results of each strategy. This kind of modeling is called *simulation modeling* because the results of each alternative considered are simulated by the model. For example, a firm may be considering a new regional distribution center but is having difficulty deciding between two feasible locations. In this situation, a firm might build a *simulation model* of the problem, simulating the costs and delivery times using one location and then the other. An *optimization model* might also be used. An optimization model states the problem mathematically and finds the solution. As discussed in chapter seven, the use of an optimization model requires a high quality mathematical understanding of all the variables and relationships which characterize the problem. This has not prevented the successful use of this kind of model. Complex linear programs have been applied to the optimization of aircraft scheduling in the post deregulation environment.

Crossing National Boundaries

The information perspectives discussed above are essentially the same when crossing national boundaries. All of the forms of information gathering remain useful. However, the realities of international communications and operations will require substantial adjustments.[10]

To begin with, operating in several different national environments will require *more complex information flows* within the firm. Primary and secondary data, internal and external data bases, reporting and analytical procedures, must all reflect the fact that multiple environments are being treated. *Organizational adjustments* will be required in order to deal with this. For example, the firm may elect to form an international division, or design the international perspective into its existing organizational structure.

The firm will have to deal with straightforward *translation difficulties* as introduced in chapter six in the context of outbound communications. Without careful translation and cross checking using *back translation*, the instruments used to gather primary data would be severely compromised.

Human communication goes far beyond the spoken or written word. Substantial national and cultural differences exist in the area of *nonverbal communications*. Information flows can be compromised by individuals who are insensitive to differences of this kind. For example there is a great deal of implicit communication in the timing or style of a report, or in the time of arrival at a meeting. The meaning which is appropriately attributed to these nuances differs substantially from culture to culture. The organization should take steps to ensure that misunderstandings in this area do not compromise information flows and analysis. The identification, training and appointment of individuals with cultural sensitivity will go some distance toward the solution of this problem.

Another important adjustment which must be made when crossing international boundaries is the recognition that *types of information will have different cost versus benefit relationships* in different environments. Thus the financial commitment to differing kinds of information gathering would not logically be made in the same proportions in different places. For example, in one nation there may be great return on investment in telephone research and in another country, little return. It would logically follow that telephone research would receive a higher proportion of funds in the first country than it would in the second. For example, it may be virtually impossible to derive two hundred telephone interviews about an intimate subject in some nations. Few homes may be equipped with phones, and discussion of the subject may be seen as taboo. In this way, the percentage of calls completed would be low and the costs of successful interviews would be extremely high. The benefits received from the completed interviews might be lower as well. Few phones might mean that the results were less representative, and cultural taboos might mean that responses were less candid.

The above example also illustrates the *differing information infrastructures* in the international environment. Communications capabilities such as those of the mail and telephone systems will differ greatly in reach and efficiency. In the United States most households may be reached with reasonable efficiency using the mail or the telephone. This is augmented by elaborate data bases which can cross reference the purchase behaviors that become a matter of record where an individual uses a credit card. In some nations, the consumer will buy with greater anonymity. They may be unreachable by telephone, and may exchange on a cash or barter basis.

The telephone interview example also illustrates *differing cultural responses to the attempt to collect primary data.* Residents of the United States are uncommonly willing to discuss personal purchase decisions with interviewers. Residents of other cultures might legitimately find such interviews offensive. The *integrity of secondary data* will also differ as national boundaries are crossed. In some nations, such things as population and income statistics may be characterized by guesswork, or may be adjusted by government agencies in order to create politically desirable impressions.

Finally, there are many kinds of *specialized international information*. These are information sources having no direct parallel in domestic information. They would include published indices of risk such as the Business Environmental Risk Index (BERI). This kind of report attempts to assess the political risk to companies operating in an overseas environment.

The Normative Versus Empirical Perspective

Clearly, accurate and appropriate communication of information is critical to the survival and growth of the firm. The identification, gathering, analysis, and synthesis of incoming information should be directed toward the selection of appropriate strategies. These strategies should then allow the defense and expansion of the market niche within legal and ethical guidelines. This is *a normative and rational set of assumptions about the firm's information gathering and analysis behaviors.*

Empirical observation of corporate marketing information activities would suggest that there are several *sources of deviation from* such *normative rationality*. First among these is *lack of understanding*. The information requirements and methodologies of the large organization quickly become complex. Such perspectives as those embodied in parametric and non parametric statistics, multivariate statistics, and data base design are slowly becoming a part of corporate information lore. It is simply difficult for individuals whose backgrounds do not include extensive training in these areas not to become confused when making decisions involving the appropriate use and interpretation of these perspectives and tools.

Another source of deviation from normative rationality is the set of *coordination difficulties* usually found in firms. Due to lack of care in management and organizational design, information flows may become redundant and competitive. Differences between data sources then become a source of political discord within the firm. The set of coordination difficulties would also include problems with the timing and specification of information flows among departments. These problems might become evident when one department's information output constitutes another's information input. For example, the marketing group might specify a need for C.O.E. numbers for the product line. These may be supplied by the finance group which in turn is dependent upon the computer services group. Under these circumstances it would take an unusual combination of political and data base understandings on the part of a market analyst to be able to identify and correct improper cost allocations to a product.

Deviation from normative rationality might also occur as a function of *differences between individual and group interests* within the firm. The normative and rational set of assumptions seems to include a "team play" assumption concerning information handling within the organization. At the same time, it is empirically observable that such team play will often fall victim to a need to protect individual interests and to subgroup "empire building." In this context, slowing information delivery, withholding information, and the biased presentation of information becomes understandable, if not in the best interest of the organization.

Akin to this kind of behavior is the deviation from normative rationality which can be expected when using *third party information suppliers*. Third party information suppliers, such as market research firms, may or may not have any real interest in the success of the organization purchasing the information. They may have little concern about the integrity of the information they are vending. Their relationship to the firm in need of information is that of a vendor to a buyer. The time and profit pressures of competitive information industries often force compromises in information integrity. Unless the analyst is very aggressive in monitoring every activity of the supplier, such problems in basic information integrity are likely to go undetected.

Marketing information activities should be managed with an awareness of these kinds of problems. Guided by an awareness of the nature of individual, group and supplier motivations, a team spirit and long term vision might still be fostered which would result in timely and accurate information gathering and analysis.

Chapter Summary

Organizations vary greatly in their information gathering and analysis behaviors. The entrepreneur may favor the intuitive approach, while the major firm will involve itself in many systematic information gathering efforts. These efforts often include environmental scan behaviors designed to provide an ongoing understanding of the evolving environment. They might also include directed information gathering, focusing upon a particular problem or opportunity. A commonly used form of directed information gathering is market research. Firms will also attempt to understand the future environment, extending past trends and creating models of future situations. Creative adjustments will be required when working with other cultures and when diagnosing misalignments between organizational interest and individual or subgroup interests in information gathering and analysis.

---

[1] An in-depth discussion of the appraisal of environments is available in George A. Steiner, *Top Management Planning* (New York: Macmillan, 1969), pp. 199-233. See also Philip Kotler, *Marketing Management*, 5th ed. (Englewood Cliffs, N.J.: Prentice Hall Inc., 1984), pp. 76-119. See also Francis J. Aguilar, *Scanning the Business Environment* (New York: Macmillan, 1967). See also Derek F. Abell and John S. Hammond, *Strategic Marketing Planning: Problems and Analytical Approaches* (Englewood Cliffs, N.J.: Prentice Hall, Inc., 1979). See also Jerry Connolly, "Information Processing and Decision Making in Organizations," in *New Directions in Organizational Behavior*, eds. Barry M. Staw and Gerald R. Salncik (Chicago: St. Clair Press, 1977), pp. 205-209. See also Bo Hedberg, "How Organizations Learn and Unlearn," in *Handbook of Organizational Design, Vol. I, Adapting Organizations to Their Environments*, eds. Paul C. Nystrom and William H. Starbuck (New York: Oxford University Press, 1981), pp. 3-17. See also Chris Argyris and Donald A. Schon, *Organizational Learning, a Theory of Action Perspective* (Reading, Mass.: Addison Wesley, 1978).

[2] The generalizations in this section are derived from the perspective of IS-LM analysis. For an in-depth discussion of this area see William H. Branson, *Macroeconomic Theory and Policy*, 2nd ed. (New York: Harper and Row, 1979).

[3] Development of information for marketing, such as that treated in this section has also been treated by authors using such concepts as "intelligence systems," "audits," "decision support systems," and "marketing support systems." See for

example, Philip Kotler, "A Design for the Firm's Marketing Nerve Center," *Business Horizons* 9 (Fall 1966), pp. 63-74. See also, William R. King and David I. Clelland, "Environmental Information Systems for Strategic Marketing Planning," *Journal of Marketing* 38 (Oct. 1974), pp. 35-40. See also William T. Kelly, "Marketing Intelligence for Top Management," *Journal of Marketing* 29 (Oct. 1965), pp. 19-24. See also Robert Hershey, "Commercial Intelligence on a Shoestring," Harvard Business Review 58, No. 5 (Sept.-Oct. 1980), p. 22. The relationship of incoming information to decision making is treated by perspectives such as those of Argyris, Hedberg, and Connolly.

[4] The importance of the perspective held by the dominant power structure in the organization is approached by the concept of the "dominant coalition." See John Child, "Organizational Structure, Environment and Performance: The Role of Strategic Choice," *Sociology* 16 (1972), pp. 1-22.

[5] See Norman H. Nie, C. Hadlai Hull, Jean G. Jenkins, Karin Steinbrenner, and Dale H. Bent, *Statistical Package for the Social Sciences*, 2nd ed. (New York: McGraw Hill, 1975).

[6] Students interested in the statistical discussion might consult the following general references: Gouri K. Bhattacharyya and Richard A. Johnson, *Statistical Concepts and Methods* (New York: John Wiley and Sons, 1977); John Neter and William Wasserman, *Applied Linear Statistical Models* (Homewood, Ill.: Richard D. Irwin, 1974); Paul E. Green and J. Douglas Caroll, *Mathematical tools for Applied Multivariate Analysis* (New York: Academic Press, 1976).

[7] Students interested in the market research discussion might consult the following general references: David A. Aaker and George S. Day, *Marketing Research*, 3rd ed. (New York: John Wiley and Sons, 1986); David J. Luck, Hugh G. Wales, Donald A. Taylor, and Ronald S. Rubin, *Marketing Research*, 6th ed. (Englewood Cliffs, N.J.: Prentice Hall, 1982); and Paul E. Green and Donald S. Tull, *Research for Marketing Decisions*, 2nd ed. (Englewood Cliffs, N.J.: Prentice Hall, 1970).

[8] See Bhattacharyya, pp. 334-367.

[9] Ibid., pp. 368-399. See also Neter, pp. 214-272.

[10] Students interested in information gathering across national boundaries might consult the following general reference: Philip R. Cateora, *International Marketing*, 6th ed. (Homewood, Illinois: Richard D. Irwin, 1987), pp. 331-361.

Questions for Study, Discussion and Examination

1. Could you define or explain to a friend who has not studied marketing, each of the following terms or ideas?
    a. Entrepreneur
    b. Scanning the environment (what components of environment?)
    c. Scan behavior (internal or external)
    d. Demographics
    e. Directed information gathering
    f. Common demographic terms in figure 73
    g. General level of price
    h. Inflation rate
    i. GNP
    j. Yd
    k. Ys
    l. Economic indicators, leading, coincident and lagging
    m. Syndicated service
    n. Newsletter
    o. Econometrician
    p. Technical journal or bulletin
    q. Competitive information
    r. Market shares
    s. Lobbyists and governmental contacts
    t. Competitive activities
    u. Selling access to a data base
    v. Data bases concerning competition; concerning consumers
    w. Information clearing house
    x. Competitive intelligence
    y. Internal scan or audit
    z. Modern data base technology
    aa. C.O.E. report
    ab. Reporting and analysis of marketing activities
    ac. Report by exception principle
    ad. Solicitation of marketing ideas, information and suggestions

ae. Situation analysis
af. Problems and opportunities
ag. Marketing services staff
ah. Marketing planning staff
ai. Corporate level strategic planning staff
aj. Secondary data
ak. Primary data
al. Market research project
am. The management problem
an. The research problem
ao. Experiment
ap. Observe behavior versus communication
aq. Form of communication (in market research)
ar. Qualitative technique
as. Quantitative technique
at. Statistical inference
au. Focus group interview
av. Discussion guide
aw. Depth interview
ax. Pilot study
ay. Sample frame
az. Random sampling
ba. Questionnaire
bb. Open ended question
bc. True false question
bd. Multiple choice question
be. Statistical test and procedures
bf. Sample size
bg. Confidence interval
bh. The effect of sample size upon precision
bi. Threat to validity (internal vs. external)
bj. Reliability
bl. Statistical package
bm. SPSS
bn. Field research house
bo. One source information house

bp. Statistical significance of differences
bq. Measures of association
br. Multivariate statistical technique
bs. Duties of the market analyst
bt. Trend extension
bu. Modeling
bv. Historical analogy
bw. Simple trend extension
bx. Simple regression
by. Multiple regression
bz. Complex trend line
ca. Underlying trend, seasonality, cycles and a random component
cb. Model
cc. Scenario writing
cd. Alternate scenarios
ce. Expert polling
cf. Brainstorming
cg. Delphi Technique
ch. Simulation model
ci. Optimization model
cj. Organizational adjustments (international)
ck. Translation and back translation
cl. Nonverbal communications (international context)
cm. Differing cost/benefit relationships for types of information (international context)
cn. Differing information infrastructure (international)
co. Differing cultural responses to the attempt to collect primary data (international)
cp. Integrity of secondary data (international)
cq. specialized international information
cr. A normative and rational set of assumptions about the firm's information gathering and analysis behaviors
cs. Lack of understanding
ct. Coordination difficulties
cu. Differences between individual and group interests
cv. Problems with third party information suppliers.

2. What is an entrepreneur? What role does this individual play in the society? Compare and contrast this individual's behavior with that of the major corporation. What do you see the strengths and weaknesses of each approach to be?
3. What is involved in an environmental scan? Compare and contrast this behavior with directed information gathering.
4. Why scan markets, won't market research be enough? What role does the understanding of demographics play in this scan behavior?
5. Give an example of the use of demographics to (a) characterize an existing market; (b) discover a new market.
6. Give an example of the use of each of the terms in figure 73 to either (a) characterize an existing market or (b) discover a new market.
7. Of what use is a scan of the political and legal environment? How might it be accomplished? Give a specific example of its usefulness.
8. Why scan the economic environment? What is the relationship of the general economy to a firm trying to succeed in an individual market?
9. How is the general condition of the economy measured? (In what terms is it seen?)
10. Describe current economic conditions in terms of P, GNP or Y, Yd, Ys, government spending, taxation, money supply, consumer spending, and business investment. What would you expect P and GNP or Y to do in the next year and why? Relate this to the profitability of an individual firm or industry with a specific example.
11. Of what use are economic indicators?
12. Relate the activity of scanning the technical environment to the innovation life cycle and profit. What does this mean for the firm which has gained control of a useful innovation? What does this mean for that firm's competitors?
13. Relate the activity of scanning the competitive environment to the concept of market structure (chapter 3) and the main ideas brought out in chapter 5 (product-price), 6 (promotion), and 7 (place).
14. Demonstrating your understanding of how the various components of an environmental scan combine to describe one reality by demonstrating how information picked up in one aspect of the scan might be important to the understanding of another aspect.
15. Describe a realistic environmental scan for a firm or organization you are familiar with; select your college if you prefer. Describe in detail

what you would look at and what information sources you would use.

16. What do you think the effect of the rapid improvement in the technology of information will be upon environmental scanning? Upon internal scanning or audits?

17. Describe a data base application for each aspect of the environmental scan.

18. If the computer and information group were designing a data base for the firm's accounting information, what would you as a marketing person want them to include? How would you want the data to be accessed (or how would you want it to be arranged)?

19. If you were the senior marketing executive in a firm or organization, what marketing activities would you want included in an internal audit or internal scan. How would you want it reported and why? Why might you consider the use of the "report by exception" principle?

20. As data bases describing individual consumer behavior become more complete what opportunities are made available to marketers? What social problems might result? Describe a consumer data base of the future.

21. What analytical capabilities might you want included in a computer terminal which accesses a data base describing individual consumers? In one describing your firm's accounting data? In one describing your firm's marketing activities? (Hint: Consider the various analyses throughout the chapter)

22. Go to fellow employees or fellow students and develop a list of marketing suggestions for your firm or college.

23. (As a class project) conduct an environmental scan and an internal audit (if data are available) for your college. Then develop a situation analysis identifying problems and opportunities for the institution.

24. Given the people who develop formal written situation analyses in the firm, and given the final decision making power of top executives and board members, how do you believe that a situation analysis should be communicated? As a report? Oral or written? As a data base?

25. How is directed information gathering "directed"?

26. What are the roles of primary and secondary data in scanning? In directed information gathering?

27. (As a class project) conduct a market research project using fellow students as a handy convenience sample. Present the findings to the class and be ready to discuss the things you learned during the project. (As an individual question, suggest how this should be accomplished.)
28. (As a class project) try to predict the future of your college or another institution or firm you are familiar with. Break the class into small teams with each team exploring a different approach to predicting the future. (As an individual question, suggest how this should be accomplished.) Present your results to the class.
29. (As a class project) choose a firm or institution you are familiar with.
    a. Design an international environmental scan.
    b. Specify data for an international internal audit
    c. Design a market research project to investigate an overseas market.
    d. Design a methodology for predicting the future environment in another nation. (As an individual question, suggest how this should be accomplished.)
30. What kinds of things go wrong with information gathering and analysis? Why? What do you think can be done about it?

CHAPTER NINE

INFORMATION SYNTHESIS AND ORGANIZATIONAL STRATEGY

Having gathered information and analyzed it, the organization must now draw information together, synthesize it into a whole understanding of how the organization's fit with its environment is evolving, and decide upon a strategy to defend and expand the market niche. This chapter will examine how information may be synthesized and how that facilitates the organization's strategic choices.

For the entrepreneur, the approach is intuitive. While information may have been gathered by reading or listening to others, the synthesis of information into strategy takes place in the thought process. At some point, after rumination, the entrepreneur has put the picture together and has the essential idea for the project. Further information might then be sought out and an overt and observable planning process begun. But, the synthesis of information into a whole understanding of the market opportunity is not an observable process. It constitutes the essence of entrepreneurial genius.

For the major firm the process is observable, varied, imperfect and every bit as critical to survival as genius is for the entrepreneur. This chapter will describe typical corporate approaches to information synthesis and strategic choice.

Marketing Organization

Several organizational forms are specific to marketing. These facilitate the synthesis of information for strategic choice. Product management is the first to be discussed.

The *product manager concept* is a team leadership idea which has arisen out of a need for coordination. Management is commonly organized by function as depicted in figure 83. Functional structure such as this provides coordination within each functional hierarchy. However, coordination across functions is uncommon until such time as the leaders of the hierarchies find time to get together. The product manager's job is to form a team which provides coordination across the various functions. The focus of the team is the improvement of the market niche of an existing product or service. The team includes representatives from the various functional areas.

The creation of this cross functional team in turn creates a set of reporting relationships commonly referred to as a *matrix*. In this matrix situation, team members report to their functional managers as well as to the product manager. The reporting relationship with the product manager is confined to contributions relevant to the individual product or service. While multiple reporting relationships such as this can be confusing, they can work successfully if the people involved are self motivated professionals who are used to operating in a "matrix culture."

Companies vary greatly in the degree of authority and responsibility given to product managers. In some firms, product managers have complete authority for the product and responsibility for the bottom line, the C.O.E. of the product. In this kind of operation, the product or service may be seen as a *profit center* or center of focus for management effort where the criterion for the evaluation of management is some measure of profit. In other firms, the product manager may need upper management approval for the slightest decision and may be viewed only as an advocate or "cheerleader" for the product.

A product manager may also be referred to as a *brand manager*. This may be done in firms where there are several brand variations on a general product type and where each variation requires detailed attention and management.

While the product manager concept has provided coordination among functional groups with a focus on the individual product, the coordination of different products into a given target market can still be a problem. In order to address this problem, the *market manager concept* was developed. It is the job of the market manager to focus company efforts on a single target market. Like the product manager, the market manager is a team leader. This team

Chapter 9 315

**Figure 83
Hierarchical Structures
Organized by Function**

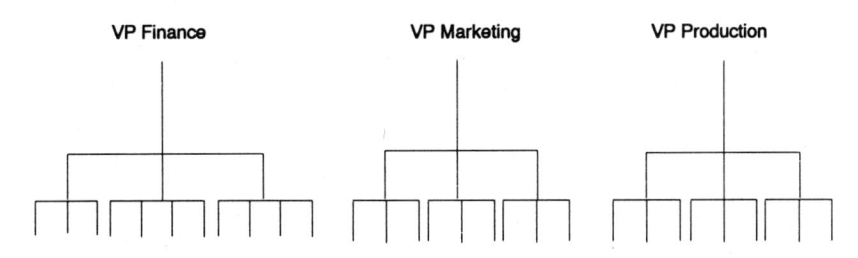

**Figure 84
The Product Manager in a
Matrix Context**

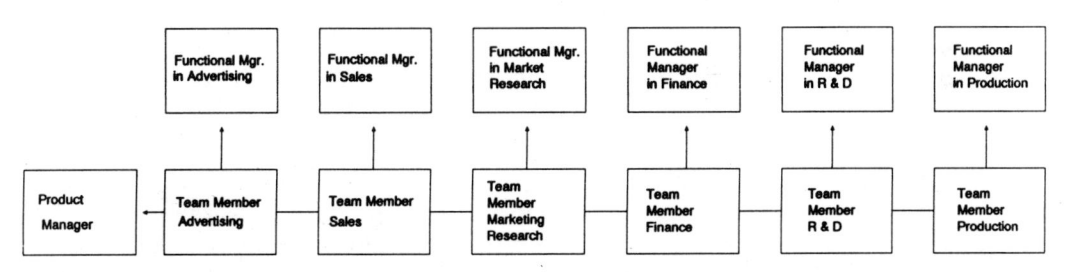

adds a new dimension to the organization's matrix, as the reporting relationships are drawn across product lines as well as across functional lines of authority. This form of organization allows the market manager to lead teams which understand the various product strategies as well as the various functional areas. It is the job of the market manager to understand the nuances of the particular target market and lead team members and upper level decision makers toward success in that market. With the addition of the market manager, the organizational matrix takes on the new dimension illustrated in figure 85.

The need for coordination of areas with different perspectives has also created the *new product manager*. Often drawn from the ranks of experienced product managers, the new product manager has the job of coordinating the activities of the research and development group with those of the marketing group. The job requires the translation of the technical understandings of R&D into the commercial understandings of marketing. The new product manager often becomes involved with the product during the early testing of its commercial viability and then takes the responsibility of product management as the product is launched. After the product is considered to be a successful established product, the new product manager may entrust the product to a product manager and begin the development of another new product. The new product manager's relationships are depicted in figure 86.

A primary source of information for the managers whose jobs have just been described is the *marketing services staff*. This staff exists to provide information and analytical services for marketing decisions and often consists of the market research, venture research, sales analysis and strategic planning groups.

The *market research group* exists to monitor and investigate secondary data as well as to gather and analyze primary data. The workforce is comprised of *market analysts* who are responsible for the gathering of data and the generation of preliminary analyses and reports. Market analysts may be assigned to product management or market management teams and often are responsible for the selection of third party information suppliers such as market research houses.

The *venture research group* is a specialized market research group which evaluates the commercial potential of future products, often working in support of the new product manager. In some firms this work may be a responsibility of the market research group. The *sales analysis* group is responsible for information derived from the firm's sales data. This may include the conversion of sales data to C.O.E. reports, and may include the projection of future sales figures.

Figure 85
The Market Manager in a Matrix Context

```
                    ┌──────────────────┐              ┌──────────────────┐
                    │ Functional Manager│              │ Functional Manager│
                    └──────────────────┘              └──────────────────┘
┌───────────────┐        Team Member                      Team Member
│Product Manager│───────────────────────────────────────────────────────
└───────────────┘
          ┌───────────────┐    Team Member                  Team Member
          │Product Manager│──────────────────────────────────────────────
          └───────────────┘
                              ┌───────────────┐
                              │Market Manager │
                              └───────────────┘
```

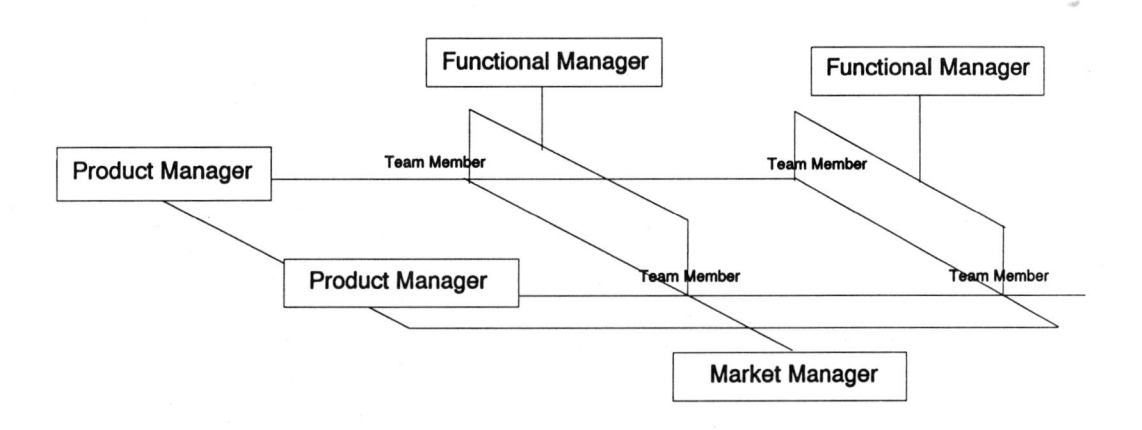

Figure 86
The New Product Manager

```
┌──────────────┐      New         ┌──────────┐
│ Research and │◄── Product ──►  │ Marketing│
│ Development  │    Manager       │          │
└──────────────┘                  └──────────┘
```

Venture Research
Market Management
Product Management, etc.

Responsible for coordinating the planning perspectives and activities of the various groups is the *strategic planning group*. Sometimes placed in marketing services, the strategic planning group assists top management in synthesizing the various information held and understood in different parts of the firm. The objective of this synthesis is a whole understanding of the firm's evolving relationship to its environment. This is accomplished by designing, initiating, coordinating and monitoring various strategic planning steps and procedures.

The *communications group*, sometimes called the *advertising group*, often stands as a separate group within the marketing staff. The responsibility of this group is the design and placement of communications efforts such as those outlined in chapter five. This group should logically include a *public relations staff* and a *government relations staff* to carry out communications efforts with important publics and government officials. However, it is common that these functions are not located within marketing. The communications group works with advertising agencies to place messages in appropriate media and then works with market research to determine the effectiveness of these efforts.

The *sales management group* is another group which often stands as a separate entity within a marketing staff. In many industries it is a very powerful group and is sometimes headed by an individual at the director or vice president level. This group is usually comprised of individuals who have worked their way up through the sales ranks. The group is responsible for that part of the communication effort which is undertaken by the firm's sales force. It guides the sales force in the directions provided by corporate strategy and manages the various sales offices, regions and territories. It also conducts research on and through the sales force, usually in collaboration with the market research group.

Flexibility in Marketing Organization

The foregoing paragraphs have developed an outline of what might be a *typical marketing organization for a major corporation*. It is intended only to develop a *benchmark understanding* for the student, as differing firms will evolve in different ways and changing circumstances will dictate different adaptations. For example, some firms are now moving toward more precise targeting of markets. Using available data bases which provide demographic and purchase record information for households, marketing is becoming ever more individualistic. This has resulted in the increasing use of *direct response* forms of communication such as direct phone or mail solicitation. It has also resulted in the use of *specialized media* such as small circulation magazines and catalogues. These developments will be reflected in adjustments within the organization, perhaps in the establishment of *direct marketing or catalog departments*. In a specific example, Campbell's Soup has recently decided to adjust the product mix substantially on a store by store basis. This has resulted in marketing strategy decisions which must now be made on this new microcosmic basis. To facilitate this kind of decision making, some marketing staff people will be moving from the corporate headquarters into the field.[1]

The need to integrate or synthesize many functional and product perspectives has brought substantial use of the *matrix organizational form*. Matrix forms violate the management principle of unity of authority and responsibility. That is, a team member working in a matrix is in the confusing position of having multiple bosses. While this creates a situation which can be abused by employees, those employees who are sufficiently professional in orientation are allowed their freedom to move about in the firm and accomplish things without constant reference to authority. The sets of personal and professional expectations which allow the matrix form to work have been referred to as *matrix culture*.

Developments in information technology are also changing marketing management. Review of the various middle management positions described above should illustrate the idea that these are largely information handling positions. Information is first gathered, then analyzed and finally synthesized into whole understandings. As information technology progresses, some of these jobs will be altered or eliminated. To the extent that the job involves routine data gathering, analysis and reporting chores, it is a candidate for replacement by automated information processing. To the extent that the job requires a unique human understanding or synthesis that is essential to a whole understanding of the firm's situation, the job should probably be retained. In making decisions in this area, top marketing managers will have to weigh unique human intellectual contributions against the unfortunate human tendency to manipulate information in support of their own interests. In this context, the concept of matrix culture may be worth further exploration. A matrix operates well in an environment of open information sharing toward team goals. Fostering the matrix culture may allow top management to retain the best human contributions to information gathering, analysis and synthesis.

Procedures to Facilitate a Whole Understanding and Strategic Choice

Each individual and group in the organization possesses a unique information base and a unique perspective. Each is therefore likely to have a unique idea about which activities will best defend and enhance the market niche of the firm. In order to create a synthesis and choose a strategic direction, firms engage in planning procedures. These are activities which encourage synthesis, whole understanding and strategic choice.

Again, to gain a benchmark understanding, activities which might be typical of a major corporation are described, but practice is very individualistic. Organizational forms similar to the ones described earlier in the chapter are presumed to exist for purposes of the illustration.

To begin a strategic planning cycle, top management may instruct the strategic planning group to create an *environmental scenario*. This is a written description of the future environment of the firm and is a result of environmental scan activities and attempts to gain information about the future. Several alternative scenarios might be used if environmental directions are unclear. The environmental scenario articulates the environmental planning assumptions that the organization is willing to make. The environmental scenario should be accompanied by a situation analysis which relates the environment to measures of the firm's success and which identifies *problems and opportunities*. The situation analysis may also restate previous corporate statements of mission, goals, objectives, and strategies for reference.

The environmental scenario and the situation analysis are then circulated to those in the firm with some responsibility for strategic choice. Department heads, product managers and market managers should be included. These individuals then review the materials together with any suggested plans and supporting budgets that have been given to them by their subordinates. After this review, they write suggested *plans* for their area of responsibility, as well as requested *budgets* supportive of these plans. In this way, a group of roughly coordinated suggested plans and budgets, reflecting perspectives by product, by market, by sales division and by department, are readied for submission to top management.

These *plans and budgets are then reviewed* at meetings of upper level managers. This results in adjustments to the plans which reflect the priorities and perspectives of top management and the board of directors. Final review activities should insure that the firm is guided by:

1. *A mission statement*
   A statement of general direction and focus
2. *Statements of goals, objectives and strategies*
   A statement of what the firm is aiming to accomplish (goals)
   A statement of how that accomplishment is to be judged and measured in time sequence (objectives)
   A specific statement of how the firm is going to proceed toward its goals and objectives through the allocation of its resources and efforts (strategies)
3. *Subordinate statements of goals, objectives and strategies*
   Statements parallel to those described in point 2 above, for each division, department, group and individual in the organization
4. *Budgets which reflect the time sequenced objectives in items 2 and 3.*

Strategic Choice

The goals of the planning exercise just described have been information synthesis to accomplish appropriate strategic choices, resulting in statements and budgets for the direction and control of marketing activities. It is appropriate to carefully evaluate the concept of *strategy* so as to be sure that the organization has actually made strategic choices as a result of its planning process. Webster defines strategy in the following ways:[2]

1A(1): Employing the political, economic, psychological and military forces of a nation or group of nations to afford maximum support to adopted policies in peace or war

1A(2): The science and art of military command, exercised to meet the enemy in combat under advantageous conditions

1B: A variety or instance in the use of strategy

2A: A careful plan or method or a careful strategy

2B: The art of devising and employing plans and stratagems toward a goal

These standard and accepted definitions of strategy suggest several components which should be a part of organizational choice if that choice is to be genuinely strategic in nature.

First (from 1A(1)), strategy involves employing *all the forces* which the organization can bring to bear (political, economic, psychological, etc.) to afford maximum support for some higher adopted policy. This higher policy would logically be the *mission statement*, if one has been adopted and not made subject to review in the planning process. If there is no stated and accepted mission statement, the defense and expansion of the market niche would be the implicit mission. Often, the mission statement of a firm is nothing more than a very general statement of the social role the firm intends to play, and thus the exchanges it intends to enter into while defending and expanding its market niche.

Second [from 1A(2)], strategy has a military flavor, involving the direction of an organization in conflict and maneuver with the intent of placing the organization in *a position of advantage*.

Third (from 1B), strategy may be used to refer to a *particular form* of the activity (such as a price cutting strategy).

Fourth (2A and 2B), strategy refers to the act of *carefully planning and directing activities toward some higher goal*.

All of these perspectives are commonly and appropriately used when referring to general corporate strategies and marketing strategies. When choosing strategies, decisions are being made concerning *how to employ forces or resources* of the organization in order to *defend and enhance the market niche of the firm or in order to support an adopted mission statement*. It is expected that the firm's activities will involve some elements of conflict, and it is the intent of the organization to employ resources in order to gain a *position of advantage*. The organization must be aware of particular *varieties of strategy or maneuver* so as to defend against them and utilize them when appropriate. All activities should be undertaken in an atmosphere of *careful planning*.

Marketing strategy has traditionally been viewed as involving a *match which identifies a target market and approaches the target market with a marketing mix (product/service, price, promotion and place)*.[3] In this context, the *forces or resources employed* are those used to understand the target market, create a product or service, say things about it and place it so that the price retrieved and the units sold yield revenues exceeding incremental costs. Conflict is seen primarily in terms of competition in the market place. *Advantage* is viewed in the context of gaining an advantage over competitors by offering the consumer either a better product, a lower price or both. There are some instances in marketing practice when advantage will be seen in terms of gaining an advantage over the consumers. This view of gaining advantage may create ethical problems. This will be discussed in the next chapter, legal and ethical guidelines. Awareness of *varieties of strategy* requires an understanding of such marketing ideas as portfolio management, positioning and segmentation. These will be introduced in this chapter. The atmosphere of *careful planning* is fostered through the design of the marketing organization and its planning procedures, introduced earlier in this chapter.

The defense or enhancement of the market niche can clearly be accomplished by means that are not within the traditional definition of a match between a target market and a marketing mix. Lobbyists can affect the regulatory environment, substantially changing the market niche. For this reason, marketing strategy may have to be more broadly construed than it has been traditionally, encompassing any employment of forces or resources of the organization in order to defend and enhance the market niche of the firm. This broad construction is very close to the concept of general corporate strategy. This would not be a new observation, as some writers have felt that the two concepts of strategy are so close as to be almost synonymous.

Marketing is so basic that it cannot be considered a separate function. [It is the business], seen from the final result; that is, from the customer's point of view.[4]
—*Peter Drucker* (brackets supplied)

Varieties of Strategy: Conceptual Aids to Strategic Choice

The primary conceptual aid to the understanding of strategic choice used in this book was introduced in the first few chapters. An understanding of the *market niche of the firm* as it is a function of the psychology and economics of human exchange and as it may be measured and understood financially is critical to the understanding of marketing strategy. Numerous other conceptual aids are useful as well. They help in the process of strategic choice by demonstrating *varieties of strategy* and the implications of different strategic choices. These conceptual aids include portfolio models, PIMS, game theory, positioning, segmentation and the philosophical approach embodied in the marketing concept. This section introduces these ideas.

Portfolio Models

Portfolio models provide a way of viewing strategic choice. They also demonstrate a particular philosophy of strategic choice. The nature of the philosophy is evidenced by the name portfolio model. The various product lines which are held by the firm are viewed as investments, to be bought, sold, emphasized or deemphasized the way individual stocks or bonds might be considered in an investment portfolio. Components of a business which are isolated and treated this way are sometimes termed *strategic business units* (SBUs). A product line might be viewed this way by the corporation or an entire corporation might be viewed this way by a corporation involved in the purchase and sale of other firms.

One important portfolio model is the *Boston Consulting Group (BCG) Model*. The BCG Model analyzes strategy by placing products (or SBUs) of the company on axes which describe the relative market share which the product enjoys and the growth of the market. Both relative market share and growth are categorized as being high or low. A 10% share might be categorized as high in a market with many competitors as the criterion used is relative market share rather than absolute market share.

Products or SBUs which fall into a category of high relative market share in a high growth market are seen to be in a favorable position. The model will suggest specific movements of capital resources in order to bring more products into this position. Products in the high growth, high relative market share position are referred to as "stars." This is depicted in figure 87.

Products with a high relative market share in low growth markets are referred to as "cash cows." This is because the model suggests managing this kind of a product, not for long term success in its market, but rather for the generation of the maximum amount of cash (cash throw off). Thus investments will not be made for innovation or improvement in the cash cow product, service or SBU. The cash cow's position of strength in its market will be traded (or milked) for immediate cash.

The model also suggests that the cash be reinvested in low relative market share products which participate in the high growth markets. This reinvestment is depicted by the arrow in figure 87. The re-investment would then presumably allow the product or company receiving the investment (the "problem child" in figure 87) to make investments designed to attain the high market share or star position. Products occupying the low relative market share, low growth position ("dogs") are to be spun off or sold.

The BCG Model makes more complex prescriptions than those noted here, but it is important to see that this model is a way of describing and prescribing the capital allocations that were discussed in chapter four and depicted in figures 49 and 50 in that chapter. The BCG Model assumes that the greatest advantage to the firm will accrue when investments result in the attainment of high market share positions in high growth markets. While this is probably a good assumption across an average of many investments, there are also ways of defending and expanding a market niche which are not high market share strategies. There may be attractive opportunities in low growth markets.

The *General Electric Planning Grid* is another example of a portfolio model. It is also another view of the capital allocation process presented in chapter four and figure 49. The G.E. Grid uses the more general concept of market attractiveness instead of market growth on one axis, and the more general

Figure 87
The BCG Matrix
Source: George S. Day, "A Strategic Perspective on Product Planning," *Journal of Contemporary Business*, 1975, p. 1-34. Used by permission.

Market Growth

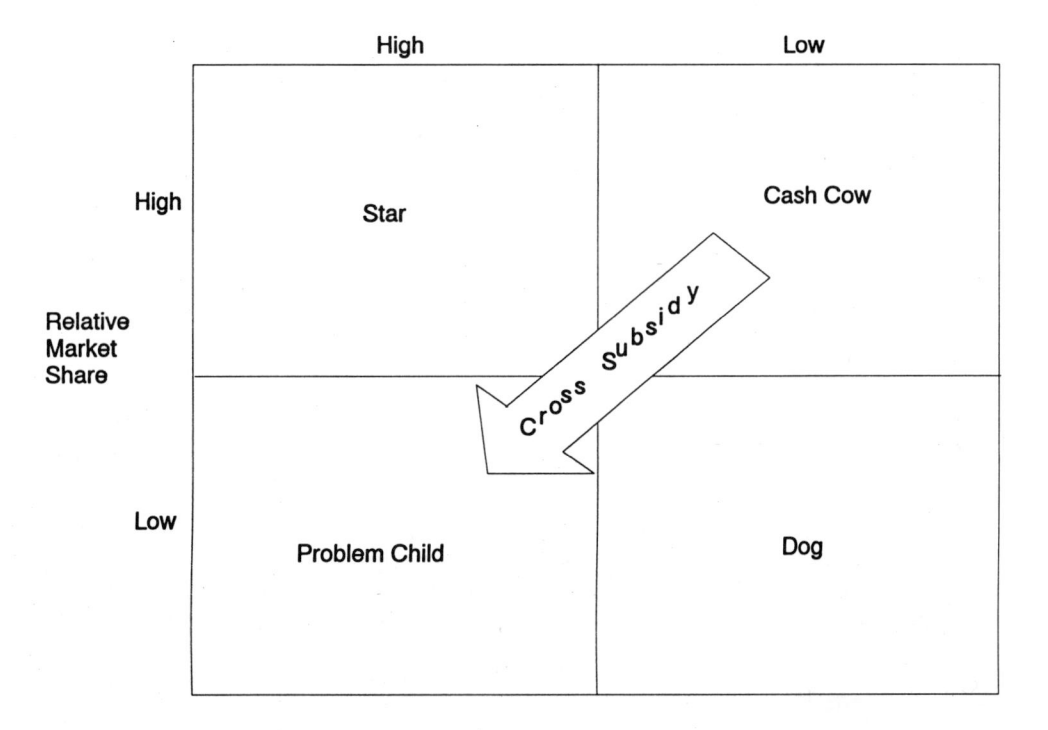

	High	Low
High	Star	Cash Cow
Low	Problem Child	Dog

Relative Market Share

Cross Subsidy (arrow from Cash Cow to Problem Child)

concept of business strength instead of relative market share on the other. The use of these more general concepts avoids the simplifying assumption that the greatest advantage to the firm comes with high growth, high share situations, but brings the complexity of deciding what constitutes market attractiveness and business strength. This is treated through the use of sets of questions which management must address when placing a particular opportunity into the G.E. Grid. The G.E. Planning grid is a 3x3 grid as illustrated in figure 88. Investment opportunities which are placed in the upper left corner of the grid are the most attractive as they represent a highly attractive market where great business strength can be brought to bear. They therefore appear to be an attractive *match* between the market and the business. Investment opportunities which are placed in the lower right corner of the grid are the least attractive, as they represent an unattractive market where little if any business strength can be brought to bear, a poor match between a market and the business.

Many other portfolio style strategic planning models exist. In general they can be seen as an attempt to shed some light on the capital allocation problem. For example, the *directional policy matrix* forces the categorization of an investment according to the prospects for sector profitability (attractive, average, unattractive) and the company's competitive capabilities (strong, average, weak). This matrix then makes specific suggestions for investment candidates or products falling into each of the resulting nine categories. The recommendations include try harder, disinvest and cash generation as illustrated in figure 89.

While such portfolio models have been popular and serve as useful conceptual aids, they harbor great potential for misuse. They greatly simplify the description of the market problems, opportunities and strategies available to the firm. They may distract management from the need to carefully build a substantial competitive advantage over a period of time.[5] In this way they may be partially responsible for some of the managerial failures in U.S. business.[6]

PIMS Results

Another approach to the analysis of strategy is to study large numbers of businesses and attempt to associate measures of profitability with characterizations of business strategy and environment. The School of Business at Harvard University has been conducting an extensive set of such studies, the results of which have come to be known as *PIMS or the Profit Impact of Marketing Strategies*. This set of studies has established a large data base which has allowed the study of strategy and results for over two thousand

Figure 88
The General Electric Planning Grid

Source: Philip Kotler and Gary Armstrong, *Principles of Marketing*, 4th ed. (Englewood Cliffs, NJ: Prentice Hall, 1989), p. 33. See also E. Jerome McCarthy and William D. Perreault Jr., *Basic Marketing*, 9th ed. (Homewood, Illinois: Richard D. Irwin, 1987), p. 117. See also Subhash C. Jain, *Marketing Planning and Strategy*, 3rd. ed. (Cincinnati, OH: Southwestern Publishing Co., 1990), p. 299.

	Market Attractiveness		
Business Strength	High	Medium	Low
High			
Medium			
Low			

328   Part III

Figure 89
The Directional Policy Matrix

Sources: *The Directional Policy Matrix* (London: Chemical Planning and Economics, Shell International Chemical Co., Ltd., September 1979). See also Subhash C. Jain, *Marketing Planning and Strategy* (Cincinnati, OH: Southwestern Publishing Co., 1990), p. 306. See also William Lazer and James D. Culley, *Marketing Management* (Boston, Mass.: Houghton Mifflin Co., 1983), p. 154. See also D. E. Hussey, "Portfolio Analysis: Practical Experience with the Directional Policy Matrix," *Long-Range Planning* (August 1978), pp. 1-9.

Prospects for Sector Profitability

Company's Competitive Capabilities	Unattractive	Average	Attractive
Weak	Disinvest	Phased Withdrawal	Double or Quit
Average	Phased Withdrawal	Custodial / Growth	Try Harder
Strong	Cash Generation	Growth / Leader	Leader

businesses. Each of the businesses has provided information concerning over one hundred aspects of the business and its environment. This has allowed the development of a management report called the *par report* which provides estimates of the return on investment which would be normal for a business given its market environment, competitive position, production structure, budget allocations and historical pattern of strategic moves.[7] The PIMS data base also provides other reports which allow management to compare its results with the pooled experience of many firms. Data such as those available from PIMS have allowed an understanding of the strengths which accrue with large market share strategies.[8]

Contingency Models: A Product Life Cycle Example

The product life cycle or innovation life cycle which was discussed in chapter three has been used as a conceptual aid for strategy selection. The basic innovation life cycle model is reproduced as figure 90. The innovation life cycle illustrates the idea that a firm's strategy should be contingent upon (dependent upon or conditioned by) the situation. For example, the innovation life cycle model suggests that a firm's pricing strategy could include higher prices during the growth period, a period of higher monopoly power, than might be charged during maturity, a period of competitive entry. Contingent approaches to understanding strategy may be designed to be contingent upon the situation as described by any model, not just the product life cycle model.

The Experience Curve

The concept of economies of scale was introduced in chapter one as a basic reason for the existence of modern specialization and exchange economies. The experience curve is a similar source of reduced costs with increased production. Beyond the usual economies of scale effects which reflect the results of larger sized operations, experience effects reflect the reduced costs which result from practice and learning.[9] Reliance upon experience effects has allowed some firms to make the bold move of pricing the coming year's product below its historical costs.[10] This will still result in a profit in the coming year if practice and learning reduce costs according to the expected *experience curve*.

330   Part III

**Figure 90
The Innovation Life Cycle or
the Product Life Cycle**

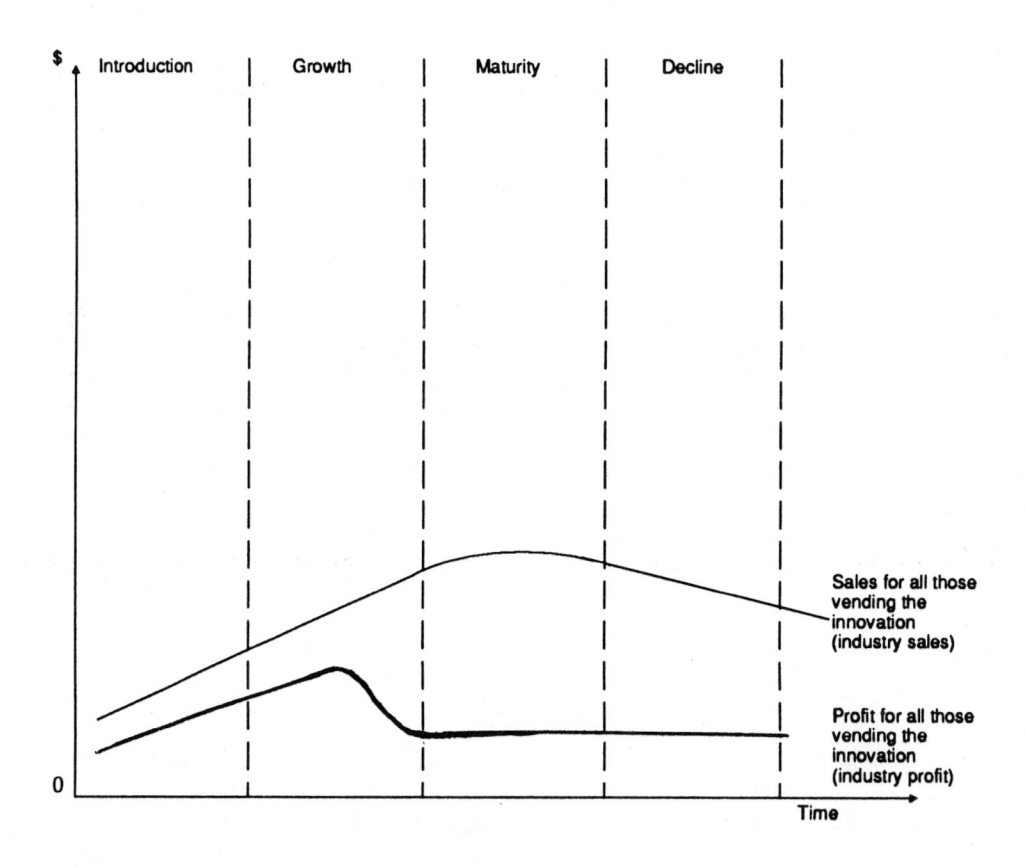

Military Analogy

The market niche of the firm is expanded by encouraging economically successful exchanges with the individuals who comprise the target market. However, no matter how well a firm understands and serves its market, no matter how efficient it becomes in lowering its costs, the profitability of its offerings can be substantially diminished by the advent of increasing competition.

Selecting strategic directions whereby an organization will survive and grow in the context of competition brings forth the elements of conflict and advantage which have been seen to be inherent in the definition of strategy. Competition implies a form of conflict, and the essential heterogeneity of suppliers insures that there will be opportunities to create advantage out of the natural differences among the suppliers.

Among the military principles which have been adopted by marketing are the *principle of objective* and the *principle of mass*. The principle of objective holds that every military operation must be directed toward a clearly defined, decisive and attainable objective.[11] Marketing acceptance of this principle is seen in the use of objective statements, describing intended objectives for the company as a whole, as well as objectives for divisions, departments and individuals. Direction, control and budgeting activities are often tied into management by objective (MBO) systems which will be discussed later in this chapter.

The principle of mass holds that superior combat power must be concentrated at the critical time and place for a decisive purpose.[12] Experienced marketers have demonstrated their understanding of this principle by arranging and allocating resources so as to create competitive superiority at critical times and places. This sometimes involves identifying a competitor's weakness and amassing strength to develop an advantage vis-a-vis that weakness. For example, an auto manufacturer might find that the competitor's otherwise excellent car has a weakness, such as poor fuel mileage. In arranging and allocating resources to create strength at a critical place, the auto firm might fund research and development to design a more fuel efficient car. The new strength might then be brought to bear against the competitor at an advantageous time, perhaps as the Environmental Protection Agency (EPA) is preparing fuel mileage figures for the next year, or as gasoline prices are rising. The result of these aggressive competitive efforts will benefit the customer, as the customer may now choose between an excellent car and one designed to be better, according to certain evaluative criteria.

Other military concepts adopted by marketing include the ideas of *attack and defense*. An attack is typified by an entry into a market already being addressed by a competitor, while defense is seen as the responses to such an attack. Specific attack and defense strategies are outlined in figures 91 and 92.

Marketing has also adopted the military's *differentiation between the concept of strategy and the concept of tactics. Strategy* carries the broader connotation of the placement of resources in order to gain a position of advantage. Something which is tactical in nature is defined by Webster as of or relating to the planning or execution of small scale actions as a part of a larger purpose.[13] Thus *tactics* are small scale actions in support of the larger (strategic) purpose. In a marketing example, the decision to increase market share by increasing field sales efforts is a strategic choice. An individual sales person's planning and execution of activities in a sales territory are tactical in nature.

Game Theory

The focus upon outguessing competition that permeates the military perspective is also reflected in game theory. Game theory is a set of perspectives which focuses on the outcomes of strategy given the strategic moves of the competition. It is useful in understanding the different kinds of reasoning that apply in conflict situations.[14]

A few game theory perspectives useful in the formulation of marketing strategy may be illustrated using the payoff matrices which comprise figure 93. In this figure, the market share payoff matrix demonstrates the results of possible strategy combinations in terms of market share. If both competitors hold their price at a high level each will be rewarded with a fifty percent share of the market. If one initiates a price cut and the other does not follow suit, the competitor initiating the price cut will gain an additional forty percent of the market, entirely at the expense of the other. If both cut prices, the market shares will remain at fifty percent for each.

The second matrix in figure 93, the profit payoff matrix, displays the results of the same possible strategy combinations in terms of profit for each competitor. By holding the price level high the industry as a whole takes the most profit with each competitor making $1 million dollars. If one elects to cut the price and take a full 90% of the market, the price cutter, perhaps through economies of scale, can increase profit to $1.1 million, while the firm holding the higher price sees profits reduced to $.1 million. When both involve themselves in price cutting, equal shares of the market result in profits of $.2 million apiece.

Figure 91
Attack Strategies, Governing Principles and Marketing Examples

Reprinted with permission from *Journal of Business Strategy*, Volume I, No. 3, copyright 1981. Warren, Gorham, and Lamont, 210 South Street, Boston, MA, 02111. All rights reserved.

Strategy of Attack	General Principle	Marketing Example
Frontal attack	Attack the competitor's strength (often fails without a substantial advantage in resources).	Match product for product, advertisement for advertisement. Meet a high gas mileage car with another high gas mileage car. Hope to prevail on greater strength and endurance.
Modified frontal attack	Attack the competitors strength plus bring one advantage to bear.	Match product for product, advertisement for advertisement for the frontal attack, but bring an advantage to bear such as a product feature or the ability to translate a cost advantage into a lower price.
Flanking attack	Concentration of strength against weakness, as in attacking the flanks or the rear of a military deployment. Often accompanied by a feint in another direction to encourage weakness in the target area. Higher probability of success than frontal attacks.	Address market needs left uncovered or poorly covered by a competitor. These may be identified geographically as in going to cities that the competitor serves poorly. They may be identified segmentally as addressing a segment of the market unserved or poorly served by competition.
Encirclement or envelopment	Grand offensive on several fronts. May include attacks on the front, flanks, and rear simultaneously. (Hits the enemies' strengths and weaknesses.) Used to encourage quick capitulation when the aggressor has superior resources.	Hitting the mark on every evaluative criterion that is relevant to the customer, regardless of whether it constitutes a competitor's strength or weakness. For example, producing a superior product in the consumer's eyes *and* giving it a lower price.

\	Figure 91 Continued	
Bypass attack	Adopt a more global view of competition. Do not necessarily infringe on markets currently held by competitors.	Avoid head on competition. Diversify, enter new geographic (overseas) markets.
Guerilla warfare	Small intermittent attacks to attack, demoralize, secure concessions, weaken, awaiting changes in the balance of force.	Selective price cuts, supply interference, executive raids, intense promotional bursts, legal actions.

Figure 92
Defense Strategies
Governing Principles and Marketing Examples

Reprinted with permission from *Journal of Business Strategy*, Volume I, No. 3, copyright 1981. Warren, Gorham, and Lamont, 210 South Street, Boston, MA, 02111. All rights reserved.

Defense Strategy	General Principle	Marketing Example
Position defense	Fortify existing positions	Assume that current offerings can be defended. This can be risky as the inevitable market dynamics will ensure change of some kind.
Mobile defense	Move to a new domain	Shift capital to new domains. Broaden offerings within a market, diversify.
Preemptive defense	Attack when another's attack is anticipated	Move to block or render powerless those who are building threatening positions. This would utilize any form of attack per Figure 91.
Flanking positioning defense	Invest and build positions on the potential enemy's flanks.	Start divisions or offer products which have the potential of bringing a strength to bear against a competitive weakness. Do not emphasize them.

Figure 92 Continued

Counter offensive	Following an attack, evaluate it and attack at the evident weak points.	U.S. auto manufacturers evaluate new small cars from overseas and design their new cars only after careful study of the new competitors.
Strategic withdrawal	Consolidate strength and attempt to concentrate mass.	Drop products when they are under successful attack and concentrate efforts on the remaining products.

In the terms of game theory the market share situation is a *zero sum game or a constant sum game* wherein one competitor's gains necessarily come at the expense of the other. When viewed in terms of profit the game is a *non constant sum game*, wherein strategies may be selected which do not reflect one party gaining exactly what the other loses. Note that market share payoffs always add up to the constant sum of 100% market share while adding the profit payoffs will result in non constant sum of .4, 2.0 or 1.2 million, depending upon the strategy combination. When evaluating one's strategy vis-a-vis competition it is always wise to consider whether one is playing a constant sum game or a non constant sum game. When playing non constant sum games, it is wise to consider antitrust law, which will be discussed in chapter ten. It is possible, depending upon the means of implementation, that the profitable strategy which involves both competitors holding prices high would be illegal in the United States.

The payoff matrices may also be used to illustrate some important types of reasoning which may be applied to strategic choice. A player may elect to play the game conservatively, selecting the strategy which places the highest absolutely defensible floor under that player's payoffs. This means selecting the strategy which guarantees the highest payoff regardless of what the competitor does. In terms of the profit-payoff matrix, competitor A's conservative strategy would be to cut the price, as $.2 million is a higher absolutely defensible floor than $.1 million. This conservative selection rule for strategy is termed a *maximin strategy* because it maximizes the minimum payoffs. Due to the way payoff matrices are sometimes constructed (in terms of what the opposition gets), this same strategy is also referred to as a *minimax strategy*, for minimizing your opposition's maximum payoffs. This is a very cautious and conservative way to approach strategic choice. It is defensive in nature and designed to protect against the worst outcomes. However, it is often the

Figure 93
Payoff Matrices

Market Share Payoff Matrix

Competitor A's Strategy / Competitor B's Strategy

	Cut Price	Hold Price High
Cut Price	50% for A / 50% for B	90% for A / 10% for B
Hold Price High	10% for A / 90% for B	50% for A / 50% for B

Profit Payoff Matrix

Competitor A's Strategy / Competitor B's Strategy

	Cut Price	Hold Price High
Cut Price	$.2 million for A / $.2 million for B	$1.1 million for A / $.1 million for B
Hold Price High	$.1 million for A / $1.1 million for B	$1.0 million for A / $1.0 million for B

prudent approach when there is insufficient competitive intelligence to allow a reasonable guess about what the competition really intends to do.

At the opposite end of the risk spectrum is a decision rule known as *regret minimization*. A regret minimizing decision requires the decision maker to determine the regrets or lost opportunities with each strategy. The strategy which minimizes regret or equivalently, provides for the highest possible gain is chosen. This striving for maximum gain is a high risk kind of strategy which typifies entrepreneurs. In the particular situation in figure 93, competitor A would again cut price, selecting the strategy with the highest possible outcomes, in order to minimize regret.

The strategist may opt for approaches which lie between these extremes. Bayesian *probabilities* might be used. This would involve attaching probabilities to the possible behaviors of the competition. For example, competitor A might be able to derive competitive intelligence which suggests that the probability of B cutting price is .4 and the probability of B holding price high is .6. This knowledge would allow competitor A to see the outcomes as displayed in figure 94. Here the decision rule is to choose the strategy with the highest *certainty equivalent*, where each possible outcome has been weighted by the probability that it will occur. In this example, competitor A would choose, in a very close decision, to cut the price. A *mixed strategy* might also be employed. Employing one strategy some of the time and another strategy at other times will keep competitors guessing and can result in higher total payoffs over a period of time.

Positioning

A way of characterizing maneuver in the context of the competition which is unique to marketing is the idea of *positioning*. The term *position* refers to the way an offering is perceived by potential customers in comparison with the other offerings which are available to them. The current position of a firm's offering may thus be diagnosed using market research. Focus groups can be used to determine the evaluative criteria which buyers utilize when judging the particular type of product or service under study. The important evaluative criteria which are found will become axes for a graphic display of the consumer's perceptions. For example, focus groups may determine that the degree to which a ginger ale is light or dark is an important evaluative criterion and the degree to which it is seen as a prestige or economy product is another. Dark-light will become one *axis* and prestige-economy will become another along which the individual offerings may be positioned. Quantitative survey research can then develop an idea of how consumers view the offerings. The researcher may ask the consumer how he or she sees the various

**Figure 94
Probable Outcomes**

Competitor A's Strategy

Cut Price:

$1.1 million × .6 (B holds price high) = $ .66

$.2 million × .4 (B cuts price) = $ .08

Certainty Equivalent Payoff = $ .68 million

Hold Price High:

$1.0 million × .6 (B holds price high) = $ .60

$ .1 million × .4 (B cuts price) = $ .04

Certainty Equivalent Payoff = $ .64 million

offerings with respect to the axes which have been identified. For example, the consumer might be asked to estimate the extent to which two brands are similar or different with respect to prestige or economy. A statistical procedure might then be used to display the resulting similarities and differences among the products in terms of distances in space. One possible result is shown in figure 95.

Here, offering A is perceived to be greatly different than offering B along the axis of (in the context of the evaluative criterion of) prestige versus economy. Offering A is perceived to be a prestige ginger ale, while offering B is perceived to be an economy ginger ale. At the same time, no difference is perceived between the two offerings in terms of color.

This diagnosis may not yet be strategically useful, but it does illustrate the concept of positioning. Product A is "positioned" as a prestige product and product B is currently "positioned" as an economy product. Both are "positioned" as light products. As the firm seeks ways to allocate resources so as to defend and enhance its market niche, it may want to invest in *repositioning* the product. In other words, it may want to invest in adjustment of the four p's of the offering to alter the way the product is perceived by the consumer.

Suppose for example, the firm wanted to invest in "repositioning product B" as a prestige product. A logical set of alterations would be product alterations (if necessary) to allow the discussion of fine ingredients, promotion in media catering to the affluent, physical distribution in a more exclusive set of outlets and price increases. If these investment activities were successful in changing perceptions, product B would be repositioned in the direction of product A. This is illustrated in figure 96.

While positioning and repositioning have now been illustrated, the strategic desirability of an *investment in repositioning* has yet to be fully considered. Is it wise to reposition product B? Positioning and repositioning must now be seen in the context of other perspectives in marketing strategy.

If the firm were to reposition product B to occupy product A's position with respect to all of the axes (or evaluative criteria) that are seen as relevant by the consumer group of interest, that would constitute a frontal assault on product A. In other words, this strategy amounts to moving product B directly into the market niche occupied by product A. Not only are such attacks risky, they imply increased competition for the market niche. This means both products must endure the downward pressure on prices and profits that accompany increased competition. Product B would have to drive product A entirely out of the market or force it to reposition substantially before these downward pressures on price and profit would subside.

**Figure 95
Product Positioning**

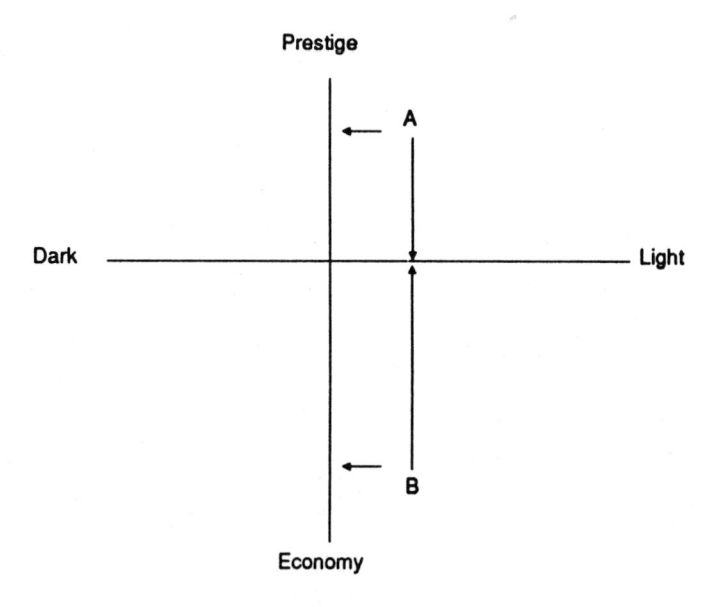

**Figure 96
The Repositioning of Product B**

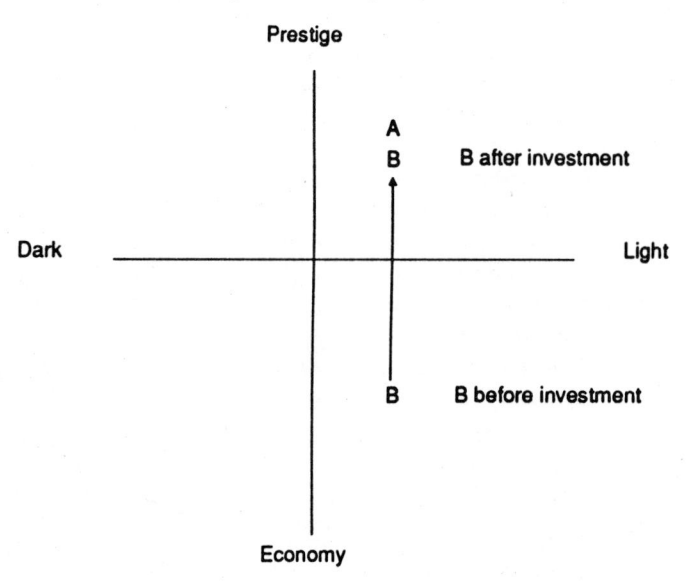

More profitable market niches are often entered through a flanking attack—addressing market needs left uncovered or poorly covered by the competition. Consider figure 97. This figure illustrates the same offerings as the previous figures have illustrated (offerings A and B) but also illustrates the positions of other competitors, C, D and E. Importantly, figure 97 displays the results of research questions which have asked consumers to characterize their "ideal ginger ale," as well as competitive offerings A through E.

Study of the demographics and consumption habits of this group might indicate that satisfying the group's preferences would be profitable. Suppose it is a segment of affluent individuals who consume a lot of ginger ale. In this case, the firm would be in a position to generate high marginal utility by successfully addressing the group's evaluative criteria. There would be little competitive pressure on price or profit because a dark prestige ginger ale (the ideal product is a dark prestige ginger ale) would be *successfully differentiated* from the competition.

At this point the firm might want to consider repositioning product B into the ideal position for this market segment. A financial comparison of the market niche implicit in the position currently occupied by product B and the potential market niche at the ideal position would have to be made. The costs of repositioning and the probabilities of success would have to be considered as well as the expected behavior of competitors. How long will competitors leave this position open? It might be decided that the market niche at B's current position is too good to be sacrificed and so a new product (B-1) might be introduced in the ideal position.

Alternatively, the interest in repositioning may have been generated by a dissatisfaction with the profitability of B in its current position. In this case B might be profitably repositioned to the ideal position. Investments in a changed product formula, in promotion of a dark prestige ginger ale, in alteration of distribution, (dropping discount outlets) and a price increase might be in order. The analysis of this set of investments should show a positive net present value and an internal rate of return exceeding the company's cost of capital. This repositioning is illustrated in figure 98 and may be viewed as a flanking attack upon competitors. If the poor profitability of the market niche at position B was the result of a frontal attack by product D (illustrated by the dotted line) then the repositioning of product B could also be seen as a mobile defense.

The positioning and repositioning of product B has been discussed in terms of two dimensions, prestige versus economy and dark versus light. These dimensions or consumer evaluative criteria have been represented as axes in figures 95-98. Representation of positions in terms of axes in this way is typical of the output of a commonly used multivariate statistical procedure,

**Figure 97
Identification of a New Potential
Market Niche**

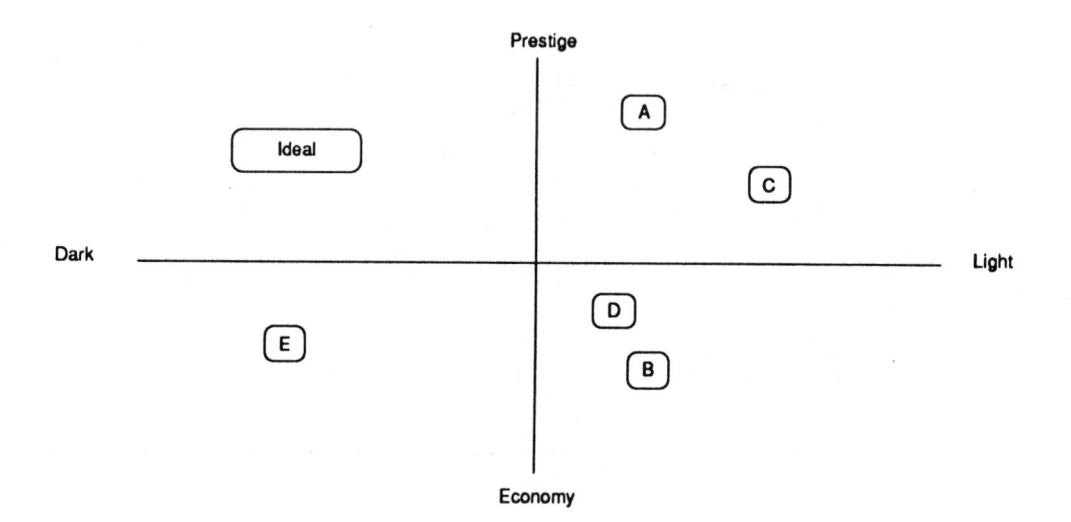

Chapter 9 343

**Figure 98
Repositioning Product B to
The Ideal Position**

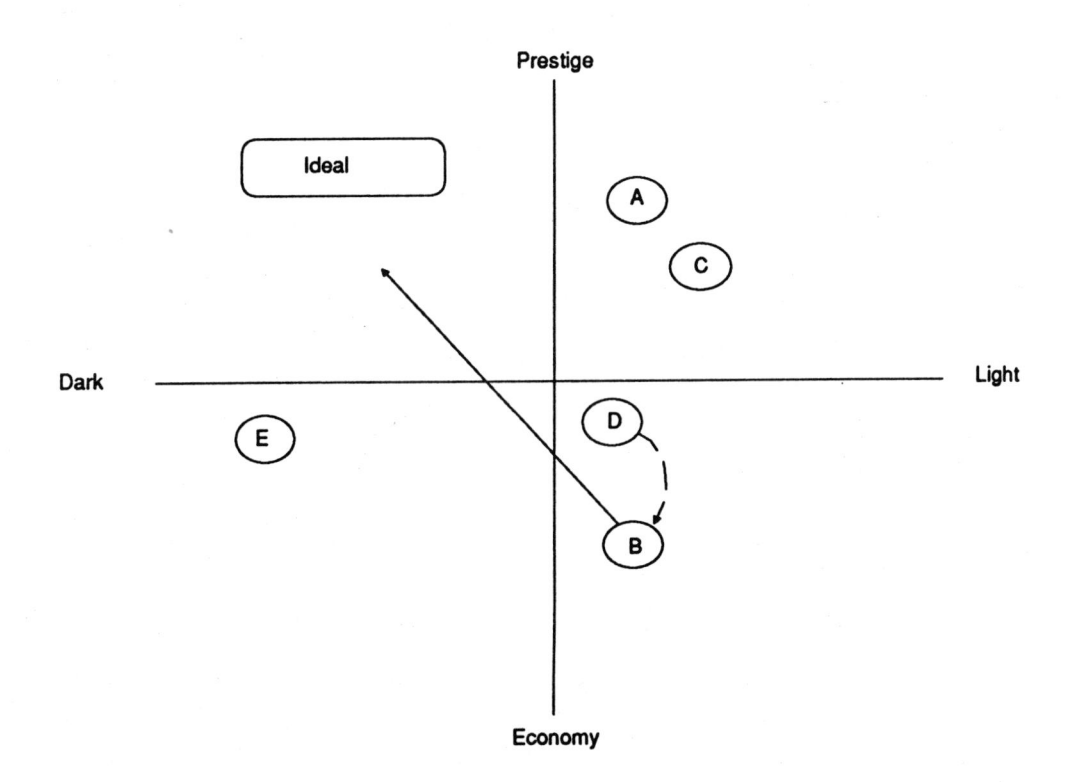

multidimensional scaling. The use of more axes simply requires multiple two-way comparisons.

While multidimensional scaling is a useful way to display positioning strategy, it is important to understand that positioning can be diagnosed using any of a number of measurement tools and statistical procedures. Linear models or conjoint measurement, both introduced earlier in the book, would be alternative means of evaluating how different offerings measure up in terms of the consumer's evaluative criteria.

Segmentation

The concept of a market segment was introduced early in the book. Chapter two defined a *market segment* as an aggregation of individuals whose response to a product offering was sufficiently similar as to allow management to make useful generalizations about their behavior. For example, in the discussion above the graphic representations of perceived product positions were for a particular market segment, the group that was researched. A given aggregation of individuals saw the competitors and the ideal product in the way that was depicted and this generalization was useful to management.

The principle of *segmentation* as a perspective in strategy is straightforward. Segmentation represents a compromise which is part and parcel of the matching of heterogeneous supply with heterogeneous demand. The two realities which encourage the compromise are:

1. People have individualistic needs and preferences
2. Economies of scale in production exist

These realities dictate that satisfying everyone on an individual basis with such things as individually crafted custom built automobiles would be too costly. On the other hand, forcing everyone to consume the identical offering would result in poor matches and low satisfaction. Because of the existence of these two realities, marketers seek to group individuals into market segments. These segments should be aggregations of individuals whose response to the product offering is similar enough that it makes sense to approach them with the same marketing mix. The segments should be large enough so that economies of scale will allow the individuals in the segment to afford the product. The segments should be small enough so that people with substantially different views and preferences are not grouped together and approached with the same marketing mix.

Financial viability is a most important criterion used in making judgments concerning who should comprise market segments, how big the segment should be and what the appropriate marketing mix should be. The use of profitability in this way is illustrated in the following example.

Consider the automobile market. If an automobile producer had corporate overhead of $1 million per year it would be necessary to generate $1 million per year in contribution to overhead and earnings just to break even. This situation is illustrated in figure 99. Here, either of two dissimilar market segments would provide enough C.O.E. for the firm to break even. In option one, a custom car is built for a very affluent individual. The costs of producing this vehicle are very high as there are no economies of scale involved. However, this is fully compensated by the psychological impact that the custom vehicle has on the affluent consumer. The vehicle is exactly what that person wants. So the affluent customer willingly pays the two million dollars which is required to cover incremental costs and the needed $1 million of C.O.E.

In the opposite extreme example, option two, lukewarm enthusiasm about a modest product is compensated by the significant economies of scale which are achieved with a production run of one million cars per year. In this case, the market segment consists of one million individuals who would rather buy a modest new car for three thousand dollars than purchase a used car for the same amount. The modest little car stirs enthusiasm in few of them, but at a price of three thousand dollars, the offer is accepted and one million units are sold. Generating C.O.E. of only one dollar per unit, this market segment has the *same financial viability as the first segment*. According to this critical criterion, these dissimilar segments of the auto market are equally attractive.

Segmenting involves finding these kinds of financially viable matches between groups of customers (market segments) and specific offerings of the firm. Generalizing from the two extreme examples above, it can be said that a financially viable market segment is a function of:

1. The utility the product generates in the mind of the consumers in the segment
2. The money the customers have to convert utility to demand
3. (Thus) the units demanded at given levels of price
4. The incremental costs at different levels of unit movement

Segmentation strategies which are targeted at extremely large segments have traditionally been referred to as *mass marketing* strategies, while strategies aimed at smaller groups have been referred to as *target marketing*. Market segments are identified and characterized according to segmenting dimensions. A *segmenting dimension* is a measurable characteristic of a buyer which allows that buyer to be grouped with others in a market segment. Without

Figure 99
Financial Viability of
Alternative Segments

Option Two

An extremely broad market segment of 1 million individuals

Product: A minimum new car; a modern Model "T"

Economies of scale allow low incremental cost per unit

Relatively low utility of this simple car is compensated for by low price

It is a viable offering

$3,000.00 price
$2,999.00 inc. cost

$1.00 C.O.E. per unit

x 1 million units

$1 million in C.O.E.

Option One

An extremely narrow market segment of one individual

Product: A custom-built 4-door, 4-wheel-drive, armor-plated convertible

No economies of scale
High incremental cost

High utility of the custom product for an individual who can afford it

It is a viable offering

Only one unit produced and sold

$2 million price
-1 million incremental cost

$1 million in C.O.E.

$1 million
In Corporate overhead which must be covered

such useful measurements to determine who belongs in the segment and who does not, the segment is not *operational*. That is, there would be no practical way to identify the segment in day to day marketing practice.

A segmenting dimension can be a physical dimension. A man who is 6 feet 6 inches tall may appropriately be grouped in a big and tall segment for men's clothing. This segment is often approached with separate clothing stores or separate departments in larger stores. *A segmenting dimension may be a geographic dimension.* Where a person lives helps to determine his or her preference for climate and culturally dependent purchases such as 4x4 vehicles, surfboards and specific styles of clothing. *A segmenting dimension can be a demographic dimension.* Knowledge about a person's age, sex, family size, income, occupational or other demographic dimensions can be used to place the individual into a group with similar responses in the market. Demographics are commonly used segmenting dimensions and often inexpensively obtained from secondary data.

A segmenting dimension can be a psychological dimension. A person's social class, life style, personality or specific motivation can be used to characterize their likely responses in the market. Psychological dimensions may be long lasting characteristics which are intrinsic to a person as a personality or life style. Alternatively they may be more superficial and a function of the person's relationship to the offering under immediate consideration. Examples of this later type of psychological dimension would include the psychological benefits which are sought from the purchase, the readiness to purchase, and the attitude toward the product.

A segmenting dimension can be a characterization of industry type and size. Industrial vendors will often classify their target markets according to the nature and size of their activities. For example, classifications might include large boat manufacturers and small boat manufacturers. *A segmenting dimension can be a description of intraorganizational and interpersonal relationships.* Group influence purchases such as the family selection of a college for their child, a corporation's selection of the aluminum to be used in the construction of boats, or a hospital's selection of specific pharmaceutical products can be characterized according to which individuals had what kind of influence at what time. For example, when hospitals purchase pharmaceuticals, the purchasing procedures can be quite different. In some situations formulary committees are very powerful; in other situations individual physicians are more powerful. Pharmaceutical companies will have to approach these different kinds of hospitals in different ways.

Any kind of segmenting dimension may be seen as a *qualifying dimension* or a *determining dimension*. A qualifying dimension simply allows the measurement of whether or not a buyer is qualified (or able) to buy the product.

Income is a common qualifying dimension and good salespeople will "qualify" a potential customer early in the conversation by asking about their profession in order to obtain an estimate of their income. After a person is qualified (or able) to buy something, other dimensions "determine" just what it is that he or she prefers to buy. Determining dimensions which may be any kind of segmenting dimension, determine a buyer's special selections from among the items he or she is qualified to buy.

Segmenting dimensions are usually combined in order to describe a market segment. Rarely is one dimension sufficient. The segment known as yuppies (young upwardly mobile urban professionals) uses four segmenting dimensions.

It is the task of marketing management to ensure that the firm successfully addresses financially viable market segments with appropriate marketing mixes. This requires substantial knowledge of the market segments and their preferences. It also requires substantial knowledge of the firm's capabilities and costs. These pieces of knowledge must be translated into estimates of the revenue and incremental costs which are reasonable to associate with each market segment under consideration.

Mergers, Acquisitions and Spinoffs

The discussion thus far has described the defense and expansion of the market niche through the efforts of the individual firm or organization. The discussion has centered upon the offering of new products and services, and the modification and pruning of the product line. *Market niches can also be expanded, pruned, and adjusted through the purchase and sale of entire companies.* In fact, these activities may be viewed simply as alternative means of expanding, modifying and pruning product lines. This perspective is so straightforward that several of the portfolio models discussed earlier may be used to analyze entire companies as opposed to product lines. The companies owned are simply substituted for products in each of the grid's classifying squares. The Boston Consulting Group matrix in figure 100 illustrates this use of a portfolio model.

An important effect that this perspective will have upon marketing strategy results from the fact that purchases and sales of major corporate entities are usually transacted at least in part with the exchange of stock. As marketing activities and results such as the success and failure of products will have an effect on the value of the company's stock, it makes sense that some consideration would be given to the adjustment and timing of marketing activities so as to affect stock values. This can place the firm in a stronger

Chapter 9   349

Figure 100
The Boston Consulting Group Matrix
Classifying Firms or
Subsidiaries Held

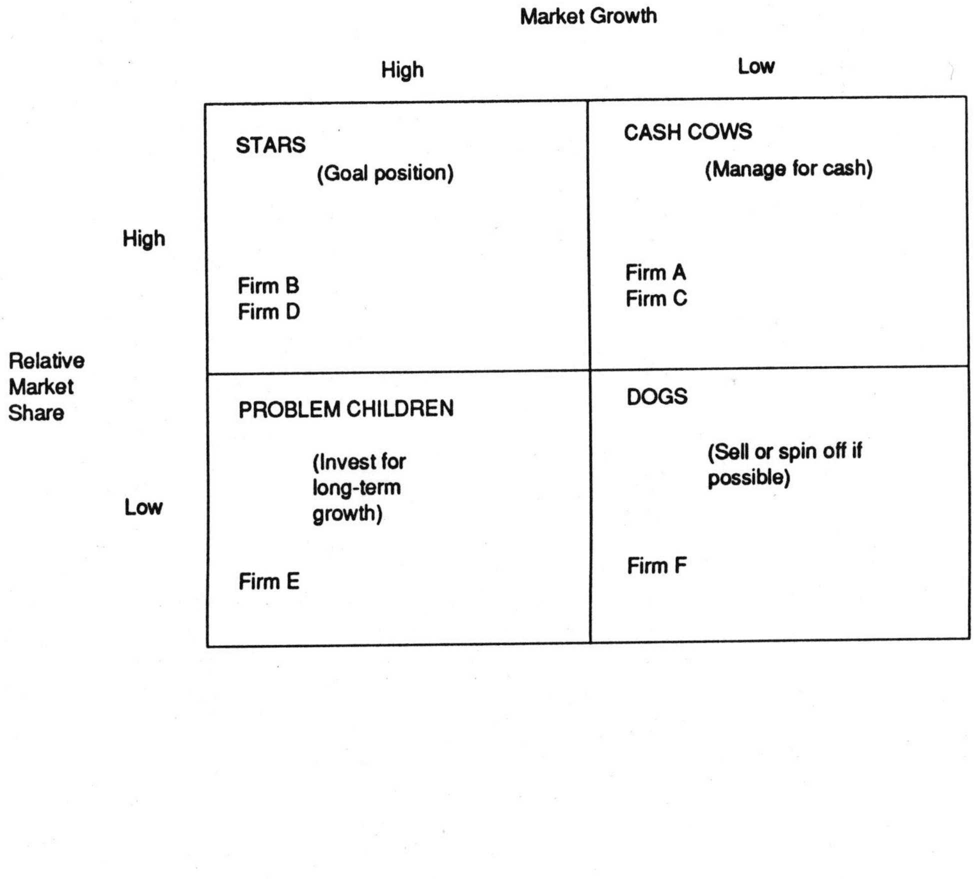

Market Growth

	High	Low
High Relative Market Share	STARS (Goal position) Firm B Firm D	CASH COWS (Manage for cash) Firm A Firm C
Low	PROBLEM CHILDREN (Invest for long-term growth) Firm E	DOGS (Sell or spin off if possible) Firm F

position when negotiating mergers, acquisitions and spinoffs or sales of corporate entities.

The Marketing Concept and Capital Shifting

The *marketing concept* is a prominent conceptual aid in marketing. There are several roughly similar statements of the marketing concept. In general the marketing concept is a statement about the preferred strategic orientation of the firm. According to the marketing concept the firm should coordinate its activities toward satisfying the customer while taking a profit for doing this. Popular statements of this idea include those of McCarthy and Kotler.[15]

> The marketing concept means that an organization aims all of its efforts at *satisfying* its customers—at a profit
>
> —E. Jerome McCarthy

> The marketing concept holds that achieving organizational goals depends on determining the needs and wants of target markets and delivering the desired *satisfaction* more effectively and efficiently than competitors.
>
> —Philip Kotler (this author's italics)

Acceptance of the marketing concept implies a high organizational priority placed upon customer *satisfaction*. It is an idealistic position which is appropriate for the development of long term relationships with markets. However, within the firm the marketing concept must compete with financial pressures which may favor a short term capital shifting strategy.

In contrast with the marketing concept, a short term *capital shifting strategy* would advocate treating offerings as components of an investment portfolio. They would be acquired, managed and sold with a higher priority placed upon short term profit than is implicit in the marketing concept. Portfolio models have encouraged a capital shifting concept, and often inadvertently, organizational design may encourage a capital shifting perspective as well. For example, it is common in U.S.-owned corporations to place an individual in a middle level marketing position with a "wait and see" attitude concerning whether the person will be allowed to stay in the job. U.S. firms are proud of their "no-nonsense, results" orientation. Given this system of rewards and punishments, it is not rational to expect that these mid level managers will make decisions where short term benefits, realized within their probationary period, are sacrificed for the longer term benefits which might be realized after the probationary period.

In contrast, Japanese firms have demonstrated greater commitment to individual job security. This together with their resulting slower promotion schedules may encourage their managers to take a longer term view. Perhaps as a function of cultural expectations rather than overt choice, the Japanese have opted for organizational forms which encourage a long term view and the marketing concept strategies which bring customer satisfaction. This has had substantial payoff. Honda, a manufacturer first known for a line of small motorcycles, is now producing an extensive line of high quality automobiles. This auto line has been slowly built from the most modest beginnings into a broad line which competes successfully with a broad range of cars, from the Ford Escort to the smaller BMWs and Mercedes. Honda, like other Japanese auto manufacturers, has concentrated on high quality, durable products which deliver customer satisfaction.

The marketing concept emphasizes customer satisfaction and yet the organization, profit or non profit, must garner more resources than it consumes if it is to survive and grow. In some instances there is no conflict between these perspectives. But it is often the case that a higher level of customer satisfaction could be delivered if a lower level of contribution margin were taken from the market. Advocates of a capital shifting strategy will argue for taking the profit from the market now and reinvesting it in more fertile fields. Middle level managers will work to survive in the short run, and may be pressed to show short term improvements in C.O.E.

Management commitment to a marketing concept or long term customer satisfaction strategy must therefore be evident in more ways than just its appearance in mission statements. It must take the form of organizational design which rewards marketing concept behaviors, and it must take the form of financial commitment to long term consumer satisfaction which is supported by the firm's owners.

Risk and Product Market Expansion

It is useful to view alternative strategies in terms of the risks which are inherent in them. *The product market expansion grid* illustrates common marketing strategies in terms of whether the product and the market are new or old. Figure 101 illustrates a product market expansion grid.[16]

When the firm seeks to grow through the more successful vending of old products in old markets, the strategy is referred to as *market penetration*. This strategy is a relatively low risk strategy because the organization knows a great deal about both the product and the market. On the other hand, this

Figure 101
Product-market Expansion Grid

Source: H. Igor Ansoff, *Corporate Strategy* (New York: McGraw Hill, 1964), p. 128. See also E. Jerome McCarthy and William D. Perreault Jr., *Basic Marketing*, 10th ed. (Homewood, ILL: Richard D. Irwin, 1990), p. 66. See also Thomas C. Kinnear and Kenneth L. Bernhardt, *Principles of Marketing*, 3rd ed. (Glenview, ILL: Scott Foresman/Little Brown, 1990), p. 49. See also Philip Kotler and Gary Armstrong, *Marketing: An Introduction*, 2nd ed. (Englewood Cliffs, NJ: Prentice Hall, 1990), p. 33.

	Product Old	Product New
Market Old	Market Penetration	Product Development
Market New	Market Development	Diversification

strategy is likely to involve the vending of innovations which are late in their life cycle, with the resulting adverse effects on profit. Should Ford elect to expand its market niche by taking more of the traditional family car market, expanding sales of the older rear wheel drive LTD Crown Victoria at the expense of the Chevrolet Caprice, it would be an example of a market penetration strategy. Should Ford seek to expand its market niche by exporting the LTD Crown Victoria to Saudi Arabia, a new geographic market, it would be an example of a *market development strategy*. Such a strategy balances the risks involved in understanding a new market against the potential rewards of the new match being proposed. In similar fashion *product development* entails the risks of a new product for a market that is already well understood. When Chevrolet developed the front drive Lumina as an offering for the traditional American family car market, it selected a product development strategy. *Diversification* entails the creation of a new product for a new market. The strategy entails both forms of risk, new products and new markets, balanced against the potential profitability of this high degree of innovation. Ford's development of an Aerospace division is an example of a diversification strategy.

Strategic Response Patterns in a Changing Environment

As the environment of the organization changes, the strategic choices which are appropriate change. Differing kinds of firms have demonstrated different degrees of creativity and initiative when facing this challenge. Those demonstrating a great deal of creativity and initiative, aggressively changing their product-market matches as the environment changes, have been termed *prospectors*. *Defenders* are firms which tend not to venture beyond their established set of product-market matches. *Analyzers* combining these two activities defending a core set of product market matches while prospecting for new opportunities in peripheral or fringe markets. *Reactors* lack a strategic orientation and simply respond to environmental pressures.[17]

Results of Strategy Selection

Once the firm has made a selection of strategy, the broad statements of mission, goals, and objectives must be translated into *budgets*. Budgets are a tool which provide day to day direction and control for marketing activities by specifying in time sequence how resources are to be allocated. The process of translation of missions, goals, and objectives into budgets can take any of several forms.[18] Budgeting can be a *top down/bottom-up* (TDBU) decision process. In this process the total size of the marketing budget is decided by top management and is then divided up among the organizational subunits in marketing. In a *bottom-up/top-down* (BUTD) decision process, managers of the subunits submit budget requests which are often parallel to and supportive of their specific plans. Top management then adjusts budgets, approving or disapproving plans, in order to support the organization's broader missions, goals and objectives. An important form of the bottom-up/top down decision process is *management by objective or MBO*. In this objective setting and budgeting process, individuals become involved in their own planning, direction and control. Individual workers and organizational groups propose objectives to their superiors in the organization. These proposed objectives are then reconciled with broader organizational objectives, approved and formalized. Budgets are approved in support of these specific objectives and become a basis for the direction and control of daily activities.

Crossing National Boundaries

Adjustments to both the organizational forms and the conceptual aids used to facilitate strategic choice will be required as the firm's activities become international. *Organizational adaptation* is extremely individualistic, but several general organizational forms exist which facilitate international activities. A firm may use an *international division structure*. This structure is a logical adaptation early in the firm's international activities. With international division structure, a new vice presidency or directorship is established and an international division is begun. Generally it is a division with responsibilities which encompass all international products, markets and functions. Coordination within this type of division may be adequate, but the division can become an enclave, a group cut off from the rest of the firm.

Attempts to better coordinate the international activities of the firm have led to organizational structures which integrate the international and domestic activities of the firm.[19] *International product structure* coordinates product activities across international boundaries, while *international functional structure* coordinates functions across international boundaries. The weakness in these organization forms lies in what is not well coordinated. In product structure, functional coordination suffers and in functional structure, product coordination suffers.

As in domestic marketing, a response to coordination difficulties lies in the idea of *matrix structures*. Coordination problems along functional lines can be approached by creating product teams similar to those led by the domestic product manager. As the market manager was added to the domestic matrix, so other teams might be constructed to focus upon particular aspects of international marketing. This can result in extremely complex matrices in organizations operating in the international environment.[20] Forms of organization for international activities comprise figure 102.

The appropriate form of organization will depend to some extent on the *type of international involvement* which the company chooses. Forms of international involvement include:[21]

1. *Import-Export*

    This involves selling domestically produced goods overseas or bringing foreign manufactured goods to the US.

2. *Licensing*

    This involves allowing an overseas company to use an exclusive design, process, trademark, etc. in return for a fee or royalty.

3. *Joint Venture*

    Entering into contracts with overseas companies to jointly accomplish a business venture and divide the profits or losses.

4. *Management Contract*

    Selling management services by agreeing to manage someone else's operation.

5. *Contract Manufacturing*

    Separating manufacturing from marketing and distribution by manufacturing for other's distribution.

6. *Wholly Owned Subsidiary*

    Conducting overseas operations using a separate company which is owned by the parent company.

If a firm is only involved in a small amount of import-export activity an international division may be more than adequate to handle operations. Complex matrices may not be workable when coordinating activities with independent firms such as would be required in licensing, joint venture, management contract and contract manufacturing, but may be appropriate when coordinating with a wholly owned subsidiary.

Conceptual aids to strategy selection also require adjustment when considering the international environment. For example, in chapter four, the concepts used to measure the financial dimensions of the market niche were modified to be seen as the result of translation to a reference currency. Psychological and therefore economic reactions to specific offerings are a function of how the offering is viewed in the culture, and these contributions to the market niche

Figure 102
International Organizational Forms

Source: Stefan N. Robock, Kenneth Simmonds, *International Business and Multinational Enterprises* (Homewood, Ill.: Richard D. Irwin, Inc., 1989), pp. 252-279. Used with permission.

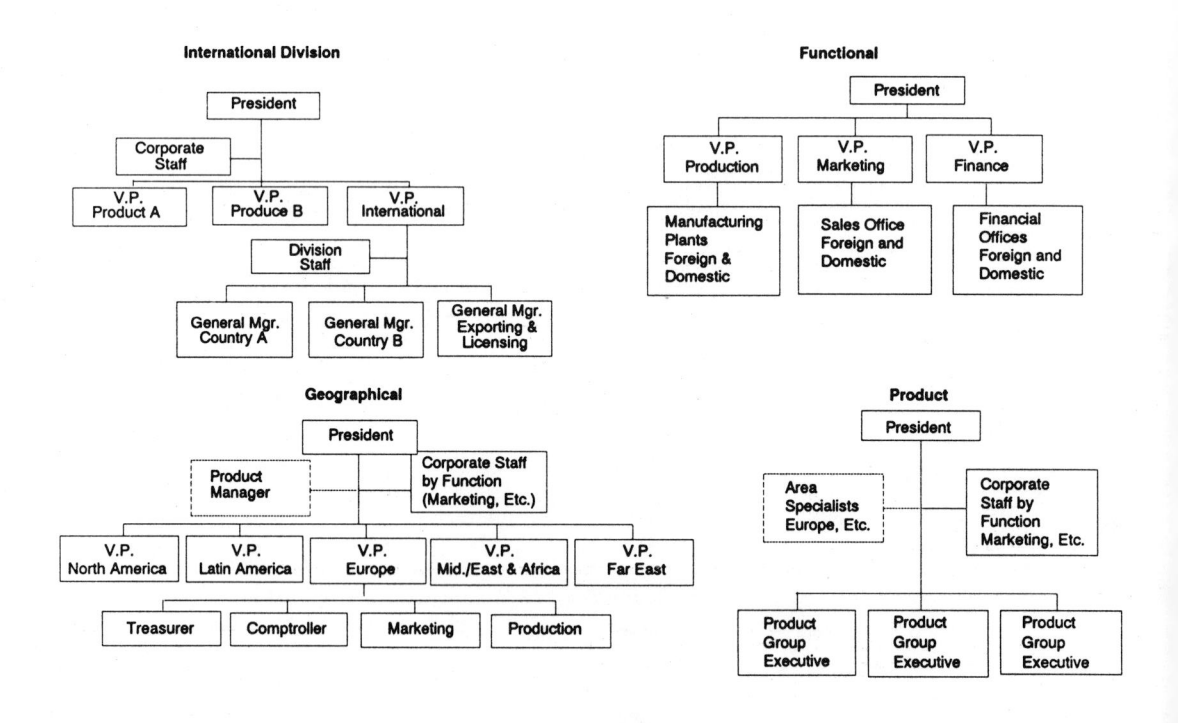

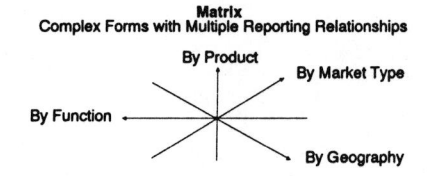

International Division

President
- Corporate Staff
- V.P. Product A
- V.P. Produce B
- V.P. International
  - Division Staff
    - General Mgr. Country A
    - General Mgr. Country B
    - General Mgr. Exporting & Licensing

Functional

President
- V.P. Production — Manufacturing Plants Foreign & Domestic
- V.P. Marketing — Sales Office Foreign and Domestic
- V.P. Finance — Financial Offices Foreign and Domestic

Geographical

President
- Product Manager
- Corporate Staff by Function (Marketing, Etc.)
- V.P. North America
- V.P. Latin America
- V.P. Europe
- V.P. Mid./East & Africa
- V.P. Far East

Treasurer | Comptroller | Marketing | Production

Product

President
- Area Specialists Europe, Etc.
- Corporate Staff by Function Marketing, Etc.
  - Product Group Executive
  - Product Group Executive
  - Product Group Executive

Matrix
Complex Forms with Multiple Reporting Relationships

- By Product
- By Market Type
- By Function
- By Geography

of the organization must be adjusted as well. Other conceptual aids have also been modified. An international adaptation of the portfolio approach has been designed by Harrell and Kiefer.[22] Like the GE Planning Grid, this approach places investment candidates in various grid catagories. This is illustrated in figure 103.

As discussed earlier, the product life cycle concept has also been adapted to the international environment.[23] In the *international product life cycle*, a new product is assumed to originate as a relatively high tech product. It is initially produced in the advanced economy which demanded it. Later, new markets are sought and the product is exported to those markets. Production is then started in the new overseas markets. As the product matures and the technology of the product and its production is more commonly understood, production is moved to the lowest cost point, often a less developed country (LDC). Markets are then served by exporting from this point.

Perhaps the most important conceptual aid is the idea of *global strategy*. After a period of time in the international arena, the firm ceases to see itself as associated with a single nation. It begins to allocate resources without regard to national frontiers, and becomes an efficient vehicle for international specialization and exchange.[24]

The Normative Versus Empirical Perspectives

In the foregoing discussion, elaborate examples of *teamwork* were depicted. The organization synthesized information through a complex set of job descriptions, reporting relationships, and planning procedures. Information was characterized and evaluated using conceptual aids. The strategic plan was chosen and detailed planning, direction and control begun.

The problem with this view is that *the organization is a complex social system. It is a power structure and a communications structure* that functions in an informal social and political fashion as well as through its designed procedures.[25] Individuals often do not share the stated or actual mission of the firm. The pursuit of individual self interest within the firm does not always contribute to the firm's progress. Both formal and informal incentive systems within the organization need to be well understood. Formal systems need to be carefully designed and well synchronized with the organizational mission.

The individual's interest within the firm often leads to the establishment of a *personal power base*, a network of communication and influence which allows the individual to defend and expand his or her niche within the firm regardless of the effects these activities may have on the organization's

Figure 103
International Product Market Portfolios

Source: Gilbert D. Harrell and Richard D. Kiefer. "Multinational Strategic Market Portfolios." MSU Business Topics, 29, 1 (Winter 1981), pp. 5-16. Reprinted by permission.

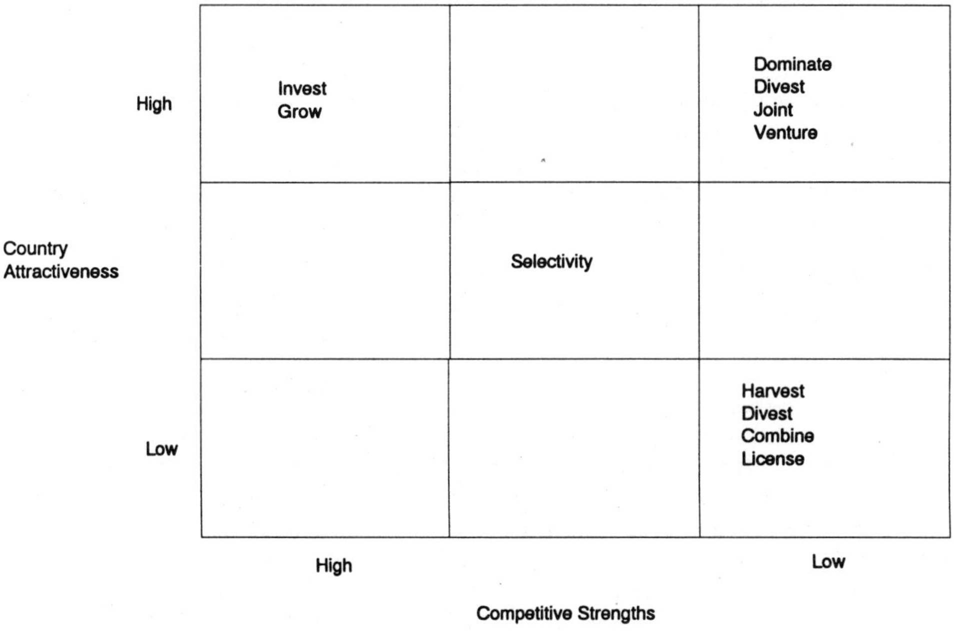

	High		Low
High	Invest Grow		Dominate Divest Joint Venture
Country Attractiveness		Selectivity	
Low			Harvest Divest Combine License

Competitive Strengths

strategic direction. The *establishment of power bases and empires* consisting of subordinates and other resources can adversely affect the information synthesis and decision making in the firm.

Some attempt has been made to study these phenomena. According to one school of thought, *power*, defined as the ability to influence another's behavior, can be measured by the degree to which individuals influence specific decisions in the firm. Some well-accepted sources of power are expert power, reward power, and coercive power as detailed by French and Raven and outlined in figure 104.[26] Another source of an individual executive's power may be the degree to which the executive is perceived as capable of protecting the firm from an external contingency or threat. In this way, the chief attorney becomes more powerful when the firm comes under legal attack, and the chief marketing executive becomes more powerful when there is competitive entry or other market based threats.[27] Through this mechanism the organization would demonstrate an interesting adaptive capacity which would derive from the informal power and communication structure rather than from the formal organization. As a threat is recognized, individuals with greater perceived expertise in the area of a threat would become more influential in the decision making process. In the context of these models of power and influence in the organization *the role of marketing has been advanced as being the advocacy of the consumers' viewpoint and interests within the firm.*[28]

In addition to identifying the power dynamics within the firm, the empirical observer would also point to another problem with the organized planning approaches. Such approaches may become bureaucratic and lose entrepreneurial vigor. In order to cope with this, firms such as 3M have encouraged *entrepreneurship* or risk taking advocacy of new products within the firm. This is unlike the new product management concept wherein the job was to bring products out of R&D to a point of marketability and then turn them over to a product manager. The entrepreneur is put in a position of having a great deal to gain should the product succeed. The entrepreneur identifies his or her career with the success of a product, advocating the firm's commitment to it. Should the firm's commitment bring success, the entrepreneur remains in charge, even if this means becoming the president of a new major division within the firm.[29]

Chapter Summary

Once information is gathered and preliminary analyses are performed, the information is then synthesized into a whole understanding of the firm's evolving alignment with its environment. This synthesis is performed as individuals exchange information in the firm. In this way, the design of the

Figure 104
Sources of Power

Adapted from J. R. P. French and B. Raven. "The Bases of Social Power," in Studies in Social Power, ed. D. Cartwright (Ann Arbor: University of Michigan, 1959). Adapted with permission.

Legitimate power
    Formal authority and position

Rewards
    Control of reward

Expertise
    Knowledge relevant to the problem at hand

Referent
    Subordinate identification with leader

Coercive
    Control of punishment

firm's organizational structure and the realities of the political relationships form the synthesis of information. Information synthesis informs strategic choice and strategic choice may also be guided by any of the conceptual aids which are available to describe marketing strategy. These aids include portfolio models, contingency models, military analogies, game theory, positioning and segmentation concepts. When crossing international boundaries, organizational forms may change and differing conceptual aids may become useful.

---

[1] See "Marketing's New Look," *Business Week*, January 26, 1987, pp. 64-69.

[2] See Webster's Third New International Dictionary (unabridged) (Springfield, Massachusetts: G. & C. Merriam Company, 1967), p. 2256.

[3] The traditional definition of marketing strategy as the target market and a marketing mix may be found in E. Jerome McCarthy and William D. Perreault, Jr. *Basic Marketing*, 9th ed. (Homewood, Illinois: Richard D. Irwin, 1987), p. 35. The concept of the match is taken from Wroe Alderson, *Marketing Behavior and Executive Action* (Homewood, Illinois: Richard D. Irwin, 1957), pp. 195-228.

[4] Peter Drucker as cited in James M. Higgins and Julian W. Vincze, *Strategic Management* (Chicago: The Dryden Press, 1989), p. 164.

[5] See Robin Wensley, "Strategic Marketing: Betas, Boxes, or Basics," *Journal of Marketing* 45, No. 3 (Summer 1981), pp. 173-182.

[6] See Robert H. Hayes and William J. Abernathy, "Managing Our Way to Economic Decline," *Harvard Business Review* (July-August, 1980), pp. 67-77.

[7] See George S. Day, "Analytical Approaches to Strategic Market Planning," in *Review of Marketing 1981*, eds. Ben M. Enis and Kenneth J. Roering, (Chicago: American Marketing Association, 1981), p. 95. See also Derek F. Abell and John S. Hammond, *Strategic Market Planning: Problems and Analytical Approaches* (Englewood Cliffs, N.J.: Prentice-Hall, 1979).

[8] See Robert D. Buzzell, Bradley T. Gale, and Ralph G. M. Sultan, "Market Share—A Key to Profitability," *Harvard Business Review* 53 (January-February, 1975).

[9] Day, p. 93.

[10] Texas Instruments has been credited with the use of this strategy.

[11] This section was developed with reference to Philip Kotler and Ravi Singh, "Marketing Warfare in the 1980s," *Journal of Business Strategy* (Fall 1980), pp. 30-41.

[12] Kotler.

[13] Webster, p. 2327.

[14] For a discussion of Game Theory see William J. Baumol, *Economic Theory and Operations Analysis*, 3rd ed. (Englewood Cliffs, N.J.: Prentice Hall, 1972), pp. 553-573. See also John von Neumann and Oskar Morgenstern, *Theory of Games and Economic Behavior*, 2nd ed. (Princeton, N.J.: Princeton University Press, 1947).

[15] McCarthy, p. 28. Copyright 1990. Philip Kotler, *Marketing: An Introduction*, 2nd ed. (Englewood Cliffs, N.J.: Prentice Hall, 1987), p. 13.

[16] McCarthy, p. 65.

[17] This typology is developed in R. Miles and C. Snow, *Organizational Strategy, Structure and Process* (New York: McGraw-Hill, 1978). Reproduced with permission. It is evaluated in the marketing context in Stephen W. McDaniel and James W. Kolari, "Marketing Implications of the Mills and Snow Strategic Typology," *Journal of Marketing* 51 (October 1987), pp. 19-30.

[18] The budget discussion was developed with reference to Nigel F. Pierce, "The Marketing Budgeting Process: Marketing Management Implications," *Journal of Marketing* 51 (October 1987), pp. 45-59. Reprinted with permission of the American Marketing Association, Chicago, IL.

[19] The discussion of organizational forms was developed with reference to Stefan N. Robock, Kenneth Simmons, and Jack Zwick, *International Business and Multinational Enterprises* (Homewood, Illinois: Richard D. Irwin, 1977), pp. 432-444.

[20] A discussion of complex matrices in the management of the international firm is provided by Y. L. Doz, "Strategic Management in Multinational Companies," *Sloan Management Review* (Winter 1980), pp. 26-46.

[21] McCarthy, pp. 575-578. Reprinted with permission.

[22] Gilbert D. Harrell and Richard D. Kiefer, "Multinational Strategic Market Portfolios," *MSU Business Topics* 29 (Winter 1981), pp. 5-16.

[23] See Louis T. Wells Jr. (ed.), *The Product Life Cycle and International Trade* (Boston: Harvard Business School Division of Research, 1972). See also Raymond Vernon, "International Investment and International Trade in the Product Cycle," *Quarterly Journal of Economics* (May 1966), pp. 1-16. Copyright 1966 by John Wiley and Sons, Inc. Reprinted by permission of John Wiley and Sons, Inc.

[24] Robock, pp. 399-426.

[25] See for example Alderson, pp. 40-51.

[26] J. R. P. French and B. Raven, "The Bases of Social Power," in *Studies in Social Power*, ed. D. Cartwright (Ann Arbor: University of Michigan, 1959).

[27] See for example Donald C. Hambrick, "Environmental Strategy and Power within Top Management Teams," *Administrative Science Quarterly* 26 (June 1981), pp. 253-275. See also, D. J. Hickson, C. R. Hinings, C. A. Lee, R. E. Schneck, and J. M. Pennings, "A Strategy Contingencies Theory of Intra-organizational Power," *Administrative Science Quarterly* 16, pp. 216-219.

[28]See Paul F. Anderson, "Marketing, Strategic Planning and the Theory of the Firm," *Journal of Marketing* 46 (Spring 1982), pp. 15-26.

[29]3M Corporation has been credited for taking this approach.

QUESTIONS FOR STUDY, DISCUSSION AND EXAMINATION

1. Can you define or explain to a friend who has not studied marketing, each of the following terms or ideas?
    a. The entrepreneurial approach to information
    b. Product manager
    c. Hierarchical structure by function
    d. Matrix structure
    e. Profit center
    f. Brand manager
    g. Market manager
    h. New product manager
    i. Marketing services staff
    j. Market research group
    k. Market analyst
    l. Venture research group
    m. Sales analysis group
    n. Strategic planning group
    o. Communications group
    p. Public relations staff
    q. Government relations staff
    r. Sales management group
    s. Matrix culture
    t. Developments in information technology
    u. Planning procedures
    v. Environmental scenario
    w. Situation analysis
    x. Plans and budgets for an area of responsibility
    y. Mission statement
    z. Statement of goals, objectives and strategies
    aa. Subordinate statement of goals, objectives and strategies
    ab. Budgets which reflect time sequenced objectives
    ac. A strategic choice
    ad. Employing forces or resources

ae. Defense and enhancement of the market niche or support of an adopted mission statement
af. Elements of conflict
ag. Position of advantage
ah. Varieties of strategy
ai. Atmosphere of careful planning
aj. Marketing strategy
ak. Conceptual aid to strategic choice
al. Primary conceptual aid used in this book
am. Portfolio model
an. SBU
ao. BCG Model
ap. General Electric Planning Grid
aq. Directional Policy Matrix
ar. Potential for misuse of portfolio models
as. PIMS
at. Par report
au. Contingency model
av. Experience curve
aw. Military analogy
ax. Principle of objective
ay. Principle of mass
az. Attack (in marketing)
ba. Defense (in marketing)
bb. Strategy versus tactics
bc. Game theory
bd. Zero sum game or constant sum game
be. Non constant sum game
bf. Maximin/minimax
bg. Regret minimization
bh. Certainty equivalent
bi. Mixed strategy
bj. Positioning
bk. Axes in positioning
bl. A product's current position
bm. Repositioning
bn. Strategic desirability of investment in repositioning

bo. Positioning or repositioning for successful differentiation
bp. Successful differentiation and competitive pressure on price and profit
bq. Multidimensional scaling
br. Market segment
bs. Segmentation
bt. Appropriate size for a market segment
bu. Financial viability of a segment
bv. Mass marketing
bw. Target marketing
bx. Segmenting dimension
by. Operational segment
bz. Physical, geographic, demographic, psychological dimensions
ca. Industry type and size as a segmenting dimension
cb. Intraorganizational and interpersonal relationships as segmenting dimensions
cd. Qualifying dimension
ce. Determining dimension
cf. Combination of segmenting dimensions
cg. Mergers, acquisitions and spinoffs as relating to marketing strategy
ch. The marketing concept
ci. Capital shifting strategy
cj. Product Market Expansion Grid
ck. Market penetration
cl. Market development
cm. Product development
cn. Diversification
co. Prospector
cp. Defender
cq. Analyzer
cr. Reactor
cs. Budget
ct. TDBU
cu. BUTD
cv. MBO
cw. International division structure
cx. International product structure
cy. International functional structure

cz. Complex matrices (international context)
da. Types of international involvement (6)
db. International product life cycle
dc Global strategy
dd. Teamwork
de. Complex social system
df. Power structure
dg. Communications structure
dh. Personal power base
di. Empire (corporate political context)
dj. Power
dk. Role of marketing in the context of power and influence within the firm
dl. Entrepreneurship

2. Compare and contrast information synthesis and strategic choice on the part of the entrepreneur and in the major firm.

3. Evaluate the complex matrix in figure 85 in terms of strengths and weaknesses in facilitating information synthesis and strategic choice.

4. Why might product management be good training for greater marketing responsibility? How much authority and responsibility should a product manger have and why?

5. What would you see the advantages and disadvantages of the new product manager concept to be when compared with the entrepreneur concept?

6. Evaluate the typical groups and jobs described in marketing in terms of the impact of the development of information technology. What changes might occur? What choices might have to be made?

7. Look up the word benchmark in the dictionary. What is meant by a benchmark understanding of marketing organization?

8. (Group Project) Organize the class as a marketing organization. Develop descriptions of each job and planning procedures designed to arrive at strategic choices. Run through your planning procedure once and then critique it and make improvements. Present your impressions of the experience to the class as a whole. Note: It might be more realistic and enjoyable if you took on a real problem, such as a strategic plan for your college or university.

9. How do the following relate to one another? Environmental scenario, situation analysis, plans and budgets. Should things usually work this way or is this a "benchmark" understanding?
10. How do the following relate to one another? Mission statement, statement of goals, objectives and strategies; subordinate statements of goals, objectives and strategies; budgets which reflect time sequenced objectives.
11. Relate the components of Webster's definition of strategy to marketing strategy. What is the difference if any between corporate strategy and marketing strategy?
12. What is a variety of strategy? Can you give a military example? A marketing example?
13. In what ways might portfolio models encourage the adoption of capital shifting strategies? Is this good or bad? Is it entirely good or bad?
14. What kind of strategic suggestions are made by the BCG matrix? Compare and contrast these with the strategic suggestions made by the GE Planning Grid.
15. How might a par report be used? What is the origin of a par report?
16. In what sense does the product life cycle, military analogy, and game theory support the concept of strategy "contingent upon the situation"?
17. How is it possible to make money by setting prices which are below the cost figures which you have in front of you?
18. Give examples of a marketing use of the military principles of objective and mass, of attack and defense, of frontal attack, flanking attack, and mobile defense.
19. Give marketing examples of the difference between strategy and tactics.
20. Explain how game theory might help an oligopolist make a marketing decision. Demonstrate using a payoff matrix. Use this opportunity to demonstrate your understanding of the ideas of constant versus non constant sum games, maximin-maximax, regret minimization, expected value, certainty equivalents and mixed strategy.
21. (May be a group project) Discuss the pros and cons of repositioning a specific product or service. Bring as many useful perspectives to bear as you can. In a step by step fashion explain how you would

make this decision beginning with how you would determine the position the product or service now occupies.

22. (May be a group project) Describe possible market segments for your college or university. Do this carefully and in detail. What strategies make sense for each market segment? Have you been creative in the use of segmenting dimensions?
23. Relate the economics of market structure with its implications for price and profit to the ideas of successful differentiation, positioning and segmentation.
24. In what sense does market segmentation arise out of the facts that (1) people have individualistic needs and preferences. (2) Economies of scale in production exist. How does this help to determine the size of a market segment?
25. How is the financial viability of a segment dependent upon (1) psychology, (2) demographics (income in particular), (3) economies of scale?
26. Give an example of a segment that is operational, one that is not.
27. Why might the timing of a new product introduction be adjusted if the firm is thinking of acquiring another firm?
28. Compare and contrast marketing concept strategies with capital shifting strategies. What do you see the pros and cons of each to be? How might internal organization structure and policy affect the selection of one of these policies?
29. With reference to the product market expansion grid in figure 101, which of the four strategies would have to show the most profit to compensate for its degree of risk? The least? Why?
30. Is the organization you work for or the college or university you are attending a prospector, defender, analyzer or reactor? Why?
31. What is the relationship of a budget to marketing strategy? Compare and contrast the TDBU and BUTD Decision processes. How does MBO support strategy?
32. (May be a group project) Evaluate each cell in the matrix below. Do you think each would constitute a good fit between structure and form of international activity? What strengths and weaknesses do you see?

	International Division Structure	International Product Structure	International Functional Structure	Matrix Structure	Geographic Structure
Import Export					
Licensing					
Joint Venture					
Management Contract					
Contract Manufacturing					
Wholly Owned Subsidiary					

33. How is the market niche affected by the fact the firm is operating in an international environment?
34. Give an example of a product following the international product life cycle.
35. Select a firm whose activities you think typify the global strategy approach. Why do you think this is a good selection?
36. Give an example of how the political realities of the firm as a complex social system might foil an elaborately designed planning process. Is it true that the important decisions are really made on the golf course?
37. Use your imagination or rely upon your organizational expertise to describe what you think a strong personal power base might consist of. What effect would the existence of such power bases have on the selection of the firm's strategy?
38. How might the existence of an external threat confer power upon an individual in the organization?
39. In a context of conflicting political power bases within the firm, how would you see the role of marketing?
40. What is the role of the entrepreneur?

CHAPTER 10

LEGAL AND ETHICAL GUIDELINES

Marketing management is not free to enhance the market niche of the organization without constraint or guidance. A substantial body of *laws* exists which both *constrains and guides* marketing decisions. Beyond that, a substantial body of *ethical thought* and expectation should also serve to *constrain and guide* marketing choice.

The concept of constraint has been introduced earlier in the book. In the discussion of profit across the product line, profit was maximized subject to limits or constraints. The linear programming example in figure 48 illustrated this logic mathematically. *Constraint is a statement of what cannot be done.* For example, management of a firm may be able to decide upon a level of production for a certain product, but cannot choose to produce more than the factory's three shift capacity. They are free to do what they want subject to the constraint. Philosophers refer to the idea of constraint as *negative injunction*, something which cannot or should not be done. In general, democratic western societies, with their commitment to individual freedom, have preferred legal systems which couple individual freedom with a system of negative injunctions. Under certain circumstances however, these societies have accepted *positive injunctions*. A positive injunction is a statement of what must or should be done, and can take the form of a law or an ethical expectation.

In this way marketing management is left fairly *free to defend and expand the market niche subject to important positive and negative injunctions.* These take the form of *laws and ethical expectations*. Law will be discussed first, and both will be discussed in the context of strategies for enhancement of the market niche.

Marketing Law in the United States

Marketing law in the United States consists of the antitrust laws, consumer protection laws, intellectual property protection laws, contract law, and the laws which create and direct the regulation of specific industries.

Antitrust Laws

The philosophy and development of the antitrust laws in the United States can be well understood by recalling the nature of the polar extreme market structures of monopoly and competition, by recalling western society's preference for freedom and negative injunction, and by understanding the political and economic climate of the era in which the laws were enacted. While the monopolist exists in a highly defensible market niche, protected from competition by barriers to entry and often rewarded with high and continuing profit, the pure competitor has a much more difficult life. There are no long term economic profits in pure competition. In the long run the competitor delivers the product at a price which equals the minimum average total costs of production. This is an excellent situation for society as a whole, but a very difficult situation for the competitive producer.

In the late nineteenth century, the rail industry and others conspired to avoid competition within their industries. These alliances were known as "*trusts.*" The result was high and stable profits in the industries, but a crippling economic burden for those who had to pay for their products and services. The social response was to take the form of negative injunction. Rather than making the positive statement that suppliers "had to compete so that consumers did not have to pay for excessive profits," the *Sherman Act of 1890 prohibited monopoly or conspiracy in restraint of trade.* Controlling products, prices, or distribution channels so as to create a monopoly or a restraint of trade was now illegal.[1]

Corporate attorneys and practitioners were not long in discovering ways to avoid competition which also avoided conflict with the specific negative injunctions in the Sherman Act. One can almost feel the frustration in the Congress when a second act, also carefully formed as negative injunction, was passed. *The Clayton Act of 1914 made anything which substantially lessened competition illegal.* This included the practice of forcing the sale of some products with others (tying contracts) and agreements which limited the number of suppliers with whom a buyer might choose to do business (exclusive dealing contracts).[2] Throughout this evolution of law, what the Congress might have wanted to say to industry was "behave competitively, and deliver products at prices which are closer to costs." But these are positive injunctions and the society's commitment to freedom was to continue to favor negative injunction.

Also enacted in 1914, the *Federal Trade Commission Act* established the FTC, an independent federal agency which is responsible to the Congress. Perhaps to further close the door on creative evasion of the Sherman Act, the agency was given the broad mandate to police *"unfair" methods of competition*. This included unfair policies as to channel activity, deceptive advertising or selling practices, and deceptive pricing.[3] "Unfair" is a very broad word and is subject to a great variety of interpretations. This fact, together with the agency's broad mandate and considerable power to identify and prosecute offenders before its own administrative law judges, makes the FTC Act of 1914 a powerful piece of legislation. It is consumer protection legislation as well as antitrust legislation, as the agency prosecuted "unfair or deceptive acts or practices" as well as "unfair methods of competition."[4]

By 1936 the political and economic climate had been altered considerably. The country was attempting to recover from a great depression, and was experimenting with new ideas. *The Robinson Patman Act of 1936 amended the Clayton Act*. A major focus of this act was upon the practice of *price discrimination*. Price discrimination on goods of "like grade and quality" was made illegal unless the difference could be justified through one or more of several acceptable defenses. These included the arguments that the price difference was justified by differences in costs of serving the customers involved, that the price was set in good faith to meet the equally low price of a competitor, or that competition was not adversely affected by the price difference.[5]

The Robinson Patman Act was passed during the depression and was intended to protect competition by protecting the many small competitors who were the likely victims of price discrimination by the firms supplying them. This made some political sense in an era when great, unusual and innovative steps were being taken to save businesses from bankruptcy. But, some of the net effects of the law appear to have been anticompetitive. The law is in conflict with two pricing perspectives which follow from principles developed earlier in the book. These perspectives are: 1) prices will naturally differ where elasticities and/or degrees of competition differ, and 2) some attrition among the individual competitors is expected in competitive markets. This attempt to protect competition by protecting competitors has created some confusion and has resulted in marketing executives who are afraid of aggressive price cutting. Individual executives and salespeople can be penalized for infractions. Therefore marketing people often prefer to avoid a price cut where there is any chance of a Robinson Patman violation.

By 1950 the merger activity of large firms had caused concern about the loss of competition in individual markets. The *Anti-Merger Act of 1950* prohibited mergers which lessened competition and made the purchase of competitors, producers or distributors subject to this competitive test.[6] Since 1980 a concern about the effects of overregulation on business innovation and productivity has resulted in a relaxation in the interpretation and enforcement of the antitrust laws. One argument in support of this has been that competition must now be considered in world markets rather than just in terms of the numbers of domestic competitors.

The antitrust laws are *enforced by the antitrust division of the Department of Justice and by the Federal Trade Commission.* They have been born of painful economic experience which has supported an observation made by Adam Smith, an early proponent of the free market economy. Smith characterized businessmen as:[7]

> ... an order of men whose interest is never exactly the same with that of the public, who have generally an interest to deceive and even to oppress the public and who accordingly have, upon many occasions both deceived and oppressed it
>
> —*Adam Smith.*

The antitrust laws have utilized the powerful economics of competition to more closely align the interests of business with that of the public. The governing philosophy has been stated by the U.S. Supreme Court.[8]

> Subject to narrow qualification it is surely the case that competition is our fundamental national economic policy, offering as it does the only alternative to cartelization or governmental regimentation of large portions of the economy.
>
> —*U.S. Supreme Court, Philadelphia Bank Case, 1938.*

Consumer Protection Laws

Competition is a good protector of the consumer, as it keeps prices and costs in reasonable control. But as the society moved to encourage competition through the antitrust acts, specific abuses occurred which were not prevented by simply increasing the degree of competition. This has resulted in specific consumer protection laws and related governmental agencies to oversee their enforcement. Many consumer protection laws and agencies now exist. The following discussion identifies important examples. Many of the abuses which these laws and agencies deal with seem to derive from either ill advised attempts at product differentiation which have involved deception, or attempts at cost reduction which have resulted in products or services of unacceptable quality.

By 1900, the industrial cities had grown to the point where they were supporting a large processed food industry, and a large patent medicine industry had also developed. These industries frequently abused the consumers' trust. Prepackaged foods sometimes contained filth, and patent medicines for dieting might contain tapeworms. The *food and drug administration* (FDA) was established by the *Pure Food and Drug Act of 1906*. The FDA is responsible for the creation and enforcement of specific regulations to prevent the adulteration of foods, drugs and cosmetics and to prevent the marketing of items in these categories which are harmful to health.[9]

The broad mandate of the *Federal Trade Commission* includes consumer protection. The FTC protects consumers from "deceptive" and "unfair" practices. The FTC also provides enforcement for other consumer protection acts.[10] The original *FTC Act of 1914* was amended and strengthened by the *Wheeler Lea Act of 1938*, which *prohibited unfair or deceptive practices* such as deceptive packaging or branding.[11] The *Federal Fair Packaging and Labeling Act of 1966* has supported these earlier laws, requiring that consumer goods be *labeled in a clear and understandable fashion.*[12]

Numerous accidents involving consumer products caused Congress to pass the *Consumer Product Safety Act in 1972*. Created by this act, the *Consumer Product Safety Commission* is responsible for the safety testing of consumer products. It may also ban the sale of dangerous consumer products and set standards for product safety. Misrepresented warranties and corporate avoidance of warranties which the courts have found to be implicit or implied, resulted in the *Magnuson Moss Warranty Act of 1975*. Under this act, firms must fully disclose and explain the terms of any warranty in simple and readily understood language.[13]

Consumer protection law is a broad area. Many enabling laws are involved as well as the thousands of resulting regulations. These regulations usually have the force of their enabling law. The departments of agriculture, commerce, energy, housing and urban development, transportation, treasury and the Environmental Protection Agency (EPA) are all involved in the regulation of some aspect of consumer goods marketing.[14] In addition, an *Office of Consumer Affairs* (OCA), has been established to handle consumer complaints.[15] Consumers *are also protected by their right to sue* producers and marketers for product related injury. This area of *product liability* rests on *tort law*. Tort law is "concerned with compensating one person for harm caused by the wrongful conduct of another."[16]

Intellectual Property Protection

As consumers must be protected from suppliers' ill advised attempts to differentiate a product, contain costs or limit competition, suppliers must occasionally be protected from unfair competition. Recognition of a legal monopoly exists in the *patent laws* and *copyright laws*. When a person produces a unique piece of intellectual property such as an original invention, thought or synthesis of thoughts, the society grants the individual the right to vend with monopoly power. Inventions are protected by patents and original thoughts or synthesis of thoughts are protected by copyright laws. This system is designed to encourage people to assume the risks and costs of bringing these ideas to the society. In marketing, this protection extends beyond the offering itself to include its brand name or trademark. The *brand name* is a word, letter or group of words or letters, while the *trademark* may include unique symbols, shapes or marks under copyright protection.[17] Brand names and trademarks are protected by the *Lanham Act of 1946*.[18]

Contract Law

Marketing practitioners must also be aware of the provisions of *contract law*, the law governing agreements. The form of a contract can influence marketing strategy. For example, contracts may be excused if an act of God (natural event) such as flood or drought prevents execution of the contract. Firms may then declare *force majeur* or "act of god" to excuse them from such performance. These kinds of events can result in actual strategies and tactics which differ substantially from those which were planned.

Direct Economic Regulation

In the late 1800s, abuse of monopoly power by the railroads led to many of the legal and regulatory precedents which allow government to directly regulate industry today. During that period, rail freight rates reflected the fact that rail competition existed between main terminal points, but did not exist between intermediate points and the main terminal points. This is illustrated in figure 105. Midwestern farmers mounted political opposition to these rates, forming an influence group known as the "Granger Movement."[19] State regulation of rail rates followed, and the federal *Act to Regulate Commerce* was approved in 1887.[20] The act established the *Interstate Commerce Commission* or ICC. In a fashion similar to that of the legal evolution which formed antitrust legislation, several other pieces of legislation were required as the constitutional basis of regulation was established, and the ICC was brought to a position of real power.[21] By 1920 the ICC was empowered to set minimum as

Chapter 10   377

**Figure 105
The Nature of Rail Monopoly**

Three competitors between Minneapolis and Chicago
Monopoly between grain elevator A and Chicago

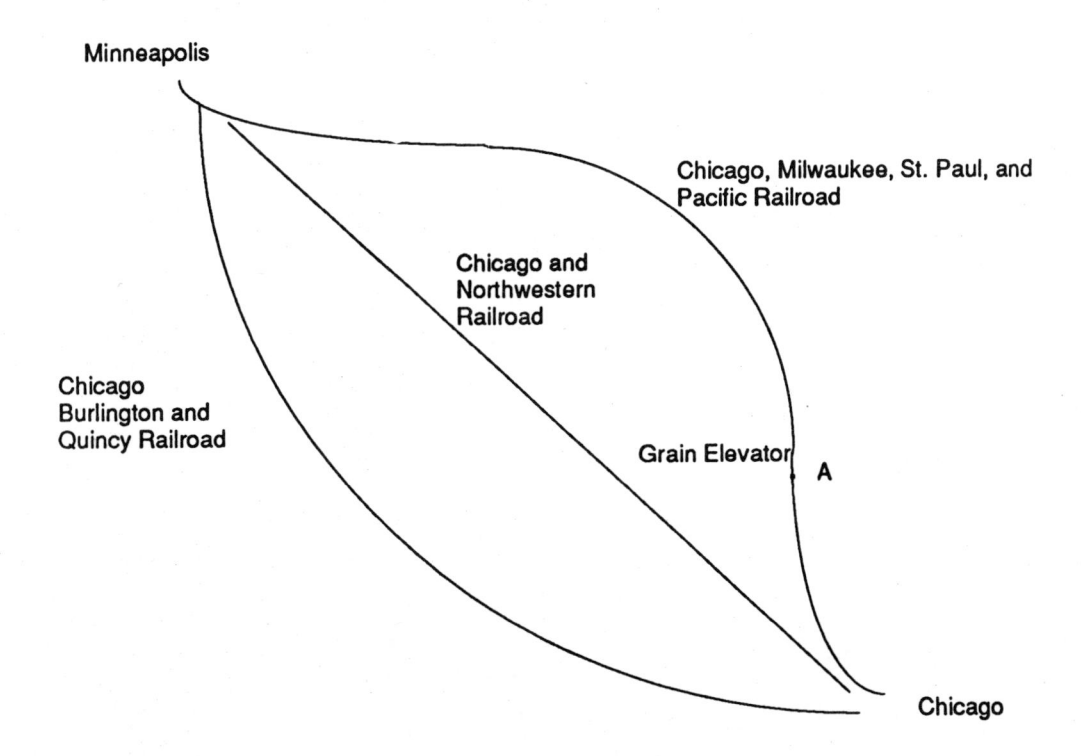

Minneapolis

Chicago, Milwaukee, St. Paul, and Pacific Railroad

Chicago and Northwestern Railroad

Chicago Burlington and Quincy Railroad

Grain Elevator A

Chicago

well as maximum rail rates and to control railroad additions and abandonments.[22] Once these precedents were established, *other regulatory commissions* such as the Federal Maritime Commission (FMC), the Civil Aeronautics Board (CAB), the Federal Communication Commission (FCC), and the Securities and Exchange Commission (SEC) were established. Through these legal precedents and using the regulatory commission, *the federal government retains the legal right and the capability to assume much of the marketing management decision making for an industry.* Maximum and minimum prices can be regulated, characteristics of the offering can be regulated, and much of physical distribution can be affected by the regulation of transportation industries. What cannot be controlled through this type of direct economic regulation may be approached using antitrust or consumer protection legislation. Thus, *government may control product, price, promotion and place.*

General dissatisfaction with the results of direct government regulation of industry has led to the *deregulation movement.* Airlines were substantially deregulated in 1978, followed by the motor carrier, rail, banking and communications industries. These are not complete deregulations as the legal framework and much of the administrative framework for regulation remains intact. But, they have forced major changes within industries which had not developed marketing skills during the era when the government made many of their marketing decisions. Marketing management should constantly be aware of the fact that *state and federal governments retain the right to assume more influence in the firm's marketing decisions or to return marketing decision making to the firm.*

Law and Ethics

Adequate sensitivity to the political environment of the firm and to the economic and ethical expectations of the society could serve to alter the picture of marketing law substantially. Much of marketing law has been developed in response to abuses or actions which have been seen as abuse according to the ethical expectations of society. Ethical expectations are of a higher order than the expectation of simple conformity to existing law, and offended ethical expectations will often result in the creation of new law. Marketing management which operates in an ethical vacuum is almost certain to lose much of its decision making prerogative.

Marketing Ethics

> The law is usually the lowest common denominator of ethical behavior, although many persons fall prey to the fallacy of believing that if they do not violate the law, they are ethical.[23]
>
> —J. H. Westing

Ethics is defined by Webster as "the study of standards of conduct and moral judgement; moral philosophy."[24] Ethical expectations are separate from the law in the sense that what is legal may or may not be ethical and what is ethical may or may not be legal. At the same time, ethics are associated with the law in the sense that a society's laws do in some general way reflect the ethical expectations of that society. This reflection is often brought about after a period of lag and political compromise. In this compromise process the evolving law may well become the lowest common denominator, reflecting only what a diverse group is able to agree upon. In a culture as diverse as that in the United States, the lowest common denominator may be low indeed.

Ethics should therefore be considered separately from the law, and the individual marketing practitioner should conduct his or her life and make life decisions according to his or her chosen set of ethics. There is no reason to exclude marketing decisions from the set of decisions guided by ethical expectations. The psychological, economic and financial realities which characterize human exchange and which govern the ways in which a market niche might be enhanced are powerful realities. The behaviors which they suggest might in some instances be behaviors which would be in conflict with an individual's ethics. In these instances individual feelings of conflict and tension are appropriate. These feelings should be resolved by changing the nature of one's employment, either by influencing the organization or by leaving it. The feelings should not usually be resolved by making changes in one's ethical system. In general, it is within the framework of most ethical systems to be involved in the marketing of something that one genuinely believes in. In this way, advocacy of a particular product or service for use by an individual or group would not be in conflict with a love and compassion for that individual or group.

The powerful realities of exchange and profit, together with the pressures for short term success on the job should not be allowed to compete with a soft and irresolute ethical commitment. Should that occur, the individual's ethics will surely be compromised. The rules of the marketplace may become the individual's ethics. The realities of human exchange and the realities of the market niche of the organization are powerful. They must be balanced by powerful ethical commitment.

Secular Ethics

Some ethical systems do not entail religious understanding or commitment. These may be referred to as *secular ethical systems*. An ethical system may be made up of an *all encompassing system of rules*, or it may rest upon a *general decision rule*, a broad based perspective for making difficult decisions. The *utilitarian ethic*, attributed to Jeremy Bentham and J.S. Mill is an example of the latter type of ethical system. The broad based decision rule or *maxim* (rule of action) underlying the utilitarian ethic is to "maximize the greatest good for the greatest number of people." Good is seen in terms of happiness, pleasure or *satisfaction*. The utilitarian ethic is an example of a *teleological* or *consequence focused* ethical perspective. The focus is on the ends rather the means of activity. If a decision hurts a few but benefits the many, it can be defended from a utilitarian point of view.[25] In marketing, an example of a decision which would conform with utilitarian ethics would be to go ahead with the marketing of a pharmaceutical product which had healing properties for many, but which had harmful side effects in a small percentage of cases.

Other secular ethical systems are not consequence focused but focus upon *means*, or how something is accomplished. Such ethical systems are referred to as *deontological ethical systems*. An example of such a system is Kant's *categorical imperative*.[26] This system focuses on means rather than end, holding that each person is a "bearer of moral worth." Each person should make their decisions in such a way that they could will that their maxim or rule of action should become a universal rule. Kant's position also holds that persons should never be treated as means to an end but rather as an end in themselves. In this ethical view, the act of keeping a costly verbal commitment to a customer even though it is not legally necessary to do so would be to will that verbal promises be kept, that a person's word be a bond. In another marketing example, to adopt a marketing concept strategy, focusing upon the long term satisfaction of the consumer may be to choose the consumer as an end, rather than simply as a means to profit. This ethical property of the marketing concept may underlie its continuing popularity.

The secular ethical discussion has also identified situations wherein positive injunction may be ethically equivalent to negative injunction. That is, in some situations it may be as powerful an ethical requirement that you do something good as it is that you simply refrain from doing something bad. The *Kew Gardens Principles*, so named for a place in New York where thirty-eight passive bystanders allowed a woman to be beaten to death, set forth the situations wherein the positive injunction (to do something) is as ethically binding as the usual negative injunction.[27] The following four conditions serve to identify these situations:

1. Need

    It must be a case of need, if there is more need there is more responsibility.

2. Proximity

    It must be a situation where you are in a position to take notice.

3. Capability

    It must be a situation you can do something about.

4. Last Resort

    It must be a fair assumption that no one else will take care of the problem. There is more responsibility as it is less likely that someone else will provide aid.

In general, it is held that all four of these conditions must be present for the Kew Gardens Principles to elevate positive injunction to the moral equivalent of negative injunction.

In a *marketing example*, executives may be discussing the design of a new automobile. Some in the group of executives have concerns that the steering column as currently designed will not collapse well enough in a crash to prevent serious injury to the driver. A faction in the group argues for a delay of the car's introduction to the market in order to improve the steering column design. An opposing faction argues that car as it is currently designed will pass the minimum legally required safety standards. Besides, this group argues, the company needs the contribution margin from the new car now.

Here there is a *need*, some drivers will die as a result of a decision to bring the car to market in its current form. There is *proximity*, the executives know of the situation and no one outside the company is in a position to know of the situation. There is *capability*, this group is certainly in a position to have the steering column redesigned. There is the element of *last resort*. While the government may eventually step in and force the company to redesign the steering column to safer standards and while the market might eventually discipline the maker of a car that has proven itself to be unsafe, these actions would no doubt occur only after many drivers had died. For these pioneering drivers, individuals willing to trust the company's new car design, the marketing executives making the decision are the last resort. According to the Kew Gardens Principles, a failure of these executives to redesign the steering column to safer standards would be as ethically offensive as willfully breaking a law against some kind of unsafe auto design.

Religious Ethics

The majority of the world's population is not governed strictly by secular ethics but rather by religious ethics or some combination of religious and secular ethics. *Religious ethics* specify standards of conduct which follow from the belief in a divine power and the understandings of that power which are set forth in the teachings of a particular religion. Marketing practitioners not professing a religious faith are wise to understand the ethical expectations which derive from the faiths professed in the societies where they expect to engage in exchange. Practitioners professing faith should be fully aware of what their faith teaches concerning exchange behavior. Marketing is not simply a technical understanding as a pure science might be. It is a social understanding. It has to do with exchanges, wealth, communication, the employment of the earth's resources and the employment of other people. As such it cannot and should not escape religious evaluation.

The world's great religions include Christianity, Judaism, Islam, Hinduism, Buddhism, Confucianism, Taoism, and the Shinto faith. Each will be discussed in the context of the part of the world where its teachings can be expected to be particularly influential. The *Judeo-Christian Ethic* will be discussed in the context of the United States and Canada.

An ethic is defined by Webster as a particular theory or system of moral values.[28] The Judeo-Christian ethic is the system of ethics derived from Scriptures or the Bible. The Hebrew Scriptures or Old Testament of the bible contains the Torah which is the law describing the covenant between God and Israel, as well as history, songs, poetry and prophecy. The New Testament (or covenant) describes the coming and the teachings of Christ, His crucifixion and resurrection, the history and teaching of the early Christian church, and prophecy. Within faith communities following the Judeo-Christian ethic there are many interpretations and divisions. Judaism does not accept the new covenant, while Christians divide themselves as to its mode of interpretation and the relative importance of Scripture in providing daily ethical guidance. The purpose here is not to probe or exacerbate these differences, but to provide a preliminary view of the guidance that Scripture can provide for those individuals and groups who are engaged in exchange behavior.

Scriptural Ethics

From Scripture it may be derived that a certain management or control of the earth's environment is expected of the human race. People are expected to have *dominion* over the earth (Genesis 1:27, 9:2). At the same time this dominion is not to be abused, it is to be exercised as a careful and conscientious *stewardship* (Genesis 2:15, Exodus 19:5, Leviticus 25:23, Psalm 24:1, 1 Corinthians 4:2, 1 Timothy 6:20). People are expected to engage in exchanges because the rules for exchange behavior are carefully set out in Scripture. These rules are cast as both positive and negative injunction. The Scriptural perspective does not share the preference for negative injunction which the Western democracies have demonstrated in their attempt to order societies while maintaining a great deal of individual liberty. At the same time, freedom from oppression and spiritual *freedom* are a part of Scriptural tradition (Exodus 12:31-42, Psalm 119:45, Isaiah 61:1, and Luke 4:18, Romans 8:21, Galatians 5:1). This Scriptural introduction will be organized according to positive and negative injunctions.

Positive Injunction

Positive expectations of people include the expectation that they are willing to work for what they receive. The *work ethic* is revealed in Genesis 3:19, Proverbs 6:6-11, 10:4, 12:24, 13:4, 14:23, 20:4, 24:30-34, 28:19, Ecclesiastes 10:18-19, 1 Thessalonians 2:9, 2 Thessalonians 3:8, 10 and 12 as well as in other Scripture.

Stewardship of *wealth is not negative per-se* or in and of itself, as it is seen to be a *blessing* (Genesis 24:35, 26;12, 39:2, 39:23, Proverbs 13:21) but people are to take a balanced view of wealth and *place many things ahead of wealth in the selection* of life's effort or *work*. People are expected to place wisdom before wealth (Proverbs 4:7, 8:10 and 11), peace before wealth (Proverbs 17:1), friends before wealth (Proverbs 19:4, Luke 16:9), integrity before wealth, (Proverbs 22:1, 28:6), and *practice moderation in the acquisition of wealth* (Proverbs 23:4) as the accumulation of great wealth is *unlikely* to bring *peace of mind* (Ecclesiastes 5:9-6:12). While some degree of prudent frugality can be expected in making provision against future hunger (Genesis 41:35 and 36; Proverbs 21:20; John 6:12), *faith in wealth should be renounced for faith in the higher values of the kingdom of God* (Matthew 6:19-34, 19:18, Mark 10:17-31, Luke 12:13-21 and 18:20). The acquisition and stewardship of wealth is also subject to a large number of negative injunctions in Scripture.

Care for employees is a positive injunction in Scripture. The employer has a responsibility for employees (Genesis 16:6) and is expected to pay fair wages (Genesis 29:15, Matthew 10:10, Luke 10:7). *Care for the poor* is also a positive injunction. The poor are to receive preference in lending (Exodus 22:25), the use of fallow land (Exodus 23:11), the fallen harvest (Leviticus 9:9-10, 23:22), and are to be cared for in a positive way (Leviticus 25:25, 35-54, Deuteronomy 15:7-11, 24:17-22, 26:12-13, Nehemiah 5:1-12, Proverbs 14:21, 31, 22:22). The New Testament sees the poor as blessed (Luke 6:20-26, James 2:5) because they are less oriented toward material gain. The poor are to be the object of much aid and hard work (Acts 20:30-34).

Voluntary restitution for gains made in unethical fashion is also a positive injunction in Scripture. Gains made through *deception* are to be restored (Leviticus 6:2-5) and injuries are to be repaid (Leviticus 24:18-21, Exodus 21:16-19, 33-36, Luke 19:8-9). The *private property (or stewardship) of others is to be carefully respected* (Exodus 22:1-5, 23:4-5, Deuteronomy 19:14, 22:1-4, Proverbs 22:28, Leviticus 25:23-34) and careful *rules for inheritance*, property allocation and property transfer are set out (Leviticus 25:23-34, 25:34, Numbers 26:52-56, 27:8-11, 33:50-54, 36, Deuteronomy 21:15-17, Ruth 4:1-8, Nehemiah 5:1-12).

Negative Injunction

Exchange behavior is subject to a substantial amount of negative injunction in Scripture. *Stealing is prohibited* (Exodus 20;15, Leviticus 19:11, Deuteronomy 5:19, Ephesians 4:28, Zachariah 5:3, Proverbs 28:24) as is *bearing false witness* (Exodus 20:16, Deuteronomy 5:20) and *coveting* the possessions of others (Exodus 20:17, 5:21). There are also prohibitions of *greed* (Ephesians 5:3, Isaiah 57:17, Psalm 119:36), *faith in money* (Matthew 6:19-34, 1 Timothy 2:6, Luke 12:13-21, Ezekiel 18:18, Psalm 52:7, 62:10) and *love of money* (2 Timothy 3:1-5, Hebrews 13:5, Matthew 6:19-20).

Some of the negative injunction in Scripture is very specific. *Deception* is prohibited (Leviticus 19:35-36, Deuteronomy 25:13-16) as is the use of *dishonest standards or measures* (Leviticus 19:35-36, Deuteronomy 25:13-16, Proverbs 11:1, 16:11, 20:10). *Taking advantage when selling* is prohibited (Leviticus 25:14) as well as *taking unfair advantage of the poor or making gains at the expense of the poor* (2 Samuel 12:1-6, Deuteronomy 24:14-15, Proverbs 22:16, Isaiah 3:14-15, Amos 2:6-7, 5:11-13, 8:4-6). *Unfair acquisition of property* (1 Kings 21), *unfair representation in trade* (2 Kings 5:20-27), *bribery* and *usury* (Job 36:18-19, Psalm 15:5) are also subject to negative injunction.

The mode and motive of gain is important in Scripture. *Gains are not to be made at the expense of the worker* (Deuteronomy 24:14-15, Jeremiah 22:13-19, Matthew 10:10, Luke 10:7). Any gain which is *selfish* (Psalm 119:36) *involves sin or is otherwise ill-gotten* (Proverbs 1:19, 10:2, Micah 3:9-11) or *dishonest* (Proverbs 13:11, 21:6-7) is prohibited. Slow and honest accumulation is a preferred means of gaining wealth (Proverbs 13:11).

Governing Perspectives

Beyond specific positive and negative injunctions which apply to marketing practice, the Scripture provides broader decision rules or maxims which apply across a broad spectrum of behavior. A complete discussion of these is beyond the scope of this book, but the marketer who wishes to practice where the Judeo-Christian ethic is influential should understand these as well as the specific injunctions which apply directly to marketing. The broad maxims are typified by the laws as given in the Hebrew Scriptures which include prohibitions of idolatry, profanity, murder, adultery, stealing, false witness, and covetousness (Exodus 20:1-17). New Testament maxims are typified by the commandment to love (Matthew 5:43-48, 22:39), the blessing of specific spiritual conditions as set forth in the Beatitudes (Matthew 5:3-11), the identification of the critical nature of the thought or heart condition (Matthew 5:21-22, 27-29) the identification of God with love (2 Corinthians 13:11, 1 John 4:8), and the commandment that admonishes that in all things do to others what you would have them do to you (Matthew 7:12, Luke 6:31).

Implications to Marketing Strategy

The expectations communicated in the Judeo-Christian ethic should affect the choice of marketing strategy. In the United States more than half of the population reads from the Bible at least on a monthly basis.[29] For secular practitioners, avoiding conflict with the teachings of the Judeo-Christian ethic is simply a matter of cultural sensitivity as 67% of the North American population and 22% of the world population subscribes to some form of the ethic.[30] For Jews and Christians, it is a matter of religious principle.

The powerful realities of human exchange and their implications to the selection of strategy may in some instances require no ethical compromise. In other instances they may tempt practitioners into unethical behavior. *Marketers should learn to ask the critical ethical questions which are derived from Scripture.* For example, the market niche of the firm may be enhanced by lowering costs. Often a real service to society, cost reductions may take the form of ingenious sales commission or remuneration plans which result in many hours of labor being donated to the firm. The marketing decision maker should learn to ask: *Is this a gain at the expense of the worker?* In another example, the avoidance of the unprofitable economics of pure competition may lead the firm into attempts to differentiate its product. Product differentiation drives the innovative process and provides real improvements for society. However, the marketing decision maker should ask *whether it amounts to deception or unfair representation in trade* as it is practiced. Careful study of the consumer's demographic and psychological characteristics can lead the marketing practitioner to insights about the consumer which the consumer himself may not share. Can this lead to *taking advantage when selling*? The economics of risk can make a good argument for vending at higher prices in poor neighborhoods where losses from theft and vandalism are more likely to occur. Can this reasonable economic calculation ever lead to *gains at the expense of the poor*?

Marketing decisions will present continuing ethical problems. The psychological, economic and financial realities which govern the organizations existence are powerful. Temptations to engage in exchange behaviors which offend ethical expectations will be ever present in marketing practice.

Crossing National Boundaries

When engaging in international marketing, the environment of legal and ethical expectation will change considerably. This should not require that the individual change his or her set of ethics, but should require increased sensitivity to the expectations of others.

Law

The antitrust statutes, very strong components of U.S. law, *are not duplicated* to any significant extent *in the rest of the world*. West German law comes the closest to duplicating the U.S. antitrust position.[31] As a general statement, the U.S. is the major capitalist power most committed to competition, favoring the consumers' interests over the suppliers' interests. In contrast, cartels, oligopolies and associated oligarchy (ruling power in the hands of a few) can be expected in many nations. This has often resulted in the economic benefits available in these nations being allocated largely to the ruling few. This in turn has impoverished the workers, disenfranchising them as consumers, and has resulted in political instability. While another nation may not have such legislation, the antitrust laws and the internal revenue service (IRS) codes follow U.S. firms overseas. This is to protect competition in U.S. markets and to insure that U.S. firms and citizens will continue to pay U.S. tax.[32]

Consumer protection laws can be greatly different. Often they are more stringent. While the United States has historically been tolerant of "puffery" or exaggerated praise of a product or service some countries will not tolerate it. For example the law in Canada reads:[33]

> All claims and statements must be examined to insure that any representation to the public is not considered false or misleading. Such representation can be made verbally in selling or contained in anything that comes to the attention of the public. . . .

Courts in Canada are to take into account the "general impression" conveyed as well as the "literal meaning" when examining individual cases.[34] Thus, something which might be excused as puffery in the United States could be found to be illegal in Canada.

Intellectual property protection in overseas environments will differ from that found in the U.S. Its nature will depend on the basis of the nation's legal system. In common law nations such as the U.S., U.K., and Canada, the basis of law is tradition, past practice and legal precedent.[35] In the code law nations which comprise the rest of the world, the law is based upon an inclusive system of written rules. From a marketing point of view, the differences between these systems can be substantial. For example, in common law nations, trade names and trade marks are established by *use*. In code law nations they are established by *registration*.[36] Thus it is possible to be the first to register a major international trademark or trade name in a code law nation and have the legal right to use that name in that country, despite its use elsewhere by its originator.

Contract law differs substantially between common law and code law countries. In a common law country, existence of a contact may be established by almost any proof of an agreement, but can only be excused by an act of God (force majeur). In code law countries, a contract may require notarization and registration, but the contract may be excused relatively easily.[37] These kinds of differences can put the firm in difficult situations. For example a U.S. contract between a U.S. importing firm and its U.S. distributors can only be excused by an act of god. Another contract which specifies delivery from a Japanese manufacturer to the U.S. importing firm might be excused much more easily. Should the Japanese exercise an option to terminate the contract which is short of the definition of an act of god, the U.S. firm would still have a binding contract with its distributors.

Control of industry by governments of other nations can go well beyond direct economic regulation. The firm may be subject to anything from *entry and takeover controls*, wherein government approval may be required for new investments or takeovers, *to expropriation* (dispossession with compensation) or *confiscation* (dispossession without compensation).[38] While the legal precedents necessary for direct economic regulation had to be laboriously worked out in the freedom minded United States, other nations have often found it easier to gain control over industry. It is a safe assumption that a foreign government which decides that a company's activities are not in its interest, will have the power to either adjust the company's behavior or take control of the company away from its owners.

Ethics

In other cultures, ethical expectations which are drawn from religions or systems of thought other than the Judeo-Christian ethic may be expected to have substantial influence. The following provides a short summary of major religions or systems of thought which may guide these ethical expectations.

Buddhism Buddhism is an influential religion in much of Asia and also claims a small but active group of followers in the United States.[39] Buddhism advocates that believers follow the noble eightfold path. This consists of right views, right intention, right speech, right action, right livelihood, right effort, right mindfulness and right concentration.[40] The disciple is to seek Nirvana, a condition wherein all desire, hatred and ignorance are extinguished.[41]

Positive injunctions in Buddhist thought include the development of an understanding of suffering, its cause, cessation and the path to cessation (right views).[42] The follower is to follow an occupation which causes no harm to any living thing (right livelihood), and is to arouse and maintain personal tendencies which are wholesome and good (right effort). Right mindfulness involves keeping watch over the states of the body and mind so as to rightly control them. The mind is to be concentrated in meditation to allow the individual to achieve higher states of consciousness and insight.

Negative injunction includes the avoidance of lust, ill will, cruelty and untruthfulness (right thought). Lying, talebearing, harsh language and vain talk are to be avoided in right speech, and right action prohibits killing, stealing and sexual misconduct. Right effort involves avoiding and overcoming one's evil tendencies.[43]

Followers of Buddhism are estimated to number over 247 million, most of them living in Asia. As some marketing practitioners may become involved in creating desire or arousing latent desire, and as some practitioners may become involved in untruthfulness, Buddhist ethical expectations may be offended.

Hinduism Hinduism is the primary religion in India where 90% of its almost 500 million followers live.[44] The Hindu scriptures recognize that wealth and power (artha) and pleasure or the satisfaction of desires (kama) are legitimate objectives in life. However, these kinds of objectives should be made secondary to right conduct (dharma) and release from the cycle of an unending rebirth (moksha). D'harma and the paths to the achievement of moksha may be characterized in terms of positive and negative injunction.

Positive injunction includes speaking the truth, performing meritorious acts and selfless deeds without regard to satisfaction of personal desire, and attainment of insight into the truths of the universe. The attainment of insight may be expected after periods of spiritual and physical discipline, involving the renunciation of all worldly attachments. *negative injunction* includes prohibition of lying, taking life and disrespect for priests or scriptures.[45] It would appear that materialism and puffery would be as likely to offend Hindu ethical expectations as to offend Judeo-Christian or Buddhist ethical expectations.

Islam

Islam is a religion claiming a large number of adherents, with numbers estimated from 500-800 million.[46] Islam is influential throughout the world but is particularly powerful in the Middle East and Africa. Islam expects that the individual will place Allah (God) ahead of himself and work to achieve righteousness.[47]

Positive injunctions in Islam include the duties of reciting the creed, worship and prayer, almsgiving and a pilgrimage to Mecca. The Muslim or individual following Islam can be expected to give to the poor, spend for the welfare of future generations, and to promote and perpetuate goodness.[48] Muslims are expected to "keep their trusts and promises and bear true witness."[49] Negative injunctions include abstinence from food, drink or sexual activity during certain periods of the year. The Koran (Holy Book) forbids the consumption of pork and liquor and the act of gambling. Muslims are expected to conduct business affairs without charging interest.[50]

Taoism

Taoism is a religion of China which was founded in the sixth century B.C. Taoist thinking remains influential in the Orient although the religion itself now claims only some 20 million followers.[51] *Positive injunctions* in Taoism include the understanding and personal absorption in "Tao," the ultimate reality in the changing world. The follower is to achieve an "inward quiet" and live in harmony with the principles which govern the universe. *Negative injunctions* include the avoidance of human striving and action. Taoists also avoid reliance upon reason and knowledge in attempting to understand the principles that govern the universe.[52]

Shintoism Shintoism is a religion of ancient Japan which still claims some 32 million followers.[53] The Shinto religion teaches that people are the children of the power of harmony and creation (kami), but must purify their heart to exhibit that essence. The best attitude toward life is "magokoro" or the true heart. *Positive injunctions* include sincerity, purity of heart, uprightness or the "bright pure upright and sincere mind," respect for family, love and faithfulness. *Negative injunction* derived from this would prohibit bearing false witness, being deceitful, and indulging in shallow opportunism.[54]

Confucianism *Confucianism* which claims over 150 million followers, is a system of thought which has its largest influence in Asia.[55] Confucius (551-479 B.C.) emphasized the importance of the Chinese concepts of Li or "proper conduct" and Te which is "moral force or inner power." *Positive injunctions* in this system includes respect for family and authority, modesty, appreciation of others, cultivation of a broad perspective, learning and contemplation, truth, restraint in competition, love of fellow man, imperturbability, resolution, slowness to speak and diligence.[56] *Negative injunction* includes the avoidance of clever talk, pretentious manners, frivolity, hypocrisy, one sided bias, love of mastery, vanity, resentment, and covetousness.[57]

Marxism *Marxism* is a system of political and economic thought which has wide influence in the world. It was originally atheistic and based upon a labor theory of value. The labor theory held that profit was derived from underpaying the workers, and so the followers of Karl Marx attempted to fashion societies which made minimum use of profit and its associated market mechanisms. Labor theory has been criticized from both theoretical and pragmatic or practical perspectives, and modern marxist societies have undertaken reforms which allow them to make much greater use of markets for the allocation of resources and the provision of incentives for production and allocation. Such reforms in the People's Republic of China have been rewarded with large increases in agricultural productivity, and the Soviet Union has followed suit with the institution of market mechanisms in agriculture.[58] However, some Marxist societies have yet to adopt the essential logic of the market. In Ethiopia where economic problems have been aggravated by drought conditions, the marxist regime continues to organize agriculture in collective farms. The government then forces farmers who can grow more than they can consume to sell to the state at prices that are below the costs of production.[59] The combination of war, a difficult ecological situation and ignorance of the power of the market has resulted in starvation. *Positive and negative injunctions* which might be derived from the consideration of Marxism would center around the work ethic and care for the worker. Marxism appeals to the arguments that one should work for what one gains and one should not achieve gains at the expense of others. Insuring that one is providing high integrity offerings to society and is involved in exchanges which are free, voluntary and characterized by accurate information would insure that both parties to the exchange would gain. They would both gain or the exchange would not be voluntary. Provision of a high standard of living to those employed could insure that profit or organizational survival would not be extracted from the sacrifice of the workers.

Ethical Marketing

The *role of marketing in society* is to match heterogeneous supplies with heterogeneous demands. It is a necessary role and one which must be accomplished effectively and efficiently if the material requirements of life are to be available. Failure of resource allocation systems brings starvation, and the world population is expected to grow from 1 billion to 10 billion people in the late twentieth and early twenty-first century.[60] The best understanding of markets and marketing will be needed if this frightening population explosion is not to lead to human misery. Marketing people busy themselves on a daily basis by finding needs in the society which might be filled and filling them. In so doing, they provide work for the many who become involved in supplying these needs, transforming the disposable and discretionary incomes of consumers into the wages of workers. This is a modern solution to poverty which rests upon free and voluntary exchanges and the work ethic. It may be augmented by government action, but can also be destroyed by government action. Together with sensitive and constructive government activity it may be seen as a modern implementation of an old solution to poverty. In considering poverty the Reverend John Wesley said:[61]

> What remedy is there for this sore evil? Many thousand poor people are starving. Find them work and you will find them meat. They will earn and eat their own bread. But how can the masters [employers] give them work without ruining themselves? *Procure vent* [sale] *for what is wrought* [made] and the masters [employers] give them as much work as they can do. (This author's italics)

Wesley went on to suggest that the price of provisions or food should be kept low to facilitate this process. By keeping the price of food low "people would have money to buy other things."[62] Thus, *marketing people "procure vent for what is wrought"* and in so doing transfer *discretionary income* (income over and above that required for necessities such as food) to willing workers. Marketers involved in the vending of necessities such as food, are involved in a similar transfer of *disposable income* (that left after tax) to workers.

Most informed ethical complaint about marketing therefore stems from specific practices rather than from *the process* itself. *Marketing is the matching of supplies with demands and such matching is necessary. Marketing feeds people by finding goods and services that some are willing to pay for and transferring that money to others willing to produce those goods or services. Marketing relies upon voluntary exchanges and is therefore more compatible with individual liberty than authoritarian alternatives.* It is when this process becomes involved in violations of the specific positive and negative injunctions discussed earlier that it becomes offensive. Sensitivity and love of one's fellow man is expected of marketers as it is of anyone else.

Despite expectations of love and sensitivity, there remains the expectation of some level of *competition*. It is perhaps a statement about the nature of man that one's greatest effectiveness and highest efficiency is often found in competition with others. *The matching process occurs vertically in the channel of distribution*, between supplies and demands. Horizontal cooperation among suppliers has been demonstrated to bring a great economic burden to the consumer as it makes the matching process far less efficient. This has been illustrated in the discussion of market structures. *Competition should be constructively viewed* as a means of measuring one's effectiveness and efficiency in the society's matching process. If other participants in the process prefer your offerings to those of competitors even when you charge a higher price, you have been more *effective* in meeting people's needs. If your offerings are preferred because you can afford to sell them for less than your competitors can, then you have been more *efficient* in meeting people's needs. Given the nature of man, some level of competition will remain a necessary component of a working market allocation process, whether it be found in capitalist or socialist environments. *Competition* should, therefore, be seen as a means of measuring the effectiveness and efficiency of one's contributions, *rather than* as a vent for conceit, provocation, and envy (Galatians 5:26).

Chapter Summary

Marketing management is not free to engage in exchanges according to the dictates of the market alone. Both the law and systems of ethics provide positive and negative injunctions which concern marketing activity. In the United States, the law consists of the antitrust laws, consumer protection laws, intellectual property protection laws, contract law and the laws which regulate specific industries. Outside of the United States, the specifics of the law will differ substantially and few nations will share the U.S. emphasis on antitrust. The development of much of marketing law can be seen as a social response to marketing activities which have been seen as "abuses." The degree of sensitivity which marketers display toward the ethical expectations of a society will say much about the degree of decision making prerogative which that society will allow the marketers to exercise. Ethical expectations are seen to be of a higher order than simple conformity to the law, and may be drawn from secular reasoning or religious teaching. Secular perspectives include the utilitarian perspective and Kant's categorical imperative. Religious ethics include those standards of conduct drawn from Judeo-Christian, Buddhist, Hindu, Islamic, Taoist, and Shinto beliefs. Confucianism and Marxism also contribute to these expectations, although these are systems of thought rather than religions.

When marketing activities are governed by the law, the path that marketing decision makers must follow narrows considerably. When ethics are considered the path continues to narrow. The marketer should undertake the necessary and stimulating challenge of resource allocation with strong ethical convictions and with great sensitivity toward the ethical expectations of others.

---

[1]Louis W. Stern and Thomas L. Eovaldi, *Legal Aspects of Marketing Strategy* (Englewood Cliffs, N.J.: Prentice Hall, 1984), p. 3.

[2]Ibid.

[3]Ibid., p. 7.

[4]Ibid.

[5]Ibid., p. 3.

[6]E. Jerome McCarthy and William D. Perreault, Jr., *Basic Marketing*, 9th ed. (Homewood, Illinois: Richard D. Irwin, 1987), p. 111.

[7]Adam Smith, *Wealth of Nations*, Book I, Chapter XI.

[8]374 U.S. 321 (1963).See also E. T. Grether, "Galbraith Vs. the Market: A Review Article," in *Society and Marketing*, ed. N. Kangun (New York: Harper and Row, 1972), pp. 9-13.

[9]For a discussion of the F.D.A. see Stern, pp. 103-106.

[10]Stern, p. 7.

[11]McCarthy, p. 111.

[12]Ibid., p. 320.

[13]See Stern, pp. 84-89, especially p. 86.

[14]Ibid., pp. 100-102.

[15]McCarthy, p. 113.

[16]Stern, p. 90.

[17]McCarthy, p. 235.

[18]Stern, p. 3.

[19]See Dudley F. Pegrum, *Transportation Economics and Public Policy*, 3rd ed. (Homewood, Illinois: Richard D. Irwin, 1973), p. 270.

[20]See D. Philip Locklin, *Economics of Transportation*, 7th ed. (Homewood, Illinois: Richard D. Irwin, 1972), pp. 224-227.

[21]Pegrum, p. 287.

[22]See Locklin, pp. 244-253.

[23]J. Howard Westing, "Some Thoughts on the Nature of Ethics in Marketing," in *Changing Market Systems*, ed. Reed Moyer (Chicago: American Marketing Association, 1967), pp. 161-163. Reprinted with permission of the American Marketing Association, Chicago, IL.

[24]Webster's *New World Dictionary of the American Language*, College Edition (New York: The World Publishing Company, 1958), p. 499.

[25]Discussions of Utilitarianism in the context of business ethics would include Gene R. Laczniak, "Frameworks for Analyzing Marketing Ethics," in *Marketing Ethics*, eds. Gene R. Laczniak and Patrice E. Murphy (Lexington, Massachusetts: Lexington Books, 1985), p. 14. See also David J. Fritzsche, "Ethical Issues in Multinational Marketing," in Laczniak, pp. 87-88. See also, Robert C. Solomon and Kristine R. Hanson, *Above the Bottom Line, an Introduction to Business Ethics* (New York: Harcourt Brace Jovanovich, Inc., 1983), pp. 201-206. See also W. Michael Hoffman and Jennifer Mills Moore, *Business Ethics* (New York: McGraw-Hill Inc., 1954), pp. 7-9. For an original discussion see John Stuart Mill, *Utilitarianism* (New York: Longmans, Green, 1861).

[26]Discussion of Kant in the context of business ethics would include Fritzsche, p. 88. See also, Solomon, pp. 194-201, and Hoffman, pp. 9-11. For an original discussion see Immanuel Kant, *Fundamental Principles of the Metaphysics of Morals*, trans. T. K. Abbott (New York: Longmans, Green, 1898).

[27]For a discussion of the Kew Gardens principle see John G. Simon, Charles W. Powers, and Jon P. Gunneman, "The Responsibilities of Corporations and Their Owners," in *Ethical Theory and Business*, eds. Tom L. Beauchamp and Neuman E. Bowie (Englewood Cliffs, N.J.: Prentice Hall, 1979), pp. 160-168. See also John E. Simon, Charles W. Powers, and Jon P. Gunneman, *The Ethical Investor: Universities and Corporate Responsibility* (New Haven, Conn.: Yale University Press, 1972).

[28] Webster's *Third New International Dictionary*, unabridged (Springfield, Massachusetts: G & C Merriam Company, 1967), p. 780.

[29] "We Search for 'Spiritual Well Being,'" *USA Today*, September 3, 1987, pp. 1A, 2A.

[30] Mark S. Hoffman (ed.), *The World Almanac Book of Facts 1987* (New York: Pharos Books, 1987), pp. 339-340.

[31] See Philip R. Cateora and John M. Hess, *International Marketing* (Homewood, Illinois: Richard D. Irwin, 1979), p. 206.

[32] Ibid., p. 202. See also Stefan H. Robock, Kenneth Simmonds, and Jack Zwick, *International Business and Multinational Enterprises* (Homewood, Illinois: Richard D. Irwin, 1977), p. 467.

[33] Cateora, pp. 194-195.

[34] Ibid. See also Henry R. Ross and Keith K. Warne, "Canada's Laws on Communications Raise Barriers to Advertisers," *Industrial Marketing* (January 1977), p. 66.

[35] Cateora, p. 186.

[36] Ibid., pp. 186-187.

[37] Ibid., p. 187.

[38] Robock, pp. 232-241.

[39] Hoffman, p. 340. See also James Hastings (ed.), *The Encyclopedia of Religion and Ethics*, Vol. 2 (New York: Charles Scribner's Sons, 1958), pp. 881-887. See also William D. Halsey and Bernard Johnston (eds.), *Colliers Encyclopedia*, Vol. 4 (New York: Macmillan Educational Company, 1987), pp. 659-670.

[40] Frank S. Mead and Samuel S. Hill, *Handbook of Denominations in the United States* (Nashville, Tennessee: Abingdon Press, 1985), p. 69.

[41] Ibid.

[42] Halsey, p. 664.

[43] The discussion of Buddhism is derived from Hastings, Halsey, and Mead.

[44] William D. Halsey and Bernard Johnston (eds.), *Colliers Encyclopedia*, Vol. 12 (New York: Macmillan Educational Company, 1987), p. 127.

[45] The discussion of Hinduism is derived from Halsey, Vol. 12, pp. 127-129.

[46] William D. Halsey and Bernard Johnston (eds.), *Colliers Encyclopedia*, Vol. 13 (New York: Macmillan Educational Company, 1987), p. 310.

[47] Hastings, p. 437.

[48] Monzer Kahf, "A Contribution to the Theory of Consumer Behavior in an Islamic Society," in *Studies in Islamic Economics*, edited by Khurshid Ahmad (Jeddah: International Center for Research in Islamic Economics, 1980), pp. 22-23.

[49] *The Koran*, 70:22 (New York: Viking Penguin Inc., 1986), p. 58.

[50] Except as noted, the discussion of Islam is derived from Hastings, Halsey, and Mead.

[51] Hoffman, p. 340.

[52] Except as noted, the discussion of Taoism is derived from Otto T. Johnson, (ed.), *Information Please Almanac* (New York: Houghton Mifflin, 1984), p. 385.

[53] Hoffman, p. 340.

[54] Except as noted, the discussion of Shintoism is derived from Mircea Eliade (ed.), *The Encyclopedia of Religions*, Vol. 13 (New York: Macmillan, 1987), pp. 280-293.

[55] Johnson, p. 385.

[56] Confucius, *The Analects of Confucius*, trans. Arthur Waley (Franklin Center, Pennsylvania: The Franklin Library, 1980), pp. 110, 118, and 124.

[57] The discussion is taken from Confucius, especially pp. 1-20 and 104-124.

[58] Except as noted, the understanding of Marxism is derived from Jacob Oser and Stanley L. Brue, *The Evolution of Economic Thought*, 4th ed. (San Diego: Harcourt Brace Jovanovich, 1988), pp. 170-191. Popular media reports of the reforms in the Soviet Union and the People's Republic of China have also influenced this section.

[59] "Famine," *Time*, December 21, 1987, pp. 34-43, especially p. 43.

[60] This projection is based on the rapid growth of the world's population from 1 billion to 5 billion since World War II.

[61] The Reverend John Wesley as cited in Charles L. Allen, *Meet the Methodists* (Nashville: Abingdon Press, 1986), p. 65.

[62] Ibid.

QUESTIONS FOR STUDY, DISCUSSION AND EXAMINATION

1. Can you define, or explain to a friend who has not studied marketing, each of the following terms or ideas?
    a. Constraint
    b. Guidance
    c. Negative injunction
    d. Positive injunction
    e. Trust
    f. Antitrust law
    g. Sherman Act of 1890
    h. Clayton Act of 1914
    i. Federal Trade Commission Act of 1914
    j. Unfair methods of competition
    k. Robinson Patman Act of 1936
    l. Price discrimination
    m. Anti-merger Act of 1950
    n. Consumer Protection Law
    o. Pure Food and Drug Act of 1906
    p. Food and Drug Administration (FDA)
    q. Wheeler Lea Act of 1938
    r. Federal Fair Packaging and Labeling Act of 1966
    s. Consumer Product Safety Act of 1972
    t. Consumer Product Safety Commission
    u. Magnuson Moss Warranty Act of 1975
    v. Tort law
    w. Patent law
    x. Copyright law
    aa. Lanham Act of 1946
    ab. Contract Law
    ac. Force Majeur
    ad. Act to Regulate Commerce, 1887
    ae. Interstate Commerce Commission, ICC
    af. Regulatory Commission

398 Part III

- ag. Deregulation Movement
- ah. Ethics
- ai. Secular Ethical System
- aj. All encompassing system of rules
- ak. General Decision Rule
- al. Utilitarian ethic
- am. Maxim
- an. Satisfaction
- ao. Teleological ethical perspective
- ap. Deontological ethical perspective
- aq. Categorical imperative
- as. Need, proximity, capability, last resort (Kew Gardens context)
- at. Religious ethics
- au. Judeo-Christian ethic
- av. Dominion
- aw. Stewardship
- ax. Freedom (in Judeo Christian tradition)
- ay. Work ethic
- az. Wealth as blessing
- ba. Priority of wealth
- bb. Care for employees
- bc. Care for the poor
- bd. Voluntary restitution for gains made in unethical fashion
- be. Deception
- bf. Respect for others' property or stewardship
- bg. Stealing
- bh. Bearing false witness
- bi. Coveting
- bj. Greed
- bk. Faith in money
- bl. Love of money
- bn. Deception
- bo. Dishonest standards or measures
- bp. Taking advantages when selling
- bq. Taking unfair advantage of the poor
- br. Making gains at the expense of the poor

bs. Unfair acquisition of property
bt. Unfair representation in trade
bu. Bribery
bv. Usury
bw. Gains at the expense of the worker
bx. Selfish gain
by. Gain involving sin or otherwise ill-gotten gain
bz. Dishonest gain
ca. Governing perspectives in scriptural ethics
cb. Critical ethical questions for marketers
cc. Antitrust law in other nations
cd. "Puffery" in the US and other nations
ce. Intellectual property protection in code law vs. common law countries
cf. Control of industry in other nations
cg. Entry and takeover controls
ch. Expropriation
ci. Confiscation
cj. Buddhism
ch. Hinduism
ci. Islam
cj. Taoism
ck. Shintoism
cl. Confucianism
cm. Marxism
cn. The role of marketing in society
co. Procuring "vent" for what is "wrought"
cp. The marketing process from a social point of view
cq. competition constructively viewed

2. Compare and contrast the terms positive injunction, negative injunction, and constraint. How free are marketing executives?

3. Why have Western democracies traditionally preferred laws which are cast as negative injunction to those cast as positive injunction?

4. Characterize the development of the Antitrust Laws in the United States. How is the development characterized by "abuse," negative injunction and the understanding of market structure?

5. In view of the Antitrust Laws, what kinds of activities should marketing decision makers avoid and why?
6. If the Antitrust Acts could be phrased as positive injunction how might they be phrased? Is this good advice for marketers, why or why not?
7. What is an unfair method of competition? Who decides this and how is it decided? How would you decide in the case of a marketing decision?
8. In what sense is the FTC Act of 1914 consumer protection legislation as well as antitrust legislation?
9. The Robinson Patman Act of 1936 is an unusual piece of antitrust legislation in that it seeks to protect competition by protecting competitors. In what ways might this legislation be confusing to marketing decision makers?
10. How does the Anti-Merger Act of 1950 reflect an understanding of market structure on the part of the Congress?
11. What logic prompted the relaxation of antitrust enforcement during the 1980s? Do you agree or disagree with this logic? What would happen if domestic antitrust enforcement were relaxed at the same time the U.S. enacted substantial tariff barriers to imports?
12. Adam Smith was an early proponent or advocate of a largely free market economy. Does this mean that Smith believed that business people would naturally serve the interests of the public? How does this mechanism work? How does this relate to antitrust law in the United States?
13. Is competition sufficient to protect the consumer? Why or why not? Discuss the evolution of consumer protection legislation in the U.S. in this context. Under what circumstances would you judge consumer protection laws to be necessary? Excessive? Can you come up with a maxim or decision rule to guide decisions to establish new consumer protection laws?
14. In what sense is a copyright or a patent an exception to the fundamental national economic policy of competition? How might this encourage real innovation?
15. What is required of a warranty by the Magnuson Moss Warranty Act of 1975?
16. Describe the evolution of direct economic regulation in the United States. Using direct economic regulation, antitrust and consumer

protection legislation, how can the government affect the marketing mix of the firm?

17. What caused the deregulation movement? What industries did it affect? How did it affect them?

18. What is the relationship of law to ethical expectations? In what sense are they related? In what sense are they separate?

19. How have marketers lost their decision making prerogatives in the past? Do you see a way for marketers to retain general freedom?

20. In what sense might the law be a "lowest common denominator" in describing expectations about behavior?

21. What is likely to happen when the powerful realities of exchange and profit together with the pressures for short term success on the job come in conflict with a marketer's ethical commitment which is only "soft and irresolute"?

22. What is a secular ethical system? Compare and contrast the utilitarian ethic with the categorical imperative. Give examples of marketing decisions which might have been made using each of these ethical perspectives. How is the "marketing concept" compatible with the categorical imperative?

23. Develop a marketing example of a situation wherein the Kew Gardens principles would suggest that a positive injunction is as ethically binding as the negative injunction.

24. Why should marketers who profess faith in a particular religion study the specific ethical injunctions of their religion? Of another religion? Why should a marketer who is an atheist or an agnostic study religious ethical expectations?

25. (Group project) Consider each of the specific injunctions underlined in the text (or listed in items 1-av through 1-bz above) which come from Judeo-Christian scripture. Investigate their meaning and context in as much detail as you wish; consult with a clergy person if you wish. Then characterize a modern marketing practice which serves as an example of what the scripture is discussing.

26 (Group project) Consider each of the religions or systems of thought other than the Judeo-Christian perspective which are outlined in the text. What parallels do you see with the Judeo-Christian ethic? What differences? What guidance would you give to marketers who expect to open up new markets where one of these religions or systems of thought is dominant?

27. How might the "governing perspectives" found in scripture affect marketing practice?
28. The text suggests that "marketers should learn to ask the critical ethical questions which are derived from scripture," and gives several examples. Give several more examples of critical ethical questions about marketing practice which may be derived from scripture.
29. The text suggests that the marketing process itself is essentially ethical and that most informed criticism of marketing stems from specific practices. How is the marketing process seen as an essentially ethical practice?
30. Why is a market allocation process viewed as compatible with individual liberty?
31. What does "procuring vent for what is wrought" have to do with the problem of poverty?
32. What is the essential role played by the marketing process in society?
33. How does the text suggest that we should resolve the need for some element of competition in modern societies with the scriptural mandate for love of our fellowman? What does this have to do with the way in which the matching process occurs in the channel of distribution? What does it have to do with antitrust law and market structure? How might competition be constructively viewed? According to the text, what view of competition should be avoided?
34. Review the discussion of aggregate demand in the economy which is included in chapter eight. Could marketers' attempts to stimulate demand ever be socially useful? Under what circumstances might attempts to stimulate demand be ethically offensive? The Engle Blackwell model of consumer behavior introduced in chapter two defines problem recognition in terms of the difference that the consumer perceives between the ideal state and the actual state. When should problem recognition defined in this way be resolved by enhancement of the actual state? By a reduction of the expectations embodied in the ideal state?
35. If people are starving in Ethiopia and the government forces the farmers to sell at prices which are below costs, what signal is the government sending to the farmers through the price system? You may wish to review portions of chapter three.

Index

A

Abuse, 378
Acceptance, 196
Accepting, 195
Account, 198
Accounting,
Accumulation, 384
Acquisitions, 347
Act of God, 376
Act to Regulate Commerce, 376
Action, 388
Activities interest and opinion, 18
Adam Smith, 374
Advantage, 321-322, 329
Advertising, 193
Advertising agencies, 198
Advertising group, 318
Affordability, 202
Agency or distributorship plans, 209
Agent, middle persons, 236
Aggregate demand, 280
Aggregate supply, 280
Air, 256
Alternative evaluation, 25
Alternative scenarios, 299
Ambiguity, 14
Analyzers, 351
Anti trust laws, 89
Anti-Merger Act of 1950, 373
Antitrust division of the Department of Justice, 374
Antitrust laws, 248, 335, 372, 374
Antitrust legislation, 373
Antitrust statutes, 385
Aristotle, 20
Aspirational group, 16
Associations, 17, 18, 197, 199
Associative learning, 18
Attack, 331
Attention, 193, 195
Average costs, 251
Average revenue, 74
Average total cost, 5, 68
Average variable cost, 74

B

Back translation, 211, 300
Backhaul, 258
Backward integration, 249
Balance of resources, 99
Balance of tensions, 19
Balance of trade deficit, 148
Balance of trade surplus, 148
Basis for exchange, 32
Bayesian probabilities, 335
BCG model, 130, 324
Bearing false witness, 383
Bible, 381
Big ideas, 198
Black" market, 92
Blend of communications, 191
Board members, 284
Boston Consulting Group, 130

Boston Consulting Group (BCG) Model, 323
Boston Consulting Group matrix, 347
Brainstorming, 299
Brand familarity, 176
Brand manager, 314
Brand name, 176, 177, 211, 375
Branding, 173
Break bulk" activities, 261
Breakeven analysis, 112
Bribery, 383
Broad perspective, 389
Broker, 238
Buddhism, 387
Budget, 33, 320, 351
Budgets: bottom-up/top-down, 352-353
Budgets: top down/bottom-up
Buyer Behavior Model, 24

C

C.O.E., 117, 121-122, 133-134, 167, 208, 243, 249, 286, 344, 350
C.O.E. reports, 284
C.O.E. Within an Individual Offering, 122
Cable television, 201
Capability, 380-381
Capital, 126
Capital Allocation, 130, 324
Capital Market, 129
Capital shifting strategy, 348
Care for employees, 383
Care for the poor, 383
Care for the worker, 389
Carload, 258
Cartel, 89
Cash flow benefit, 140
Categorical imperative, 379
Ceiling prices, 92
Chain, 241
Channel decisions, 231
Channel leader, 234, 248
Channel members, 232
Channel of distribution, 231
Channels, 231
Channels: creative flexibility, 234
Channels: administered system, 234
Chunk, 197, 199
Classical conditioning, 17
Clayton Act of 1914, 372
Clever, 389

Clinical psychologists, 18
Cognitive dissonance, 16, 196
Cognitive learning, 18
Coincident indicators, 280
Commissions, 208
Communication, 357
Communication Feedback, 209
Communication group, 318
Communications design, 210
Communications structure, 355
Communications: adjustment when crossing national boundaries, 210
Comparative advertising, 199
Competition, 248, 283, 329, 331, 372-373, 376, 389, 391
Competition Among Brands, 176
Competitive activities, 283
Competitive advertising, 199
Competitive environment, 283
Competitive information, 283
Competitive intelligence, 284
Competitive offerings, 165
Competitive parity, 202
Complex commission formulae, 209
Complex exchange, 53
Complex matrices, 353
Complex systems, 206
Complex trend lines, 296
Confidence interval, 289-291
Confiscation, 386
Conflict, 322, 329
Confucianism, 389
Conjoint measurement, 163, 341
Conscious parallelism, 90
Consequence focused, 379
Conspiracy, 372
Constant sum game, 334
Constraints, 126, 371
Consumer Behavior, 24, 37, 241
Consumer goods classes, 173
Consumer optimum, 33
Consumer Product Safety Act in 1972, 375
Consumer Product Safety Commission, 375
Consumer protection, 373, 375, 385
Consumer Protection Laws, 374
Consumer surplus, 81
Consumer trust, 234
Consumers, 283
Containerization, 259
Contingency Models, 326
Contract law, 376, 386

Index 405

Contract Manufacturing, 354
Contributing margin space, 121
Contribution, 133
Contribution Margin, 112, 117, 121, 161, 243, 249-251, 350, 381
Contribution margin across the product line, 121
Contribution margin in time, 121
Contribution margin of the individual offering, 121
Contribution to overhead and earnings, 117, 133
Contributions to customer service, 251
Control of industry, 386
Convenience store, 241
Cooperation, 248
Cooperative chains, 243
Coordination, 314
Coordination difficulties, 302
Copy thrust, 199
Copyright laws, 375
Corporate chain, 243
Corporate level strategic planning staff, 284
Cost effectiveness, 199
Costs, 251, 257, 263, 284, 329, 339, 373, 374, 375, 389
Costs of turnover, 203
Counter arguments, 195
Coveting, 383
Covetousness, 389
Creative destruction, 100
Creative flexibility, 247
Creative mixing, 49
Creativity, 198
Credit strategy, 247
Cross subsidy, 130
Cues, 18
Currency fluctuations, 133, 134, 146
Customer service, 257, 263
Customer service characteristics, 251, 262
Customer service level, 249
Customs brokers, 264 - 265
Customs officials, 265
Cycles, 296

D

Dangerous consumer products, 375
Data base systems, 246
Data base technology, 201, 283

Data bases, 318
Deception, 374, 383
Deceptive packaging, 375
Decision making process, 198
Decisions in transportation and storage, 262
Declining marginal utility, 30, 32
Defenders, 351
Defense, 331
Delphi Technique, 299
Demand, 5, 13, 77, 390-391
Demand curve, 39
Demographics, 39, 195, 201, 278
Deontological ethical systems, 379
Depth interview, 288
Deregulation movement, 376
Derived, 53
Diagnostic Models, 210
Diagnostic questions, 193
Differentiated Product, 161
Differing information infrastructures, 301
Diminishing marginal utility, 33
Direct mail, 201
Direct response, 201
Directed information gathering, 278, 285
Directional policy matrix, 324
Discount house, 244-246
Discrepancies of place, 259
Discrepancies of time, 259
Discretionary income, 390
Discussion guide, 287
Dishonest gain, 384
Dishonest standards or measures, 383
Disposable income, 390
Dissonance, 16, 195
Dissonant element, 196
Distributor, 209
Diversification, 351
Diversion in transit, 259
Divine power, 381
Dominion, 382
Drive, 18

E

Ecological model, 99
Ecological niche, 99
Econometricians, 283
Economic environment, 278
Economic growth, 280
Economic indicators, 280

Economic profit, 76, 85-86
Economics,
Economies of Scale, 5
Edwards Personal Preference Inventory, 291
Edwards Personal Preference Schedule, 18
Effective, 391
Efficiency, 199
Efficient, 391
Empire building, 302
Empires, 355
End, 380
Engle Blackwell High Involvement Model, 24
Engle's Laws, 37
Entrepreneur, 277, 313
Entrepreneurship, 359
Entry controls, 386
Environment, 283
Environmental scan, 277
Environmental scenario, 320
EPPI, 291
Equilibrium, 77
Equilibrium point, 77
Estimates, 167
Ethical commitment, 379
Ethical expectations, 371, 378, 381, 385
Ethical questions, 384
Ethics, 378, 387
Evaluative criteria, 25, 30, 163, 250-251, 286, 331, 337, 341
Evoke, 17
Evoked set, 198
Example, 5
Exchange rates, 134, 179
Exclusive dealing contracts, 372
Experience curve, 329
Experience effects, 329
Expert polling, 299
Exposure, 195, 201
Expropriation, 386

F

Factor, 237
Faith, 383
Faith in money, 383
Family choice process, 25
FDA, 374
Federal Fair Packaging and Labeling Act of 1966, 375

Federal Trade Commission, 374-375
Federal Trade Commission Act, 372
Feedback, 209
Field research house, 291
Field sales, 205
Finance,
Financial implication, 201
Financing, 8
Flexibility in MarketingOrganization, 318
Focus group interview, 287
Focus groups, 337
Food and drug administration, 374
Force majeur, 376
Forces, 321-322
Forces or resources, 322
Forms of channel organization, 232
Forward integration, 249
Four "ps" of the offering, 49
Franchise operation, 243
Free, 391
Freedom, 5, 372, 382
Freight forwarder, 259
Frequency, 201
Freudian theory, 19
Friends, 382
Fringe markets, 351
FTC, 372
FTC Act of 1914, 375
Functions, 248, 314
Functions of marketing, 4, 7
Future environment, 295
Future Pattern of C.O.E., 124

G

Gain at the expense of the worker, 384
Gain involving sin, 384
Gains at the expense of the poor, 385
Gains made in unethical fashion, 383
Game theory, 331
GATT, 265
General Electric Planning Grid, 324
Geodemographic information, 201
Geographic territory structure, 206
Gestalt, 195
Global strategy, 355
GNP, 280
God, 384
Government, 193
Governmental agencies, 374
Governmental contacts, 283

Granger Movement, 376
Grants, 133
Greed, 383
Gross national product, 280
Group Effects, 52
Group interests, 302
Groups, 15-16

H

Heart condition, 384
Hebrew Scriptures, 381
Heterogeneity, 4, 98
High unit movement, 246
Hinduism, 387
Historical analogy, 295
Homogeneous product, 158
Horizontal cooperation, 391
Horizontal integration, 248
Howard Sheth Model, 24
Human exchange, 32
Human exchange behavior,

I

ICC, 376
Ideal state, 25, 198
Ill-gotten gain, 384
Impact, 201
Import-Export, 354
Improve their satisfaction, 4
Inbound communication, 191
Income, 37
Income effect, 36 - 37
Income expansion path, 37
Incremental costs, 5, 112, 117, 122, 249
Incremental revenues, 122
Individual interests, 302
Industrial goods classes, 173
Inferior goods, 39
Inflation rate, 280
Information clearing house, 283
Information sources, 283
Information synthesis, 313
Information technology, 319
Innovate, 173
Innovation, 99, 258
Innovation life cycle, 100, 247, 326
Innovative process, 385
Inputs, 53
Insistence, 176

Institutional advertising, 199
Integrated Physical Distribution, 261, 262
Integrity, 382
Intellectual property protection, 386
Interest, 388
Intermodal service, 259
Internal rate of return, 124, 142, 341
International division structure, 353
International functional structure, 353
International product life cycle, 178, 355
International product structure, 353
International transport companies, 264-265
Interstate Commerce Commission, 376
Invest, 124, 337
Investment, 124, 203-204, 324-326
Investments, 167, 250-251, 323-324
Inward quiet, 388
Islam, 388
Iso-utility curve, 32

J

J.S. Mill, 379
Jeremy Bentham, 379
Job of management, 262
Job of marketing management, 52
Job security, 350
John Wesley, 390
Joint Venture, 354
Judaism, 382
Judeo-Christian Ethic, 381-382
"Just in time" delivery systems, 247

K

Karl Marx, 389
Kew Gardens Principles, 380
"Kinked" demand curve, 90
Knowledge, 388
Koran, 388

L

Labor theory of value, 389
Lagging indicators, 280
Lanham Act, 176
Lanham Act of 1946, 375

Last Resort, 380-381
Law of downward sloping demand, 41
Laws, 371
Leadership, 248, 314
Leading indicators, 280
Learning, 17, 329
Legal monopoly, 375
Legal newsletters, 283
Less than carload, 258
Less than truckload, 258
Letters of credit, 265
Level of compensation, 208
Level of costs, 166
Licensing, 354
Lifestyle, 18
Likert Scale, 291
Linear models, 163, 341
Lobbying, 193
Lobbyists, 283
Long term constraint, 129
Love, 384, 389, 391
Love of money, 383
Low cost producers, 159
Low involvement purchase, 25
Low unit movement, 246
Lying, 387-388

M

Magnuson Moss Warranty Act of 1975, 375
Make price, 161
Making gains at the expense of the poor, 383
Management by objective, 329, 352-353
Management Contract, 354
Management problem, 285
Maneuver, 322
Manufacturers representative, 209
Marginal costs, 5, 68, 71
Marginal revenue, 71, 74
Marginal utility, 30, 158, 239
Market, 77
Market analyst, 293, 316
Market coverage, 203
Market development, 351
Market information, 8
Market manager, 208, 314
Market match, 67
Market mechanisms, 389

Market niche, 67, 83, 85, 96, 111, 134, 248-249, 262, 322-323, 337, 347, 354, 371-372, 379
Market penetration, 350
Market price, 74, 83
Market Research, 285
Market research group, 316
Market research:
    Differing cultural responses, 301
    Experiment, 286
    Internal threats to validity, 291
    Observe behavior, 287
    Communication, 287
    Data AnalysisInterpretation and Communication, 293
    External threats to validity, 291
    Field Work, 291
    Research Design, 286
    The Management, 285
    Threats to validity, 291
Market resource: size of the sample, 288
Market segment, 41, 341
Market segment reaction, 162
Market segments, 342-344
Market share, 90, 283
Market specialist sales force, 206
Market structure, 71, 166, 391
Marketing activities, 284
Marketing concept, 348, 350
Marketing mix, 52, 322
Marketing Organization, 314
Marketing planning staff, 284
Marketing services staff, 284, 316
Marketing strategy, 52, 322, 331
Marxism, 389
Maslow's hierarchy of needs, 20
Mass marketing, 345
Mass merchandiser, 246
Mass, 329
Match, 248, 322, 324, 390
Matches, 344
Matching, 4-5, 80-81, 341
Matching process, 391
Material handling, 247
Matrix, 208, 314, 318-319, 325-326
Matrix culture, 314, 319
Matrix structures, 353
Maxim, 379, 384
Maximin strategy, 335
MBO, 329, 352-353
Means, 380
Measure, 99
Measures of association, 293

Index 409

Media habits, 193
Media options, 201
Membership group, 16
Memory, 195, 197
Merchant wholesalers, 236
Mergers, 347, 373
Message appeals, 198
Microeconomics, 31-32
Microeconomist, 25
Military, 321, 329
Minimax strategy, 335
Minimum average total cost, 76
Mission statement, 320, 322, 350
Missionary sales people, 205
Misuse of portfolio models, 326
Mix, 49, 239
Mixed car, 259
Mixed strategy, 335
Model, 296, 323
Modeling, 295-296
Moderation, 382
Modern data base technology, 284
Modesty, 389
Monopolist, 161, 372
Monopolistic competition, 86
Monopoly, 81, 85-86, 372
Monopoly power, 375-376
Monopoly Product, 172
Motives, 20
Motor Carriers, 255
Multidimensional scaling, 341
Multiple choice questions, 288
Multiple regression, 295-296
Multiple stages of communication, 197
Multivariate statistical techniques, 293
Murray, 20, 24

N

National accounts manager, 208
National accounts sales force, 206
Need satisfaction approach, 206
Needs, 20, 380-381, 391
Negative injunction, 371, 372, 383, 387-389
Net, 52
Net present value, 124, 140, 142
New patents, 283
New product manager, 316
New Testament, 382
Niche of the firm, 384
Non constant sum game, 334

Non profit, 350
Non Profit Organizations, 130
Non recognition, 176
Non tariff barriers, 265
Nonverbal communications, 300
Normal goods, 37

O

Objectives, 202, 329
OCA, 375
Office of Consumer Affairs, 375
Old Testament, 381
Oligopoly, 86, 89, 96
One source information houses, 292-293
Open ended questions, 288
Operant conditioning, 17
Operational segment, 345
Opinion leaders, 195
Opportunity, 285
Optimization model, 300
Optimization models, 263
Options for Management Initiative, 166
Order getting, 205
Order taker, 205
Order taking, 205
Organizational buying, 25
Organizational design, 350
Organizational options, 206
Outbound communication, 191
Outhaul, 258
Outside sales, 205
Overhead, 114

P

Package express, 259
Packaging, 177
Packaging, physical implications, 177
Packaging, strategic implications, 177
Par report, 326
Patent laws, 375
Payback, 125-126, 142
Peace, 382
Peace of mind, 383
People's needs, given the, 391
Perception, 14, 18
Perceptual defense, 14, 196
Perceptual organization, 14
Perceptual sets, 14
Perceptual vigilance, 14

Perfect elasticity, 158
Perfectly inelastic demand, 42
Personal power base, 355
Personal Selling, 202 - 203
Personality, 18
Physical distribution, 249
Physical distribution system, 261
Physical Exchange, 249
Physiological psychologists, 24
Pilot study, 288
PIMS, 326
Pipeline, 252
Place, 49, 231
Planning, 322
Planning and directing, 321
Planning assumptions, 320
Planning procedures, 319
Plans, 320
Policy, 321
Political and legal environment, 278
Pool car, 259
Portfolio models, 323
Positioning, 337
Positive injunctions, 371, 382, 387-389
Poverty, 390
Power, 234, 357
Power structure, 355
Preference, 176
Prepared sales presentation, 205
Present value, 341
Press, 192
Prestige demand curve, 42
Pretentious manners, 389
Price, 30, 158, 280, 339
Price changes, 36-37
Price controls, 92
Price discrimination, 373
Price elasticity, 286
Price elasticity of demand, 46
Price maker, 86
Price supports, 94
Price system, 79-81
Price taker, 86, 158
Price theory,
Prices, 373, 389
Pricing, 158, 161, 165, 172, 329
Pricing in Transportation Services, 258
Pricing Objectives, 172
Pricing power, 92, 161-162, 164-165, 176
Primary data, 285
Private property (or stewardship) of others, 383
Private warehouse, 260

Problem, 195, 285
Problem recognition, 25, 198
Problems and opportunities, 284, 320
Product advertising, 199
Product and communication strategies, 178
Product Classes, 173
Product design, 165
Product development, 351
Product differentiation, 49, 86, 98, 157, 176, 374, 385
Product liability, 375
Product life cycle, 100, 326
Product management, 314
Product manager, 208, 316
Product manager concept, 314
Product market expansion grid, 350
Product or service offering, 49
Product portfolio models, 130
Product safety, 375
Product specialist sales force, 206
Product-price interaction, 157
Profit, 99, 111-112, 117, 314, 339, 350, 389
Profit center, 314
Profit: Impact of Marketing Strategies, 326
Profit maximization, 71, 172
Promotion, 49, 192
Prospectors, 351
Proximity, 380-381
Psychological dynamics, 163
Psychology, 30
Psychometrics, 18
Public relations, 192
Public relations staff, 318
Public warehouse, 260
Publicity, 192
Puffery, 385
Purchasing agent, 53
Pure competition, 74, 81, 159
Pure competitor, 372
Pure Food and Drug Act of 1906, 374

Q

Qualitative technique, 287
Quantitative research, 288
Quantitative techniques, 287
Questionnaire, 288

R

Rail, 254
Random component, 296
Random sampling, 288
Reach, 201
Reactors, 351
Recognition, 176
Reference currency, 134
Reference groups, 16, 195
Regional distribution center, 261
Regret minimization, 335
Regulation, 92
Regulatory commissions, 376
Reinforcement, 18
Rejection, 176
Relatively elastic demand, 46
Relatively inelastic demand, 46
Reliability, 291
Religion, 381
Religious Ethics, 381
Religious evaluation, 381
Reminder advertising, 199
Report by exception principle, 284
Repositioning, 337, 339, 341
Research problem, 286
Resource allocation, 165
Resources, 322
Response, 18
Response of the Market Niche, 167
Retail chains, 243
Retailer, 239
Retailer strategy, 243
Reteailer strategy, 241
Retrieval, 198
Return on assets managed, 209
Return on investment, 146
Revenue, 114, 249
Revenues, 117, 284
Risk, 350, 375
Risk adjusted return to capital, 69
Risk taking, 8
Robinson Patman Act of 1936, 373
ROI, 146
Role of marketing, 357
Role of marketing in society, 390
Rules for inheritance, 383

S

Salary, 208
Salary plus commission, 208
Sales, 318
Sales analysis group, 316
Sales approach, 204
Sales management group, 318
Sales manager, 208
Sales oriented objective, 172
Sales position, 205
Sales presentation, 205
Sales promotion, 192, 209
Sales task, 205
Salesperson, 204
Salespersons:
    compensation and motivation, 208
    formula, 208

level, 208
Sample frame, 288
Satisfaction, 4, 13, 17, 19, 24-25, 195, 350, 379-380, 387-388
Satisfaction: satisfying the customer, 348
SBUs, 323
Scan behavior, 277, 284
Scenario writing, 299
Scriptural Ethics, 382 - 383
Scriptural Ethics: Governing Perspectives, 384
Scriptures, 381
Search behavior, 193
Seasonality, 296
Secondary data, 285, 301
Secular Ethics, 379
Segmentation, 241, 341
Segmenting, 344
Segmenting dimension, 345
Segmenting:
    Demographic dimension, 345
    Description of intraorganizational and interpersonal relationships, 345
    Determining dimension, 347
    Geographic dimension, 345
    Industry type and size, 345
    Physical dimension, 345
    Psychological dimension, 345
    Qualifying dimension, 347
Selection and training, 206
Selective demand, 199
Selfish gain, 384

Selling formula, 205
Sensitivity, 391
Sherman Act of 1890, 372
Shifting and sharing functions, 247
Shintoism, 388
Shopping stores, 241
Shortage, 92
Simple regression, 295
Simple trend extension, 295
Simulation model, 263, 299
Simulations, 167, 263
Sincerity, 389
Situation analysis, 284, 320
Social psychologists, 14
Social reward structure for the suppliers, 67
Social system, 355
Source of power, 234
Special interest magazines, 201
Specialization and exchange, 4-5
Specialized international information, 301
Specialty shop, 243
Spinoffs, 347
SPSS, 291
Standardization, differentiation problem, 178
Standardizing and grading, 8
Statements of goals, objectives and strategies, 320
Statistical inference, 287
Statistical package, 291
Statistical Package for the Social Sciences, 291
Statistical significance of differences, 293
Statistical tests and procedures, 288
Status quo objective, 172
Stealing, 383
Stevedores, 263
Stewardship, 382
Storage, 249, 259
Storage cost, 260
Storage costs per unit, 260
Straight commission, 209
Strategic business units, 323
Strategic choice, 313, 321
Strategic direction, 170
Strategic planning group, 316
Strategy, 331
Striving, 388
Subsidies, 133
Substitution effects, 36-37
Successful brand, 176

Sullivan, 19
Superior goods, 37
Supermarket, 243
Superstore, 243
Supplies, 390-391
Supply, 5, 13, 76-77
Supply curve, 74, 76
Supporting salespeople, 205
Syndicated services, 283
Synthesis, 313, 319
System of rewards and punishments, 208
Systems of ethics, 391

T

Tactics, 331
Take price, 161
Takeover controls, 386
Taking advantage when selling, 383, 385
Taking unfair advantage of the poor, 383
Taoism, 388
Target market, 52, 322
Target marketing, 345
Target markets, 278
Target return, 172
Tariff, 265
Tasks, 202
Tax effects, 140
TDBU decision process, 351
Team, 314, 319
Team selling, 205
Teamwork, 355
Technical environment, 280
Technical journals, 283
Technical representatives, 205
Technological Change, 246
Telemarketing, 201
Teleological, 379
Temptations, 385
Tension, 17, 19, 196
Tension system, 19
Thematic Apperception Test, 18
Theoretical units, 20
Third party information suppliers, 303
Time value of money, 140
Ton-mile, 251
Top executives, 284
Torah, 381
Tort law, 375
Trademark, 176, 375
Traditional channel, 232, 248

Transfer price, 179
Translation, 211
Translation difficulties, 300
Transportation, 249, 259, 265
Transportation and storage, 8, 249
Transportation Options, 251
Transportation Ownership, 257
Transportation:
    Ability to handle a variety of goods, 251
    Dependability in meeting schedules, 251
    Frequency of scheduled shipments, 251
    Number of locations served, 251
    Door-to-door delivery speed, 251
Trend extension, 295
Truckload, 258
True heart, 389
True-false questions, 288
Trusts, 372
Truth, 388-389
Two human decisions,
Tying contracts, 372
Types of advertising, 199

U

Underlying trend, 296
Understanding, 196, 302
Unfair acquisition of property, 383
Unfair representation in trade, 383, 385
Unfair" methods of competition, 373
Unfair" practices, 375
Unit movements, 161
Unit pricing, 177
Universal product code, 177
Untruthfulness, 387
Usury, 383
Utilitarian ethic, 379
Utility, 13, 17, 19, 25

V

Vain talk, 387
Varieties of strategy, 322-323
Venture research group, 316
Vertical integration, 249
Vertical marketing systems, 232, 248
Visual image personality, 197
Voluntarily demanded, 67

Voluntary chain, 243
Voluntary exchange, 67
Voluntary exchange behaviors, 7

W

Warranties, 375
Water transportation, 252
Wheel of Retailing, 247
Wheeler Lea Act of 1938, 375
Wholesaler, 236, 243
Wholly Owned Subsidiary, 354
Wisdom, 382
Witness, 388
Work ethic, 382
Worldly attachments, 388

Z

Zero sum game, 334